Permanent Disability Benefits
in
Workers' Compensation

Monroe Berkowitz
and
John F. Burton, Jr.

D1198339

1987

W. E. Upjohn Institute for Employment Research

Library of Congress Cataloging-in-Publication Data

Berkowitz, Monroe, 1919-
    Permanent disability benefits in workers' compensation / Monroe
Berkowitz and John F. Burton, Jr.
        p. 459 cm.
    Includes bibliographies and index.
    ISBN 0-88099-051-1.   ISBN 0-88099-050-3 (pbk.)
    1. Insurance, Disability—United States.   2. Workers'
compensation—United States.   I. Burton, John F.   II. Title.
HD7105.25.U6B47 1987
368.4'1'00973—dc19   87-22874
                                                                        CIP

Copyright © 1987
by the
W. E. UPJOHN INSTITUTE
FOR EMPLOYMENT RESEARCH

300 South Westnedge Ave.
Kalamazoo, Michigan 49007

Authors

Monroe Berkowitz has recently retired from his teaching duties as professor of economics at Rutgers, the State University of New Jersey. He maintains his connection with the Bureau of Economic Research where he directs the Disability and Health Economics Research section and he will continue arbitrating labor-management disputes. A graduate of Ohio University, Professor Berkowitz received his Ph.D. degree in economics from Columbia University. His interest in workers compensation issues began with his study of the New Jersey system, which was published in 1960. Since then he has published numerous articles on various aspects of the field, with recent concentration in the field of rehabilitation. He is the editor of *Measuring the Efficiency of Public Programs,* to be published in 1988 by Temple University Press.

John F. Burton, Jr. is a professor in the New York State School of Industrial and Labor Relations at Cornell University. He formerly was professor in the Graduate School of Business of the University of Chicago and chairman of the National Commission on State Workmen's Compensation Laws. He has published widely on public sector collective bargaining and workers' compensation, including (with Alan B. Krueger), "Interstate Variations in the Employers' Costs in Workers' Compensation," which was included in *Current Issues in Workers' Compensation,* published by the Upjohn Institute in 1986. Burton received his undergraduate education at Cornell University and received both an LL.B. and Ph.D. in economics from the University of Michigan. His dissertation research, which examined workers' compensation costs, was partially supported by the Upjohn Institute.

Acknowledgements

The origin of this study was a research project conducted by Workers' Disability Income Systems, Inc. with support from the National Science Foundation under the title "An Evaluation of State Level Human Resource Delivery Programs: Disability Compensation Programs" (No. APR75-01067). The final report for that project, *Permanent Disability Benefits in the Workers' Compensation Program,* was completed in 1979.

The authors of the 1979 NSF final report were the authors of the present volume plus Wayne Vroman. Other staff members of Workers' Disability Income Systems, Inc. who were essential to the report were Katherine Hagerty, who conducted much of the field work for the Ten-State Study (part II of the present volume), and Bruce Vermeulen, who supervised much of the data collection for the Wage-Loss Study (part III of the present volume). We wish to express our appreciation again to all who assisted in the preparation of the NSF final report, including Wayne Vroman, Katherine Hagerty, and Bruce Vermeulen, plus the three National Science Foundation program managers who had responsibility for the project: Lynn Dolins, James Cowig, and Frank P. Scioli, Jr.

After submitting the NSF final report, we decided to revise and update the manuscript. This task has taken considerable effort because of the rapid pace of change in the 10 jurisdictions we selected for scrutiny. As an example, Florida completely revised its statutory aproach to permanent disability benefits subsequent to the submission of our final report to the National Science Foundation. The present volume contains a chapter devoted entirely to Florida because of the significance of the recent changes. Although changes elsewhere have not been as dramatic, in almost all states some statutory or judicial developments of note have occurred since 1979, or proposals for substantial revisions of the law are pending. We have attempted to include all significant developments or proposals through 1986 involving the permanent disability benefits of the workers' compensation progrms in the 10 jurisdictions.

Various persons in the 10 jurisdictions, many of whom are acknowledged in the notes to the various chapters, aided in the preparation of the present volume. We thank those who aided our efforts, whether specifically named or not. Two persons were critical to the preparation of the manuscript: Nancy Orchard, who typed most of the manuscript in draft form and then entered the entire study into a word processing program, and Brian Keeling, who, as copy editor, shortened and polished the text. Finally, we express our appreciation to H. Allan Hunt, Manager of Research at the W. E. Upjohn Institute, who demonstrated a most admirable mixture of patience and support as this study progressed.

Monroe Berkowitz
John F. Burton, Jr.
October 1987

v

Preface

More than five million persons suffer work-related injuries or diseases each year.[1] Most of these incidents require only medical treatment or involve brief interruptions of work, but annually over two million workers experience work-related injuries or diseases that disable them for more than a day. For at least 100,000 of these workers (more likely, for over 250,000) the consequences include permanent disabilities: that is, losses of actual earnings or of earning capacity even after maximum medical recovery. These permanent disabilities are usually partial, rather than total: the workers continue to have some earnings or retain some of their preinjury earning capacity.

Benefits for workers who are permanently and partially disabled are the most expensive portion of workers' compensation, the program for work-related injuries and diseases.[2] Although permanent partial cases account for less than 25 percent of the workers' compensation cases paying cash benefits, the cash benefits in these cases account for more than 60 percent of all such payments (Price 1984, table 4).

Permanent partial benefits not only are the most expensive part of workers' compensation, they are the most controversial and complex aspect of that program. The statutes and practices used to compensate partial disability vary widely among states. To mention but one example, cash benefits for minor permanent partial cases represent less than 10 percent of all payments in ten states, but more than 30 percent in seven others.[3]

The overall expense of permanent partial benefits, the considerable variations in their costs among states, and the many controversies over the procedures and standards used to determine the benefits make them a crucial area for reform. Indeed, the National Commission on State Workmen's Compensation Laws concluded in its 1972 report that reforming permanent partial benefits was one of the two problems "so important that the vitality of the state systems will be tested by the ability of states to resolve them satisfactorily" (National Commission 1972, p. 129). Nonetheless, because the issue was so intractable and the time available to the National Commission so limited, in its 19 essential recommendations the Commission refrained from making precise recommendations for restructuring permanent partial benefits, concentrating instead on expansion of coverage to previously unprotected workers and increases in the amount and duration of benefits for total disability and death (National Commission 1972, p. 67).

Workers' compensation developments in the years 1972-86 bear the imprint of the National Commission's report. Impediments to coverage, such as the exemption of small employers, were eliminated in many jurisdictions, and the proportion of employees covered by workers' compensation increased from 84 percent in 1972 to 88 percent in 1980 (Price 1984, table 1). Perhaps even more impressive is the improvement in benefits. In 1972, for example, only six of 51 jurisdictions had temporary total maximum weekly benefits that were at least 66 2/3 percent of the state's average weekly wage.[4] This meant that the majority of workers did not receive the nominal replacement rate for total disability found in most statutes—namely 66 2/3 percent of preinjury wages—but received less because the maximum held down their benefits. By 1986, benefits generally were much more adequate. Thirty-one jurisdictions (out of 51) in 1986 had maximums for temporary total disability that were at least 100 percent of the state's average weekly wage, and only 9 had maximums less than 66 2/3 percent of the state's wage. Durations of benefits also improved. For example, whereas in 1972 only 17 jurisdictions paid benefits for life or the entire period of disability in permanent total cases, in 1986, 35 jurisdictions paid for the extended duration.

These improvements in coverage and benefits were accompanied by a surge in the costs of workers' compensation. Benefits paid in 1972 totalled $4.1 billion; by 1984 (the latest year for which data are available) the total was $19.5 billion (Price 1984, table 3, and Price 1987, table 1). The costs to employers, including insurance premiums and administrative expenses, were $5.8 billion or 1.14 percent of payroll in 1972; by 1984 they were $25.3 billion or 1.66 percent of payroll (Price 1984, table 7, and Price 1987).

These escalating costs caused apprehension among employees, carriers, and state legislators. One particular area of concern is permanent partial disability benefits, the cost of which appears to have grown proportionately faster than the costs of benefits for death and total disability since 1972 despite the National Commission's emphasis on the latter types of benefits. Permanent partial benefits accounted for 65.20 percent of all cash benefits in 1968, declined to 62.64 percent by 1973, and then rebounded to 64.96 percent by 1982.[5]

The result of these cost developments is that a second wave of reform has been sweeping through workers' compensation in recent years. Whereas the first wave primarily focused on improvements in coverage and adequacy of benefits, the current wave is emphasizing efficiency in the delivery system and restrictions on benefits to those workers who are perceived as receiving awards far in excess of their lost wages. Some aspects of the current reform movement, such as the use of open competition in the rate-setting process for workers' compensation insurance, are beyond the scope of this study. Much of the recent reform effort, however, has centered on permanent partial disability benefits, with a number of jurisdictions reassessing, and in some cases changing, the procedures or criteria for these benefits.

The pressures for reform of permanent partial benefits often relate to practices that were tolerable only so long as workers' compensation was relatively inexpensive. For example, in states that paid benefits on the basis of the workers' physical impairments, such as Florida and New Jersey, the long-standing approach of litigating almost all cases involving permanent disabilities and routinely making settlements with substantial benefits for minor injuries increasingly became anathema to employers. And in Michigan and other states that conditioned permanent benefits on the occurrence of actual wage loss, the frequency with which substantial benefits were awarded when actual wage losses were questionable—especially in the case of retirees—spurred employers to increasingly feverish efforts for change.

In some states, the first wave of reform was accomplished without triggering the second. In Wisconsin, permanent partial disability benefits had never been out of control, and thus the higher benefits did not produce excessive costs. In other states, the improvements in benefits and coverage resulted in cost increases that precipitated the permanent partial reforms. Florida is the classic example of this sequence. In other states, such as California, the first wave of reform either never was accomplished or was delayed for many years because the concern about misallocation of resources in permanent partial cases surfaced early, forestalling the benefit improvements.

Our research on permanent partial disability benefits began in 1975 and 1976, when we conducted extensive field work for a report submitted to the National Science Foundation (Berkowitz, Burton, and Vroman 1979). The time of this investigation corresponded roughly with the end of the first wave of reform. We updated our information between 1982 and 1986, at a point well into the second wave. Several of the states we examined had made extensive changes between our initial contacts and the 1980s, and part of what we will do is to review the dynamics of reform in recent years. We believe that the current handling of permanent partial disability benefits in many jurisdictions can be understood only by knowing where those jurisdictions were in 1975-76, because it is the responses to problems as they were then perceived that led these states to their current positions.

The problems that existed in the mid-1970s and still exist today are not unique—many are common across states and many are old problems in new guises. Nor are the solutions that the states have endorsed or considered in recent years unique or new—many of them are old palliatives in new garb. We have seen some states turn to "innovative" approaches that are simultaneously being abandoned in other jurisdictions as deficient. If the states are laboratories of experiment, to use Brandeis's phrase, then it would be nice if they learned from the failures elsewhere. We hope to provide a systematic catalogue of approaches that were discarded with good reason.

Plan of This Volume

The basic concern of our research is the adequacy and equity of permanent partial disability benefits, and the efficiency of the procedures and standards used to provide these benefits. The report contains four parts.

Part I is a general introduction to permanent partial disabilities. Chapter 1 presents a conceptual framework used to view disability among the working age population: terms such as "impairment," "work disability," and "functional limitations" are defined so as to facilitate comparisons among different jurisdictions. Chapter 2 first presents the rudiments of workers' compensation, then reviews the objectives of the workers' compensation program and explains the criteria of adequacy, equity, and efficiency used in this report.

Part II contains our Ten-State Study. The 10 jurisdictions in our sample, which were selected to provide a good representation of the various procedures and standards used to provide compensation payments for permanent disabilities, are California, Florida, Michigan, Nevada, New Jersey, New York, Ohio, Pennsylvania, Wisconsin, and the District of Columbia.[6] An introduction (chapter 3) is followed by chapters examining the states' procedures for permanent partial disability benefits and the criteria used by the states for scheduled benefits and for nonscheduled benefits. (For convenience, we will often refer to the District of Columbia as a state.) Because of the national attention the 1979 changes in Florida's law have received, a separate chapter is devoted to that state.

Part III presents a summary of our Wage-Loss Study. In three of the states in our sample—California, Florida, and Wisconsin—we examined the relationships among workers' disability ratings, the workers' compensation benefits they received, and their actual losses of earnings caused by work-related injuries.

In Part IV we draw on the conceptual materials and data from parts I-III to evaluate the adequacy, equity, and efficiency of the permanent partial disability benefits in the jurisdictions examined. The study concludes with a discussion of possible reforms for permanent disability benefits in workers' compensation.

NOTES

1. The sources of data in the first paragraph are provided in Burton and Vroman 1979, footnote 1.

2. The basic nature of the program is described in chapter 2.

3. See table 3.5, below.

4. The 51 jurisdictions are the 50 states and the District of Columbia. The data on benefits in this paragraph are from U.S. Department of Labor (1987), as supplemented by a quarterly release dated January 1, 1986.

5. See table 3.3, below.

6. Chapter 3 explains why these 10 jurisdictions were selected.

CONTENTS

Part I
Introduction to Permanent Partial Disability
and Workers' Compensation

Part II
The Ten-State Study of Workers' Compensation
Procedures and Standards

Part III
The Wage-Loss Study

Part IV
Evaluation and Possible Reforms

List of Tables

List of Graphs and Charts

Part I
Introduction to
Permanent Partial Disability
and Workers' Compensation

Chapter 1
Disability Among the
Working-Age Population
A Conceptual Framework

Our ultimate purpose in this study is to prescribe benefits and services for workers who experience permanent disabilities because of work-related injuries or diseases. That prescription is possible, however, only if we provide a proper framework for analysis. Not only do the criteria and procedures used to provide benefits and services to workers with permanent disabilities vary substantially among jurisdictions, but different jurisdictions, as well as different groups and individuals, use different terms to describe the same phenomena. Some, though not all, of the apparent differences among various programs are due to the inconsistent use of terminology.

In describing the conceptual framework to be used throughout this book, we will employ much of the terminology in use within the workers' compensation field, including the terms in the glossaries of *The Report of the National Commission on State Workmen's Compensation Laws* (1972, p. 137) and of the American Medical Association's *Guides to the Evaluation of Permanent Impairment* (1984, pp. 225-27). However, we also take some concepts from literature concerned less with workers' compensation *per se* than with disability programs in general, including the disability insurance program under Social Security.

Causes of Injury or Disease

Chart 1.1 briefly categorizes injuries and diseases. We define an injury as damage to the body resulting from an acute traumatic episode, and a disease as damage to the body resulting from a cause other than an injury. These definitions differ from those usually used within the workers' compensation program. *Injury,* for example, is commonly defined so as to include disease. In some states, this broad use of *injury* results from court interpretations. The original intent of the framers of the legislation, to cover only traumatic episodes, was extended to cover diseases as well, even though these often result from cumulative

3

nontraumatic episodes. In some other instances, the term *injury* has been broadly applied by design. For example, the model Workmen's Compensation and Rehabilitation Law, prepared by the Council of State Governments in the mid-1960s, defines injury so as to encompass virtually all diseases. We follow the *Report* of the National Commission in treating injury and disease as mutually exclusive (rather than making disease a subset of injury) because this use of the terms is more consistent with generally accepted usage in the medical literature.

An injury or disease can result from one or more of the causes listed in chart 1.1. There are many possible taxonomies, but, consistent with our particular interest, we have indicated a primary division between (1) work-related causes and (2) nonwork-related causes.

Chart 1.1
Causes of Injury or Disease

1. Work-Related	2. Nonwork-Related
(a) employer at fault	(a) congenital
(b) employee at fault	(b) degenerative
(c) neither at fault	(c) other nonwork-related
	(i) other person at fault
	(ii) no other person at fault

One way to subclassify work-related causes is by assignment of fault: in some cases the employer is at fault (1a), in some cases the employee (1b), and in some cases neither party (1c). The term *fault,* of course, can be variously interpreted. For example, it could be taken to mean the standard of negligence defined by traditional tort law; or one could resuscitate the definition of fault acted on in most states in the days before workers' compensation, when employers made effective recourse to several extraordinary defenses against liability in tort suits.

In general, the fault issue is no longer of major significance in workers' compensation (as is discussed in chapter 2, below). It is of some importance, however, when we consider the workers' disability income system and not just the workers' compensation program. For instance, work-related injuries that result from the negligence of a third party, such as a supplier to an employer, can lead to successful causes of action by employees against the third party under the legal doctrines used in many states.

Several types of nonwork-related causes of injury and disease affect the working-age population. Some workers have congenital conditions, such as blindness, that affect them throughout their lives. Others have degenerative conditions that reflect hereditary predispositions and the toll of aging; heart disease often, though not always, is in this class. Other nonwork-related causes can be divided between those for which a person other than the injured worker is at fault (2c-i in chart 1.1) and those for which no one other than the injured worker is at fault (2c-ii). For example, an off-the-job automobile accident in which a worker is injured may be the fault either of another driver (2c-i) or of the worker himself (2c-ii).

This classification system is designed with an analysis of the workers' compensation program in mind. It reflects the division between work-related and nonwork-related causes, a key element in the workers' compensation program, and it indicates the necessity to go beyond a two-way classification even in workers' compensation. As discussed below, determining whether an injury or disease is work-related, as a criterion for awarding compensation, is not always a straightforward matter, particularly since the causes catalogued in chart 1.1 are *not* mutually exclusive categories. Indeed, for certain types of injuries and diseases, notably back injuries and heart diseases, the relative importance of work-related and nonwork-related factors in explaining the occurrence of the injury or disease is often at issue.

Consequences of Injury or Disease

The various consequences of injury and disease (chart 1.2) can be categorized as temporary and permanent, a distinction that has an important bearing on the types of benefits provided under workers' compensation. The differentiation we utilize between temporary and permanent is consistent with the use of those terms in the *Report* of the National Commission. *Temporary* refers to the period from the onset of injury or disease until maximum medical improvement (MMI) has been achieved; *permanent* refers to the period following MMI.[1] Not every statute would draw the dividing line between permanent and temporary this way. Further, in practice, that line may be unclear. For example, in California the "permanent" status is equated with a permanent and stable medical condition, but in fact permanent partial benefits may have to be paid before such a medical condition is reached.

In this book, *temporary* and *permanent* refer to mutually exclusive time periods. All workers who have an injury or disease temporarily experience some or all of the consequences indicated in chart 1.2. A minority of workers also permanently suffer some of those consequences.

Chart 1.2
Possible Consequences of an Injury or Disease

Impairment	Functional Limitations	Work and Nonwork Disability	Other Influences

Impairment and Functional Limitation

The initial consequence of an injury or disease is an impairment. An impairment "is an anatomical, physiological, intellectual or emotional abnormality or loss" (Nagi 1975, p. 8). Similarly, the National Commission *Report* (1972, p. 137) defines permanent impairments as "any anatomic or functional abnormality or loss after maximum medical rehabilitation has been achieved."[2] Examples of impairments are an amputated limb and an enervated muscle.

An impairment can be manifested (and perhaps measured) in several ways. Some manifestations, such as restricted motion or ankylosis, may be regarded as "objective." Subjective manifestations include pain, which may be constant, intermittent, or dependent on the activities undertaken by the worker. Other subjective manifestations are weakness and limited endurance.

The impairment experienced by the worker may *not* lead to functional limitations, the next concept shown on chart 1.2. When it does not, we term it "nonlimiting." More often, however, impairments do give rise to functional limitations (or limitations in the worker's performance).[3]

Although overlapping in some respects, three dimensions of performance are . . . separable: physical, emotional and mental. Physical performance refers to sensory-motor functioning of the organism as indicated by limitations in such activities as walking, climbing, bending, reaching, hearing, etc. Emotional performance refers to a person's effectiveness in psychological coping with life stress and can be manifested through levels of anxiety, restlessness, and a variety of psycho-physiological symptoms. Mental performance denotes the intellectual and reasoning capabilities of individuals which have been most commonly measured through problem-solving (I.Q.) tests. (Nagi 1975, p. 3)

A few examples may clarify some of the terms we have introduced:

(1) *Temporary nonlimiting impairment.* A worker is injured by flying glass, which inflicts a minor laceration on his arm. The result is a physiological disturbance of the skin (impairment). However, the wound is cleaned and bandaged, and is completely healed in a few weeks. Even during the healing period, the impairment is not limiting; that is, there are no resulting functional limitations.

(2) *Temporary limiting impairment.* A falling box breaks a worker's great toe. The result is a physiological disturbance of the bone structure (impairment), which manifests itself in pain and, after the bone is set, in temporary ankylosis. During the healing period, the impairment limits the worker's ability to walk and climb (functional limitations). After the healing period is over, however, there is no residual impairment.

(3) *Temporary limiting impairment and permanent nonlimiting impairment.* A worker is scalded on his back by hot acid. The temporary result is burnt tissue (impairment), accompanied by pain and weakness, which results in temporary inability to bend and lift (functional limitations). After the healing period, the worker's back is still scarred (impairment) and painful when touched, but the worker is able to bend, lift, and perform all other activities he could before his injury.

(4) *Temporary and permanent limiting impairments.* A falling box strikes a worker's back and causes a compression fracture of a vertebra (impairment), which manifests itself in pain and complete loss of motion in the back. During the healing period, the worker is unable to walk, bend, and so on (functional limitations). Even after maximum

medical rehabilitation is reached, a physical abnormality (impairment) remains and the worker has limited motion in his back. Moreover, when the worker is asked to lift a 25-pound object, he is weak (barely able to lift the object), he experiences increasing levels of pain with continued lifting, and he is only able to lift the object twice (limited endurance). These manifestations of his impairment (weakness, pain, and limited endurance) are indications of a functional limitation (inability to lift).

These examples enable us to contrast the varying approaches to the assessment of impairment and functional limitations. The AMA *Guides,* for example, largely confine the measurement of impairment to objective manifestations, such as restricted motion. The reason given (1971, p. iii) is that "competent evaluation of permanent impairment requires adequate and complete medical examination, accurate objective measurement of function, and the avoidance of subjective impressions." Subjective manifestations of impairment, however, are considered important for certain types of injuries and diseases by workers' compensation programs in a number of jurisdictions, such as California. Thus a medical examiner following the AMA *Guides* approach in evaluating the extent of permanent impairment in example (4) above would confine himself to determining the limitations of motion in the back, whereas, following the California approach, he would also consider the subjective manifestations of pain, weakness, and limited endurance.

Disabilities

As a result of functional limitations, a worker may experience a disability. A broad definition of disability is offered by Nagi (1975, pp. 3-4): "inability or limitations in performing social roles and activities such as in relation to work, family, or to independent community living." We distinguish two types of disability in chart 1.2, namely, work disability, a loss of actual earnings or earning capability as a consequence of the impairment, and nonwork disability, the other consequences for the worker included in Nagi's broad definition.

In much of the literature on disability, including the *Report* of the National Commission, that term has been treated as synonymous with *work disability* as defined above. *Nonwork disability,* as defined above, is not included in the glossary of the *Report,* but for our purposes it is worthwhile to recognize the consequences for workers resulting from functional limitations other than the consequences for the work role. In later chapters, however, when we use the term *disability* without the modifier *work* or *nonwork,* we intend it to mean *work disability* as defined here.

As mentioned, not all impairments are attended by functional limitations. Similarly, not all functional limitations are attended by a disability; some functional limitations are "nondisabling." For example, an impairment may render a worker unable to lift heavy objects, but lifting ability may be irrelevant to the worker's job (college professor).

Other Influences on Disabilities

One aspect of both the work disability and the nonwork disability concepts is that the extent of a given worker's disability depends not only on the extent of his functional limitations but also, as indicated in chart 1.2, on other influences. For example, the loss of actual earnings or decrease in earning capacity (that is, work disability) depends not just on functional limitations, but on the worker's personal characteristics (age, education, experience, and other factors), the labor market conditions in which he must compete for employment, and the sources of assistance available to him (including cash benefits, such as workers' compensation and welfare, and other assistance, such as medical care and rehabilitation services).

Age, education, and previous work experience are examples of personal characteristics that might interact with a worker's functional limitation to affect the extent of his work disability. Thus an older worker with a given impairment may have more difficulty finding employment than a younger worker with the same impairment. An employer may be reluctant to pay for retraining the older worker, given his relatively short expected job tenure. Also, a given functional limitation may affect a highly educated worker less than a poorly educated worker, because the more educated worker is likely to rely on mental rather than physical skills for his job market success. Similarly, a worker with greater experience prior to his work-related injury or disease, who can draw on this reservoir of skills to overcome a functional limitation, may also have an easier adjustment.

The relationships among functional limitations, workers' personal characteristics, and work disabilities are complex, and only relatively few hypotheses describing them have been adequately tested in terms of actual labor market experience; great care must therefore be taken in making judgments about them. An important general point, however, and one that appears quite likely on the basis of what we know about the operation of the labor market from studies by economists, is that any factor that may influence the employability of a worker, whether it be a functional limitation, age, education, or other personal characteristic, will interact with the other factors in determining the earnings experience of that worker.

The actual work disability experienced by workers with functional limitations will also be affected by general labor market conditions. It seems likely that workers with functional limitations will be more adversely affected when labor market conditions deteriorate than workers who are otherwise equivalent except for the functional limitations.

The extent of work disability (and nonwork disability) that results from a particular functional limitation also depends on the sources of assistance for disabled workers. Here it is useful to draw a distinction between work disability in the sense of loss of wage-earning capacity and disability in the sense of loss of actual earnings. The actual loss of earnings for a worker with a given functional limitation will certainly depend in part upon the alternative sources of income for the worker and his family. Thus, as workers' compensation benefits are increased, at least beyond certain limits, a worker's incentive to overcome a given functional limitation and return to work may decline. Because of this effect, disability (earnings loss) may increase as workers' compensation benefits increase. The same relationship can be expected for increased availability of benefits from programs such as disability insurance, welfare, and private pension plans.

We do not want to suggest that we are opposed to increases in benefit levels for these programs. Indeed, one of the purposes of workers' compensation benefits is to reduce the pressures on workers to return to work under onerous conditions. There are complex policy issues (discussed later in this book) concerning the proper trade-off between the work disincentive effects of higher benefits and the purpose of providing workers adequate support in a period of adversity. The main point here is simply that the extent of disability (as measured by earnings loss) in the working age population is affected by the nature of the income programs available to disabled workers.

Disabled workers have sources of assistance other than cash benefits, including medical care and rehabilitation services. At a conceptual level, it is again important to stress that the quality and quantity of these other forms of assistance are interrelated with the extent of work disability and nonwork disability that will occur for a worker with a functional limitation. For example, a worker whose work-related back injury makes it impossible to continue a previous job involving lifting may, after rehabilitation, find a new job, such as sales work, in which his functional limitation does not affect his work performance.[4]

Actual Loss of Earnings

Graph 1.1 illustrates an example of the actual loss of earnings resulting from a work-related injury or disease. In this example, wages increased through time from A to B, reflecting the worker's increasing productivity, as well as economywide inflation. At point B, the worker experienced a work-related injury that permanently reduced his earnings. Had he not been injured, his earnings would have continued to grow along the line B-C. Although these potential earnings cannot be observed, they can be estimated from information such as the worker's preinjury earnings, age, occupation, and work experience. The worker's *actual* earnings in this example dropped from B to D and continued

Graph 1.1
Economic Consequences of a Work-Related Injury
(for Workers with Permanent Disabilities)

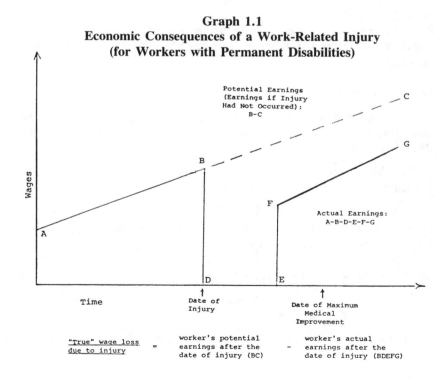

at this zero earnings level until point E, when the worker returned to work at wage level F. Thereafter, actual earnings grew along the line F to G. As this example is drawn, it is assumed that the worker's actual earnings never return to the potential earnings (line BC) that he would have earned if he had never been injured.

Of course, not all workers with permanent impairments or permanent functional limitations have wage histories that correspond to the example in graph 1.1. Some may return to their old jobs at the wages they would have earned if they had never been injured; others may experience a total loss of earnings after their injuries. The example shown illustrates an intermediate case, in which the worker has a partial but not total loss of earnings.

As previously discussed, permanent disability cases are defined as those for which the worker has consequences that extend beyond the date of maximum medical rehabilitation, or maximum medical improvement (MMI). In a workers' compensation program, the date of MMI is when the worker's medical condition is considered stable, so that he can be rated for the purposes of deciding the permanent disability benefits to which he is entitled. For the case illustrated in graph 1.1, MMI occurs after the worker returns to work, which is a typical sequence.

Questions To Be Answered

The conceptual framework presented in this chapter raises several questions which must be answered by any program that compensates disability. These include:

(1) Which causes of injuries and diseases (as shown in chart 1.1) should be covered by the program?

(2) Which of the consequences of an injury or disease (as shown in chart 1.2) should be compensable? That is, should temporary consequences or permanent consequences or both be compensable? And which of impairments, functional limitations, work disability, and nonwork disability should be compensable?

(3) What should be the amount of compensation for those consequences that are compensable?

(4) How should compensation benefits be distributed among workers?

(5) How should the delivery system for compensation benefits be evaluated?

The next chapter develops some answers to these questions.

NOTES

1. The glossary of the 1972 National Commission *Report,* in defining permanent impairment, indicates that permanent means the medical condition must be declared stable or nonprogressive by a physician (p. 137).

2. The definition of permanent impairment contained in the glossary of the National Commission's *Report* is virtually identical to the definition in the 1st edition of the AMA *Guides* (1971, p. iii). The 2nd edition of the AMA *Guides* (1984, p. 225) defines impairment as "the loss of, loss of use of, or derangement of any body part, system or functions" and permanent impairment as "impairment that has become static or well stabilized with or without medical treatment, or that is not likely to remit despite medical treatment of the impairing conditions."

3. We rely on the classification system developed by Nagi (1975), which distinguishes among impairments, functional limitations, and disability. The definition of impairment in the AMA *Guides* (1984, p. 225) includes functional limitations, and thus has only two consequences of an injury or disease: impairment and disability. Another three-consequence classification system published by the World Health Organization (1980) utilizes impairment (which includes functional limitations), disability, and handicap. The Nagi system is the most useful in explaining the operational approaches in workers' compensation.

4. Medical care and rehabilitation services will also affect the extent of impairment and functional limitation that result from a given injury or disease, a relationship not shown in chart 1.2. Although this is an important relationship, it is largely beyond the scope of this study.

Chapter 2
The Objectives
of Workers' Compensation

The Basic Nature of Workers' Compensation

There is a workers' compensation act for each of the 50 states and for the District of Columbia. There also are two federal workers' compensation programs.[1] No two acts are exactly alike, but most have similar basic features.[2]

Workers' compensation provides cash benefits, medical care, and rehabilitation services for workers who suffer work-related injuries and diseases. To be eligible for benefits, normally an employee must experience a "personal injury by accident arising out of and in the course of employment." All of the laws provide benefits for workers with occupational diseases, although many states restrict the coverage of occupational diseases through provisions such as minimum duration of exposure rules.

In general, the effect of the phrase "personal injury by accident arising out of and in the course of employment" is to exclude some injuries and diseases from the scope of the program. However, the distinguishing feature of workers' compensation is that it provides benefits for many workers who could not win suits for damages under the common law because of the difficulty of proving that the employer was at fault. Workers' compensation benefits are paid even when the employer is free of negligence or other fault; they are the employer's exclusive liability for work-related injuries and diseases.

When an injury or disease falls within the scope of the workers' compensation program, the employer must furnish medical care, usually unlimited in time and amount. Most states also provide vocational and medical rehabilitation services, or supervise the services if they are furnished by the employer. In addition, all states require the employer to pay cash benefits to the worker if certain conditions are met.

15

Cash benefits usually are classified as temporary total, temporary partial, permanent total, permanent partial, and death benefits. After a specified waiting period, temporary total benefits are paid if the employee is unable to work. The benefits continue as long as the worker remains totally but temporarily disabled. Temporary partial benefits are paid during a period of reduced earnings and continue until the worker returns to full wages or is found eligible for permanent total or permanent partial benefits. Permanent total benefits are paid to a worker disabled completely for an indefinite time. *Permanent partial benefits are paid if the worker incurs an injury or disease that causes a permanent impairment or if the worker experiences a permanent but partial loss of wages or wage-earning capacity.* Death benefits include burial expenses and benefits to specified dependent survivors. For each category of benefits, each state prescribes a maximum weekly benefit and usually a minimum weekly benefit. Some states prescribe limits on the duration or total amount for certain benefits, including permanent partial, permanent total, and death benefits.

In all but four jurisdictions, an administrative agency adjudicates disputes concerning eligibility for benefits and extent of disability. Decisions of these agencies may be appealed for review by the courts. In four states, the courts decide all of the disputed claims.

Despite the role of the states in workers' compensation, it is largely a privately administered and funded program. The workers' compensation statutes provide that each employer shall compensate disabled workers using specified formulas for benefits, but normally the employer has some choice about how to provide these benefits. In all but three states, the employer, if it can meet the state financial standards, may self-insure the risk of work-related injuries and diseases. In 45 jurisdictions, the employer may purchase workers' compensation insurance from private insurance carriers. There are 19 states that operate insurance funds, but 13 of these compete with private carriers. Faced with these choices, employers usually make private insurance arrangements to meet their statutory obligations. In 1984, private insurance carriers were responsible for 59.3 percent of all benefits paid, self-insurers for 20.3 percent, and government funds for 20.4 percent.[3]

Workers' compensation benefits are financed by charges in the form of insurance premiums and rates related to the benefits paid. The relationship between benefits paid and the employers' costs is most direct for self-insuring employers. Other employers are rated on the experience of their class by state insurance funds or private carriers. Typically, several hundred insurance classifications are used in each state. The individual employer usually pays a rate related to the benefits paid by all employers in his class, but employers with sufficiently large premiums can have their rates modified to reflect their own record of benefit payments relative to other firms in their class.[4]

This brief description of workers' compensation serves as a starting point for answering the questions posed in chapter 1.

Which Causes of Injuries and Diseases Should Be Covered?

Which of the several causes of injuries and diseases enumerated in chart 1.1 should be covered by the workers' compensation program? The origin of the workers' compensation program provides some guidance to the answer.[5]

Industrial accident rates reached their all-time peak in the first decade of this century. For example, in 1907 over 7,000 workers were killed in just two industries—railroading and bituminous coal mining. Especially in view of the enormity of the industrial injury problem, the schemes available to compensate disabled workers were deficient.

Employees were required to bring legal actions against their employers based on the common law. The worker was the plaintiff in such cases, and therefore had the burden of proving the employer's negligence. Given the complexity of the work situation and the reluctance of fellow workers to testify for fear of losing their jobs, the worker often found himself unable to carry this burden of proof. Moreover, the employee was at a disadvantage because of the availability to the employer of

> that "unholy trinity of defenses": (1) *contributory negligence*—the worker could not recover if he himself had been negligent in any degree, regardless of the extent of the employer's negligence; (2) *the fellow-servant doctrine*—the employee could not recover if it could be shown that the injury had resulted from the negligence of a fellow worker; (3) *assumption of risk*—the injured man could not recover if injury was due to an inherent hazard of the job of which he had, or should have had, advance knowledge (Somers and Somers 1954, p. 18).

The grossest deficiencies of the common law soon became apparent, and dating from the 1850s there were legislative attempts, known as employers' liability laws, to modify these common law defenses. These laws still forced the employee to prove employer negligence, however, and their contribution to the ability of injured workers to recover from their employers was minimal.

Several shortcomings of the common law and the employers' liability laws were generally acknowledged. A system that protected workers only when someone was negligent was an anachronism: accidents were often an inevitable result of hazards inherent in industrial employment. Awards were glaringly inconsistent, ranging from nil to substantial. Society was forced to assume a burden in the form of "charity" for uncompensated injured workers. In short, as Arthur Larson has observed, "the coincidence of increasing industrial accidents and decreasing remedies had produced in the United States a situation ripe for radical change" (National Commission 1972, p. 34).

Most of the numerous objectives for a new system of compensating injured workers took their inspiration from the weaknesses of the common law. The new program was to provide benefits that were predetermined and adequate. The payments were to be prompt and certain, primarily to eliminate wasteful litigation. Adequate medical and rehabilitation services were to be provided. And the most radical objective was the establishment of an entirely new economic and legal principle—liability without fault. This principle would make it much easier for employees to recover. In turn, employers were to receive a limit on their liability. Workers' compensation benefits were to be the only recovery against the employer, and there was to be no possibility of a negligence suit against the employer.

The origins of the program thus support the idea of broad coverage of work-related injuries and diseases, since that approach helps overcome the deficiencies of the common law. More recently, the National Commission on State Workmen's Compensation Laws has endorsed the approach. One of the five objectives for a modern workers' compensation program spelled out in the Commission's *Report* (1972, p. 35) is broad coverage of employees and work-related injuries and diseases: "Workmen's compensation protection should be extended to as many workers as feasible, and all work-related injuries and diseases should be covered."

Workers' compensation statutes generally meet the objectives of broad coverage of work-related injuries and diseases. Several qualifications must be added, however. The idea of broad coverage includes the notion that fault of the employer or employee is irrelevant. Nonetheless, some states do permit extraordinary recoveries for workers whose damages result from particularly egregious conduct by employers. Conversely, some states will reduce the worker's benefit under workers' compensation when the worker's injury or disease can be traced to his own gross misconduct.

The counterpart of making all work-related injuries and diseases compensable is to make all injuries and diseases arising from nonwork-related causes noncompensable in the workers' compensation program. The argument for noncompensability provided by the National Commission *Report* (1972, p. 51) is that the function of workers' compensation

> is not to protect against all sources of impairment or death for workers. One of its objectives is to provide incentives to employers to improve their safety record. Impairments to his workers from non-work-related sources are largely beyond an employer's control. Moreover, there are many private and public benefits which are available to workers and their families regardless of the source of disability or death. Therefore, despite our sympathy for resolving doubts in favor of employees, we would not extend workmen's compensation to cover impairment and deaths that are not work-related.

A particularly difficult matter, at least conceptually, is establishing the extent of the employer's liability when an injury or disease is determined to be a result of both nonwork- and work-related causes. The National Commission noted that "in general an employee has been eligible for full workmen's compensation benefits if any nontrivial portion of his disability was due to a work-related source" and recommended that full workers' compensation benefits be paid "if the work-related factor was a significant cause of the impairment or death" (National Commission 1972, p. 51). Although this policy has been accepted in principle in most jurisdictions, substantial practical problems remain in determining causality. In most states, the issue of cause must be resolved by deciding whether the fact situation in a particular case meets the "arising out of and in the course of" tests. Often the "facts" are complex or ambiguous or both, and it is difficult to decide. In most jurisdictions, however, once work-related factors are established as being of some significance, the relative importance of the work-related and nonwork-related factors becomes secondary.[6]

Despite the general practice and the Commission's recommendation, some states, such as California, adjust the amount of workers' compensation benefits according to the relative importance of work-related and nonwork-related causes of damages. Among the more important and common cases in which factual determination of the relative importance of each factor can become quite difficult are those involving heart damage, which may result from an interaction of congenital, degenerative, and work-related factors; and those involving diabetes, which, although its etiology includes hereditary and degenerative processes, can be aggravated by an incident or a condition of work.

The complexities of workers' compensation and its concern with determining the causes of injuries or diseases are considerable. Putting those complexities aside for the present, it is sufficient to restate two simple generalizations about the treatment in workers' compensation laws of the causes of injuries or disease: eligibility is conditioned upon the presence of a work-related cause of injury or disease; and, with minor exceptions, once that cause is established, determination of whether the work-related cause was due to the employee's or employer's fault, and of whether there were also nonwork-related factors present, are irrelevant.

Which Consequences Should Be Compensable?

As outlined in chapter 1, the permanent consequences of work-related injuries and diseases include impairments, functional limitations, work disability, and nonwork disability. This section reviews some of the judgments made about which of these consequences should be compensable.

This review is complicated by two factors. First, those who comment on the goals of workers' compensation generally do not use a conceptual framework as elaborate as the one used in this report. Second, and more serious because the consequences are sequential and interdependent, a particular consequence may be endorsed as compensable because it serves as a convenient proxy for other consequences that are the primary concern of the commentator. Thus, a commentator may argue that impairments should be compensated when the real concern is for work disabilities and nonwork disabilities that generally flow from the impairments. An indirect route to compensate these disabilities may be chosen because impairments may be easier to measure than disabilities. Unfortunately, the commentators who favor payment for impairments do not always make clear whether this payment is for the existence of an impairment by itself or as a proxy for a disability.

The National Commission on State Workmen's Compensation Laws considered the question of which consequences of work-related injuries and diseases should be compensable. The Commission defined two types of cash benefits (1972, p. 54): *impairment benefits,* paid to a worker with an impairment caused by a work-related injury or disease, whether or not any wage loss results; and *disability benefits,* paid when an employee has impairment and actual or potential wage loss, both due to a work-related injury or disease. The *primary basis* for permanent partial benefits, the National Commission concluded, should be disability, although impairment can also serve as a secondary basis for this type of benefit.

The National Commission placed primary emphasis on disability as a basis for benefits because it concluded that one of the basic objectives of a modern workers' compensation program is the substantial protection against loss of income. Both the National Commission's description of disability benefits and its rationale for those benefits indicate that its concept of disability accords with the concept of "work disability" as used in this study.

It is necessary to reconcile the National Commission's "impairment benefits" with the concept used in this paper. The glossary of the National Commission's *Report* defines impairment in terms virtually identical to those used in chapter 1. The rationale offered by the National Commission (1972, p. 38) for impairment benefits, however, is that "many workers with work-related injuries or diseases experience losses which are not reflected in lost remuneration. Permanent impairment involves lifetime effects on the personality and on normal activity"—a description broad enough to include some of the aspects of functional limitations and nonwork disability as defined in chapter 1. The National Commission thus appears to have based its impairment benefits not on impairment *per se* but on impairment as a convenient proxy for the functional limitations and nonwork disability that result from the impairment.

Arthur Larson, the leading legal scholar in workers' compensation, stresses the primary importance of work disability (as that term is used in this study) as the basis for benefits (1973, pp. 33-34). He recognizes that some jurisdictions pay benefits based on evaluations of impairments, but argues that such evaluations are made only as rough estimates of actual or potential disability. The jurisdictions, in short, compensate the impairment because it serves as a proxy for work disability. Larson sees disability benefits as serving the social purpose of allowing workers to maintain their incomes in periods of distress, but payments for impairments *per se* as in the nature of recompense for damages, a concept more appropriate to negligence cases than to a social insurance program. Workers' compensation should cover medical and legal expenses related to the work injury, however, lest the income-sustaining purpose of the benefits be undermined.

The National Commission's and Larson's views on compensability do not represent the full range of approaches that have been offered. They are typical, however, in their argument that work disability should be the primary, if not exclusive, basis for permanent partial benefits. The National Commission's argument that impairment (and, inferentially, functional limitations and nonwork disability) is also a suitable basis for permanent partial benefits, although unusual, is not without precedent.

What Should Be the Amount of Compensation?

Once the issue of which permanent consequences of work-related injuries and diseases should be compensated has been decided, the next question is how much compensation to award. One criterion for evaluating permanent partial benefits is that they should be adequate.

Adequacy of Disability Benefits

The National Commission defines *adequate* as "delivering sufficient benefits and services to meet the objectives of the program." For disability benefits, the relevant objective of the program is to "provide substantial protection against interruption of income." The rationale for providing *substantial* benefits, tied to the worker's loss of income, rather than an amount tied to the worker's economic needs, is that workers' compensation is an insurance program, not a welfare program (National Commission 1972, pp. 36-38). The history of workers' compensation, which distinguishes that program from other forms of social insurance, supplies the justification for offsetting a substantial proportion of the loss of income in the form of benefits. In exchange for the benefits provided by workers' compensation, workers surrendered their right to sue their employers in common law for full damages including pain and suffering. (One reason for limiting workers' compensation cash benefits to less than the full amount of lost income, on the other hand, is that benefits nearly equal to lost income might seriously reduce workers' incentive to return to employment.)

The National Commission did not make specific recommendations for permanent partial disability benefits that would permit a translation of providing "substantial protection against interruption of income" into a numerical or quantitative standard. For temporary total and permanent total disability, the National Commission recommended that, subject to the state's maximum weekly benefits, the total disability benefits be at least two-thirds of the worker's gross weekly wage.[7] If a similar degree of protection were provided for permanent partial disability, the permanent partial disability benefits would be two-thirds of the difference between the worker's earnings (or earning capacity) before and after the injury or disease.

This definition of adequacy can be visualized by use of graph 2.1, which is a modified version of graph 1.1.

The measure of earnings loss used in the discussion of graph 1.1 corresponds to what is labeled on graph 2.1 as "true" wage loss. This measure of wage loss is equal to the worker's potential earnings after the date of injury (BC) minus the worker's actual earnings after the date of injury (BDEFG). Although this version of wage loss is appropriate for many purposes, including the assessment of the total consequences of a work-related injury, it is not the measure of wage loss typically encompassed in a workers' compensation statute. Rather, the statute usually measures what is termed in graph 2.1 as "restricted" wage loss. That is, the worker's earnings as of the date of injury, which were at level B, are projected into the future at that level, namely along the line BH. Then the "restricted" wage loss that serves as a basis for workers' compenation benefits is measured as the difference between the line BH and the worker's actual earnings after the date of injury (BDEFG). As is obvious, the "restricted" wage loss is smaller than the "true" wage loss. Indeed, there is a date at which the actual earnings line FG crosses the line BH, which means there is no additional "restricted" wage loss after this date even though there is continuing "true" wage loss.

Adequacy for temporary total disability benefits using this restricted definition of wage loss requires that 66 2/3 percent of the area lying above DE and below BH be replaced by benefits. Adequate temporary partial disability benefits requires that 66 2/3 percent of the area between BH and FG be replaced between the time the employee returns to work (EF) and the date the medical condition stabilizes (the date of maximum medical improvement, or MMI). For permanent partial disability benefits to be adequate, 66 2/3 percent of the area between BH and FG must be replaced after the date of MMI.[8] (These examples assume the worker's benefits are not affected by maximum or minimum weekly benefit amounts.)

Graph 2.1
Actual Loss of Earnings for a Worker with a Permanent Disability

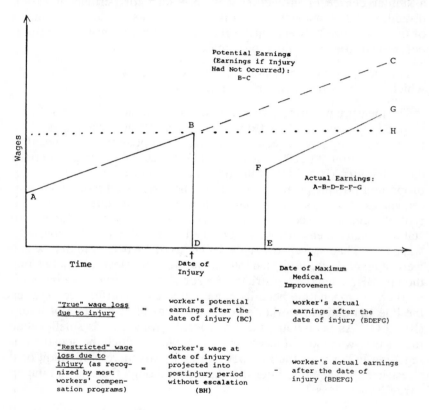

"True" wage loss due to injury	=	worker's potential earnings after the date of injury (BC)	−	worker's actual earnings after the date of injury (BDEFG)
"Restricted" wage loss due to injury (as recognized by most workers' compensation programs)	=	worker's wage at date of injury projected into postinjury period without escalation (BH)	−	worker's actual earnings after the date of injury (BDEFG)

Adequacy of Impairment Benefits

Adequacy for impairment benefits is not well defined by the National Commission. The *Report* (1972, p. 38) indicates that impairment benefits "should be of secondary importance" and "limited in number and amount." In a discussion of suggestions for restructuring permanent partial benefits (pp. 68-70), a scheme for impairment benefits is offered which relates the duration of the benefits to the extent of the worker's impairment compared to total impairment. If total impairment were defined as warranting 400 weeks of benefits, a worker with 50 percent impairment would receive 200 weeks of benefits. The *Report* does not, however, suggest an appropriate amount of weekly benefits, which leaves the scheme incomplete.[9]

The National Commission, although obviously not specifying exactly what was meant by "limited," did offer several reasons why the impairment benefits should be limited. One is the historical exchange, or *quid pro quo,* which established the principle of liability without fault in exchange for limited benefits (National Commission 1972, p. 38). Another reason for limited impairment benefits is a concern for efficiency. Since the determination of the degree of impairment is inherently complicated and expensive, by limiting impairment benefits the Commission felt it would be providing for "far less time consumed in evaluating such claims" (National Commission *Report,* p. 38). Presumably, time would be saved because the relatively low amount of the impairment benefits would reduce the incentives for litigation, or because benefits for minor permanent impairments would be proscribed. (See National Commission 1972, p. 70.)

How Should Compensation Benefits Be Distributed Among Workers?

The second criterion for permanent partial benefits is that they should be equitable. The National Commission defines *equitable* as "delivering benefits and services fairly as judged by the program's consistency in providing equal benefits or services to workers in identical circumstances and its rationality in providing benefits and services in proportion to the impairment or disability for those with different degrees of loss" (1972, p. 137).[10]

Equity of Disability Benefits

The application of the equity criterion to disability benefits is fairly straightforward at an abstract level. Workers with equal losses of earnings (or losses of earning capacity) should receive equal benefits; workers with different losses should receive benefits proportionate to their losses. The difficulties become much more severe when the equity criterion is applied to real-world situations (a generalization also true of the adequacy criterion). As indicated in chart 1.2, the extent of work disability proceeds not only from the workers' functional limitations, but from their interaction with a variety of other influences (age, education, and so on). For a given worker who is earning less after a work-related injury or disease than before, the drop in earnings may be due to a work disability (caused by his functional limitations interacting with the other influences) or to factors entirely unrelated to his work-related injury or disease (he won the Illinois lottery and decided to retire, or was arrested for gambling and incarcerated). Until the cause of the drop in earnings is ascertained (and there are likely to be multiple causes), it is not possible to determine if the assigned benefits are equitable compared to other workers' benefits (or, for that matter, adequate).

Equity of Impairment Benefits

The application of the equity criterion to impairment benefits also is fairly straightforward at an abstract level. Workers with equally serious impairments should receive equal benefits, and workers with different degrees of impairment should receive proportionately different benefits. One problem is that the measurement of impairment is at best controversial and at worst almost impossible (some of the difficulties are discussed in part II). Another problem is that sometimes impairment benefits are meant to compensate not only for impairment *per se* but also for a worker's functional limitations and nonwork disabilities, and it is exceedingly difficult to determine the extent of these other losses. For example, the extent of nonwork disability is a result of complex interactions among such factors as the worker's functional limitations, age, education, and family situation. The problem of determining the extent of nonwork disability makes it difficult to assess the adequacy and equity of benefits that are meant, at least in part, to compensate for nonwork disability.

How Should the Delivery System for Compensation Benefits Be Evaluated?

The benefits and services in workers' compensation are provided by a delivery system comprising employers, carriers, state agencies, attorneys, and doctors that was briefly described in the first section of this chapter. How should this delivery system be evaluated? The third criterion for permanent partial benefits is that they should be provided efficiently. The term *efficiency* is used in this study to describe two concepts, which are illustrated in graph 2.2. The horizontal axis measures the administrative costs of providing benefits incurred by the participants in the workers' compensation delivery system, including employers, insurance carriers, workers, attorneys, and state agencies. The vertical axis measures the quality of the workers' compensation benefits, where quality is assessed on the basis of one or more criteria such as adequacy and equity. Graph 2.2 is constructed so that the desired outcomes (high quality and low costs) are furthest from the origin.

Graph 2.2
The Efficiency of Workers' Compensation Benefits

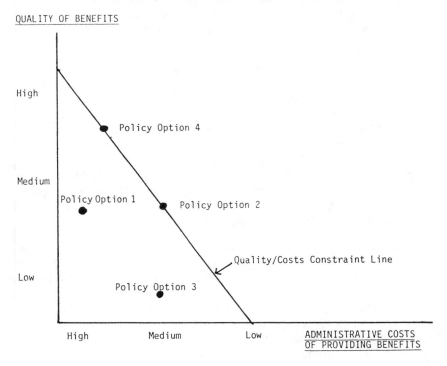

One meaning of efficiency, which will be termed *panoramic efficiency*, is that benefits of a particular quality are provided at the least possible administrative costs. A complementary definition of panoramic efficiency is that benefits of the highest possible quality are obtained for a given amount of administrative costs. Panoramic efficiency is illustrated by the difference between policy option 1, which has high administrative costs and medium-quality benefits, and policy option 2, which also has medium-quality benefits but lower administrative costs. Moving from policy option 1 to policy option 2 (perhaps by ending unnecessary litigation) improves panoramic efficiency. Policy option 2 lies on the quality/costs constraint line, which means that the administrative costs cannot be further reduced for medium-quality benefits.[11]

Panoramic efficiency is also illustrated by the difference between policy option 3, which has medium administrative costs and low-quality benefits, and policy option 2, which has medium administrative costs and medium-quality benefits. Moving from policy option 3 to policy option 2 (perhaps by increasing the level of benefits in a state with inadequate benefits) improves panoramic efficiency.

Another meaning of efficiency, which will be termed *myopic efficiency,* is only concerned with reducing administrative costs, without concern for the quality of the program. Myopic efficiency is illustrated by the difference between policy option 2, which has high administrative expenses, and policy option 4, which has medium administrative expenses. Moving from policy option 4 to policy option 2 thus reduces administrative costs. Because it is impossible to move outside the quality/cost constraint line, however, the movement from policy option 4 to policy option 2 requires a reduction in the quality of benefits. Myopic efficiency means that the move from policy option 4 to policy option 2 is made, regardless of the decline in quality of benefits, solely because of the reduction in administrative costs.[12]

As indicated by graph 2.2, the three criteria—adequacy, equity, and efficiency—are to some extent competitive. A reduction in litigation expenses can improve efficiency without reducing equity if a horizontal move can be made toward the quality/costs constraint line. But eventually, further reductions in administrative expenses can be achieved only by movements along the constraint line, which represents only a gain in myopic efficiency because of the reduction in the quality of the program. These trade-offs among the criteria are examined at length in part IV of this study.

NOTES

1. The federal programs are the Federal Employees' Compensation Act, which is applicable to federal employees, and the Longshoremen's and Harbor Workers' Compensation Act, which is applicable to employees working on navigable waters, excluding the master or crew of a vessel. These federal programs are beyond the scope of this study, which is concerned with the 51 jurisdictions—the 50 states and the District of Columbia. As used in this study, the term *state* includes the District of Columbia.

2. This section is adapted from material at pp. 32-33 of the National Commission *Report* (1972). Current data are from U.S. Dept. of Labor, *Administration Profiles* (1985) and U.S. Dept. of Labor, *State Laws* (1986).

3. The percentages are for data excluding the federal black lung program and are from Price (1987). Competitive state funds were authorized in 1983 in Minnesota and in 1985 in Hawaii, but the Hawaiian fund is not in operation.

4. More information on the insurance arrangements in workers' compensation is included in Burton and Krueger (1986).

5. This section is adapted from material at pages 33-35 of the National Commission *Report* (1972).

6. The relative contributions of work-related and nonwork-related causes may be relevant if the case qualifies for partial payment of the benefits from the second injury fund. Under stipulated statutory conditions that vary from state to state, these funds will pay for a portion of the workers' compensation benefits when the injury or disease experienced by the worker interacts with impairments that existed prior to the worker's current employment. See Larson and Burton (1985).

7. Although the National Commission supported a benefit formula that replaces 66 2/3 percent of the worker's gross weekly wage, the formula preferred by the Commission makes total disability benefits at least 80 percent of spendable earnings (National Commission 1972, pp. 60, 64). Spendable earnings are gross earnings minus deductions for the social security payroll tax and the federal income tax. Variants of the spendable earning approach are used in the Alaska, District of Columbia, Iowa and Michigan workers' compensation programs.

8. The National Commission also recommended that permanent total benefits be increased through time in the same proportion as increases in the state's average weekly wage. Similar protection for permanent partial disability would require permanent partial disability benefits to be escalated through time, reflecting the increase in the worker's earnings (or earning capacity) that would have occurred if he had not been affected by a work-related injury or disease. This definition of adequacy requires permanent partial disability benefits to replace 66 2/3 percent of the area between BC and FG after the date of MMI (graph 2.1).

9. One difficulty in establishing the appropriate amount for impairment benefits is the lack of an objective measure of the nonwork disability that results from the impairment. The standard for disability benefits is the worker's loss of earnings, which can be measured (although with some difficulty). An equivalent standard for impairment benefits is lacking since the disutility associated with nonwork disability cannot be directly measured.

10. The National Commission's definition of *equitable* implies that vertical equity requires a strict proportionality of benefits to losses. That is, a worker with twice the losses of another worker should receive exactly twice the benefits. More generally, vertical equity only requires that there be a consistent relationship between losses and benefits. Society may decide, for example, that the proportion of benefits to losses should decrease (or increase) as losses increase. The desired

relationship between benefits and losses may be nonlinear, which is consistent with the use of minimum and maximum benefits. Evaluation of workers' compensation benefits becomes much more complicated when the test for vertical equity is something other than strict proportionality between losses and benefits. Nonetheless, even the National Commission did not strictly adhere to its own definition of equitable (because the *Report* at p. 38 concluded "there is an uneasy case for maximum and minimum benefits"), and part IV of this report will consider the implications of using a more general test of vertical equity when the performance of workers' compensation programs is evaluated.

11. In order to provide permanent partial benefits that are reasonable and equitable—e.g., benefits that vary among workers reasonably with respect to their varying work disability—a certain amount of supervision by the workers' compensation agency is necessary. Cutting administrative costs by reducing the agency budget will, after a certain point, jeopardize the supervisory role and reduce equity.

12. A move from policy option 1 to policy option 4 increases both panoramic and myopic efficiency, as those terms are defined in the text.

Part II
The Ten-State Study of Workers' Compensation Procedures and Standards

Chapter 3
An Introduction
to the Ten-State Study

The previous chapters provided a general introduction to workers' compensation and to permanent disability benefits. In this part of the study, we provide a detailed examination of the procedures and standards used to provide compensation for permanent disabilities in 10 jurisdictions.

An Overview of Permanent Disability Cases

The national experience with permanent disability cases in recent decades provides a useful backdrop for our intensive examination of the experience in 10 jurisdictions. The best data on permanent disability cases are available from the National Council on Compensation Insurance (NCCI), the organization that helps establish workers' compensation insurance rates in most states.

The NCCI data are collected for use in the rate-making procedure for workers' compensation insurance and bear the imprint of that use. The data are national only to the extent that they are provided by private insurance carriers and some competitive state funds. Excluded entirely from the data are six states with exclusive state funds, plus the experience of self-insuring employers and of some competitive state funds. Despite these exclusions, the data encompass most benefit payments in the United States and represent the most comprehensive available national and state information on benefits broken down by type of case.

The NCCI data used in this chapter are based on reports on the experience of carriers with insurance policies sold during particular policy years. Because of the time lag between the issuance of the policies for a given policy year and the compilation of the statistical reports pertaining to that year, the most recent data as of the writing of this study (summer 1986) are for policies written in 1982.[1]

The data collected by the NCCI distinguish among five types of cases with indemnity (cash) benefits: death, temporary total, and, of particular interest to us, permanent total, permanent partial major, and permanent partial minor. The distinction between permanent partial major and permanent partial minor relates to the seriousness of the injury. The procedure used to distinguish between major and minor has changed through time.[2] Currently, permanent partial disability cases are classified as major or minor depending on the amount of cash benefits paid in the case, with the critical values varying by state.[3] Comparisons through time and among jurisdictions of the proportion of cases classified as major or minor permanent partial must be used with caution, but the data provide a rough guide to the distribution of such cases.

Table 3.1 shows the number of permanent disability cases for selected years since 1958. Permanent total cases have never totalled as many as 2,000 cases per year, and have represented from 0.10 percent to 0.16 percent of all cases. Their relative lack of frequency helps explain why the main focus of this study is on permanent partial disability benefits.

There were 20,994 major permanent partial disability cases in 1958, which was about 3 percent of all cases. By 1982, the number of major permanent partial disability cases had increased to 82,687, about 6.5 percent of all cases. Minor permanent partial disability cases have always been the most common type among permanent disability cases, although the absolute number in 1982 of 217,736 only represented about 17 percent of all cases, down from about 24 percent of all cases in 1968.

The combined total of all permanent disability cases (consisting almost entirely of permanent partial disability cases) was 188,653 in 1958, representing 26 percent of all cases. The percent of cases accounted for by permanent disability peaked in 1968 at almost 29 percent, and then declined to about 24 percent of all cases in 1978 and 1982. In short, there is evidence that permanent disability cases have become numerically less prevalent than other cases (almost all of which are temporary total disability).

Although the number of permanent disability cases has been declining relatively in recent decades, the average costs of such cases have been increasing in both absolute and (at least through 1978) relative senses (see table 3.2). In 1958, the national average cost of indemnity benefits for permanent total cases was $19,322, which represented 6,490 percent of the average cost of a temporary total case ($298) that year. By 1978, permanent total cases cost on average $78,788, which was 8,602 percent of the average cost of a temporary total case ($916) that year. Between 1978 and 1982, the average cost of a permanent total

Table 3.1
Number of Permanent Disability Cases,
U.S. Totals,[1] 1958-82

Year	Type of Cases				
	Permanent total	Major permanent partial	Minor permanent partial	All permanent disability	All with indemnity benefits
1958[2]					
Number	808	20,994	166,851	188,653	715,999
Share of all cases (%)[3]	0.11	2.93	23.30	26.35	100.00
1968[2]					
Number	919	39,207	217,854	257,980	895,847
Share of all cases (%)[3]	0.10	4.38	24.32	28.80	100.00
1973[2]					
Number	1,692	42,114	213,228	257,034	1,030,740
Share of all cases (%)[3]	0.16	4.09	20.69	24.94	100.00
1978[2]					
Number	1,876	71,576	259,945	333,397	1,392,192
Share of all cases (%)[3]	0.13	5.14	18.67	23.95	100.00
1982[2]					
Number	1,869	82,687	217,736	302,292	1,259,770
Share of all cases (%)[3]	0.15	6.56	17.28	24.00	100.00

SOURCE: National Council on Compensation Insurance, ''Countrywide Workers' Compensation Experience Including Certain Competitive State Funds—1st Report Basis,'' exhibits dated: for 1958, no date; for 1968, March 15, 1972; for 1973, July 1976; for 1978, April 1982; and for 1982, June 1986.

1. U.S. refers to the states that provide data to the National Council on Compensation Insurance, and thus excludes Nevada, North Dakota, Ohio, Washington, West Virginia, and Wyoming. California no longer provides certain data to the National Council, and so California 1981 policy year data are used for the columns pertaining to 1982. The 1982 data thus pertain to 44 states plus the District of Columbia. For these 45 jurisdictions, the data encompass the experience of private insurance carriers and some competitive state funds; excluded are data for self-insuring employers and some competitive state funds.

2. The data shown are for the insurance industry policy years that most closely correspond to the calendar years shown. For Pennsylvania, e.g., the 1982 data are for insurance policies in effect between April 1982 and March 1983.

3. The share is the number of the type of cases shown as a percentage of all cases paying indemnity (cash) benefits. Types of indemnity cases not shown individually are death and temporary total disability.

case increased in dollars to $92,055, but declined relative to the average cost of a temporary total case to 7,293 percent. Major permanent partial disability costs went from an average of $6,879 in 1958 to $21,456 in 1978, both figures roughly 2,300 percent of the average cost of temporary total cases in the corresponding years. In 1982, the major permanent partial cases had an average cost of $25,139, almost 2,000 percent of the cost of a temporary total case. Minor permanent partial disability costs averaged $1,253 in 1958 and $4,013 in 1978, both about 430 percent of the average cost of temporary total cases in those years. The minor permanent partial cases had an average cost of $4,953 in 1982, about 390 percent of the average cost of a temporary total case. The weighted average of all permanent disability cases went from $1,957 in 1958 to $8,178 in 1978 to $11,013 in 1982, increasing the relative costs compared to temporary total cases from 657 percent to 893 percent followed by a modest decline to 872 percent. This substantial escalation in relative costs between 1958 and 1982 reflects, in part, the increasing proportion of permanent disability cases accounted for by major permanent partial disability cases (see table 3.1), which are considerably more expensive than minor permanent partial disability cases.

The total costs of permanent disability cases, shown in table 3.3, reflect the developments in the numbers of such cases and their average costs as shown in the previous two tables. The share of all benefit payments represented by payments for permanent total cases increased from 2.64 percent to 3.54 percent between 1958 and 1982. Major permanent partial disability cases increased their share of all benefit payments from 24 percent to almost 43 percent, primarily because of the increasing share of all cases accounted for by these serious injuries. In contrast, minor permanent partial disability cases' share of all costs dropped from 35 percent to 22 percent, due to the numerical decline of such cases compared to other cases. Overall, the 24-year period saw permanent disability cases increase their share of all benefit payments from 62 percent to 68 percent, while the dollar amounts for permanent disability cases increased from $369 million to $3,329 million.

Two additional observations are warranted. Since 1968, the approximately two-thirds share of all cash benefits accounted for by permanent disability cases has been quite stable. Also, the notion sometimes advanced that too much of workers' compensation resources are dissipated on minor permanent partial disability cases seems increasingly less accurate, since the share of all benefits going to such cases has declined in each successive subperiod shown in table 3.3. This obser-

Table 3.2
Average Costs of Permanent Disability Cases,
U.S. Averages,[1] 1958-82

Year	Permanent total	Major permanent partial	Minor permanent partial	All permanent disability	Temporary total
		Type of Cases			
1958[2]					
Cost (dollars)[3]	19,322	6,879	1,253	1,957	298
Cost relative to temporary total (%)	6,490	2,310	421	657	100
1968[2]					
Cost (dollars)[3]	35,606	9,983	2,055	3,379	434
Cost relative to temporary total (%)	8,207	2,301	474	779	100
1973[2]					
Cost (dollars)[3]	37,544	13,265	2,627	4,599	560
Cost relative to temporary total (%)	6,704	2,369	469	821	100
1978[2]					
Cost (dollars)[3]	78,788	21,456	4,013	8,178	916
Cost relative to temporary total (%)	8,602	2,342	438	893	100
1982[2]					
Cost (dollars)[3]	92,055	25,139	4,953	11,013	1,262
Cost relative to temporary total (%)	7,293	1,992	392	872	100

SOURCE: National Council on Compensation Insurance, ''Countrywide Workers' Compensation Experience Including Certain Competitive State Funds—1st Report Basis,'' exhibits dated: for 1958, no date; for 1968, March 15, 1972; for 1973, July 1976; for 1978, April 1982; and for 1982, June 1986.

1. U.S. refers to the states that provide data to the National Council on Compensation Insurance, and thus excludes Nevada, North Dakota, Ohio, Washington, West Virginia, and Wyoming. California no longer provides certain data to the National Council, and so California 1981 policy year data are used for the columns pertaining to 1982. The 1982 data thus pertain to 44 states plus the District of Columbia. For these 45 jurisdictions, the data encompass the experience of private insurance carriers and some competitive state funds; excluded are data for self-insuring employers and some competitive state funds.

2. The data shown are for the insurance industry policy years that most closely correspond to the calendar years shown. For Pennsylvania, e.g., the 1982 data are for insurance policies in effect between April 1982 and March 1983.

3. The cost is the average cost of indemnity (cash) benefits for the type of cases shown. The cost of medical benefits is excluded.

Table 3.3
Total Costs of Permanent Disability Cases,
U.S. Totals,[1] 1958-82

Year	Type of Cases				
	Permanent total	Major permanent partial	Minor permanent partial	All permanent disability	All with indemnity benefits
1958[2]					
Cost ($ millions)[3]	15.612	144.418	209.103	369.133	590.709
Share of all costs (%)[4]	2.64	24.45	35.40	62.49	100.00
1968[2]					
Cost ($ millions)[3]	32.722	391.384	447.578	871.684	1,286.793
Share of all costs (%)[4]	2.54	30.42	34.78	67.74	100.00
1973[2]					
Cost ($ millions)[3]	63.524	558.630	560.246	1,182.400	1,786.198
Share of all costs (%)[4]	3.56	31.27	31.37	66.20	100.00
1978[2]					
Cost ($ millions)[3]	147.807	1,535.737	1,043.063	2,726.607	4,042.086
Share of all costs (%)[4]	3.66	37.99	25.81	67.46	100.00
1982[2]					
Cost ($ millions)[3]	172.051	2,078.689	1,078.366	3,329.107	4,860.672
Share of all costs (%)[4]	3.54	42.77	22.19	68.49	100.00

SOURCE: National Council on Compensation Insurance, "Countrywide Workers' Compensation Experience Including Certain Competitive State Funds—1st Report Basis," exhibits dated: for 1958, no date; for 1968, March 15, 1972; for 1973, July 1976; for 1978, April 1982; and for 1982, June 1986.

1. U.S. refers to the states that provide data to the National Council on Compensation Insurance, and thus excludes Nevada, North Dakota, Ohio, Washington, West Virginia, and Wyoming. California no longer provides certain data to the National Council, and so California 1981 policy year data are used for the columns pertaining to 1982. The 1982 data thus pertain to 44 states plus the District of Columbia. For these 45 jurisdictions, the data encompass the experience of private insurance carriers and some competitive state funds; excluded are data for self-insuring employers and some competitive state funds.

2. The data shown are for the insurance industry policy years that most closely correspond to the calendar years shown. For Pennsylvania, e.g., the 1982 data are for insurance policies in effect between April 1982 and March 1983.

3. The cost is the total cost of indemnity (cash) benefits for the type of cases shown. The cost of medical benefits is excluded.

4. The share is the total cost of indemnity benefits for the type of cases shown as a percentage of all indemnity benefits. Types of indemnity cases not shown individually are death and temporary total disability.

vation must be used with caution, however, since the dividing line between major and minor permanent partial disability cases is somewhat arbitrary, and the trend showing relatively less importance for the minor category may in part be a statistical artifact.[4] Most of our analysis in this report relies on the total costs of all permanent disability cases in various states, a statistic that is not affected by the division between the major and minor permanent partial disability categories.

Limitations in the data shown in tables 3.1 to 3.3 make some qualification necessary. One limitation is that the information is all derived from the first reports from insurance carriers on the policies written in the given policy years. The first report is submitted 18 months after the policy begins, and obviously only covers developments in cases to that point, although reserves for expected future payments in the cases are recorded. Subsequent developments in these cases or for new cases that can be traced back to the particular policy year are reported on an annual basis thereafter.[5] Between the first and subsequent reports, some cases that were initially classified as minor permanent partial disability or temporary total are reclassified as major permanent partial disability or permanent total.[6] In some cases that are not reclassified as to type, the amount of benefits paid or reserved for future payments is increased. The result is that between the first and subsequent reports, typically the number of permanent disability cases increases, while the average costs for these cases also increase, both in dollars and relative to the costs of temporary total disability cases.

Table 3.4 shows changes in 1982 permanent disability cases between the actual first report on these cases and the simulated ultimate report basis.[7] Several results are apparent. The most dramatic change involves permanent total cases, for which the number almost doubled and total costs more than doubled. Indeed, permanent total cases on the ultimate report basis account for more than 7 percent of all cash benefit payments.

Major permanent partial disability cases also show a marked increase in numbers and costs, accounting for almost 52 percent of all benefit payments on the ultimate report basis. Permanent partial disability minor cases, in contrast, show almost no increase in absolute numbers between the first and ultimate report basis, in part because some of these cases are transformed into permanent total or major permanent partial disability cases. As a result, permanent partial disability minor cases account for about 16 percent of all costs in the ultimate report, down from about 22 percent on the first report basis.

Table 3.4
Permanent Disability Cases, 1982
Comparisons of First Report Basis and Ultimate Report Basis

Type of cases and report basis	Number of cases	Share of all cases (percentage)	Average cost[1] (dollars)	Cost relative to temporary total (percentage)	Total costs[2] ($ millions)	Share of all costs (percentage)
Permanent total						
First report	1,869	0.15	92,055	7,293	172.051	3.54
Ultimate report	3,640	0.28	137,021	9,881	498.756	7.07
Major permanent partial						
First report	82,687	6.56	25,139	1,992	2,078.689	42.77
Ultimate report	99,855	7.66	36,638	2,642	3,658.445	51.85
Minor permanent partial						
First report	217,736	17.28	4,953	392	1,078.366	22.19
Ultimate report	218,853	16.78	5,210	376	1,140.291	16.16
All permanent disability						
First report	302,292	24.00	11,013	872	3,329.107	68.49
Ultimate report	322,348	24.72	16,434	1,185	5,297.493	75.08

SOURCE: National Council on Compensation Insurance, "Countrywide Workers' Compensation Experience Including Competitive State Funds—1st Report Basis," and similar exhibit on "Ultimate Report Basis," both June 1986. California data from the 1981 policy year were added since California did not provide the 1982 policy year data to the National Council on Compensation Insurance.

1. The cost is the average cost of indemnity (cash) benefits for the type of cases shown.

2. The cost is the total cost of indemnity (cash) benefits for the type of cases shown.

The overall significance of permanent disability cases is magnified by moving from the first to ultimate report basis. They are more numerous, more expensive on average, and account for 75 percent of all cash benefits, more than 6 percentage points higher than on the first report basis.

Although the data on an ultimate report basis provide a more accurate picture of the number and cost of permanent disability cases, the balance of this report will focus on first report data for two reasons. First, the National Council on Compensation Insurance only began to develop the countrywide exhibits on a simulated fifth report basis in 1979 and on the simulated ultimate report basis in 1984, and therefore data on an historical basis comparable to those shown in table 3.4 are unavailable. Second, the procedures used to develop the simulated ultimate report basis from the first report data are not comparable among all states. In particular, the development procedures for three of the states examined intensively in this report—California, New Jersey, and New York—are inconsistent with those used for the other states for which the NCCI provides data.[8]

Another limitation to the data provided in tables 3.1 to 3.3 that affects the previous observations is that the information pertains to national experience and thus masks significant differences in developments in permanent disability benefits at the state level. Table 3.5 provides an introduction to the diversity that underlies the national averages. In 1982, for example, the percentage of benefit costs accounted for by permanent total cases ranged from zero percent in South Dakota to 13.10 percent in Hawaii. For major permanent partial disability cases, the range was from 5.39 percent in Missouri to 79.63 percent in Rhode Island. For minor permanent partial disability cases, the percentages varied from 3.01 percent in Rhode Island to 49.10 in New Jersey. The percentages for particular types of permanent disability benefits were partially offsetting (as in Rhode Island), but the share of all costs accounted for by all types of permanent disability benefits ranged from 40.59 percent in Arizona to 84.21 percent in Rhode Island, each a considerable distance from the U.S. average of 68.49 percent. A major purpose of this study is to explain some of the reasons for this diversity.

The Selection of Ten States

Each state controls its workers' compensation program, and there are substantial differences among jurisdictions in the criteria and procedures

Table 3.5
Costs of Permanent Disability Cases, by Jurisdiction, 1982

Jurisdiction	Permanent total Cost[1] ($ millions)	Permanent total Share of all costs[2] (percentage)	Major permanent partial Cost[1] ($ millions)	Major permanent partial Share of all costs[2] (percentage)	Minor permanent partial Cost[1] ($ millions)	Minor permanent partial Share of all costs[2] (percentage)	All permanent disability Cost[1] ($ millions)	All permanent disability Share of all costs[2] (percentage)
Alabama	1.386	3.13	19.244	43.46	8.213	18.55	28.843	65.13
Alaska	3.029	9.18	16.688	50.59	5.599	16.97	25.317	76.75
Arizona	1.197	2.05	17.794	30.43	4.744	8.11	23.735	40.59
Arkansas	0.819	2.13	21.153	55.10	5.488	14.30	27.461	71.53
California	17.782	2.79	289.126	45.29	217.269	34.03	524.177	82.11
Colorado	3.000	2.47	75.859	62.35	16.820	13.83	95.678	78.64
Connecticut	1.114	1.24	44.001	49.18	17.017	19.02	62.132	69.45
Delaware	0.495	5.22	3.203	33.77	1.822	19.21	5.520	58.21
District of Columbia	1.937	7.17	17.761	65.70	1.162	4.30	20.860	77.16
Florida	7.491	4.88	75.223	49.03	14.277	9.31	96.991	63.22
Georgia	3.434	4.01	48.362	56.43	11.934	13.92	63.730	74.36
Hawaii	5.260	13.10	20.028	49.89	7.335	18.27	32.623	81.26
Idaho	0.497	2.23	5.498	24.74	8.383	37.73	14.378	64.71
Illinois	6.770	2.04	173.783	52.43	68.475	20.66	249.028	75.12
Indiana	0.539	1.26	16.185	37.75	7.203	16.80	23.928	55.81
Iowa	1.589	2.59	29.594	48.23	9.189	14.98	40.372	65.80
Kansas	1.693	2.83	34.790	58.25	8.600	14.40	45.083	75.48
Kentucky	2.895	5.20	34.551	62.01	3.768	6.76	41.214	73.97
Louisiana	10.273	6.76	96.528	63.55	14.324	9.43	121.125	79.74
Maine	3.237	5.97	30.258	55.82	7.653	14.12	41.147	75.91
Maryland	2.889	3.31	32.229	36.93	28.642	32.82	63.760	73.07

Massachusetts	3.821	1.69	112.111	49.56	14.919	6.60	130.851	57.84
Michigan	3.952	2.54	84.690	54.37	18.444	11.84	107.086	68.75
Minnesota	1.987	1.81	56.082	51.01	18.069	16.44	76.139	69.26
Mississippi	0.448	1.54	16.389	56.29	3.414	11.73	20.251	69.56
Missouri	3.256	3.88	4.528	5.39	34.400	40.98	42.184	50.25
Montana	1.073	2.94	22.969	62.97	1.485	4.07	25.527	69.99
Nebraska	0.875	3.81	10.543	45.91	3.883	16.91	15.301	66.63
New Hampshire	1.689	5.59	18.564	61.42	1.256	4.15	21.509	71.16
New Jersey	4.847	2.75	45.007	25.58	86.391	49.10	136.245	77.44
New Mexico	1.003	2.26	25.379	57.20	7.753	17.47	34.134	76.93
New York	2.735	0.98	102.792	36.71	51.122	18.26	156.649	55.95
North Carolina	1.567	2.38	25.948	39.35	15.424	23.39	42.940	65.11
Oklahoma	4.979	3.68	54.246	40.08	37.700	27.85	96.925	71.61
Oregon	1.260	1.65	8.274	10.84	37.455	49.05	46.990	61.54
Pennsylvania	31.172	11.27	61.210	22.12	50.506	18.25	142.888	51.64
Rhode Island	0.598	1.56	30.519	79.63	1.154	3.01	32.271	84.21
South Carolina	0.791	1.72	23.767	51.64	9.239	20.07	33.798	73.43
South Dakota	0.000	0.00	2.873	38.21	1.551	20.62	4.424	58.83
Tennessee	1.387	2.06	34.697	51.48	11.779	17.48	47.863	71.01
Texas	22.384	3.97	157.629	27.94	171.603	30.42	351.616	62.33
Utah	0.244	2.11	6.946	59.93	1.136	9.80	8.326	71.84
Vermont	0.039	0.31	5.477	43.45	1.863	14.78	7.379	58.55
Virginia	1.863	2.74	31.543	46.47	9.971	14.69	43.377	63.91
Wisconsin	2.751	3.07	34.652	38.64	19.929	22.22	57.332	63.92
Total	172.051	3.54	2,078.689	42.77	1,078.366	22.19	3,329.107	68.49

SOURCE: National Council on Compensation Insurance, "Countrywide Workers' Compensation Experience Including Certain Competitive State Funds—1st Report Basis," exhibits dated June 1986.

1. The cost is the total cost of indemnity (cash) benefits for the type of cases shown. The cost of medical benefits is excluded.

2. The share is the total cost of indemnity benefits for the type of cases shown as a percentage of all indemnity benefits. Types of indemnity cases not shown individually are death and temporary total disability.

used to compensate permanent disabilities. The data in table 3.5 provide some evidence on the extent of this diversity, although even some states that devote similar percentages of benefits to permanent disability cases may reach the parity by different routes.

This study provides an examination of the approaches to permanent disability benefits used in 10 jurisdictions. It was not feasible to examine a larger number because the paucity of information on criteria and procedures made extensive field work, reviews of published and unpublished documents, interviews, and analyses of court decisions necessary.

The 10 jurisdictions were selected at the beginning of a research project sponsored by the National Science Foundation (NSF) that commenced in 1974. An advisory committee composed of academics and practitioners familiar with workers' compensation aided in the selection. The field work took place in 1975-76 in most jurisdictions, and following completion of an intensive statistical analysis of data from three states (California, Florida, and Wisconsin), a final report was submitted to the NSF in 1979 (Berkowitz, Burton, and Vroman). The information on the 10 jurisdictions was updated by correspondence and interviews between 1982 and 1985.

Among the factors considered when we chose the jurisdictions for our study were: the relative emphasis placed on impairment, as opposed to disability, as a basis for benefits; the administration procedures used to assess the extent of impairment and disability; the relative importance of litigation in determining the amounts of benefits; the comparative level of benefits; the attention devoted to rehabilitation by the state workers' compensation agency; and the relative importance of self-insurance, private insurance carriers, and state insurance funds.

Three states—California, Florida, and Wisconsin—were chosen partly because they were included in the "wage-loss study" summarized in part III of this volume, but also partly because of their distinctive attributes. California is the most populous state, and it uses a unique comprehensive schedule for rating the extent of permanent partial disability. Before 1979, when our original field work was completed, Florida had an unusual procedure that allowed workers to choose whether their permanent injuries would be rated on the basis of impairment or on the basis of disability. Since 1979, Florida has achieved fame or notoriety because of the adoption of the wage-loss approach to permanent partial disability benefits. As for Wisconsin, its workers' compensation program is widely regarded as among the best-administered in the country.

To supplement these three states, New Jersey was an obvious candidate. One of the authors (Berkowitz) had done previous work in the state, which is widely know for its practice of evaluating permanent partial disabilities on the whole man theory. New York was included for several reasons. Not only is it the second largest state and the only one with a hearing system that mandates an inquiry in each case before closure, but it also has a unique combination of approaches to permanent disability benefits. We included the District of Columbia not only because it measures loss of wage-earning capacity in the nonscheduled permanent partial cases, but because when we began this study, it was a federal jurisdiction operating under provisions of the Longshoremen and Harbor Workers' Act. Subsequently the program has been taken over by the local government.

Nevada and Ohio were included in part because we wanted to describe and analyze their experience with exclusive state funds. Another reason for Nevada's inclusion was the 1972 amendment to its law that mandated the use of the American Medical Association's *Guides for the Evaluation of Permanent Impairment.* Ohio was interesting not only because it was an exclusive fund state, but also because it was the only state besides Florida to use a choice of procedures approach for nonscheduled cases. Michigan and Pennsylvania were chosen because we thought they represented wage-loss states. We were particularly interested to learn why Michigan made more prominent use of redemption settlements (compromise and release agreements) than did Pennsylvania.

The initial reasons for selection of the 10 jurisdictions have in some cases been rendered moot by subsequent changes in state laws. Nonetheless, as we will indicate, the changes themselves in jurisdictions such as Florida, New Jersey, and Michigan have particular significance in understanding the continuing quest for an effective way to provide permanent disability benefits.

Historical Data for the Ten Jurisdictions

The historical data that follow, describing the numbers and costs of permanent disability cases in the jurisdictions included in this study, are based on National Council on Compensation Insurance information, and are therefore consistent with the data in tables 3.1—3.5. Two states in our 10-state study—Ohio and Nevada—are exclusive fund states for which the NCCI does not collect information, and therefore they are omitted from subsequent tables (as they were from earlier tables).

The shares of each state's indemnity cases accounted for by permanent total cases in 1958, 1968, 1973, 1978, and 1982 are shown in table 3.6. In 1958, the average proportion of all cases represented by permanent total cases across the 45 states for which the NCCI collects information was 0.1128 percent. Among the eight states considered here, the range in the percentage of all cases accounted for by permanent total cases was from 0.0406 percent in the District of Columbia to 0.1723 percent in Pennsylvania (36 percent and 153 percent of the U.S. average share, respectively); the eight-state average was 0.0935 percent, or only 83 percent of the U.S. average share.

Through time, the share of all cases accounted for by permanent total disability at the national level has varied in a fairly narrow range: roughly 0.10 percent to 0.16 percent. The eight-state average has fluctuated more widely, dropping from 1958 to 1968, then increasing to 1973 and again to 1978, and then dropping by 1982. In 1982, the eight-state average share (0.13 percent) was about 88 percent of the national average (0.1348 percent).

The relative importance of permanent total cases in the eight states has fluctuated considerably in some jurisdictions. In Michigan, for example, the share was 137 percent of the national average in 1958; down to 53 percent in 1968; then, by 1978, up to fully 331 percent; only to drop again to 130 percent in 1982. In Wisconsin, the figure was 51 percent in 1958, but had wound down to 29 percent by 1982. As of 1982, only Michigan and Pennsylvania had permanent total shares that were more than 20 percent above the national average share for permanent total cases; California, New Jersey, New York, and Wisconsin had shares more than 20 percent below the national average; the District of Columbia and Florida were within 20 percent of the national average.

The shares of each state's indemnity cases accounted for by major permanent partial disability cases are presented in table 3.7. As previously reported (table 3.2), the major cases share at the national level increased from 2.93 percent in 1958 to 6.56 percent in 1982. The national experience has been closely tracked by the eight-state average, which has consistently been within about 10 percent of the national figure.

Table 3.6
Number of Permanent Total Disability Cases as a Share of All Cases, 1958-82, in Eight States

Jurisdiction(s)	1958[1] Share of all cases[2] (%)	1958[1] Share in state as % of U.S. share	1968[1] Share of all cases[2] (%)	1968[1] Share in state as % of U.S. share	1973[1] Share of all cases[2] (%)	1973[1] Share in state as % of U.S. share	1978[1] Share of all cases[2] (%)	1978[1] Share in state as % of U.S. share	1982[1] Share of all cases[2] (%)	1982[1] Share in state as % of U.S. share
U.S. average	.1128		.1026		.1641		.1348		.1484	
Eight-state average	.0935	82.85	.0685	66.77	.1079	65.73	.1342	99.62	.1300	87.62
California	.0666	59.02	.0883	86.12	.0796	48.47	.0430	31.93	.0428	28.82
District of Columbia	.0406	36.00	.0227	22.12	.1543	93.99	.1217	90.33	.1492	100.58
Florida	.0820	72.67	.0742	72.35	.1253	76.33	.1161	86.17	.1582	106.63
Michigan	.1546	137.01	.0547	53.31	.2511	152.99	.4455	330.62	.1926	129.79
New Jersey	.0793	70.28	.0517	50.37	.0944	57.50	.1422	105.52	.0938	63.19
New York	.0895	79.32	.0285	27.83	.0542	33.04	.0825	61.19	.0506	34.11
Pennsylvania	.1723	152.64	.1540	150.16	.2293	139.69	.3518	261.05	.3100	208.92
Wisconsin	.0574	50.88	.0404	39.36	.0624	38.02	.0174	12.95	.0430	28.96

SOURCE: National Council on Compensation Insurance, "Countrywide Workers' Compensation Experience Including Certain Competitive State Funds—1st Report Basis," exhibits dated: for 1958, no date; for 1968, March 15, 1972; for 1973, July 1976; for 1978, April 1982; and for 1982, June 1986.

1. The data shown are for the insurance industry policy years that most closely correspond to the calendar years shown. For Pennsylvania, e.g., the 1982 data are for insurance policies in effect between April 1982 and March 1983.

2. The share is the number of permanent total disability cases as a percentage of all cases paying indemnity (cash) benefits in the state.

Table 3.7
Number of Major Permanent Partial Disability Cases as a Share of All Cases, 1958-82, in Eight States

Jurisdiction(s)	1958[1]		1968[1]		1973[1]		1978[1]		1982[1]	
	Share of all cases[2] (%)	Share in state as % of U.S. share	Share of all cases[2] (%)	Share in state as % of U.S. share	Share of all cases[2] (%)	Share in state as % of U.S. share	Share of all cases[2] (%)	Share in state as % of U.S. share	Share of all cases[2] (%)	Share in state as % of U.S. share
U.S. average	2.93		4.38		4.09		5.14		6.56	
Eight-state average	2.70	92.16	4.29	98.01	4.53	110.79	5.40	105.05	5.86	89.30
California	4.18	142.74	6.98	159.48	7.76	189.82	7.12	138.46	8.01	122.11
District of Columbia	2.23	76.20	3.43	78.29	8.92	218.26	13.75	267.52	12.06	183.76
Florida	1.91	65.00	3.28	75.04	3.84	94.04	6.71	130.58	5.03	76.63
Michigan	2.50	85.20	4.96	133.35	4.10	100.24	7.04	136.93	7.17	109.27
New Jersey	1.83	62.36	2.77	63.30	3.20	78.37	4.24	82.42	4.20	64.02
New York	2.34	79.88	2.17	49.62	2.82	68.98	4.36	84.90	5.86	89.26
Pennsylvania	3.46	117.87	4.82	110.15	1.89	46.30	1.47	27.58	1.40	21.26
Wisconsin	0.96	32.58	2.11	48.23	1.36	33.18	2.14	41.57	3.15	48.05

SOURCE: National Council on Compensation Insurance, "Countrywide Workers' Compensation Experience Including Certain Competitive State Funds—1st Report Basis," exhibits dated: for 1958, no date; for 1968, March 15, 1972; for 1973, July 1976; for 1978, April 1982; and for 1982, June 1986.

1. The data shown are for the insurance industry policy years that most closely correspond to the calendar years shown. For Pennsylvania, e.g., the 1982 data are for insurance policies in effect between April 1982 and March 1983.

2. The share is the number of major permanent partial disability cases as a percentage of all cases paying indemnity (cash) benefits in the state.

The share of all cases accounted for by major permanent partial disability cases has varied considerably through time in some jurisdictions, however. In the District of Columbia, the share was only 76 percent of the national average in 1958, but it soared to 268 percent of the national average by 1978 and was still 184 percent of the national average in 1982. The Florida share increased from 65 percent to 131 percent of the national average between 1958 and 1978, but slid to 77 percent in 1982. As of 1982, the share of all cases going to major permanent partial disability was within 20 percent of the national average only in Michigan and New York. States with shares at least 20 percent above the national average were California and the District of Columbia. At the other extreme were Pennsylvania and Wisconsin, with shares at least 50 percent below the national average share.

Table 3.8 provides the shares of all cases accounted for by minor permanent partial disability cases. Nationally, the share increased from 1958 to 1968 and thereafter declined, and this general pattern was matched in the eight states on average, with the eight-state share consistently within 10-20 percent of the national average share.

In contrast to permanent total and major permanent partial disability cases, the experience of individual states with the shares of all cases going to minor permanent partial disability has not varied dramatically through time. Only Florida had a swing in its share relative to the U.S. share in excess of 40 percent over the 1958 to 1982 period (up from 45 percent of the national average to 89 percent by 1978, and then back to 43 percent). The other states have had relatively stable shares over that period. New Jersey has consistently had a share of minor permanent partial disability cases in excess of 230 percent of the national average; California and New York have consistently been within about 30 percent of the national average; and the District of Columbia, Michigan, Pennsylvania, and Wisconsin have always been at least 30 percent below the national average.

The share of all indemnity cases accounted for by all types of permanent disability cases (permanent total, major permanent partial, and minor permanent partial) is provided in table 3.9. As previously noted (table 3.1), all permanent disability cases accounted for 26 percent of all indemnity cases in 1958. That share increased to almost 29 percent in 1968, then declined to 25 percent in 1973 and 24 percent in 1978 and 1982. This pattern was closely tracked in the eight states on average: their share consistently ran about 10-15 percent above the national

Table 3.8
Number of Minor Permanent Partial Disability Cases as a Share of All Cases, 1958-82, in Eight States

Jurisdiction(s)	1958[1]		1968[1]		1973[1]		1978[1]		1982[1]	
	Share of all cases[2] (%)	Share in state as % of U.S. share	Share of all cases[2] (%)	Share in state as % of U.S. share	Share of all cases[2] (%)	Share in state as % of U.S. share	Share of all cases[2] (%)	Share in state as % of U.S. share	Share of all cases[2] (%)	Share in state as % of U.S. share
U.S. average	23.20		24.32		20.69		18.67		17.28	
Eight-state average	25.82	110.81	27.74	114.05	24.74	119.56	21.16	113.31	16.19	93.68
California	22.35	95.92	30.53	125.56	27.11	131.01	21.42	114.73	21.89	126.67
District of Columbia	8.86	38.01	11.32	46.56	11.11	53.68	9.62	51.50	6.69	38.71
Florida	10.55	45.27	17.10	70.34	15.21	73.49	16.63	89.08	7.35	42.51
Michigan	6.58	28.25	11.53	47.40	13.48	65.13	9.60	51.42	10.27	59.40
New Jersey	67.08	287.85	58.48	240.48	49.89	241.10	49.84	266.95	40.98	237.12
New York	30.49	130.86	31.73	130.48	27.02	130.59	24.14	129.26	21.95	127.01
Pennsylvania	4.53	19.42	5.21	21.43	9.33	45.07	7.71	41.30	9.86	57.05
Wisconsin	12.13	52.04	12.50	51.39	10.86	52.48	9.34	50.04	10.54	60.97

SOURCE: National Council on Compensation Insurance, "Countrywide Workers' Compensation Experience Including Certain Competitive State Funds—1st Report Basis," exhibits dated: for 1958, no date; for 1968, March 15, 1972; for 1973, July 1976; for 1978, April 1982; and for 1982, June 1986.

1. The data shown are for the insurance industry policy years that most closely correspond to the calendar years shown. For Pennsylvania, e.g., the 1982 data are for insurance policies in effect between April 1982 and March 1983.

2. The share is the number of minor permanent partial disability cases as a percentage of all cases paying indemnity (cash) benefits in the state.

Table 3.9
Number of All Types of Permanent Disability Cases as a Share of All Cases, 1958-82, in Eight States

Jurisdiction(s)	1958[1]		1968[1]		1973[1]		1978[1]		1982[1]	
	Share of all cases[2] (%)	Share in state as % of U.S. share	Share of all cases[2] (%)	Share in state as % of U.S. share	Share of all cases[2] (%)	Share in state as % of U.S. share	Share of all cases[2] (%)	Share in state as % of U.S. share	Share of all cases[2] (%)	Share in state as % of U.S. share
U.S. average	26.35		28.80		24.94		23.95		24.00	
Eight-state average	28.62	108.61	32.09	111.45	29.37	117.77	26.69	111.46	22.18	92.44
California	26.61	100.98	37.60	130.58	34.94	140.10	28.58	119.36	29.95	124.82
District of Columbia	11.13	42.25	14.77	51.30	20.18	80.91	23.49	98.09	18.90	78.77
Florida	12.54	47.58	20.46	71.06	19.17	76.88	23.46	97.97	12.53	52.24
Michigan	9.24	35.06	16.54	57.44	17.82	71.46	17.09	71.35	17.63	73.48
New Jersey	68.99	261.82	61.30	212.88	53.18	213.24	54.22	226.43	45.28	188.70
New York	32.93	124.97	33.93	117.83	29.89	119.86	28.58	119.35	27.86	116.11
Pennsylvania	8.15	30.95	10.19	35.38	11.45	45.90	9.53	39.80	11.57	48.20
Wisconsin	13.14	49.87	14.65	50.86	12.28	49.23	11.50	48.02	13.74	57.24

SOURCE: National Council on Compensation Insurance, "Countrywide Workers' Compensation Experience Including Certain Competitive State Funds—1st Report Basis," exhibits dated: for 1958, no date; for 1968, March 15, 1972; for 1973, July 1976; for 1978, April 1982; and for 1982, June 1986.

1. The data shown are for the insurance industry policy years that most closely correspond to the calendar years shown. For Pennsylvania, e.g., the 1982 data are for insurance policies in effect between April 1982 and March 1983.

2. The share is the number of all types of permanent disability cases (permanent total, major permanent partial, and minor permanent partial) as a percentage of all cases paying indemnity (cash) benefits in the state.

average share from 1958 to 1978, and as of 1982 was about 8 percent below.

The eight states' movements in the three types of permanent disability cases as shown in tables 3.6 to 3.8 were partially offsetting. For example, in Pennsylvania the increased shares of permanent total and minor permanent partial disability cases were partially offset by a decrease in the share of major permanent partial disability cases. Nonetheless, the percentage of all cases accounted for by permanent disability cases changed dramatically in some states. The District of Columbia's share relative to the national average share increased from 42 percent in 1958 to 98 percent in 1978, and then fell to 79 percent in 1982; Florida's from 47 percent to 98 percent to 52 percent; Michigan's from 35 percent to 71 percent to 73 percent. New York and California began and ended the 20-year period with permanent disability cases accounting for shares within about 30 percent of the national average shares. New Jersey's permanent disability cases as a percentage of its total cases were always in excess of 180 percent of the national average, while the shares in Pennsylvania and Wisconsin were always less than 60 percent of the national average shares.

The average costs of the various types of permanent disability cases are analyzed in the next series of tables. Table 3.10 shows the average costs of permanent total cases in the U.S. and in the eight states in 1958, 1968, 1973, 1978, and 1982. In 1958, the national average was $19,322, compared to $24,107 (almost 25 percent more) in the eight states. The range among the eight states that year was from $17,526 in Michigan to $52,364 in Wisconsin (91 percent and 271 percent of the national average, respectively).

The average cost of permanent total cases increased nationally from $19,322 in 1958 to $92,055 in 1982. The average permanent total cost in the eight states increased more rapidly than the national average, so that by 1982 the eight-state average ($149,978) was about 163 percent of the national average.

The relative cost of permanent total cases varied widely within the eight jurisdictions between 1958 and 1982. Michigan had the lowest average cost in 1958 (91 percent of the national average) and the next to the lowest in 1982 (75 percent), but in 1968 its average cost was 164 percent of the national average, ranking it fourth among the eight jurisdictions that year. Wisconsin had the highest average cost in 1958 and in 1978 (271 percent and 180 percent of the national averages in

Table 3.10
Permanent Total Disability Cases in Eight States, 1958-82
Average Costs and Costs Relative to U.S. Averages

Jurisdiction(s)	1958[1]		1968[1]		1973[1]		1978[1]		1982[1]	
	Cost[2] (dollars)	Cost relative to U.S. cost (%)	Cost[2] (dollars)	Cost relative to U.S. cost (%)	Cost[2] (dollars)	Cost relative to U.S. cost (%)	Cost[2] (dollars)	Cost relative to U.S. cost (%)	Cost[2] (dollars)	Cost relative to U.S. cost (%)
U.S. average	19,322		35,606		37,544		78,788		92,055	
Eight-state average	24,107	124.77	53,084	149.09	56,759	151.181	94,738	120.24	149,978	162.92
California	31,420	162.61	63,673	178.83	67,525	179.86	139,745	177.37	199,803	217.05
District of Columbia	30,500	157.85	27,000	75.83	163,000	434.16	132,800	168.55	322,902	350.77
Florida	25,000	129.39	38,208	107.31	45,796	121.98	62,648	79.51	97,291	105.69
Michigan	17,526	90.71	58,238	163.56	36,988	98.52	43,686	55.68	69,339	75.32
New Jersey	32,500	168.20	66,464	186.67	63,396	168.86	87,944	111.62	107,704	117.00
New York	19,714	102.03	33,280	93.47	42,358	112.82	62,925	79.87	60,789	66.03
Pennsylvania	17,742	91.82	35,148	98.71	64,776	172.53	138,076	175.25	180,187	195.74
Wisconsin	52,364	271.01	88,364	248.17	47,333	126.08	141,667	179.81	161,812	175.78

SOURCE: National Council on Compensation Insurance, "Countrywide Workers' Compensation Experience Including Certain Competitive State Funds—1st Report Basis," exhibits dated: for 1958, no date; for 1968, March 15, 1972; for 1973, July 1976; for 1978, April 1982; and for 1982, June 1986.

1. The data shown are for the insurance industry policy years that most closely correspond to the calendar years shown. For Pennsylvania, e.g., the 1982 data are for insurance policies in effect between April 1982 and March 1983.

2. The cost is the average cost of indemnity (cash) benefits for permanent total disability cases in the state.

those years), but in 1982 ranked only fourth out of the eight jurisdictions. These fluctuations reflect in part the relatively small number of permanent total cases: a few cases can significantly affect a state's average costs. Nonetheless, a few stable patterns are evident. For example, in each of the five years, California and Wisconsin had permanent total costs at least 25 percent above the national average, while Florida and New York had costs within 35 percent of the national average.

The average costs of major permanent partial disability cases are shown in table 3.11. As previously discussed, the national average for this type of case increased from $6,879 in 1958 to $25,139 in 1982. The eight-state average also increased through time, but at a slower pace until recently. In 1958, the average cost of major permanent partial disability cases in the eight states was 119 percent of the national average; in 1968, 109 percent; in 1973, 103 percent; and in 1978, 90 percent. Then in 1982 the eight-state average cost shot up to 135 percent of the national average cost.

Major permanent partial disability costs declined relative to the national average during each of the subperiods shown in table 3.11 in three states: California, New York, and (with one exception) New Jersey. Pennsylvania was a clear exception to the pattern of declining relative costs. Pennsylvania's average major permanent partial disability costs were about 93 percent of the national average in 1958, then fell to 70 percent in 1968; but by 1982 they had soared to $78,575, more than 312 percent of the national average and far higher than in any of the other seven jurisdictions.

Table 3.12 presents the average costs of minor permanent partial disability cases. The national average increased from $1,253 to $4,953 between 1958 and 1982. The eight states on average were within 3 percent of the national average in 1958, 1968, 1973, and 1982; in 1978 their average minor permanent partial disability cost had declined to only 89 percent of the national average. In all but New Jersey and Pennsylvania, minor permanent disability cases were relatively less expensive (compared to the national average) in 1982 than in 1958. As with major permanent partial disability costs, Pennsylvania provided the most striking increase, beginning at 92 percent of the national average in 1958 and increasing through time until by 1982 its minor permanent partial disability costs were more than 185 percent of the national average. As of 1982, New York's minor permanent partial disability average

Table 3.11
Major Permanent Partial Disability Cases in Eight States, 1958-82
Average Costs and Costs Relative to U.S. Averages

Jurisdiction(s)	1958[1]		1968[1]		1973[1]		1978[1]		1982[1]	
	Cost[2] (dollars)	Cost relative to U.S. cost (%)	Cost[2] (dollars)	Cost relative to U.S. cost (%)	Cost[2] (dollars)	Cost relative to U.S. cost (%)	Cost[2] (dollars)	Cost relative to U.S. cost (%)	Cost[2] (dollars)	Cost relative to U.S. cost (%)
U.S. average	6,879		9,983		13,265		21,456		25,139	
Eight-state average	8,169	118.75	10,890	109.09	13,602	102.55	19,379	90.32	34,119	135.72
California	8,442	122.73	10,005	100.23	12,516	94.35	15,776	73.53	17,330	68.93
District of Columbia	10,900	158.45	11,987	120.08	17,242	129.99	38,266	178.34	36,620	145.67
Florida	5,491	79.82	9,692	97.09	12,070	90.99	19,276	89.84	30,728	122.23
Michigan	8,705	126.55	18,209	182.41	20,226	152.48	26,666	124.28	39,892	158.68
New Jersey	8,451	122.85	10,308	103.26	11,713	88.30	15,344	71.51	22,314	88.76
New York	8,897	129.34	12,368	123.90	14,337	108.08	18,534	86.38	19,730	78.48
Pennsylvania	6,413	93.23	6,956	69.68	20,062	151.24	54,904	255.89	78,575	312.56
Wisconsin	10,448	151.88	10,899	109.18	15,775	118.92	20,890	97.36	27,766	110.45

SOURCE: National Council on Compensation Insurance, "Countrywide Workers' Compensation Experience Including Certain Competitive State Funds—1st Report Basis," exhibits dated: for 1958, no date; for 1968, March 15, 1972; for 1973, July 1976; for 1978, April 1982; and for 1982, June 1986.

1. The data shown are for the insurance industry policy years that most closely correspond to the calendar years shown. For Pennsylvania, e.g., the 1982 data are for insurance policies in effect between April 1982 and March 1983.

2. The cost is the average cost of indemnity (cash) benefits for major permanent partial disability cases in the state.

Table 3.12
Minor Permanent Partial Disability Cases in Eight States, 1958-82
Average Costs and Costs Relative to U.S. Averages

Jurisdiction(s)	1958[1] Cost[2] (dollars)	1958[1] Cost relative to U.S. cost (%)	1968[1] Cost[2] (dollars)	1968[1] Cost relative to U.S. cost (%)	1973[1] Cost[2] (dollars)	1973[1] Cost relative to U.S. cost (%)	1978[1] Cost[2] (dollars)	1978[1] Cost relative to U.S. cost (%)	1982[1] Cost[2] (dollars)	1982[1] Cost relative to U.S. cost (%)
U.S. average	1,253		2,055		2,627		4,013		4,953	
Eight-state average	1,235	98.54	2,119	103.12	2,589	98.57	3,558	88.67	5,014	101.24
California	1,972	157.36	2,611	127.10	3,180	121.06	4,205	104.78	4,767	96.25
District of Columbia	2,083	166.18	2,459	119.68	3,353	127.64	4,496	112.05	4,318	87.19
Florida	1,486	118.57	2,399	116.77	2,763	105.20	3,703	92.27	3,992	80.61
Michigan	2,221	177.24	4,077	198.44	4,270	162.56	4,723	117.71	6,069	122.54
New Jersey	904	72.16	1,566	76.20	1,918	73.03	2,482	61.86	4,392	88.68
New York	1,044	80.10	1,722	83.83	1,819	69.24	2,351	58.58	2,619	52.87
Pennsylvania	1,156	92.24	2,038	99.21	3,648	138.86	7,843	195.46	9,176	185.28
Wisconsin	1,951	155.67	2,298	111.87	2,868	109.20	3,703	92.28	4,779	96.50

SOURCE: National Council on Compensation Insurance, "Countrywide Workers' Compensation Experience Including Certain Competitive State Funds—1st Report Basis," exhibits dated: for 1958, no date; for 1968, March 15, 1972; for 1973, July 1976; for 1978, April 1982; and for 1982, June 1986.

1. The data shown are for the insurance industry policy years that most closely correspond to the calendar years shown. For Pennsylvania, e.g., the 1982 data are for insurance policies in effect between April 1982 and March 1983.

2. The cost is the average cost of indemnity (cash) benefits for minor permanent partial disability cases in the state.

costs were more than 40 percent below the national average; Pennsylvania's were more than 85 percent above; and costs in the other five states were within 25 percent of the national average.

Table 3.13 provides the average cost for all types of permanent disability cases from 1958 to 1982. The increase in the national average during this period was from $1,957 to $11,013; these figures reflect the dominant number of minor permanent partial disability cases. The eight-state average cost for all permanent disability cases was within 4 percent of the national average in 1958, 1968, and 1973, declined to only 88 percent of the national average in 1978, and then soared to 133 percent of the national average in 1982.

Average permanent disability costs declined relative to the national average in each of the successive subperiods between 1958 and 1982 in California and New York. In Wisconsin, costs were lower in 1982 than in 1958, although between 1978 and 1982 costs did increase. In Michigan and New Jersey, costs increased between 1958 and 1968, then declined in 1973 and 1978, and finally increased between 1978 and 1982; in both states average costs relative to the national average were lower in 1982 than they were in 1958. In the District of Columbia (up from 202 percent of the national average in 1958 to 249 percent in 1982), Florida (up from 115 percent to 145 percent), and Pennsylvania (up from 191 percent in 1958 to 201 percent in 1982) the relative costs increased during the 24-year period.

As of 1982, the eight states could be divided into three distinct groups in terms of their average costs for permanent disability cases compared to the national averages. Michigan, Pennsylvania, and the District of Columbia had permanent disability costs that on average were 80 percent or more above the national average; New Jersey and New York had costs more than 40 percent below the national average; and California, Florida, and Wisconsin all had costs within 45 percent of the national average.

The total costs of permanent disability cases in the eight jurisdictions, shown in tables 3.14 to 3.17, reflect the developments in the number of such cases and their average costs shown in the two previous sets of tables.[9]

Nationally, the share of all cash benefits accounted for by permanent total disability cases increased from 2.64 percent in 1958 to 3.54 percent in 1982 (table 3.14). In the eight states, the permanent total share

Table 3.13
All Types of Permanent Disability Cases in Eight States, 1958-82
Average Costs and Costs Relative to U.S. Averages

Jurisdiction(s)	1958[1] Cost[2] (dollars)	1958[1] Cost relative to U.S. cost (%)	1968[1] Cost[2] (dollars)	1968[1] Cost relative to U.S. cost (%)	1973[1] Cost[2] (dollars)	1973[1] Cost relative to U.S. cost (%)	1978[1] Cost[2] (dollars)	1978[1] Cost relative to U.S. cost (%)	1982[1] Cost[2] (dollars)	1982[1] Cost relative to U.S. cost (%)
U.S. average	1,957		3,379		4,599		8,178		11,013	
Eight-state average	1,964	100.39	3,400	100.62	4,485	96.44	7,218	88.26	14,693	133.41
California	3,064	156.57	4,127	122.14	5,398	117.38	7,290	89.14	8,407	76.34
District of Columbia	3,956	202.19	4,707	139.29	10,711	232.89	24,933	304.87	27,447	249.22
Florida	2,249	114.92	3,699	109.49	4,910	106.75	8,450	103.33	15,898	144.35
Michigan	4,231	216.25	8,494	251.40	8,397	182.58	14,784	180.78	20,519	186.31
New Jersey	1,141	58.29	2,015	59.64	2,617	56.90	3,711	45.38	6,269	56.92
New York	1,616	82.60	2,430	71.92	3,072	66.81	4,997	61.10	6,322	57.41
Pennsylvania	3,735	190.86	4,866	144.01	7,585	164.91	19,903	243.37	22,133	200.97
Wisconsin	2,789	142.54	3,775	111.73	4,520	98.27	7,107	86.90	10,549	95.79

SOURCE: National Council on Compensation Insurance, "Countrywide Workers' Compensation Experience Including Certain Competitive State Funds—1st Report Basis," exhibits dated: for 1958, no date; for 1968, March 15, 1972; for 1973, July 1976; for 1978, April 1982; and for 1982, June 1986.

1. The data shown are for the insurance industry policy years that most closely correspond to the calendar years shown. For Pennsylvania, e.g., the 1982 data are for insurance policies in effect between April 1982 and March 1983.

2. The cost is the average cost of indemnity (cash) benefits for all types of permanent disability cases (permanent total, major permanent partial, and minor permanent partial) in the state.

Table 3.14
Total Costs of Permanent Total Disability Cases as a Share of All Cash Benefits 1958-82, in Eight States

Jurisdiction(s)	1958[1]		1968[1]		1973[1]		1978[1]		1982[1]	
	Share of all costs[2] (%)	Share in state as % of U.S. share	Share of all costs[2] (%)	Share in state as % of U.S. share	Share of all costs[2] (%)	Share in state as % of U.S. share	Share of all costs[2] (%)	Share in state as % of U.S. share	Share of all costs[2] (%)	Share in state as % of U.S. share
U.S. average	2.64		2.54		3.56		3.66		3.54	
Eight-state average	2.59	97.95	2.26	89.01	3.23	90.77	4.55	124.32	4.43	125.14
California	1.98	74.79	3.01	118.42	2.36	66.31	2.35	64.20	2.79	78.69
District of Columbia	1.68	63.72	.57	22.34	9.27	260.68	2.26	61.68	7.17	202.47
Florida	4.11	155.47	2.28	89.82	3.88	109.21	2.62	71.58	4.88	137.95
Michigan	2.83	106.92	1.38	54.45	3.84	108.02	5.07	138.52	2.54	71.68
New Jersey	2.74	103.79	1.86	73.25	2.90	81.64	4.61	126.18	2.75	77.82
New York	1.84	69.63	.66	25.96	1.43	40.08	1.99	54.31	.98	27.60
Pennsylvania	5.19	196.47	4.98	195.93	9.13	256.65	13.58	371.25	11.27	318.30
Wisconsin	5.18	195.99	4.26	167.45	3.12	87.61	1.68	45.87	3.07	86.65

SOURCE: National Council on Compensation Insurance, "Countrywide Workers' Compensation Experience Including Certain Competitive State Funds—1st Report Basis," exhibits dated: for 1958, no date; for 1968, March 15, 1972; for 1973, July 1976; for 1978, April 1982; and for 1982, June 1986.

1. The data shown are for the insurance industry policy years that most closely correspond to the calendar years shown. For Pennsylvania, e.g., the 1982 data are for insurance policies in effect between April 1982 and March 1983.

2. The share is the total cost of indemnity (cash) benefits for permanent total disability cases as a percentage of all indemnity benefits in the state.

increased even more rapidly, rising from 2.59 percent of all cash benefits in 1958 (98 percent of the national share) to 4.43 percent in 1982 (125 percent).

Among individual states, the shares of all cash benefits accounted for by permanent total cases are quite volatile, reflecting in part the relatively small number of such cases. Every state had a swing in its share (as a percentage of the national average share) of at least 40 percent during the 20-year period. An extreme example is the District of Columbia, where the permanent total share was 22 percent of the national average in 1968, 261 percent in 1973, 62 percent in 1978, and 202 percent in 1982. Only New York had a permanent total share below the national average in all five years; only Pennsylvania was consistently above the national average. As of 1982, Pennsylvania (with a 318 percent figure) was far above the other jurisdictions in its share of cash benefits accounted for by payments for permanent total cases; Florida and the District of Columbia were also above the national average; and California, Michigan, New Jersey, and Wisconsin were from 10 to 30 percent below the national average. New York's share was almost 75 percent below the national average. The high cost in Pennsylvania is due both to its relatively large number of permanent total cases (table 3.6) and the relatively high cost of each case (table 3.10). New York achieved the lowest share of cost accounted for by permanent total benefits in 1982 (table 3.14) both because its average cost for permanent total cases was lower than in the other seven jurisdictions (table 3.10) and because permanent total cases were quite rare in the state (table 3.6).

Major permanent partial disability cases accounted for an increasing share of all cash benefits nationally through time, rising from 24 percent in 1958 to 43 percent in 1982 (table 3.15). The average share in the eight states for major permanent partial disability benefit cases was consistently within 5 percent of the U.S. share. There were, however, large swings in some states. In Florida and Michigan, major permanent partial disability costs as a percentage of the national average increased by 25 percent or more, while Pennsylvania's share dropped from 154 percent of the national average in 1958 to 52 percent in 1982. As of 1982, the District of Columbia stood apart in terms of the cost of major permanent partial disability cases: they accounted for 66 percent of all cash benefits in that jurisdiction, a share that was 154 percent of the national average share. In Michigan, the share for major permanent partial disability benefits was more than 25 percent above

Table 3.15
Total Costs of Major Permanent Partial Disability Cases as a Share of All Cash Benefits 1958-82, in Eight States

Jurisdiction(s)	1958[1]		1968[1]		1973[1]		1978[1]		1982[1]	
	Share of all costs[2] (%)	Share in state as % of U.S. share	Share of all costs[2] (%)	Share in state as % of U.S. share	Share of all costs[2] (%)	Share in state as % of U.S. share	Share of all costs[2] (%)	Share in state as % of U.S. share	Share of all costs[2] (%)	Share in state as % of U.S. share
U.S. average	24.45		30.42		31.27		37.99		42.77	
Eight-state average	25.35	103.70	29.08	95.60	32.45	103.77	37.41	98.47	42.18	98.63
California	33.38	136.52	37.38	122.90	42.61	136.25	43.85	115.41	45.29	105.90
District of Columbia	33.10	135.40	38.07	125.18	56.68	181.24	73.44	193.30	65.70	153.62
Florida	20.97	85.78	25.64	84.29	31.39	100.38	46.56	122.54	49.03	114.65
Michigan	22.68	92.76	39.27	129.11	34.26	109.55	48.65	128.05	54.37	127.13
New Jersey	16.45	67.27	15.49	50.92	18.20	58.19	23.99	63.14	25.58	59.81
New York	21.73	88.89	18.67	61.37	25.07	80.16	30.97	81.50	36.71	85.85
Pennsylvania	37.66	154.04	30.86	101.45	23.32	74.57	22.55	59.34	22.12	51.73
Wisconsin	17.19	70.33	27.45	90.27	22.56	72.12	30.30	79.75	38.64	90.34

SOURCE: National Council on Compensation Insurance, "Countrywide Workers' Compensation Experience Including Certain Competitive State Funds—1st Report Basis," exhibits dated: for 1958, no date; for 1968, March 15, 1972; for 1973, July 1976; for 1978, April 1982; and for 1982, June 1986.

1. The data shown are for the insurance industry policy years that most closely correspond to the calendar years shown. For Pennsylvania, e.g., the 1982 data are for insurance policies in effect between April 1982 and March 1983.

2. The share is the total cost of indemnity (cash) benefits for major permanent partial disability cases as a percentage of all indemnity benefits in the state.

Table 3.16
Total Costs of Minor Permanent Partial Disability Cases as a Share of All Cash Benefits 1958-82, in Eight States

Jurisdiction(s)	1958[1]		1968[1]		1973[1]		1978[1]		1982[1]	
	Share of all costs[2] (%)	Share in state as % of U.S. share	Share of all costs[2] (%)	Share in state as % of U.S. share	Share of all costs[2] (%)	Share in state as % of U.S. share	Share of all costs[2] (%)	Share in state as % of U.S. share	Share of all costs[2] (%)	Share in state as % of U.S. share
U.S. average	35.40		34.78		31.37		25.81		22.19	
Eight-state average	36.63	103.47	36.59	105.16	33.77	107.66	26.91	104.28	20.91	94.27
California	41.64	117.63	42.68	122.71	37.84	120.65	35.17	136.29	34.03	153.40
District of Columbia	25.07	70.82	25.81	74.20	13.73	43.77	6.03	23.38	4.30	19.37
Florida	31.42	88.76	33.05	95.02	28.44	90.69	22.16	85.86	9.31	41.94
Michigan	15.25	43.08	20.43	58.73	23.80	75.88	11.75	45.55	11.84	53.37
New Jersey	64.55	182.36	49.65	142.75	46.44	148.06	45.65	176.90	49.10	221.32
New York	31.92	90.19	37.98	109.19	30.50	97.23	21.72	84.16	18.26	82.30
Pennsylvania	8.89	25.11	9.78	28.11	20.90	66.65	16.90	65.50	18.25	82.28
Wisconsin	40.76	115.13	34.28	98.54	32.85	104.74	23.48	90.98	22.22	100.15

SOURCE: National Council on Compensation Insurance, "Countrywide Workers' Compensation Experience Including Certain Competitive State Funds—1st Report Basis," exhibits dated: for 1958, no date; for 1968, March 15, 1972; for 1973, July 1976; for 1978, April 1982; and for 1982, June 1986.

1. The data shown are for the insurance industry policy years that most closely correspond to the calendar years shown. For Pennsylvania, e.g., the 1982 data are for insurance policies in effect between April 1982 and March 1983.

2. The share is the total cost of indemnity (cash) benefits for minor permanent partial disability cases as a percentage of all indemnity benefits in the state.

the national average; California, Florida, New York, and Wisconsin were within 15 percent of the national average; and New Jersey and Pennsylvania were each more than 40 percent below the national average. In Pennsylvania, a high average cost for each major permanent partial disability case (table 3.11) was more than offset by the relative scarcity of such cases (table 3.7). The District of Columbia, on the other extreme, had both high average costs and a relatively large number of these cases.

Minor permanent partial disability cases represented a decreasing share of all cash benefits nationally between 1958 and 1982 (table 3.16). The importance of minor permanent partial cases declined on average in the eight states as well, with the eight-state and national shares within 8 percent of each other in each of the five years. Again there were divergences among the individual states and some dramatic movements at that level. In the District of Columbia, for example, the share of all cash benefits represented by minor permanent partial disability cases relative to the national average share decreased by more than 50 percent between 1958 and 1982, while in Pennsylvania there was a more than 50 percent increase. (Even with this increase, Pennsylvania remained below the national average in the relative importance of minor permanent partial disability benefits.) As of 1982, the shares of all cash benefits devoted to minor permanent partial disability cases were more than 50 percent above the national average share in New Jersey and California, and at the other extreme, at least 40 percent below in Michigan, Florida, and the District of Columbia. In New York, Pennsylvania, and Wisconsin, the shares were within 20 percent of the national average.

The shares of dollars accounted for by all three types of permanent disability cases (permanent total, major permanent partial, and minor permanent partial) are examined in table 3.17 and in graph 3.1. Nationally, the share increased from 62 percent in 1958 to 69 percent in 1982. The experience in the eight states on average was similar, with an increase from 65 percent in 1958 to 68 percent in 1982.

Within individual states, the percentage of total benefits represented by all permanent disability benefits combined did not undergo as much change during the 20-year period as did the percentages represented by individual types of permanent disability benefits, in part because the movements of the particular types were offsetting in some states. Nonetheless, there were some significant movements through time, and as of 1982 the individual jurisdictions diverged widely.

Table 3.17
Total Costs of All Types of Permanent Disability Cases as a Share of All Cash Benefits 1958-82, in Eight States

Jurisdiction(s)	1958[1]		1968[1]		1973[1]		1978[1]		1982[1]	
	Share of all costs[2] (%)	Share in state as % of U.S. share	Share of all costs[2] (%)	Share in state as % of U.S. share	Share of all costs[2] (%)	Share in state as % of U.S. share	Share of all costs[2] (%)	Share in state as % of U.S. share	Share of all costs[2] (%)	Share in state as % of U.S. share
U.S. average	62.49		67.74		66.20		67.46		68.49	
Eight-state average	64.57	103.33	67.92	100.26	69.45	104.91	68.87	102.09	67.52	98.59
California	76.99	123.21	83.07	122.63	82.81	125.10	81.37	120.62	82.11	119.88
District of Columbia	59.86	95.79	64.45	95.14	79.68	120.38	81.73	121.16	77.16	112.66
Florida	56.50	90.41	60.97	90.01	63.72	96.26	71.33	105.75	63.22	92.30
Michigan	40.75	65.26	61.08	90.17	61.90	93.51	65.47	97.06	68.75	100.37
New Jersey	83.74	134.01	67.03	98.91	67.54	102.03	74.25	110.08	77.44	113.06
New York	55.50	88.81	57.30	84.59	56.99	86.10	54.67	81.05	55.95	81.69
Pennsylvania	51.74	82.80	45.61	67.34	53.35	80.60	53.02	78.61	51.64	75.40
Wisconsin	63.13	101.02	65.99	97.41	58.52	88.41	55.45	82.21	63.92	93.33

SOURCE: National Council on Compensation Insurance, "Countrywide Workers' Compensation Experience Including Certain Competitive State Funds—1st Report Basis," exhibits dated: for 1958, no date; for 1968, March 15, 1972; for 1973, July 1976; for 1978, April 1982; and for 1982, June 1986.

1. The data shown are for the insurance industry policy years that most closely correspond to the calendar years shown. For Pennsylvania, e.g., the 1982 data are for insurance policies in effect between April 1982 and March 1983.

2. The share is the total cost of indemnity (cash) benefits for all types of permanent disability cases (permanent total, major permanent partial, and minor permanent partial) as a percentage of all indemnity benefits in the state.

Graph 3.1

Share of All Cash Benefits Accounted for by Permanent Disability Cases, 1958-72, in Eight States

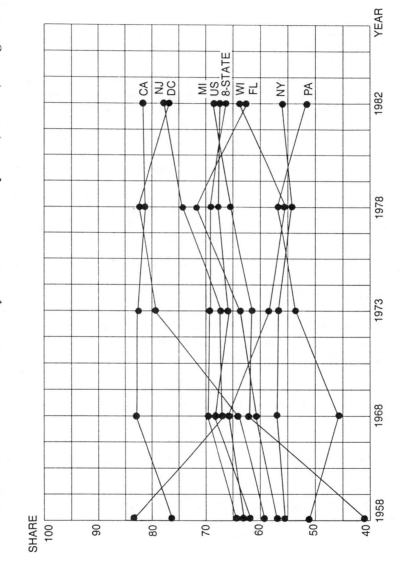

In three jurisdictions—California, New Jersey, and the District of Columbia—the share of all benefits going to permanent disability cases in 1982 was at least 10 percent above the national average share, but the three reached that status by different routes. The California share was consistently above the national average share by about 20 percent for all five years between 1958 and 1982. New Jersey began as the highest share state in 1958, dropped slightly below the national share in 1968, and has steadily increased its share since 1973 so that by 1982 it ranks only behind California. The District of Columbia has an even more volatile history, ranking below the national average share in 1958 and 1968, then increasing rapidly so that by 1978 the jurisdiction ranked first among the eight states in share of benefits devoted to permanent disability benefits, and then declining somewhat between 1978 and 1982, but still remaining about 13 percent above the national average.

In two jurisdictions—New York and Pennsylvania—the share of all benefits going to permanent disability benefits in 1982 was at least 10 percent below the national average share, a record these jurisdictions had consistently maintained over the 1958 to 1982 period.

Three jurisdictions—Florida, Michigan, and Wisconsin—were within 10 percent of the national average share of benefits going to permanent disability benefits as of 1982. Florida had always been within 10 percent of the national average share between 1958 and 1982. Michigan had been well below the national average share in 1958, but was within 10 percent of the national average from 1968 to 1982. Wisconsin had begun with a share of benefits going to permanent disability cases slightly above the national average in 1958, had seen that share steadily decline to 82 percent of the national average share in 1978, and then rebounded to 93 percent of the national share as of 1982.

Significance of the Data

The causes and significance of the movements in the numbers and costs of permanent disability benefits will be examined in more detail in subsequent chapters that deal with individual states. Here one aspect of the significance will be examined: the relationship between the share of all benefits accounted for by permanent disability benefits and the employers' costs of workers' compensation insurance.

Information on the employers' costs of workers' compensation insurance for a representative sample of employers is presented in table 3.18.[10] The figures are adjusted manual rates, which are insurance

Table 3.18

Employers' Costs of Workers' Compensation Insurance as a Percentage of Payroll, 1958–74, in Nine States

Jurisdiction	1958 Costs	1958 Costs in state as % of U.S. average	1965 Costs	1965 Costs in state as % of U.S. average	1972 Costs	1972 Costs in state as % of U.S. average	1978 Costs	1978 Costs in state as % of U.S. average	1984 high Costs	1984 high Costs in state as % of U.S. average	1984 low Costs	1984 low Costs in state as % of U.S. average
U.S. average (28 states)	0.618	—	0.791	—	0.783	—	1.420	—	1.434	—	1.368	—
California	0.707	114.4	1.183	149.6	1.102	140.7	2.135	150.4	1.936	135.0	1.936	141.5
D.C.					0.737	94.1	3.502	246.7	1.911	133.3	1.909	139.5
Florida							2.641	186.0	1.674	116.7	1.552	113.5
Michigan	0.450	72.8	0.715	90.4	0.914	116.7	1.890	133.1	1.798	125.4	1.283	93.8
New Jersey	0.911	147.4	1.039	131.4	1.224	156.3	1.687	118.8	1.231	85.8	1.231	90.0
New York					0.864	110.3	1.770	124.6	1.107	77.2	1.079	78.9
Ohio	0.627	101.5	0.820	103.7	0.885	113.0	1.550	109.2	1.521	106.1	1.521	111.2
Pennsylvania	0.355	57.4	0.386	48.8	0.387	49.4	1.173	82.6	1.339	93.4	1.235	90.3
Wisconsin	0.523	84.6	0.603	76.2	0.505	64.5	0.752	53.0	0.846	59.0	0.846	61.8

SOURCE: U.S. average: weighted observations from Burton, Hunt, and Krueger (1985), table 28. Individual state data from Burton, Hunt, and Krueger (1985), table 26.

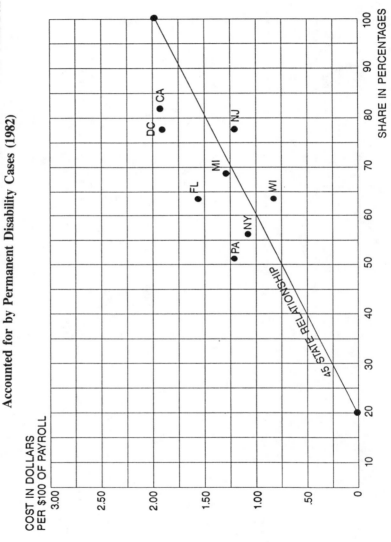

Graph 3.2
Employers' Costs of Workers' Compensation (1984) as a Function of the Share of All Cash Benefits Accounted for by Permanent Disability Cases (1982)

premiums in dollars per $100 of payroll. The adjusted manual rates can be interpreted as the percentage of payroll expended on workers' compensation insurance after factors such as experience rating and dividends are considered. The data are for selected years between 1958 and 1984 that roughly correspond to the years shown in the previous tables in this chapter dealing with numbers and costs of permanent disability benefits. The data are available for nine of the states in our study. As shown in table 3.18, data for the nine states are available only since 1978, and so the discussion focuses on insurance costs in 1978 and 1984. Two sets of data are presented for 1984—high adjusted manual rates, which reflect the traditional factors that modify insurance rates, such as experience rating and dividends, and low adjusted manual rates, which also reflect the competitive devices that have emerged in recent years in workers' compensation, including open competition and deviations. Hunt, Krueger, and Burton (1985) argue that the low adjusted manual rates are the most accurate measure of costs in 1984, and so we use these rates.

There is a considerable range in workers' compensation insurance rates in 1984 among the jurisdictions in our study, with California about 40 percent above the national average (28 states) and Wisconsin about 40 percent below. The relationship between insurance costs and share of all benefits accounted for by permanent disability cases is examined in graph 3.2. Eight of the ten states (all but Ohio and Nevada) have appropriate data and are shown in the graph. There is a general positive relationship between the share of permanent disability benefits and the cost of workers' compensation insurance. The District of Columbia and California are among the three high-share states and are the two high-cost states. Pennsylvania and New York are among the three low-share and three low-cost states.

The generally positive relationship between share and costs for the eight states shown in graph 3.2 is hardly conclusive, given the small sample size. More persuasive evidence is summarized in table 3.19. There are 45 states with data on the 1982 share of all costs accounted for by permanent disability benefits (table 3.5) for which data are available on the employers' costs of workers' compensation insurance in 1984. There is a positive correlation between the variables; the regression results suggest that a 10 percent increase in share is associated with an increase in workers' compensation premiums of $0.24 per $100 of payroll. This regression result is shown on graph 3.2 as the "45-state relationship" line. The eight states of particular concern in our study are scattered along this line (although most are above, suggesting higher costs than would be expected given the share of costs accounted for by permanent disability benefits in these states).

Table 3.19
Statistical Relationships Between Employers' Costs
of Workers' Compensation and Share of All Cash Benefits
Accounted for by Permanent Disability Cases

Data	Correlation coefficient	Regression results with costs as dependent variable[2]		
1982 share/1984 costs[1]	0.401	−0.431 (.575)	+	.024 share (.008)
1978 share/1978 costs	0.364	−0.453 (.724)	+	.028 share (.011)
1978–1982 change in share/ 1978–1984 change in costs[1]	0.381	−0.259 (.079)	+	.030 share (.011)

SOURCE: 1982 share from table 3.5; 1978 share from source cited in table 3.1, n.1; 1978 and 1984 cost data from Burton, Hunt, and Krueger (1985), table 26.

1. 1984 costs are low adjusted manual rates.

2. Standard errors are in parentheses.

The relationship between 1982 share of costs due to permanent disability benefits and 1984 insurance costs is positive and the relationship is statistically significant. Statistical results that tend to confirm the positive relationship between shares and insurance costs are included in table 3.19. For 1978 shares and 1978 insurance costs, the relationship is also positive; the regression results indicate that a 10 percent increase in share is associated with a $0.28 increase in workers' compensation premiums per $100 of payroll. In addition, there is a positive relationship between changes in shares in each state between 1978 and 1982 and changes in insurance costs in each state between 1978 and 1984; the regression results indicate that a 10 percent increase in share over time is associated with a $0.30 increase in workers' compensation premiums per $100 of payroll.

The similarity of the results for the three regressions reported in table 3.19 lend support to the view that share of costs going to permanent disability benefits and workers' compensation insurance costs are positively associated, especially since the relationships between the variables are statistically significant in each of the regressions. We do not wish to overstate the importance of the relationship between permanent disability benefits and costs. Burton and Krueger (1986) have argued that changes in the levels of all types of benefits were important determinants of insurance cost developments between 1972 and 1983 in Connecticut, New Jersey, and New York. In addition, a statistical examination by Krueger and Burton (1984) shows that interstate differences in benefit levels other than permanent partial benefits and differences among states in insurance arrangements are significant determinants of interstate differences in insurance costs. It is obvious from graph 3.2 that factors other than the share of costs accounted for by permanent disability benefits must account for some of the interstate differences in insurance costs. Nonetheless, the differences in shares appear to be one important factor in explaining interstate cost differences, which underlines the relevance of the present study's focus on permanent disability benefits.

Conclusions

The extensive data in this chapter can be viewed at several levels of aggregation. At the national level (tables 3.1 to 3.3), the numbers of permanent disability cases relative to all types of cases declined between 1958 and 1982, while the average costs of such cases relative to the costs of temporary total cases increased. The shares of all cash benefits accounted for by permanent disability cases increased from 1958 to 1978, but subsequently have consistently been about two-thirds of all cash payments. Thus, at the national level, the appearance is one of relative stability and gradual movements in the number and costs of permanent disability cases. The average experience in the eight states with permanent disability benefits also is relatively stable. Numerically, between 1958 and 1978 all permanent disability cases accounted for about a 10 percent larger share in the eight states than nationally (table 3.9); by 1982, the eight-states share was about 10 percent below the national share. Meanwhile, average costs for all permanent disability cases in the eight states declined from about 100 percent of the national average in 1958 to 88 percent in 1978 and then increased to about 33 percent above the national average in 1982 (table 3.13). The consequence of the offsetting trends is that the share of total cash benefits accounted for by permanent disability cases in the eight states has consistently been within a few percentage points of the national average share from 1958 to 1982 (table 3.17).

The relative stability and gradualness of change at the national and eight-state levels of aggregation mask a great deal of diversity among the states as of 1982 in the relative numbers and average costs of permanent disability cases and in shares of all cash benefits accounted for by those cases, and belies the significant changes that have occurred from 1958 to 1982 in many jurisdictions. The full extent of diversity and change can be appreciated only by studying the individual state experience over the twenty years, but the intermediate level of aggregation in graph 3.1 provides a useful summary.

In the balance of part II of this study we attempt to explain some of the more significant developments in numbers and costs by examining changes in procedure and criteria in the states since 1958. We also attempt to show how the changes in cost levels from 1958 to 1982 generated pressures for change in the approaches to compensating permanent disabilities that in some jurisdictions resulted in statutory or administrative changes by 1986, the terminal point in our study.

NOTES

1. The policy years vary among states and do not always correspond with calendar years. For example, the 1982 data for the District of Columbia shown in the tables in this chapter pertain to policies written between February 1982 and January 1983.

2. At one time, the distinction was based on the severity of the injury. Thus, an impairment of 50 percent or more of an arm was treated as a major permanent partial, while an impairment of less than 50 percent of an arm was treated as a minor permanent partial. Since 1967, the distinction between major and minor permanent partial has been based upon the amount of cash benefits paid in the case. For example, for policies written in the District of Columbia in 1982, the "critical value" was $10,000. The critical values are changed for each state whenever the benefit levels for permanent partial are amended.

The distinctions between major and minor permanent partial disability cases in states with independent rating bureaus may depend on procedures different from the critical value procedure used in states that rely on the National Council on Compensation Insurance for rate making. States with independent rating bureaus that are part of our ten-state study are California, New Jersey, and New York. The potential inconsistency among the jurisdictions in the procedures used to separate major and minor permanent partial disability cases is a reason why most of our analysis in this report relies on the total costs of all permanent disability cases in various states, a statistic that is not affected by the division between the major and minor categories.

3. The use of the critical values is explained in note 2, above. As of 1982, the critical value was $10,000 in the District of Columbia, $16,000 in Michigan, and $14,500 in Wisconsin.

4. The critical values discussed in the preceding two notes are changed only when there are statutory changes in permanent partial disability benefits. In most cases, the amounts of permanent partial disability benefits depend in part on the workers' preinjury wages. Thus as wages increase through time in a state without statutory changes, there is likely to be a shift in cases from the minor to the major permanent partial disability categories. For example, the critical value was $10,000 in the District of Columbia between 1972 and 1984, which probably is a factor explaining the declining share of minor permanent partial cases in the District between 1973 and 1982 shown in table 3.8.

5. Some cases may be filed two or more years after the policy year expires but are nonetheless charged to that year. This might happen, for example, for a work-related disease where the exposure took place in the policy year but the disease did not manifest itself until years later.

6. Other movements between types of cases are possible. For example, a case initially classified as temporary total may result in a payment of death benefits. Cases can also move to less serious categories.

7. The actual ultimate report on 1982 cases is not yet available because not enough time has elapsed, but a simulated ultimate report on 1982 cases has been prepared by the National Council on Compensation Insurance. The simulation is based on data showing the first to ultimate report development factors for reports from earlier policy years for which actual ultimate data are already available.

8. For exhibits on an ultimate report basis prepared by the National Council on Compensation Insurance, all states were developed by injury type to an ultimate report basis for losses and to a fifth report basis for the number of cases. There are several exceptions, including New Jersey where losses are not developed by any type of injury (just for indemnity losses for all types of injuries combined) and New Jersey and New York, where losses are only developed to a fifth report basis.

9. Actually the share of all costs within a state accounted for by permanent disability cases depends on the number of such cases and their average costs relative to the costs of other types of cases within that state, and in particular temporary total disability cases, which account for the bulk of each state's cases.

10. The methodology used to derive the data on the employers' costs of workers' compensation insurance is presented in Burton and Krueger (1986).

Chapter 4
Procedures for Permanent
Partial Benefits

Workers' compensation procedures are carried out by both private parties and public agencies. Typically five actors are involved—the injured worker, his employer, the insurer of the employer's liability, the provider of medical care, and the state agency—although one actor may double and play two roles at a time. For example, the employer may self-insure and thus dispense with the services usually provided by a private insurance carrier, although the company may still hire a service bureau to administer its claims. Or, if the state has an exclusive state insurance fund, the state agency may carry out the claims management functions usually performed by private carriers. But no matter how these roles are distributed, all workers' compensation claims involve an injured worker, his employer, the insurer of the employer's liability, the provider of medical care, and a workers' compensation agency.

Any of these actors may be represented by legal counsel. The worker may be represented at some stage of the process by a lawyer, and the carrier and the employer may also employ counsel if the case reaches the contested level. The legal aspects of the administrative process have traditionally received the most attention. We do not ignore these, but choose to emphasize the other aspects.

The process is complex, not only because of the number of parties with or without their legal representation, but because of the blending of private administration with public interest. The laws mandate specific payments but generally leave the claims management in private hands. The exact combination of public standards and private administration in workers' compensation is not encountered either in the administration of tort suits or in the public income transfer programs.

The Claims Management Function

Common to all systems, whether tort suits, workers' compensation cases, or social security claims, is the payment of a claim. The claims management function consists of the following five procedures:

(1) *Opening procedures.* Usually a claim for benefits is made, although in some instances news of the event may by itself trigger an administering agency to proceed with payment.

(2) *Validation procedures.* In all systems, the validity of the claim for payment must be scrutinized. Was the person insured, or did he otherwise fall within the population eligible for receipt of the benefits? Did the event occur as claimed? Did it result in the alleged consequence? Is the extent of the injury or monetary loss as large as is claimed? What standard shall be used to measure these losses? In some tort cases it is necessary to determine who was at fault; in workers' compensation it is sufficient to determine whether the injury was connected with the insured activity. In either case, if reserves are to be set aside, estimates must be made of the eventual total cost of the claim.

(3) *Payment procedures.* In a sense this is the heart of the matter. Whether it is cash transfers or payment in kind, the appropriate account must be debited, and the payments made and delivered in a timely fashion as prescribed by the statutes or agreement of the parties. The payment may be made in a lump sum or in periodic installments. Separate and more complex procedures are required for processing medical claims and other benefits in kind, since another party, the provider, is involved.

(4) *Contested procedures.* If the claim is denied and the injured party protests, administrative procedures must allow for reconsideration of such claims and possible modification of the initial decision. If the matter is not satisfactorily settled and the case is controverted, further legal procedures come into play. The dissatisfied claimant may hire an attorney who may perform, or cause to be performed, additional administrative procedures. Another investigation of the claim may take place, other examinations to determine medical condition may be authorized, and a whole new cadre of people may become involved.

(5) *Closing procedures.* In the event that the claim is denied, or at the expiration of the period of payment, the file is closed and the case ended.

Responsibility for Claims Management

In a public program, such as the social security system, these claims procedures become the responsibility of a governmental unit such as the Social Security Administration. The agency requires information from the applicant, the physician, and possibly vocational experts.

However, the central administrative responsibility remains with the agency that administers, supervises, and eventually pays or denies claims, subject to appeals to the courts.

In tort cases, the administration of the claims management function is usually the responsibility of a private insurance carrier whose activities are constrained by various statutes and decisional law. The claimsperson is a guardian of the assets of the carrier and, in general, seeks to minimize the amounts the carrier pays. The claimant is naturally concerned with maximizing the amounts due him. The resolution of that contest becomes a matter of public concern only in the event of an appeal to the judicial system.

The administration of workers' compensation is a blend of private and public interests. The administration of the claims management functions is the responsibility of the insurer, whether it is a private insurance company, a competitive or exclusive state fund, or (if it is self-insured) the firm itself. It is the insurer under the workers' compensation law that has the primary responsibility for the administration of the claims management function. It pays the claim. And, unless the workers' compensation agency itself administers an exclusive state fund, the state agency does not pay the claim. Thus, unlike the Social Security Administration, the workers' compensation agency does not pay benefits to injured workers, nor does it pay treating physicians or any other provider of services. Yet there comes a time, at differing stages of the claim's process depending upon the jurisdiction, when the workers' compensation agency is charged with substantial responsibility for administrative procedures.

The patient suing his physician in a malpractice suit can settle for any amount that is agreeable to him, his doctor, and the insurance carrier. No state agency will interfere with the voluntary settlement on the grounds that it is not sufficient. At the opposite end of the administrative spectrum, the person qualifying for disability insurance benefits under Social Security will receive a specific amount stipulated by statute. Nongovernmental parties have little or no influence on the amount of the benefits. Workers' compensation stands between these models. The claims management function and considerable control over the amount of the benefits rests with the insurer, which is normally in the private sector, but the state workers' compensation agency supervises the application of the statute to ensure that the objectives of workers' compensation are met. This blending of public and private roles adds to the complexity of workers' compensation administration.

The Objectives of Workers' Compensation

The National Commission on State Workmen's Compensation Laws (1972, p. 99) considered an effective delivery system to be one of the five objectives of a modern workers' compensation program. It recognized that such a system is required in order to achieve the four basic objectives: broad coverage, adequate income maintenance, necessary medical care and rehabilitation services, and safety incentives. The Commission saw an effective delivery system as a means to an end, not an end in itself. Its performance was to be evaluated relatively in comparison with other systems, and absolutely by the degree of accomplishment of the four basic objectives of workers' compensation.

The whole theory of workers' compensation administration is based on the assumption that there should be a direct public interest in the compensation paid to workers injured at work. The type and amount of such payments, the conditions under which they are to be made, and the medical care workers are to be provided are prescribed in general terms by the state statutes, which also establish an administrative agency to insure these prescriptions are satisfied.

There are, however, wide variations among states in the procedures used for permanent partial disability cases. Each state workers' compensation agency keeps records, monitors claims that are paid, provides some system to evaluate permanent partial disability, and also provides a forum for the adjudication of disputes. We will discuss each of these functions further. First we provide a general description of state agencies' administrative procedures, a description that is applicable in some measure to all states, but fully applicable to none.

General Introduction to Procedures

Uncontested Cases

A claim typically begins with an accidental injury, which triggers notice by the employee to the employer, and the filing by the employer of a First Report of Injury. In the typical state in which a private insurance carrier has the primary responsibility for paying claims, a copy of the report will go to the carrier, alerting it to the fact that a possible claim is pending, and a copy will also go to the state agency.

The EFR may be the document that initiates a claim for benefits, or a separate form may be required. In some states, it will be necessary for the carrier to file the additional report, or a simple notice to the agency that payments have actually begun may be sufficient. Initial payments typically are for temporary total disability benefits.

As noted, the payment of these benefits can begin simply by the carrier accepting the claim without further formality. In some states, the carrier is called upon either to contest the claim or to begin payments within a stipulated number of days; in other states some form of paper work, possibly an agreement with the employee, must be consummated before payments begin. Usually temporary disability benefit payments stop once an employee goes back to work, or, if he does not return, after maximum medical rehabilitation has been achieved. The extent of permanent disability is assessed at that time or (in some states) a stipulated number of weeks after that date. In a minority of cases, such as amputations without further complications, the amount of benefits may be determined exclusively by a schedule, in which case there may be no controversy and payment may be made soon after the injury occurs.

Contested Cases

In the more typical case, the fact of permanent disability is conceded, but the exact nature and extent of permanent disability, and the translation of the nature and extent of disability into a particular dollar benefit, are matters of some controversy. This is not to say that the case cannot be handled voluntarily by the carrier and without resort to the controverted procedures. In California, the extent of the applicant's impairment may be determined by the rating bureau based upon medical reports, and the carrier may pay the amount suggested by the informal rating. If accepted by the employee, the processing of the case comes to an effective end.

In other states where no rating bureau exists, the carrier might have the worker examined by a physician, who assesses the percentage of disability and consequently the benefits to which the worker is entitled. Obviously, the likelihood that that amount will be accepted is greater in a case of some uncomplicated anatomical loss than in cases involving subjective complaints. Even in simple cases, in the event of some disagreement, the impairment may be rerated by the carrier based upon whatever additional information may be supplied.

If dissatisfaction persists, in some states the case moves to an informal procedural level. A referee may hear the case and possibly have the worker examined by a state physician, and, based upon the doctor's findings and medical records contained in the file, suggest an amount appropriate for that particular permanent disability. Typically, such findings are not binding on either party, and the employee, if dissatisfied, has recourse to a more formal proceeding.

The formal procedures vary greatly among the states. Typically, the agency's file in the case will be part of the record. The hearing officer will have available to him all prior determinations made at the informal level, the contentions of the parties at the several stages through which the case may have passed, and the reports of examining and treating physicians. Although formal rules of evidence are usually not followed, a stenographic transcript may be taken, some orderly procedure will be followed, and the hearing officer will make rulings as to the relevance, materiality, and admissibility of the evidence before him. In some states, the hearing room appears much like a court room, with the judge sitting on a raised bench. In other states, an informal atmosphere prevails. For the most part, the hearing officer will make a decision based upon the evidence before him, but in some instances he may request impartial medical information.

The principal witnesses on both sides will usually be physicians. In an industrial illness case, an industrial hygienist may testify as to the conditions prevailing at the workplace. The employee's "testifying physician" will state that the claimant suffered a particular injury and that his present condition is a direct result of that accidental injury. He will then give his medical opinion as to the nature and extent of what in the compensation law is usually termed "disability." If it is a so-called schedule case, the physician will estimate the percentage of the arm or other extremity that he finds to be the extent of the residual permanent partial disability. If it is a nonschedule case, the percentage may be based on some arbitrary number of weeks selected as the sum for complete disability. If earnings capacity is the criterion, the physician may also testify as to the worker's inability to perform particular types of work and the employee's counsel may elicit corroborating testimony from a vocational expert.

The physician for the carrier or the defendant/employer will offer similar but opposing testimony. His estimate of the percentage of disability based upon the same schedule will be less than that offered by the physician retained by the plaintiff/employee. The equanimity and certainty with which one physician calls forth the numbers is usually not affected by his almost certain knowledge that his colleague on the opposite side will have equally firm contrary opinions. In some states, percentage assessments by the opposing physicians will differ by predictable amounts.

The hearing officer also has some idea of how each physician will testify, what the differences will be, and where his assessment ought to lie. The lack of scientific precision is usually taken for granted, as is the fact that the assessment will be tinged by the parties' biases.

Where the estimate is to be made based on wage-earning capacity rather than on impairment or functional limitations, the attorneys for both sides may argue their cases based upon the ''other'' attributes of the injured worker. They may refer to his age and education, and the state of the labor market. Even in states where impairment or functional limitations presumably are the sole criteria, the physicians may shade their medical judgments based upon their estimates of the worker's chances in the labor market. In some states, the assessment of the ''other factors'' explicitly falls within the purview of the physician's estimates. In other jurisdictions, both the physician and the hearing officer may take these into account in some unknown and unpredictable fashion.

If the issue is actual wage loss, rather than extent of impairment or wage-earning capacity, evidence will be forthcoming as to what the employee has been earning in the labor market. Evidence, based upon his pay stubs, may be introduced as to what his actual wage loss has been. In addition, vocational experts may testify as to what he should be earning in the labor market and physicians may testify as to the work he could be doing, had he made efforts appropriate to his physical condition.

In other wage-loss cases, the employability of the worker may be at stake. In these cases, the burden may be upon the employer to show that the employee can now, in fact, return to his former job or to some other employment. The employer may offer testimony indicating that the employee has refused job offers and buttress it with medical testimony that the employee is perfectly capable of performing the work that was offered. Or, again, testimony might be forthcoming from vocational experts indicating that jobs of a particular character are available and that the employee could fill these had he the will to do so.

In yet other cases in some states, it might be workers' compensation agencies themselves that bring the case to a hearing before a hearing officer. The screening of the so-called direct settlements made by the employer and employee may raise some questions as to equity or adequacy, and the case may be scheduled for a hearing. The usual avenue to the formal hearing, however, is a petition filed by the employee.

It is not unusual for cases to continue for more than one hearing. Crucial medical testimony may be lacking, or (as pointed out above) the hearing officer may want the employee to undergo an examination by a specialist. Eventually, the record in the case is closed. The hearing officer then has a stipulated amount of time in which to issue a formal opinion. His written decision may be buttressed by a short opinion or, in cases where new issues are raised, a lengthy exposition.

Many issues might be raised at the hearing that are not concerned with the nature and extent of disability. A controversy may arise over the wages that the employee was earning or over one of the many ancillary questions connected with where the accident occurred, whether the worker was an employee within the meaning of the Act, and so on.

Once a decision is issued and served on the parties, either party has a specified number of days in which to appeal. In states without a workers' compensation commission, such as New Jersey, the only appeal from a decision of the judge of the compensation agency is to the courts, where the cases are handled in much the same manner as other civil matters. More typically, however, there are provisions for appeal within the agency, possibly to a panel of the workers' compensation commission or board. At that point, procedures vary a great deal. The appeal may be based upon the record, supplemented perhaps by written briefs from both parties; or, in some cases, oral hearings may be held to supplement the record. In yet other cases, there is, in effect, a new hearing with completely new testimony presented at the board or commission level.

Appeals from either the hearing officer level or, if it exists, the appellate body within the agency are usually to the court system of the state. There may be a trial *de novo* before a judge, or even (as in Ohio) before a jury. Alternatively, the case may be heard on the basis of the record and the hearing officer's findings accepted if supported by the evidence, substantial evidence, or a preponderance of evidence, depending on the rule in the jurisdiction.

In those states in which there is an exclusive state fund with which employers are required to insure their liability, many of the administrative functions entrusted to the carriers are now transferred to the agency administering the fund. In the case of competitive, rather than exclusive, state funds, the procedures depend on whether or not the workers' compensation agency itself is a custodian or operator of the fund, or whether the fund merely operates as another insurance carrier. For example, in California and New York, the state funds are competitive state funds and occupy the same relationship to the workers' compensation agency as does any other insurer in the state.

Administrative Functions for Permanent Disability Cases

The procedures described in the preceding section can be grouped under four headings: record keeping, monitoring, evaluation, and adjudication. We first briefly describe these functions and then more intensively examine the four functions as they are performed in the ten jurisdictions that are the primary concern of this study.

The *record keeping function* is present in all agencies. Each workers' compensation case begins with a report to the employer of an injury or disease, a copy of which is sent to the carrier and eventually to the agency. Each state requires some subsequent reporting about the individual case and its eventual disposition. States vary greatly as to the kinds of case records the agencies maintain and the diligence with which administrators follow up requests for records that do not come to them in the normal course. However logical it may be to proclaim a public interest in these matters, the total extent of some agencies' involvement may be in recording and filing what the parties themselves have done voluntarily.

Some, possibly most, states go further and are concerned with the *monitoring* function. The state agency is concerned with the equity and adequacy of the payments made voluntarily by the insurance carrier. The agency may also be concerned with the worker's rehabilitation in cases where his return to work is delayed. The agency may police the carrier's activities designed to maximize the probability of the worker's return to his job. The monitoring function may involve procedures for checking on the carrier's general performance and providing advice or sterner strictures if the carrier's performance falls short.

A third group of procedures has to do with *evaluation* of the permanent partial disability. Some agencies have prescribed procedures to evaluate, or to aid the parties in evaluating, the extent of permanent partial disability. In some states, the agency itself will take on the responsibility of determining the extent of the permanent partial disability.

In other states, the agencies will do almost nothing in this area; the parties either reach some agreement or resort to the contested procedures.

The fourth function is *adjudication,* which is undertaken by the state agencies in almost all states. Each agency has procedures to adjudicate disputes between the parties. The disputes of primary concern in this study are those concerning the liability of the employer for permanent partial benefits and those concerned with measuring the nature and extent of permanent disability.

Variations in Procedures Among the States

The 10 jurisdictions examined in this study differ in how they perform the functions of record keeping, monitoring, evaluation, and adjudication. The differences in part reflect the magnitude of the administrative burdens assigned to the states workers' compensation agencies (table 4.1). The numbers of workers covered by the workers' compensation program and the numbers of first reports of injuries vary by a factor of 20 between the largest state (California) and the smallest jurisdictions (the District of Columbia and Nevada). The amounts of benefits for which the workers' compensation agencies are responsible to insure accuracy of payments are at least 10 times greater in California than in the District of Columbia, Nevada, and Wisconsin. The resources allocated to the workers' compensation agencies to perform the administrative functions also vary considerably among the 10 jurisdictions. The figures for Ohio and Nevada are not comparable to those in other jurisdictions since the staff and budget figures include resources devoted to administering their exclusive state funds. The New York staff figure is not entirely comparable since the personnel who administer the nonoccupational disability benefits program are included.[1]

The number of staff members per million covered workers and per thousand first reports are shown in the final columns of table 4.1. Nevada and Ohio have the highest ratios—reflecting the responsibilities of administering exclusive state funds. Among the other jurisdictions, Wisconsin stands out because of its low staff ratios—an impressive result in light of the state's reputation of excellence in administration. New York is distinguished by its high ratios—a consequence in part of its unique method of monitoring, in which each indexed case must be scheduled for a hearing before an administrative law judge prior to closing.

The balance of this section reviews the approaches to the procedural functions in the 10 jurisdictions and provides observations that represent inputs to a model for permanent disability benefit procedures.

Table 4.1
Administrative Burdens and Resources of the Workers' Compensation Agencies in Ten Jurisdictions

Jurisdiction	Covered workforce (millions)	First reports (indemnity cases)	Benefits paid 1984 (millions $)	Agency staff	Agency budget (millions $)	Number of staff members		
						Per million covered workers	Per thousand first reports	
California	9.800	408,000	2,687	816	37	83	2.0
District of Columbia	0.400	13,396	74	59	2.3	148	4.4
Florida	3.800	64,834	692	523	20.3	138	8.1
Michigan	3.290	74,045	630	197	6.6	60	2.7
Nevada	0.413	10,726	106	597[1]	25[1]	1,446[1]	55.7[1]
New Jersey	3.825	37,794[2]	446	182	4.8	48	4.8
New York	6.600	174,620[2]	857	1,627[3]	51.3	247[3]	9.3[3]
Ohio	4.625	101,315	1,121	1,383[1]	47.6[1]	299[1]	13.7[1]
Pennsylvania	5.000	127,388	888	317	11	63	2.5
Wisconsin	1.920	61,499	239	84.5	3	44	1.4

SOURCES: Benefits Paid 1984 from Price (1987, table 2); other data from U.S. Department of Labor, *Administration Profiles* (1985).

1. Includes staff and budget for exclusive state fund.

2. Includes all reports filed, not just reports on indemnity cases.

3. Includes staff that administers nonoccupational disability benefits program.

Record Keeping

Ideally, procedures should place the least burden on the parties and agency consistent with fulfilling the system's objectives. If one of these objectives is the promotion of safety, the records should allow state agencies to examine the universe of work-related injuries. However, some states, such as Wisconsin and Michigan, receive reports only on potentially compensable cases. Accidental injuries in which the worker did not lose time beyond the waiting period or sustain a permanent injury will not come to their attention. On the other hand, efficiency considerations would require not placing an undue burden on the parties. New Jersey, which requires an employer's first report on all accidental injuries involving lost time, also requires an additional report on compensable cases. The purpose of the second report is not at all clear.

The parties ought not to be required to report the same information to more than one agency. The question of duplicate reporting brings up the relationship of the workers' compensation system to the rules and regulations of the Occupational Safety and Health Administration (OSHA). All employers covered by OSHA are required to fill out a form (Form 101 or an acceptable substitute) for "OSHA-recordable" cases. These include, in addition to lost time and permanent disability cases, loss of consciousness, restriction of work or motion, transfer to another job, and medical treatment other than first aid. Employers are not required to transmit OSHA 101 forms, but the forms must be kept on file and are the source of information for the employer's annual report to OSHA.

The very existence of OSHA may have engendered an attitude in some state administrators, and perhaps some employers as well, that safety has somehow become the concern of OSHA and the federal government and need no longer occupy the attention of the state workers' compensation agencies. To perpetuate such a notion would be to deprive the state agencies of one of their traditional and essential functions. To discharge these functions, the agencies should have not only knowledge of all work-related injuries and diseases, but also the capability of preparing reports and analyses to fulfill the objective of promoting safe and healthful working conditions in the state.

The problem always is where to draw the line. To require employers to send in the forms in all OSHA-recordable cases might involve a flood of "medical only" cases and complicate the administration of the entire program. The net is cast wide in the OSHA-recordable criteria, and although it may suit OSHA's legislative purposes, it may result in a flood of forms coming to the workers' compensation agencies and discourage any meaningful analysis. In any event, none of the states under consideration here requires reports on all OSHA-recordable cases; all maintain the more traditional requirements of reporting on lost-time injuries or on some even narrower universe.

If the employer's first report is used not only for safety purposes but as the first document in the case file, there is an additional problem of confidentiality. The fear is sometimes expressed that if the document is used in case processing, employers will be less frank in recording the event, lest the information be used against them. Thus, in New Jersey and in California, where first reports are required on all cases, the analysis and the processing of these forms are not done by the same division that administers the workers' compensation statute.

More universally accepted than the safety objective is the objective of assuring the payment of adequate benefits promptly. For this purpose, the agency must be aware of all potentially compensable cases and of whether the first payment is being made within a reasonable time. In states where private insurance prevails, three general opening procedures can be identified. First is New York's unique system. The employer files a first report on all lost-time cases and agency personnel make the preliminary judgment as to whether compensation benefits will become payable. Such cases are indexed. The employer is notified and is required to respond to the notice of indexing by indicating payment or intent to controvert. Once indexed, a case cannot be closed without a hearing.

Second is the procedure in Pennsylvania, where the employer's first report on all lost-time injuries becomes the first document in the file. Within 21 days, the carrier submits another report indicating either payment or intent to controvert. Essentially the same system is followed in Wisconsin and Michigan, except that in these states the employer's first reports are filed only in potentially compensable cases. The third procedure is found in New Jersey, which calls itself a direct payment system state. There the employer must file a first report on all lost-time cases and then a form accepting liability and setting forth some details. But the second form does not report when the compensation payments are to be made, nor is any employer form routinely required if the case is controverted.

The Pennsylvania procedure places the least burden on the employer and employee consistent with the information the agency must have to discharge its functions. An employer's first report is filed in all lost-time cases; within a stipulated period, the carrier must give notice either that the employer will pay or that the employer will not pay; subsequently the carrier is required to file forms indicating any change of status; and at the close of payments, it must submit a final receipt of compensation. Further, the carrier must file annually for each open case a statement showing the compensation details and the amounts to be paid.

If the sole objective were assurance of benefits, the New York procedure would seem to be preferable. It can be criticized only on the grounds of efficiency; the resources used in conducting a final hearing or offering the opportunity for such a hearing in each case before closing might better be used elsewhere. The system also places a burden on agency personnel, who are required to decide which cases should be assembled and indexed. In the Pennsylvania procedure, the carrier is obligated to make this decision, to advise as to whether payments have begun, and, if they have not, to advise as to the reason for nonpayment.

Exclusive state-fund states have obviously different problems. Information is required on all work-related injuries that involve any type of expenditures, even for minor first aid cases. The fund must be advised on all items that will result in charges. In Ohio's exclusive state fund, detailed reports are required from employers before claims can be paid. In the case of Ohio self-insurers, however, the state's function is not to pay but to oversee payments, and reports are not required until such time as permanent partial disability is to be assessed.

Closing procedures in states are likely to differ not only because of the method of insuring liability, but also according to what criteria are used to assess disability—wage loss, impairment, or functional limitations. In New Jersey, where an assessment of impairment is the rule, the final report filed by the employer lists the percentage of disability and amount of benefits and some medical information, but it is not accompanied by a physician's report.

New York requires a physician's report on a periodic basis, in part because these reports are useful to the carrier to audit the treatment and the physician's fees. The physician is chosen by the employee in New York; in New Jersey the carrier has control over the choice of physician and the agency does not require physicians' reports.

In New York, the case cannot be closed without a hearing and consequently the agency has knowledge of the settlements reached in all cases. Even if the parties do not appear for a hearing, presumably the file information is sufficient for the agency to audit the adequacy of the payments.

To assure adequate payments to a worker where such payments are made voluntarily, the agency needs information on the amounts being paid, the reason they are being paid, medical condition, and the worker's current employment status. A further obligation of the agency is to audit and analyze these reports and take action on the basis of the information. Such considerations bring us to the next group of procedures, namely those having to do with the monitoring function.

Monitoring

The extent of monitoring that can be done in any state is crucially dependent on the type of records kept. Obviously, monitoring is difficult or impossible if no information is forthcoming from the parties. As we have seen, all states require some documents from interested parties. Most states review these documents as they come in, even if only to check the accuracy of the parties' computation.

The patterns of monitoring are quite different from state to state. In New York, all indexed cases are scheduled for a hearing, and monitoring is an integral part of the case processing. All cases presumably come under the scrutiny of an administrative law judge before they can be closed. Whether anything substantive is done in routine cases, which are handled at rates of more than 100 per day, and whether an individual judge can give very serious consideration to these cases is another matter. Nonetheless, there is at least some review.

New Jersey from time to time, depending on the availability of personnel, checks on the direct settlement made between the parties. The efficacy of such activity is dependent on the budget allocated to this process. Obviously, if the screening is entrusted to an untrained clerk, he will only be able to apply the mechanical criteria given him. On the other hand, if the screening is done by a trained administrator or physician, more significant questions might be raised as to the adequacy of the benefits paid. No field investigations are undertaken in New Jersey, and cases that are questionable can only be set down for a hearing.

Wage-loss states have other items to check. In Michigan, if payments cease and the worker is not back to work, the agency will investigate the matter, sometimes on its own initiative. The use of an investigative staff by an agency is a relatively rare event, however, except in the exclusive fund jurisdictions. The more usual procedure when discrepancies are suspected is to notify the parties and schedule the case for a hearing. In some instances, however, the hearing officer may make a judgment that further information is needed and will initiate a request for further medical testimony.

Wisconsin takes an active interest in pending cases. Formal checks of computational accuracy are made in mechanical fashion, but the agency also follows through, telephones the parties, and in general is willing to investigate questionable situations.

Another method of monitoring, used in Wisconsin and Michigan among other states, is to provide information to the employee on a routine, regular, and continuing basis. In both states, the worker is sent copies of forms so that he can check on what the employer has reported. In Pennsylvania, copies of the first reports are given to the injured employee and the reverse side of the copy lists his rights. Notices of the compensation payable must be sent to the injured employee by the carrier, and, in general, the employee is kept informed of developments in his case.

The concept of monitoring carrier performance is not appropriate in the exclusive fund states. The workers' compensation agency pays benefits and, of course, must keep a constant check on what is happening in the case so as to decide whether or not particular benefits are justified.

In California, each employer that voluntarily begins payments of compensation is supposed to file a form setting forth the basic information about the claim. Similarly, a form is supposed to be filed at the end of the case. Not all employers abide by the requirement for the first form and fewer still comply with the requirement for the final form. California has adopted a computerized system of monitoring these forms. Each goes through a basic editing process and obvious errors are spotted by the computer check. The system appears to be capable of efficient superficial checking of forms that are filed; it fails, however, to systematically check as to whether such forms are filed in the first place.

It is wasteful and inefficient to audit forms and then do nothing further. The objectives of monitoring, which may be to assure that the law is being administered in an equitable fashion or to provide reliable information to improve the administration of the law, must be clearly specified. Whatever the purpose, it is worthwhile to follow up on cases flagged for attention. In Wisconsin, employers and insurance carriers know that if their forms are not complete, or if they have deviated from established procedures, the matter will be called to their attention by a phone call, a letter, or other means. Because the administrators care about information that comes in, those who forward material are careful about what they send.

The monitoring function requires a type of administrative talent that is not always found in the state agencies, with their sharp division of personnel between clerical employees on one hand and hearing officers on the other. The monitoring function requires one or more investigators charged with following up flagged cases to see that the appropriate information is forthcoming, and to assure that the worker receives his rights.

The line between monitoring and our next category, "evaluation," is a thin one. By monitoring, we mean to include all activities deigned to provide information to the employee and to advise the parties of their rights in an attempt to deliver benefits equitably, quickly, and without litigation when no genuine dispute exists. All monitoring activities depend upon information coming from the parties and, hence, on a good record keeping and data system. Once in effect, an efficient system would audit these forms in the least-cost manner; in a larger state, auditing to check on the accuracy and completeness of the information can be computerized.

The second element of a good monitoring system is providing information and advice to the employee so that he is aware of what the employer intends to do and the basis for the action. Obviously, excessive monitoring can result in a paternalistic system. The agency should keep the employee informed about his rights and about the significance of the actions of the employer under the law; whatever actions the employee takes (or fails to take) normally are his own choice, although in some instances the agency may need to override the decision.

The third element of a monitoring system is to take active steps— field investigations to learn the facts in questionable cases, concerted attempts to advise the parties of their rights under the law—to avoid unnecessary litigation. One way to work toward this end, obviously, is to provide criteria for the evaluation of the permanent partial disabilities.

Evaluation

What procedures have been set up to allow the parties to evaluate permanent partial disability? If an employer seeks to pay permanent partial disability benefits voluntarily, can he arrive at the amounts that ought to be paid by complying with these procedures? If he does comply, does he have any assurance that the payment will dispose of the matter without further litigation?

Possibly the most developed evaluation procedures are California's. On request, the permanent disability rating bureau prepares an informal rating for a permanent disability case. If both parties accept the rating, payment of compensation due may begin without further procedures. The informal rating has no legal significance unless the parties voluntarily accept it. It does not constitute evidence of the existence of permanent disability or of the factors of disability. Available evidence suggests that the informal rating is most effective in the resolution of cases involving minor injuries. The more serious injuries are almost always the subject of disputed cases. It may have been hoped that California's rating system would assure objective disposition of cases, but the fact is that litigation has become the rule rather than the exception in California. The fault may be with the subjective nature of the criteria used in the state.

New Jersey's procedure at the informal hearing level bears some resemblance to California's rating procedure, but the differences are significant. The employer in New Jersey can begin to pay permanent partial disability benefits without securing any rating from the agency. It may, however, bring the matter to the informal level, a procedure that is voluntary on the part of both employer and employee. The referee's recommendation, made after hearing both sides, has no legal significance, but if accepted by both parties, it may be the effective end of the matter, with the employer filing a final report on the case.

In Ohio, an exclusive-fund state, a separate section of the Commission evaluates all applications for permanent partial disability benefits. The evaluation may be based on medical information in the file or the section may order an examination by a medical specialist.

The wage-loss states have no specific evaluation procedures. Evaluation of impairments and function limitations is confined to schedule-type injuries. An issue that arises more commonly in permanent partial disability cases is the question of whether an employee is able to return to his work, or to other work that is available to him.

In the scheme by which we have chosen to describe workers' compensation procedures, evaluation procedures lie between monitoring procedures (designed to insure that the law's objectives are carried out) and adjudication procedures (governing the settlement of disputes), inasmuch as they are concerned with allowing the parties themselves to settle on the amount and type of permanent partial disability benefits. If the state discourages any voluntary payment of these benefits until agency personnel have had an opportunity to rate the extent of the impairment, evaluation is close to monitoring. And to the extent that evaluation procedures substitute for adjudication, such as in the informal hearing or rating bureau procedures, evaluation becomes almost the first step in the adjudication procedures.

Even were there a perfect and universally accepted set of objective criteria with which to evaluate cases, there would remain the question whether it is necessary to have each and every case come before some tribunal or bureau of the state workers' compensation agency or whether workers need appear personally in order for their cases to be evaluated. In California, workers need not make a physical appearance at the rating bureau. The initial rating is done on the basis of medical information and forms filed by the employer, which include input from the employee. In Nevada, although it is unnecessary for the worker to appear at a hearing, a high percentage of all but the most trivial of the permanent partial benefit cases do appear before a referee for evaluation, which usually entails an examination of the employee by the state doctor.

The ideal criteria would be sufficiently clear and objective to allow the parties to comply with evaluation procedures and determine the benefit amount. Such determination could be reviewed by the agency, and only settlements that fell outside acceptable bounds would be adjudicated on the agency's motion. Whatever the ideal, the fact remains that a high percentage of cases in most states are decided on a controverted level. Each state has some provision for the adjudication of disputes.

Adjudication

Broadly speaking, the adjudication procedures of the states examined in this study are very similar. An exception is New York, in which all cases must be considered at some point by an administrative law judge (ALJ). But in New York, the adjudication procedure often begins after the ALJ's decision, when one of the parties appeals the decision to the Board.

In general, however, all contested cases begin with some type of a petition, followed by a pretrial conference, a hearing before a hearing officer, and then possibly an appeal from that hearing officer's decision.

Efficiency considerations require that adjudication procedures be used only after voluntary settlement procedures have failed. Controversy should be a last resort, and efficient procedures would allow the parties to present all their evidence fully and completely at a hearing before a competent trier of the facts. An appeals procedure would then be reserved only for the unusual case in which new and important issues are raised, or in which proceedings at the lower level are deficient.

Adjudication procedures do, of course, vary from state to state. In New Jersey there is a hearing before a judge of compensation, who operates in a fairly formal capacity and whose decision can be appealed only to the state court system. By contrast, in Wisconsin there is a less formal hearing before an attorney-examiner, with appeals to a review commission of the department in which the compensation agency is located, and from there to the court system.

In Ohio, the Commission's rulings concerning the extent of disability cannot be appealed, but other matters may be appealed to the courts, where the case may be heard *de novo* and possibly before a jury.

Differences among the states in their adjudication procedures reflect in large part the differences among state constitutions and court systems. It would be most difficult and probably not worth the effort to standardize adjudication procedures. The ideal procedures, however, would seem to require a full hearing at some stage before a hearing officer with an appeals step within the Commission. Such a decision should be dispositive of the facts, with appeals to the court system confined to interpretation of law, with findings of the fact supported if the courts find that they are based on substantial evidence.

Summary and Conclusions

We have accepted the National Commission's emphasis on the importance of the delivery system, seconding its plea for an active administrative agency that concentrates on administrative functions other than adjudication. Our concern has been with agency procedures involved in the processing of claims for permanent partial disability benefits. We have not examined all aspects of administration, but have taken many of the factors as given. We recognize that the particular insurance arrangements in effect, the civil service structure, the type of compensation system, and a great many other variables affect administration. Our focus has been on the administrative procedures of the state agency to the exclusion of the claims management functions entrusted to the insurer. We have adopted a fourfold classification of administrative functions involved in processing permanent partial disability cases.

The Record Keeping Function

An efficient delivery system requires record keeping for several purposes. The record keeping function furthers all of the basic objectives of the modern workers' compensation program. Without adequate knowledge of what is happening to all workers who become injured in the state, the agency will not be able to determine whether the program provides for broad coverage of employees with work-related injuries or diseases. Without knowing what happens to workers who become involved in industrial injuries, administrators will not be able to determine whether the system provides substantial protection against interruption of income. Without adequate reporting, it will not be able to tell whether provisions for medical care and rehabilitation are adequate; and, of course, without reporting from employers of the wide range of injuries and illnesses that are work-related, it will not be able to fulfill the objective of encouragement of safety.

Desirable though it would be to possess complete information, it is clear that in a world of limited resources most agencies must live with an information system that has obvious gaps. California has good information about the nature and type of all lost-time injuries in the state, but not about their consequences. In Wisconsin, the agency's field of vision is restricted to compensable injuries and illnesses, but for these the system develops considerable information about the types of injuries involved and the benefits paid. Both systems have defects and advantages. Pennsylvania's example shows that it is possible to have both extensive reporting of injuries and illnesses and a system that follows what happens in compensable cases.

No state has an ideal system, but pieces that could be assembled into a nearly ideal system are scattered throughout various states. It remains to bring them together and to convince the states that doing so will be worth the cost. Unfortunately, as of this writing no such eclectic design has (to our knowledge) been seriously advanced; nor are the data forthcoming that would allow for a cost-benefit analysis.

The Monitoring Function

To discharge its obligations to further the objectives of the program, a state agency must monitor the activities of the principal actors in the system. It must have sufficient information to act promptly in cases where the letter and the spirit of the law are not complied with. It must routinely monitor the system so that workers are guaranteed substantial protection against interruption of income and so that sufficient medical care and rehabilitation services are assured.

The monitoring function can range from mere checks on the correctness of arithmetic calculations to a thorough follow-up of cases. It will vary among states according to the type of law; according to the obligation of the carrier either to pay a claim or controvert, or to delay payment until after some formality; and according to the type of notice, if any, the payer must file before payments are suspended. As with the other administrative functions, much will depend on whether the agency adopts an active or passive stance. Fears of acting too paternalistically may prevent a state from adopting an active role in the monitoring function. If the agency detects something amiss, it may limit itself to scheduling a hearing and allowing the parties, if they choose, to protect their own interests.

The monitoring function can be carried out to further the program's objectives without the agency acting in an excessively paternal manner and without displacing the legitimate functions of the legal profession. As with the other categories, we cannot point to one jurisdiction as having the ideal system, and we recognize that any system, to be pronounced perfect, must pass the economic test. We can, however, suggest an eclectic system based on our examination of all 10 states.

Once a workers' compensation program grows to the point that it receives thousands of reports annually, computerization of routine procedures may be worthwhile. Computer programs are admirably suited to checking on completeness of forms, auditing computations, and conducting simple logic checks. It does not take a sophisticated program to determine when a date is omitted, when the weekly compensation rate times 10 weeks comes to less than 10 times the rate, or when the date of injury occurs after the date of first payment. Assigning such checks to a computer can free personnel for a more meaningful audit of reports.

Once potential errors are discovered, some method of rectifying them must be set into motion. An ideal monitoring system would provide a budget for phone inquiries and for field investigations. The carriers discharging their claims processing functions in a timely fashion deserve plaudits; those deficient should have their shortfalls called to their attention.

Clearly, it is not paternalistic for the worker to be kept advised of the status of his claim at all stages. An ideal monitoring system is dependent on a system of records on one hand and, on the other, a system of evaluation that affords the parties some guidance.

The Evaluation Function

The evaluation category encompasses all administrative functions designed to provide guidance to the parties in their evaluation of the nature and extent of permanent disability. Unlike some of the other categories of administrative procedures, in the case of evaluation, the particular type of procedures used may be less important than whether the agency has promulgated any guidelines to aid the party in making such determinations.

As the system now operates, the rating of a particular person's disability or impairment depends on judgmental factors, but variability can be reduced if the agency is able to provide guidance to the parties—a feat that obviously requires the formulation of standards and an active administration to promote them.

The evaluation functions can be performed in a number of ways, but if they are neglected, the result will be extensive litigation, with each case being decided on an *ad hoc* basis and with the inevitable possibility of uneven and inequitable treatment. Our examination of the evaluation procedures is developed in subsequent chapters. Whether these procedures are carried out by means of an agency rating bureau or by the promulgation of general guidelines, the assertion of interest by the agency in these matters and the requirement that settlements be made to conform to some uniform standard would go far toward the achievement of equity.

The Adjudication Function

Adjudication remains an inevitable characteristic of the administrative system of state workers' compensation agencies. Unfortunately, in many state agencies, the greatest part of the administrative energy and resources goes into discharging the adjudication function.

The claim petitions must be docketed and served on the appropriate parties. Strict controls must be kept over contested case files whose contents may be subject to subpoena. Due process requires notice to the parties. Hearing officers' time must be scheduled; decisions and opinions must be typed and sent to the parties. Appeals must be dealt with within legally specified time limits. Transcripts may be taken at hearings, and these must be preserved and distributed. The procedures are, of necessity, regularized, but they must give due attention to the legal rights of the parties. Care is also necessary because deficiencies in procedures may cause reversals of decisions at appellate levels.

The care and attention given to these adjudication procedures serve as a standard that should govern the record keeping, monitoring, and evaluation functions. It is understandable that when budgets are limited, adjudicative functions receive priority. But to the extent that the other functions are neglected, the adjudicative role becomes more necessary, extensive, and expensive.

Record keeping, monitoring, and evaluation are complementary functions. To monitor effectively requires records, and the standards that are monitored largely come from the evaluation function. But these three categories of administrative functions may substitute for some adjudicative activities. To the extent that funds for the records, monitoring, and evaluation can be found, adjudication funds might be saved. If the parties know what to do (evaluation), if they believe that what they do is a matter of concern (monitoring), and if the agency has knowledge of what they do (record keeping), to that extent, disputes (adjudication) should be minimized. The contested forum can then be reserved for genuine disputes, in which novel issues are explored and new directions taken.

NOTE

1. The annual budget of the New York State Workers' Compensation Board of $56,580,700 includes $5,258,300 to administer the nonoccupational disability benefits program (U.S. Dept. of Labor, *Administration Profiles*, 1985, p. 238). A similar breakdown of staff is not provided, but the budgetary division suggests that most Board personnel are involved in administering the workers' compensation program.

Chapter 5
Scheduled Benefits
Scheduled Versus Nonscheduled Injuries

The essential task of the workers' compensation program is to pay appropriate benefits to injured workers. In this chapter, we explore the criteria used for deciding on appropriate benefit amounts in cases involving scheduled injuries of a permanent and partial nature. In chapters 6-9 we deal with the nonscheduled, permanent partial injuries.

As is often the case in describing workers' compensation programs, the terms ''scheduled'' and ''nonscheduled'' are not used in a uniform and unambiguous fashion. The statutes in most states contain a schedule that lists the number of weeks or dollar amounts of compensation benefits to be paid for the physical loss or (in most jurisdictions) the loss of use of specified parts of the body. In addition to listing the upper and lower extremities (the arm, leg, hand, foot, fingers, and toes), states commonly schedule benefits for the enucleation of an eye and for the loss of hearing and vision. Disfigurement is also specifically mentioned in some statutes, usually without specific guidance as to how it is to be rated. We define a *scheduled* injury as any injury that is specifically enumerated in the workers' compensation statute.

Injuries to the trunk, internal organs, nervous system, and other body systems are not usually included in the lists of injuries found in the statutes, and we define these injuries as *nonscheduled*. (In some states, they are referred to as ''unscheduled'' injuries.)

The distinction between scheduled and nonscheduled injuries can be related to the possible consequences of an injury or disease illustrated in chart 1.2 and discussed in chapter 1. The worker who suffers the physical loss of a part of the body included in the schedule is evaluated in terms of the seriousness of his or her impairment. Thus in a state that equates the loss of an arm with 250 weeks of benefits, a worker who loses half of an arm by amputation will be entitled to 125 weeks of benefits. An injury that leads to the loss of use of a body part found in the schedule is evaluated in terms of the extent of functional limitations that result. Thus in a state that equates the loss of a hand with 100 weeks of benefits, a worker with an injury that causes a 50 percent loss of use of a hand will receive 50 weeks of benefits. Most states pay scheduled benefits if the worker experiences either a physical loss or a loss of use of the body part found in the schedule, but there are some states that confine scheduled benefits to amputations as opposed to loss of use.

There are three general approaches to nonscheduled injuries that can also be related to the conceptual framework found in chapter 1. (Most states use only one of these approaches, although, as we will discuss in subsequent chapters, there are exceptions.) The first approach to nonscheduled injuries evaluates them in terms of the resulting impairments or functional limitations. For example, a worker may experience structural damage to a vertebra and the spinal column, which are injuries usually not found on the schedule. The impairment itself may be evaluated (the disc is herniated) or the consequent functional limitations may be assessed (the worker is restricted in his ability to lift, stoop, or make certain motions that he was able to make before the injury). This first approach usually produces a rating in percentage terms that relates the worker's condition to that of a whole man (or to a "totally disabled" person). Thus in a state that equates a whole man to 500 weeks, a worker with an impairment rating of 25 percent would receive 125 weeks of benefits. The states that use the impairment approach to nonscheduled benefits are our category I states, and are examined in chapter 6.

The second approach to nonscheduled injuries evaluates them in terms of the loss of earning capacity. In states that use this approach (category II states, discussed in chapter 7), an assessment of the seriousness of the worker's medical condition, in light of such factors as the worker's prior education, work experience, and personal characteristics, is used to yield a rating in percentage terms of the loss of earning capacity. Thus in a state that defines a total loss of earning capacity as equivalent to 600 weeks of benefits, a worker with a 33 1/3 percent loss of earning capacity would receive 200 weeks of benefits.

The third approach to nonscheduled benefits is the wage-loss approach, which requires the worker to demonstrate that he has experienced an actual loss of earnings because of the work-related injury or disease. The states using the wage-loss approach (category III states) are examined in chapters 8 and 9.

The typical workers' compensation statute, then, distinguishes between scheduled injuries, which are listed in the statute and evaluated according to the resulting impairments and functional limitations, and nonscheduled injuries, which are evaluated in terms of impairment, loss of earning capacity, or actual wage loss. A few jurisdictions are atypical. In California, for example, the statute does not contain a list of injuries with corresponding benefits; i.e., there is no statutory schedule. However, the California workers' compensation agency issues a set of guidelines for evaluating injuries that encompasses all types of injuries, without the typical scheduled-nonscheduled distinction found in the statutes of other jurisdictions. The California guidelines are also unique because, depending on the injury, the basis for the rating can be impairment, functional limitations, or loss of earning capacity. Although California does not neatly fit into our taxonomy, we will examine the California treatment of those injuries that are normally scheduled in this chapter, and then reexamine California as an example of the category II approach to nonscheduled injuries in chapter 7.

Nevada, too, defies our classification scheme. As in California, Nevada's statute includes no list of injuries. Rather, all injuries are evaluated by use of the American Medical Association's *Guides to the Evaluation of Permanent Impairment.* In terms of the conceptual approach provided in chapter 1, the *Guides* evaluate injuries in terms of the resulting impairments and functional limitations. We treat Nevada in this chapter for those injuries that are typically scheduled; in the next chapter, Nevada is viewed as exemplifying the category I approach to nonscheduled injuries.

A final matter requiring discussion before we turn to an intensive examination of scheduled injuries is the question of whether a given injury can be compensated under more than one approach. In most states the schedule is "exclusive," that is, an injury that qualifies for scheduled benefits cannot qualify for any other type of permanent disability benefit. (An injured worker may qualify for temporary disability benefits during the healing period that are paid in addition to the scheduled benefits, and still meet our definition of "exclusive" benefits.) In some states, however, a worker who qualifies for scheduled benefits may also qualify for some other type of permanent disability benefits; such scheduled benefits are "nonexclusive." One state with nonexclusive benefits is New York, where workers with scheduled awards based on loss of at least 50 percent of the arm, hand, leg, or foot can qualify for a type of wage-loss benefit if they are still experiencing losses of earnings due to the injury when the scheduled benefits expire. Another example is Florida, where the limited scheduled benefits included in the 1979 law can be paid in addition to wage-loss benefits for the same injury (assuming the worker is experiencing an actual loss of earnings).

History of the Schedule

Arthur Larson (1986, sec. 57.14), in tracing the history of the schedule in workers' compensation, identifies the fundamental rule of liability: normally a fixed amount of compensation is paid for a particular type and severity of injury, regardless of actual wage loss. Larson recognizes that the rule cuts both ways. A worker may receive a scheduled benefit in the absence of any permanent wage loss. Conversely, he may suffer a continuing wage loss in excess of the time specified on the schedule. Larson notes that this rule was never universal and has been giving way to both judicial and legislative assaults. Despite these exceptions, the fundamental rule of liability is so pervasive that a review of its historical origins is warranted.

Ancient Precedents

A generation ago, Babylonian law, which was codified in the reign of Hammurabi, was rediscovered for the modern world. Hammurabi's code represented some amelioration of more primitive customs, because it partially substituted compensation for retaliation. Also, the principle of *talion,* a punishment identical to the offense, however brutal it might have been, at least precluded retaliations that exceeded the severity of the original offense. The code of Hammurabi includes both specified money payments for particular injuries and more direct "eye for an eye, tooth for a tooth" penalties, with the choice dependent upon the relative social ranks of the aggressors and the victims.[1]

In Hittite law, penalties, fines, and punishments were reduced, and the previous talionic and corporal penalties replaced by compensation. Punishment of the offenders became almost secondary to reparation for the damage done (Neufeld 1951, p. 99).

In the Hebrew Bible, although the law of retaliation—the measure for measure—is quoted, nonfatal physical injuries became a matter for monetary compensation to the injured party. The general rule was that these ought to be equitable and, as far as possible, equivalent. The rules allowed compensation for a good deal more than wage loss (Falk 1964, pp. 83-84) and can be considered the predecessor of tort law and nonscheduled injury awards as much as the forerunner of the schedules.

A clear illustration of how compensation replaced retaliation is found in Exodus (21.18-19):

> And if men contend, and one smite the other with a stone, or with his fists, and he die not, but keep his bed; if he rise again and walk abroad upon his staff, then shall he that smote him be quit; only he shall pay for the loss of his time and shall cause him to be thoroughly healed.

The commentaries explain that compensation is awarded on five grounds: for damage, for pain, for healing, for loss of time, and for insult. Insult apparently refers to payments made when the harm was intentionally inflicted. The liability for healing extended to payment of medical costs; the commentaries are quite specific as to when liability ceases, and under what conditions the case may be "reopened," to use the modern phrase.[2]

Payment for damages was assessed in a way that is not possible in the absence of a slave market. The instructions were to consider the injured person as if he were a slave to be sold in the market, to appraise his price before the injury, and to contrast that price with what he would be worth with the impairment. Obviously, in a perfect market the difference would be the present value of the future net product of the whole slave, as contrasted with that of the impaired one. With the examples at hand (a slave market), these capitalized values could be observed, rather than estimated by probabilistic functions dependent upon imperfect knowledge of future earning streams.

Another of the five grounds was liability for loss of time. The rabbis recognized that the injured man had already been paid for the value of his foot or leg, and consequently the amount paid for loss of time was estimated at a minimum wage—"as if he were a watchman over a cucumber field," neither an onerous nor a dangerous occupation. The duration is not clear from the commentaries. Was it payment for the healing period or "temporary total disability" in modern terms? Or was it an extended wage-loss benefit after payment of compensation for the impairment? A footnote to the commentaries implies it was the latter, and that wages of the simplest task were chosen since the injured often may have been fit for no other kind of work. It goes on to say that "in actual practice the court must take into consideration what services he will be fit to give after he has been completely cured." The ambiguity remains since the same footnote also states that compensation for lost time must be paid even in the absence of bodily injury.

Since the scheme was general, and not one of "liability without fault," the last of the five grounds was for "pain." The amounts awarded depended upon the amounts a person "would be willing to accept to suffer so much"—a startlingly modern formulation.

People in similar stages of civilization develop similar concepts to deal with such matters, but how these concepts survive, and through what transmutations, is difficult to trace. Certain developments cannot be traced on a straight upward line; retrogression and advance both take place, and it is not easy to distinguish between them. It is claimed that the Egyptian Bedouin, until quite recently, had a set of fixed payments for assaults and wounds, dealing respectively with loss of limbs, broken bones, wounds on the face, and wounds elsewhere on the body. A hereditary assessor determined the amount payable in each case in order to avoid talion or some sort of revenge (Driver and Miles 1960, pp. 408-9).

By the time the Anglo-Saxon world begins to leave its record, money reparations as a substitute for clan vengeance seem to be the rule. A definite schedule of tariffs established the official money worth of all persons, gauged principally by their rank (Malone 1970, p. 2). Thus the biblical notion specifying a definite amount for a specific injury, independent of rank, was lost sight of as status distinctions came into play.

Disfigurements, which are included in some modern schedules, were also included in the earliest laws. Malone (1970, p. 2) quotes the laws of Ethelbert to illustrate his point that the amount of tariff to be paid was determined to a large extent by the public shame that attended the wound: "If the bruise be black in part not covered by the clothes, let bot be made with thirty scaetts. If it be covered by the clothes, let bot be made for each with twenty scaetts." Such pronouncements sound much like current provisions of state compensation statutes, which specify dollar amounts due for highly visible scars but often leave less obvious scars uncompensated.

Malone cites the reference by Pound (1914, p. 198) to a pronouncement of the Welsh king, Howell the Good, that a scar on the face is worth six-score "pints," while the permanent loss of both joints of the thumb (an injury that would virtually disable the hand) brought only seventy-six "pints" and a half-penny. Thus even in the earliest times there was no ready social consensus as to the relative value of the consequences of one injury versus those of another.

We can find no organic connection between these ancient and primitive valuations and modern-day compensation schedules. The practice of levying fixed sums to compensate victims for specific injuries apparently disappeared, perhaps because of the lack of flexibility, or perhaps because the sums became unrealistically large and paid no account to the offender's ability to pay (Pollock and Maitland 1895, Vol. II, pp. 459-60).

The development of the criminal law substituted a more sophisticated method of social control, and in civil suits money damages were awarded when harm was inflicted, at first in accordance with strict liability and later according to negligence principles. Thus in the late nineteenth century, courts proudly declared that the law does not attempt to fix any precise rules for measuring damages, but "from the necessity of the case leaves their assessment to the good sense and the unbiased judgment of the jury."[3] "There can be no fixed measurement of compensation," wrote the Supreme Court in a late nineteenth century railroad case, "for . . . the permanent injury to health and body."[4]

Of course, it was the very dissatisfaction with these jury awards and the uncertainty attendant upon the tort law standards that helped persuade legislatures to adopt the first compensation statutes. The aim was to eliminate negligence concepts and substitute the concept of liability without fault. Liability was to be limited and the search was for definite rules to govern the determination of compensation benefits.

European Experience and Early State Laws

American state workers' compensation laws were influenced heavily by European experience. Germany's workers' compensation statute in 1884 was followed by Austria's in 1887. Sixteen other European nations, as well as South Australia, Queensland, and the Cape of Good Hope, had followed suit (between 1894 and 1907) before the first American act appeared (Larson 1986, sec. 57.13).

By 1913, the Bureau of Labor Statistics could report that no subject of labor legislation had gained such general acceptance throughout the world in so brief a period. Forty-one foreign countries, including all European countries except Turkey, had introduced some form of workers' compensation for industrial accidents. In the United States, the U.S. Congress passed a law in 1908 granting certain of its employees the right to receive compensation for injuries sustained in the course of employment. New York, Wisconsin, and Minnesota appointed commissions to formulate laws in 1909. Legislation was passed in Montana in 1909 and in Maryland and New York in 1910, but each of these laws was later declared unconstitutional. In 1911, Wisconsin became the first state to pass a state workers' compensation law that survived constitutional tests.

As Larson makes clear, most of these statutes did not contain schedules (1986, sec. 57.13). The New York law, for example, was modeled on the 1897 British act, which had a wage-loss provision for all permanent injuries. New Jersey's 1911 law is the first that contained a schedule from the beginning. New Jersey was the first state to adopt what Reede terms a flat rate disability schedule—"the only completely original element in American compensation scales." According to Reede (1947, pp. 117-18), the idea for the schedule was derived from the prevailing practice in private accidental and health insurance of paying specified sums for accidental dismemberment.

Dodd (1936, p. 617) maintains that the amounts specified for various types of impairments were influenced by jury verdicts in liability cases, schedules in accident policies, and legislative compromise between opposing interests.

Larson notes that schedules for compensation appeared in the United States well before the first state workers' compensation statutes: the first schedules were probably those of individual insurance policies, which began to appear in the second half of the nineteenth century.[5] Larson claims that Belgium's Industrial Accident schedule was closely associated with comparable compensation for war wounds, as was France's original schedule. It is his opinion that these historical fragments are of no use at all in explaining the origin of the fundamental rule of liability used for workers' compensation scheduled injuries—namely, the complete independence from actual wage loss within a program that justified benefits because of the existence of lost earnings (work disability, in our terminology). The schedules, especially the more limited schedules (such as Pennsylvania's early law, which was limited to major members), Larson notes, were tied in with the wage-loss rationale by the conclusive presumption of wage loss from major impairment. He contends that it was a realistic presumption, more obvious in earlier times than now because of the absence then of laws prohibiting employment discrimination. "The presumption that a one-armed or a one-legged worker would suffer eventual actual wage loss, then, was no fiction, nor was it a facade behind which to distribute payments for physical impairment" (Larson 1986, sec. 57.14).

New Jersey's example inspired the adoption of schedules in many other state workers' compensation laws. In 1912, Michigan, Rhode Island, and Maryland passed original statutes containing limited schedules; and a number of states whose original statutes had no schedules added them within a few years (Reede 1947, pp. 117-18). Ten jurisdictions had no schedules in their original acts: Arizona, California, Illinois, Kansas, New Hampshire, Ohio, Washington, West Virginia, Wisconsin, and Wyoming. By 1940, every state with a compensation law had a schedule of one sort or another.[6]

Of the 48 states in the union in 1940, only Arkansas and Mississippi were without workers' compensation laws. Of the remaining 46 states, 20 had exclusive schedules, which Reede defines as schedules under which payments represent the entire compensation with no attempt to differentiate the healing period, the permanent impairment, or any subsequent loss of earning capacity; and 22 states had schedules that Reede labels "additional," which show the number of weekly installments for permanent impairments to be paid in addition to compensation for total disability during the healing period. Maine, Massachusetts, and Rhode Island also had schedules of one kind or another, but Reede categorizes them apart from the other 42 states with workers' compensation.

Why did states follow New Jersey's lead? Reede (1947, p. 117) argues that the move was influenced, in part, by doubts about the effect of alternative plans on the worker's "will to recover" and, in part, by the difficulty of relating earning capacity at the wage level prevailing after the injury to earning capacity at the level prevailing at the time of injury.

California did not place a schedule in its statute, but authorized the workers' compensation administrator to issue a comprehensive schedule that measured disabilities as a percentage of the compensation awarded for total and permanent disability. The California schedule was borrowed from a Russian schedule, which listed 136 disabilities rated in terms of the percent of permanent total injury.[7]

The California schedule provided a standard rating for a wide range of injuries, and then adjusted that standard rating according to the occupation and age of the worker. In terms of our typology, California was basing its final award on some estimated measure of disability, since presumably the only justification for adjusting the standard rating according to age and occupation was that the same impairment or functional limitation would have different economic consequences depending upon the age and occupation of the worker affected.

What is most significant for our purpose is that no state followed California's lead. It was New Jersey's schedule that served as the model for the other states. New Jersey's schedule differs from California's in the limited number of entries and in the absence of explicit adjustments for age and occupation. In the New Jersey schedule, each of the entries (the arm, the leg, and so on) is valued at a particular number of weeks. In the California schedule, all injuries are assessed at a proportion of the single figure allocated for total disability. That difference should not be too significant, in that it is always possible to translate the assessed number of weeks for a particular part of the body into a fixed proportion of the number of weeks allocated for total disability, and yet those schedules that do base all entries on a common denominator tend to be much more comprehensive. Again, the Russian schedule, from which the California schedule was borrowed, had over a hundred entries, in contrast to New Jersey's limited schedule. It is also apparent that when one begins to list more than the extremities and the eyes, it becomes necessary to evaluate loss of use. If internal injuries or injuries to the back are listed, it is clear that the initial assessment is based not on impairment, that is, a loss of the particular limb or the eye, but rather on a functional loss or limitation.

In addition to this basic difference in schedules among the states, there is today a difference as to whether the amounts awarded are wage-related. The statutes in all states but Massachusetts, Minnesota, Washington, and Oregon make awards by first fixing a number of weeks for a particular impairment or functional limitation, then multiplying that number by a weekly compensation benefit that is a specified percentage of the worker's preinjury wage, subject to a minimum and maximum weekly amount. In Washington, losses are valued as specified dollar sums, ranging in 1986 from $2,760 for the loss of a lesser toe to $36,000 for the loss of an arm or a leg. In Oregon, losses are valued in terms of degrees, with each degree of scheduled injury calling for $125 in compensation benefits. Thus the loss of an arm is valued at 192 degrees, or $24,000.[8]

The scheduled benefits in the few "deviant" states, such as Washington and Oregon, are obviously based on the philosophy that an arm is an arm, and worth the same amount to a lawyer or truck driver, a rich man or poor man. Larson (1986, sec. 57.17) maintains that such an assessment method is the only logical one if the reason for payments is physical impairment. In the typical state, the loss of an arm is valued at a larger sum for a high-wage worker than for a low-wage worker. Presumably the reason for this method is that the sums are paid not to compensate for physical loss in and of itself (although that is the operational basis for benefits), but because, on the average, the low-wage worker will suffer a smaller future wage loss due to the impairment than will the high-wage worker with the identical impairment.

Many of the other differences in the schedules will be discussed as we make comparisons across states. It will be seen that state schedules differ in the specificity of their entries, and they also differ in the exclusivity of their awards. The latter difference among states has persisted to the present day. Most states pay benefits during the period of temporary disability, and in addition pay the scheduled benefits. In four states, the compensation for temporary disability is deducted in its entirety from the allowance for scheduled injury, and in four other states there are restrictions on the number of weeks of temporary disability benefits that can be subtracted from the duration of the scheduled awards.[9] Also, in a few states, it is possible to collect benefits after the scheduled number of weeks are paid, whereas in most states the payment of the scheduled number of weeks constitutes the full and complete payment, and is not supplemented in the absence of a change in the worker's medical condition.

Consistency of the Schedules

Durations

In the literature on workers' compensation, perhaps nothing is more frequently remarked than the extreme variations across states in durations or amounts of benefits for the same loss. In terms of number of weeks, for example, table 5.1 shows the range for the arm is from 225 weeks in Ohio to 500 weeks in Wisconsin. Comparable differences in durations for other parts of the body are also shown in the table.

Internal Consistency

Granted that the durations of benefits for any specified loss differ widely among states, we can also ask whether there is internal consistency within the states.

In table 5.2, we have set the duration of benefits for the arm in each state equal to 100. Other entries in a state's schedule are expressed as a proportion of the duration for the arm in that state. For example, in

Table 5.1
Number of Weeks of Cash Benefits Paid for Parts of Body, January 1, 1986

State	Arm	Hand	Thumb	Other fingers 1st 2nd	Other fingers 3rd 4th	Leg	Foot	Great toe	Other toe	Sight one eye	Hearing one ear	Hearing both ears
California	421.25	311	54.25	24 24	18 18	461.25	241.00	30.25	6	150.75	45.25	311
D.C.	312.00	244	75.00	46 30	25 15	288.00	205.00	30.00	16	160.00	52.00	200
Florida	Benefits paid in lump sum based upon AMA *Guides* for percentage of disability of whole man.											
Michigan	269.00	215	65.00	38 33	22 16	215.00	162.00	33.00	11	162.00		
Nevada	Benefits paid for 5 years or to age 70 (whichever is later) based upon AMA *Guides* for percentage of disability of whole man.											
New Jersey	330.00	245	75.00	50 40	30 20	315.00	230.00	40.00	15	225.00	60.00	200
New York	312.00	244	75.00	46 30	25 15	288.00	205.00	38.00	16	160.00	60.00	150
Ohio	225.00	175	60.00	35 30	20 15	200.00	150.00	30.00	10	125.00	25.00	125
Pennsylvania	410.00	335	100.00	50 40	30 28	410.00	250.00	40.00	16	275.00	60.00	260
Wisconsin	500.00	400	160.00	60 45	26 28	500.00	250.00	83.33	25-2nd 20-others	275.00	55.00	330

SOURCES: U.S. Department of Labor, Employment Standards Administration, *State Workers' Compensation Laws* (January 1986), table 9; U.S. Chamber of Commerce, *Analysis of Workers' Compensation Laws* (1986), chart VII; statutes for various jurisdictions. Durations shown are California pays lifetime benefits for disabilities rated between 70% and 99.75% following the duration of the scheduled benefits. Durations shown are based on a standard rating prior to any adjustments for age or occupation.

Michigan: Amputation or loss of use of the arm must be less than 6 inches from below the elbow, otherwise it is a hand loss. Amputation or loss of use of the leg must be less than 7 inches from below the knee, otherwise it is a foot loss. **Pennsylvania** also compensates the loss of a forearm at 370 weeks. **Wisconsin** compensates the loss of an arm at the elbow at 450 weeks. The durations given for thumb and fingers are for losses including the metacarpal bone; the durations are different for losses at the proximal, second and distal joints. The loss of a leg at the knee is 425 weeks, and the durations for the loss of toes are given as including the metatarsal bone.

Table 5.2
Scheduled Compensation Payments as a Percentage of the Loss of an Arm, January 1, 1986

State	Arm	Hand	Thumb	First finger	Leg	Foot	Great toe	Other toe	Sight one eye	Hearing one ear	Hearing both ears
					Scheduled compensation payments as a percentage of the loss of an arm						
California	100	73.8	12.9	5.7	109.5	57.2	7.2	1.4	35.7	10.7	73.8
District of Columbia	100	78.2	24.0	14.7	89.7	65.7	9.6	5.1	51.3	16.7	64.1
Florida	100	89.1	32.0	16.4	63.6	41.6	7.3	1.8	34.5	5.5	54.5
Michigan	100	79.9	24.2	14.1	79.9	60.2	12.3	4.1	60.2		
Nevada	100	90.0	36.7	23.3	66.7	46.7	13.3	3.3	40.0	10.0	58.3
New Jersey	100	74.2	22.7	15.2	95.5	69.7	12.1	4.5	68.2	18.2	60.6
New York	100	78.2	24.0	14.7	92.3	65.7	12.2	5.1	51.3	19.2	48.1
Ohio	100	77.8	26.7	15.6	88.9	66.7	13.3	4.4	55.6	11.1	55.6
Pennsylvania	100	81.7	14.4	12.2	100.0	61.0	9.8	3.9	67.1	14.6	63.4
Wisconsin	100	80.0	25.0	12.0	100.0	50.0	16.7	5.0	50.0	11.0	66.0
Average		80.3	25.3	14.4	88.6	58.5	11.4	3.9	51.4	13.0	60.5
Standard deviation		5.46	6.17	4.37	14.68	9.45	2.93	1.32	11.96	4.47	7.48
Coefficient of variation		0.068	0.244	0.304	0.166	0.162	0.258	0.343	0.233	0.344	0.124

SOURCES: U.S. Department of Labor, Employment Standards Administration, *State Workers' Compensation Laws* (January 1986), table 9; U.S. Chamber of Commerce, *Analysis of Workers' Compensation Laws* (1986), chart VII; statutes for various jurisdictions.

Nevada: Percentages are based on ratings from the AMA *Guides to the Evaluation of Permanent Impairment*.

Florida: Percentages are based on adjusted ratings from the AMA *Guides*.

New Jersey the duration of benefit payments for the loss of an arm is 330 weeks, and for the loss of the great toe, 40 weeks (table 5.1). When the arm is set equal to 100, then the great toe's "relative value" is 12.1 (table 5.2).

Since the hand is part of the arm and the fingers part of the hand, we expect fairly close correspondence among the relative values of these parts of the upper extremity, when calculated using the arm as the base. In general, the relative values show only moderate variation among states. For the hand, they range from a low of 73.8 in California to a high of 90 in Nevada, which derives its values from the AMA *Guides.* The average value of the hand relative to the arm is 80.3, and the standard deviation is 5.46. The coefficient of variation (the standard deviation divided by the average) is only .068.

If we were to set the leg equal to 100, instead of the arm, we would find a similar correspondence in relative values for the foot and the toes. Larger deviations occur in the comparisons between the two major members—the arm and the leg. California is the only state that sets a longer duration for the leg than for the arm. In two of the states, the durations are equal; and in the remaining seven jurisdictions, the duration for the leg is less than that for the arm. Florida assesses the leg at the lowest relative rate, assigning it only 63.6 percent of the duration allocated for the arm. Nevada also places a low value on the leg relative to the arm.

The Florida and Nevada low evaluations of the relative worth of a leg result from the states' use of the AMA *Guides* as the basis for rating permanent impairments. Henry Kessler, one of the formulators of the AMA *Guides,* argued that although injuries to the leg will, in general, cause a longer period of disability and absence from work than comparable injuries to the arm, the long-range prognosis for vocational rehabilitation is more favorable for leg injuries. "The activities of the leg are relatively simple and therefore more easily restored or duplicated" (Kessler 1970, p. 109). As Kessler sees it, the human leg has two major tasks: to support the trunk and upper body, and to achieve ambulation. The arm primarily acts as an auxiliary of the hand, which has the prehensile ability indispensable to carrying out basic vocational functions. Kessler's views as to the importance of the hand are also reflected in its relative valuation of 90 percent of the arm in the AMA *Guides.*

The relative valuations are influenced by basic differences in philosophy and judgment as to the importance of the extremities. Even this short discussion is suggestive of the difficulty of pricing any part of the body in an entirely objective, scientific way.

Specificity and Comprehensiveness

Subdivisions of Parts of the Body Listed. The typical schedule, which gives only maximum values for the complete loss of the extremity, does not define precisely any part of the body. This leaves the sometimes challenging task of determining ratings for partial loss of the member. Is the loss of a tip of the finger before the distal joint equivalent to the loss of one-third of the finger or one-half of the finger? Or is the loss of any part of the finger to be considered as the loss of the entire finger?

Both the degree of specificity of schedules and accompanying guidelines issued by the worker's compensation agency vary from state to state. Although most states are content with a bare listing in the schedule, with minimum detail, Wisconsin has 20 separate schedule listings covering the loss of the thumb, fingers, or parts of these digits. Four separate listings differentiate portions of the index finger alone. The loss of the finger at the distal joint in Wisconsin is valued as 25 percent of the finger; by comparison, in New York, it is taken as 50 percent of the finger. The loss of the first two phalanges in Wisconsin is defined as 60 percent of the finger; in New York it is viewed as the equivalent of the entire finger. The same range of values for partial loss occurs with the hand and the arm, or the foot and the leg.

More Than One Extremity Affected. Some schedules are explicit as to benefits due when more than one member is affected. In New York, if more than one part of the body is affected, compensation is to be awarded for each, and these awards are to run consecutively. It is recognized, however, that adding together the scheduled values may exceed the value for the next highest specified loss in the schedule. Thus, in New York, the loss of two or more fingers is proportioned to the loss of the hand, but the total duration may not exceed that which is scheduled for the loss of an entire hand.

In Wisconsin, if two fingers on the same hand are lost, the award for the first equal or lesser valued finger is increased by 100 percent; if three fingers are lost, the award for the second and third equal or lesser valued finger is increased by 150 percent. The same type of adjustment is provided in the case of toes, although at only a 20 percent rate, an amount that applies in all other cases that are not specifically mentioned in the multiple injury variation portions.

There is very nearly a perfect split of opinion among the states as to the relation of the combined value of the fingers to the value of the whole hand. Fratello (1955, Exhibit D1) compared the schedules of 39 states. In 19 of them, the sum of the values for the five individual fingers is less than the value of the hand; in 2 it is the same; and in the remaining 18 it is greater.

Combinations of impairments are also difficult to evaluate when unrelated parts of the body are involved. Most state schedules do not specify the durations for such combinations. Texas is an exception: it specifically schedules the loss of an eye and leg, the loss of an eye and hand, and so on. Some statutes presume permanent total disability in the event of multiple major losses. Michigan, for example, defines as total permanent disability the loss of any of the two members or faculties among eyes, legs, or arms.

Comparing Benefits Across States

Percentage of Wages and Weekly Maximums

Thus far, our discussion largely has been in terms of duration of benefits for various specified losses. Obviously, a person who loses an arm must be concerned not only with the duration of benefits, but with the amounts he receives. Table 5.3 shows the maximum weekly rates paid for permanent partial as well as the maximum rates for temporary total disability in 10 jurisdictions.

As seen in table 5.3, the District of Columbia, Michigan, and Pennsylvania pay the same maximum rate for temporary disability as they do for permanent partial. The other states have different maximums for permanent partial and temporary total. Thus in Wisconsin, the maximum for temporary total is set at 100 percent of the state's average weekly wage ($329), whereas the maximum weekly rate for permanent partial disability is $112 as of January 1986.

New Jersey's weekly benefits for permanent partial disability are governed by the duration of benefits. Thus minor awards are compensated according to a rate as low as 20 percent of the state's average weekly wage, while major awards (421-600 weeks) are paid on the basis of 75 percent of the state's average wage, as is the case for temporary total and permanent total disabilities.

Table 5.3
Scheduled Permanent Partial Benefits for Loss of an Arm, January 1986

State	Maximum weekly benefits temporary total disability	Number of weeks of benefits for loss of an arm	Maximum weekly permanent partial benefits for loss of an arm	Maximum amount of benefits for loss of an arm	Present value of benefits for loss of an arm discounted at 6%
California	$224.00	421.25	$140.00	58,975	46,708
District of Columbia	431.70	312.00	431.70	134,690	113,111
Florida	318.00			27,500	27,500
Michigan	375.00	269.00	375.00	100,875	86,721
Nevada	332.46	1,612.00	179.39	289,177	131,269
New Jersey	284.00	330.00	208.00	68,640	57,084
New York	300.00	312.00	150.00	46,800	39,302
Ohio	365.00	225.00	182.50	41,063	36,165
Pennsylvania	347.00	410.00	347.00	142,270	113,352
Wisconsin	329.00	500.00	112.00	56,000	42,552

SOURCE: U.S. Department of Labor, Employment Standards Administration, *State Workers' Compensation Laws* (January 1986), tables 6, 8, and 9; plus calculations by authors for Florida and Nevada.

Nevada: Benefits based on 39-year-old person who receives maximum amount of $777.36 per month until 70th birthday.

Neither the weekly rate nor the duration, considered alone, reveals the total amount of benefits. That quantity is the number of weeks times the weekly amounts.

Dollar Amounts

How do these states compare in dollar benefits? Table 5.3 shows the maximum amount paid for what normally is the gravest scheduled loss, the loss of an arm at the shoulder. The last columns of table 5.3 show the present values of the maximum weekly benefits paid for the durations shown.

It is difficult to compare Nevada and Florida with the other states because of their different methods of calculating benefits. Nevada pays six-tenths of 1 percent of a worker's wage up to the maximum amount allowable ($2,159.33 a month as of July 1, 1985) for each 1 percent of disability. The loss of an arm is rated at 60 percent and would pay, at most, $777.36 per month (.006 x 60 x $2,159.33), or $179.39 per week. The worker is entitled to receive such a sum until his 70th birthday, or for at least five years. In our calculations, we assume a 39-year-old worker. Nevada is the most generous of the jurisdictions, although the amounts shown depend, of course, on our choice of the age of the worker. Florida, like Nevada, uses the AMA *Guides* to rate the injuries, and pays $250 per 1 percent of impairment up to 10 percent and $500 for each percent above the 10 percent level.

The differences among the states are extreme, regardless of whether the maximum scheduled amount column or the present value column is used as the basis of comparison. One of the most generous jurisdictions on a present-value basis is the District of Columbia; its duration (312 weeks) is below the median among the nine jurisdictions with duration data, but it has the most generous weekly maximum. The present value of D.C.'s benefits discounted at 6 percent is $113,111. Wisconsin pays for 500 weeks, but with a considerably lower maximum weekly benefit than in D.C., and the resulting maximum scheduled amount is less than one-half of D.C.'s. Present value comparisons are probably more meaningful than comparisons of maximum amount, since they take into account not only the weekly benefit but the time over which it is received. We assume that none of the benefits paid are in a lump sum. The present value of Pennsylvania's amount discounted at 6 percent is $113,352, almost three times the amounts paid in New York, Ohio, and Wisconsin. It is here that one sees the importance of the exclusivity or nonexclusivity of the schedule. Pennsylvania pays only for scheduled benefits. New York's relatively low sum may be augmented if actual wage loss follows the scheduled number of weeks. In New Jersey the awards are also exclusive in the sense of not being influenced by possible continuing wage loss, but there always is the possibility of a nonscheduled award—for psychiatric considerations, for example—and such matters are not susceptible to exact measurement. Florida's scheduled benefits are also nonexclusive, since a worker may also be eligible for wage-loss benefits.

Utility of the Scheduled Method of Assessing Permanent Partial Disability

The schedule is a list that details the number of weeks to be paid for the loss or loss of use of a specified limb or other part of the body. It is essentially a relative value scale, which places a value on the major members, the arm and the leg, and lesser values on the parts of each of these major concerns. Provision is also usually made for loss of vision, loss of hearing, enucleation of the eye, and sometimes disfigurement.

In antiquity, such schedules as existed served the useful function of substituting a finite amount of money damages for retaliation. Even in ancient times, the amounts to be paid were rated on the basis of several factors, and not necessarily confined to the impairment or functional limitation that arose as a result of the injury. With the growth of the common law and negligence principles, the schedules gave way to an assessment of the consequences of the injury by a jury on an individual basis. Schedules were retained, however, in personal accident policies. Acting on these examples, and on the examples of European countries, when U.S. compensation laws were passed in the first and second decades of this century, all of the states—even those that began without schedules—soon adopted some sort of schedule in their workers' compensation programs.

California followed the example of Russia in issuing a comprehensive schedule with all entries based on a common denominator. The number of weeks of benefits to be paid was adjusted according to the age and occupation of the worker. New Jersey adopted a more limited schedule with relatively few entries, each with a specified number of weeks. New Jersey's law provided very little guidance to the parties as to how such schedules were to be used. Most states followed New Jersey's lead rather than California's. There are two exceptions: in recent times, Nevada adopted the AMA *Guides to the Evaluation of Permanent Impairment,* which go far beyond specifying the names of limbs and the number of weeks to be paid; and Florida, in contrast, all but eliminated its schedules when it adopted a wage-loss method of compensating for permanent partial injuries (see chapter 9).

States are not uniform in their assessment of the relative value of the limbs specified. The value of an arm varies across the states, as does the value of a leg. The value of the minor members in relationship to the corresponding major members is, however, fairly uniform.

The amounts paid for scheduled impairments vary greatly among states, not only because of differences in the number of weeks of compensation, but also because of differences in the amounts to be paid per week as measured by the maximums in the states.

The general function of any schedule, be it an advertising rate schedule, a freight rate schedule, or a workers' compensation schedule, is to provide information on amounts to be paid. In principle, a schedule will promote certainty to the extent that it is detailed, complete (containing as many entries as are likely to be needed), and joined with explicit guidance as to its proper use. Such details and guidance can be communicated via statutory provisions, rules and regulations, advice from the administrators, or possibly simply by a practice widely known among practitioners.

In workers' compensation, how the schedule is used is the most important question, and that question can be approached only with considerations such as those discussed in chapter 4, dealing with procedures. It would be naive to expect that a limited schedule, in and of itself, without rules or guidance as to its use, could provide a great deal of information—or increase significantly the level of certainty as to the benefit amounts due for a particular contingency. Even in the complete loss cases, the amputations, certainty is not guaranteed unless the loss is one exactly specified by a scheduled entry. Given the great number of possibilities as to where an amputation can take place, it is not likely that many amputations will be exactly as specified by a scheduled entry.

The more frequent consequence of an injury is not an amputation, but some degree of loss of use of a limb that remains physically present. Given the variety of functions of every limb, it is obvious that determining the extent of functional limitation is a complex task. The hand not only has functions specific to it, such as its use as a mallet or pointer in Kessler's terms (1970, p. 20), but it also acts as a sensory organ with which the brain monitors resistance, texture, temperature, weight, and so forth.

Although an injury to the hand requires a fairly sophisticated assessment to determine the resulting functional limitation, the most the typical schedule does is to provide the maximum number of weeks for the total loss of the member to be used as a benchmark. In that respect, a schedule can limit the range of values that can be paid for the consequence of an injury to a member, and hence can limit the range of values over which the parties can quarrel—but only in the special case of an injury whose consequences are confined to one member only and that do not extend to the so-called nonscheduled area by reason of some effect to the worker as a whole.

The problem is complicated further in that the physician may be called upon not only to assess the worker's physical condition, but also to judge to what extent the condition is due to the work-related injury. If the physician decides that a particular functional limitation of the arm is the result of the work injury aggravating a pre-existing impairment of the arm, then the physician may be required to assess the relative contributions of the prior impairment and the new work injury to the resulting functional limitation. Unless given specific guidance by a very comprehensive schedule, rules and regulations, guidelines issued by the agency, or some well-understood rules that have grown up as a matter of practice, different physicians are liable to arrive at very different judgments.

The rules for measuring functional limitation, no matter how they are derived, may or may not call upon the examiner to estimate the impact of a functional limitation in terms of future wage earnings. If they do, the estimates move to a consideration of "disability" factors, as we will see in the consideration of the nonscheduled injuries. In the California schedule, the guides for the assessment of back injuries call upon the rater to make a judgment as to the kind of work the injured worker should be capable of performing. In these cases, the assessment of disability factors is open and explicit. The same is true of some of the entries and rules in Wisconsin's guides. In Ohio, the loss of two or more digits of the hand may call for compensation in an amount greater than scheduled if it can be shown that the injury would cause more than the normal handicap because of the nature of the claimant's work.

How can the method of determining the amount of payments due in scheduled injuries be evaluated? If the purpose of the schedule is to provide information and increase the level of certainty with which decisions about permanent partial disabilities can be made, an appropriate question is whether using the schedule improves the reliability of rating. Can several raters, using the schedule, look at the same consequences of an injury and come up with the same number of weeks? If so, the schedule can be said to increase certainty, and presumably could have the eventual effect of eliminating litigation over the injuries it covers.

If this is the objective, it is obvious that a comprehensive schedule is necessary, and that there must be agreement as to how the schedule is to be used.

The American Medical Association *Guides to the Evaluation of Permanent Impairment* is an example of a comprehensive schedule that covers all body systems. The users are instructed to evaluate impairment or functional limitations only, without regard to the other consequences of the injury. Theoretically, it should be possible for physicians to use the method of measurement called for in the *Guides* with a high degree of correspondence among their ratings. At the same time, we ought to recognize that since it deals only with measurement of impairment and functional limitations, its desirable contributions to objectivity may be purchased at the expense of ignoring some of the consequences of the injury. The *Guides* contain no adjustment for the age and occupation of the worker, or any other proxy that measures work disability in specific cases. Neither is any attempt made to measure subjective pain, except to the extent that the physician evaluates the ability of the person to make a particular movement and infers the degree of pain associated with that movement.

Other bases for compensation benefits may be appropriate in addition to impairment and functional ratings. We examine that policy issue in part IV of this study.

NOTES

1. Driver and Miles (1960, pp. 406-11). Some of the differences between the Babylonian and Mosaic Laws are discussed in Hertz (1975, pp. 403-6).

Hertz maintains that the church's Father Augustine was one of the first to declare that taliation was the law of justice, not of hatred, in that it was one eye, not two, for an eye; one tooth, not ten, for a tooth; and one life, not a whole family's lives, for a life. He quotes authorities on international law to sustain his position that the rule enjoined, on the one hand, that a fair and equitable relation must exist between the crime and the punishment, and, on the other hand, that all citizens are equal before the law and their injuries were to be valued according to the same standards. In the Mosaic law, monetary commutation became the rule except in capital cases, and it is Hertz's contention that in the code of Hammurabi, the money compensation prevailed in the cases of injury only to the slaves. Hertz points out that the two systems are independent codifications of ancient Semitic common law, and the resemblances are probably due to the common usages of the Semitic ancestors of both Babylonians and Hebrews.

2. "If [the wound] healed up and then reopened, and healed again and opened up once more, he is liable [for all expenses] to cure him, but once it is healed up thoroughly he is no longer liable to heal him." The quotations and the information about the commentaries are from Blackman (1983, Vol. IV, pp. 62-64). The more traditional citation would simply be *Mishnayoth,* Baba Kamma, Chap. 8 (Hachovel), Mishna 2.

3. *Aldrich v. Palmer,* 24 Cal. 513 (1863).

4. *Illinois Central Railroad v. Barron,* 5 Wall. 90, 105 (1866). Both cases are cited in Dodd (1936, p. 617).

5. Larson, citing Geerts, Kornblich, and Urmson (1977, p. 110).

6. Nevada and Massachusetts, according to Reede (1947), adopted schedules in 1911. The schedule in Massachusetts was much less detailed than Nevada's, and not altogether on the basis of the New Jersey schedule. In 1912, Michigan followed New Jersey; and Rhode Island followed the Massachusetts plan, which allowed subsequent compensation for demonstrated loss of earnings. The new laws adopted in 1913, with the exception of the West Virginia law, included schedules, six of them modeled after New Jersey and one of them modeled after Massachusetts. During the same year, amendments in Illinois and Ohio added schedules similar to that of New Jersey, so that by the end of 1913, 14 laws contained partial disability schedules while 6 used exclusively the system of rating loss of earning capacity. The latter system was used in the remaining states for nonlisted injuries (Reede 1947, p. 118).

On January 1, 1915, 17 states used schedules of compensation for specific injuries. Nine states made these payments to the exclusion of any other payment for injury (Connecticut, Iowa, Louisiana, Maryland, Michigan, Minnesota, Nebraska, Oregon, and Wisconsin). These states made no distinction between the temporary total benefit paid during the healing period and the amounts that they would receive under the schedule.

Five of the laws, effective on January 1, 1915, provided scheduled payments for injuries in addition to payments for temporary total disability during the healing period: Illinois, Nevada, New Jersey, New York, and Ohio. Three of the states, Massachusetts, Rhode Island, and Texas, allowed subsequent compensation for demonstrated loss of earning capacity. What is interesting in these states, however, is that there is still an overall limitation. Under the Massachusetts law, a person could receive temporary total disability during the healing period, then a short period of scheduled payments, approximately 50 weeks, and then compensation for subsequent loss of earning capacity. The limitation on payments under all of the provisions in Massachusetts was for 500 weeks, a specified sum of $3000.

Reede then takes up the revisions between 1915 and 1940. Amendments to Texas and West Virginia provided a flat rate schedule exclusive of any kind of compensation. Twelve of the new laws adopted such a schedule, and four adopted a schedule allowing additional payments during the healing period. The schedule system was more firmly established, with 22 states employing the system exclusively, and 11 compensating total disability as well. Only five states had altogether avoided the flat rate schedule: Arizona, New Hampshire, California, Washington, and Wyoming. California is an exception, only because its schedule was not contained in the statute. In 1937, the last state with no schedule of any kind, New Hampshire, adopted a flat rate schedule of specific injuries.

7. Discussion of "Report of Committee on Statistics and Compensation Insurance Costs" of the International Association of Industrial Accident Boards and Commissions (1923, p. 87).

The Bureau of Labor Statistics published its Bulletin 126, *Workmen's Compensation Laws in the United States and Foreign Countries,* in 1914. It gave a fairly detailed description of the various foreign schedules and discussed their advantages and disadvantages.

8. U.S. Chamber of Commerce (1986, Chart VII).

9. U.S. Chamber of Commerce (1986, Chart VII).

Chapter 6
Nonscheduled Benefits in Impairment (Category I) States

Categorization of the States for Nonscheduled Injuries

We divide states into three categories according to the method used to evaluate nonscheduled injuries. In category I are those jurisdictions in which the physical impairments or functional limitations that are consequences of the work-related injury are rated as a percentage of total disability; in category II, those that assess consequences on the basis of the loss of wage-earning capacity; in category III, those in which actual wage loss is a necessary condition for benefits. We use these categories with the caution that distinctions are by no means clear-cut. We will note differences among jurisdictions within the same category and commonalities among states in different categories.

We include New Jersey and Nevada in category I. Ohio provides workers a choice of methods for assessing permanent consequences of injury. One of these choices is to base the assessment on an evaluation of impairments or functional limitations, and we discuss Ohio's method of assessing impairment in this chapter.

Nevada assesses all cases—without distinction between scheduled and nonscheduled injuries—on the basis of the American Medical Association's *Guide to the Evaluation of Permanent Impairment.* New Jersey and Ohio use schedules for those injuries that are listed and use the total number of weeks for complete disability as the referent for all cases not listed. The role of factors other than impairment in assessing the benefit amounts, and the amount of guidance given the raters, differ greatly among these states, and we comment on these differences below.

Despite our categorization, Ohio and New Jersey do not assess *solely* on the basis of impairment or functional limitation. Both states implicitly take into account the consequences of the impairment for a worker's future role in the labor market. (Nevada is a less clear-cut case.) In some states, little formal guidance is given the evaluators of nonscheduled injuries, and so the internist or other specialist may evaluate the consequences of a given heart condition quite differently for a lawyer and a truck driver, for a young man and an old man, and so on. We provide examples from our field work reports of how these adjustments are made without any particular basis in statutory or administrative rules.

Why then denominate these jurisdictions as ones that assess on the basis of impairments or functional limitations? In part, because in these states a physician is called upon to assess the physical condition of the claimant. The physician's evaluation is based primarily, even if not exclusively, on the extent of the physical or mental damage and on his estimate of the worker's residual capacity.

If the methods used in category I are contrasted with the methods used in category III, the wage-loss states of Florida, Pennsylvania, Michigan, and New York, and the alternative method in Ohio, several distinctions become apparent. However "disability" factors are taken into account in the assessment of the permanent consequences of the injury in New Jersey or Nevada, it is clear that workers in these category I states need not experience an actual wage loss in order to receive a permanent and partial disability award. In category I jurisdictions, the rater need never address the question of whether the injury under examination puts the worker at a disadvantage in the labor market. The rater instead evaluates the worker's condition against the standard of a normal unimpaired man. His concepts of normality may not be based strictly on medical factors, such as prescribed in the AMA *Guides,* and may be conditioned by factors such as age, occupation, experience, and training. Nonetheless, the rating is essentially centered on the worker's physical or mental condition. We classify the rating methods in Florida, Pennsylvania, and New York, and one of the methods in Ohio, as wage-loss methods because they endorse compensation in nonscheduled cases only in the event of actual wage loss assessed on a retrospective basis (at least that is the theoretical prerequisite for benefits in those jurisdictions). In Michigan, as we shall see, compromise enters into the handling of a great many cases, and the exact basis for settlement is not always clear. But compromises are not the rule in the other jurisdictions, and in those states the distinction between scheduled injuries (rated strictly on medical factors) and nonscheduled injuries (requiring actual wage loss) is quite clear.

California, Wisconsin, and the District of Columbia are left in an *intermediate* category II group, between actual wage loss on the one hand and impairment on the other, and are designated as states that assess on the basis of loss of wage-earning capacity. For convenience, we include California in this category even while recognizing that California is different. In California the standard rating is based on impairment factors, but is then adjusted by age and occupational factors. Taking age and occupation into account is one method of assessing wage-earning capacity.

In all three categories of states, the rater must use medical judgment to determine if at least some permanent consequences stem from the worker's injury. If not, the worker is not entitled to permanent disability benefits. Beyond that threshold determination, the three categories of states diverge as outlined above.

We will now proceed to examine the impairment and functional limitation criteria used to evaluate partial disability in New Jersey, Nevada, and Ohio.

New Jersey

Introduction

New Jersey is one of the pioneering states in the field of workers' compensation.[1] It was one of the first states to enact any type of workers' compensation law, and it was the first to adopt a schedule (see chapter 5). New Jersey also pioneered in that its statute was elective, a method designed to overcome the perceived constitutional obstacles to a compulsory law in 1911. New Jersey's original act did not provide for compulsory insurance. Insuring one's liability was altogether optional for employers. Rubinow denotes this type of insurance and liability arrangements as the "New Jersey plan" (Rubinow 1916, p. 183).

In recent decades New Jersey has been well known for its "permanent partial problem." The problem, it is safe to say, is hardly a new one. The Somers used 1951 data to show that the proportion of compensation cases in the permanent partial category was higher in New Jersey than in the industrially important states of Illinois, New York, Pennsylvania, and Wisconsin. Moreover, New Jersey had the lowest average award per case (Somers and Somers 1954, pp. 74-79). By 1956, 72 percent of all closed compensated cases involved permanent partial disability, and they accounted for 89 percent of the compensation benefits awarded. Employer groups in New Jersey complained about the ever-increasing number of permanent partial cases "where there is no apparent disability and little or no loss of time or wages" (Berkowitz 1960, p. 69). In 1957, a commission set up to study laws affecting industrial development noted, in what was to become an oft-repeated refrain during the years, that the major problem in workers' compensation was the payment of many claims for permanent partial disability in amounts up to $800 where there was no apparent disability and little or no loss of time or wages, and where the claim often rested on subjective complaints (Berkowitz 1960, p. 68).

A New Jersey study commission reported in 1973 that New Jersey was paying an enormous number of relatively small awards in permanent partial cases, which, in the aggregate, consumed a very substantial portion of workmen's compensation resources. (The charges are corroborated by the data in tables 3.8 and 3.16.) Many of these awards were for injuries that did not involve permanent disability under any of the theories familiar to the Commission (New Jersey Study Commission 1973, p. 23).

The Commission recommended substantial changes in New Jersey's law, including an increase in the rates paid for permanent partial, award of benefits on the basis of the extent of permanent impairment as established in the AMA *Guides,* and payment of continuing wage-loss benefits in cases where wage loss occurs and impairment at the initial evaluation step is rated at 20 percent or higher. No legislation resulted from the Commission's report, and it was not until 1979 that forces coalesced to bring about changes in New Jersey's statute to address the permanent partial problem. What came to be perceived as an excessive number of minor permanent partial disability awards in New Jersey stemmed from the courts' interpretation of the statutory language. New Jersey lists a limited number of injuries in its schedule, with 23 different entries. The statute (N.J.S.A. 34:15-12[22]), provides:

> In all lesser or other cases involving permanent loss, or where the usefulness of a member of any physical function is permanently impaired, the duration of compensation shall bear such relation to specific periods of time stated in the above schedule as the disabilities bear to those produced by the injuries named in the schedule. In cases in which the disability is determined as a percentage of total and permanent disability, the duration of the compensation shall be a corresponding portion of 600 weeks.

From the earliest days of the law, claimants were not required to show any present or anticipated future wage loss in order to be eligible to receive compensation for the consequences of an injury. In the case that enunciated that concept, *Brubage v. Lee,* 87 N.J.L. 36 (1915), compensable disability was defined as "any loss of physical function which detracts from the former efficiency of the body or its member in the ordinary pursuits of life." The definition was refined further in *Hercules Powder v. Morris Co. Court,* 93 N.J.L. 93 (1919), when it was established that permanent impairment of the physical entity is compensable in the absence of any showing of functional impairment. Similarly, in *Kiczko v. Baylis,* 20 N.J.Misc. 323 (1942), it was held that compensation was dependent not on loss of efficiency, but on whether there had been a loss of any portion of the scheduled member. In keeping with that concept, compensation, whether for scheduled or for nonscheduled injuries, has been awarded for impairment to the worker as a "physiological unit"; for "structural change"; for "fault akin to a traumatic injury"; for "loss of (personal) anatomy"; and for "physical loss and not industrial capacity" (Lefelt 1975, p. 597).

The term "ordinary pursuits of life" seems to have almost limitless applications. The category includes recreation, procreation, avocation, and many other activities. There does seem to be some restriction on the broad concept in *Barbato v. Alsan Masonry and Concrete, Inc.,* 64 N.J.L. 514 (1974), in which disability was defined as "loss ensuing from personal injury which detracts from the former efficiency of the workman's body or its members in the ordinary pursuits of life, in relation to the field of service to which he is suited." However, the implications of that qualification upon disability determinations have not yet been felt (Lefelt 1975, p. 598). The decision has been used to justify a permanent total award on the basis of unemployability. We discuss the changes brought about by the 1979 amendments below.

Changes in New Jersey's Law

The 1973 Study Commission raised several procedural issues about the operation of the law. The Commission observed that at every stage of the workers' compensation proceedings, factors were at work to ensure that virtually no claim relating to the existence or the extent of disability would be denied. The volume of cases and the controversies had led to delays in payments for medical services and for temporary disability. They noted the limited role of the Division of Workmen's Compensation and what they perceived to be an absence of reasonably precise standards defining disability. We document later the Commission's observations that disability evaluation techniques were developed by the physicians, who alone had custody of this knowledge. Their testimony, according to the Study Commission, was governed not only by medical considerations but by considerations of other factors, such as age, sex, education, and economic and social environments, which are much less precise and which only the physicians knew how to include in their testimony.

The 1973 Commission reviewed files of 74 workers' compensation permanent partial cases selected at random and observed that the disability evaluations of both the respondents' and the petitioners' doctors were frequently based on pure guesswork and self-serving declarations with little physiological or other logical rationale.

Amendments of the law did not come until 1979. (The 1978 data in tables 3.8 and 3.16 show that minor permanent partial cases still dominated the New Jersey program one year prior to the amendments.) Senate Bill S. 802, introduced on February 9, 1978, was originally drafted by representatives of the business community. In an effort to solicit the support of organized labor, a series of amendments was hammered out and the final version was adopted by the legislature on November 13, 1979, and signed by the governor on January 10, 1980, as P.L. 1979, Chapter 283 (Napier 1981).

One objective of the new law was to eliminate the payment of benefits for minor permanent partial disabilities and to direct the money to more seriously disabled workers. It sought to accomplish this objective, not by any radical change in the philosophy by which awards were given, but by revising the statutory definitions of permanent partial disabilities. The amendments stated (at N.J.S.A. 34:15-36):

> "Disability permanent in quality and partial in character" means a permanent impairment caused by a compensable accident or compensable occupational disease, based upon demonstrable objective medical evidence, which restricts the function of the body or its members or organs; included in the criteria which shall be considered shall be whether there has been a lessening to a material degree of an employee's working ability. Subject to the above provisions, nothing in this definition shall be construed to preclude benefits to a worker who returns to work following a compensable accident even if there be no reduction in earnings. Injuries such as minor lacerations, minor contusions, minor sprains, and scars which do not constitute significant permanent disfigurement, and occupational disease of a minor nature such as

mild dermatitis and mild bronchitis shall not constitute permanent disability within the meaning of this definition.

This statutory definition preserves the essence of the impairment theory, so New Jersey still belongs as a category I state. However, the loss-of-earning-capacity approach is also used in the new law, which moves New Jersey closer to the border between our category I and category II. In addition to reformulating the basis for benefits, the new statute requires "demonstrable objective medical evidence." As a result, cases that formerly were compensated as permanent partial impairments of a minor nature are presumably excluded under this statute.

Also changed were the criteria for compensable heart attacks. Awards based on compensable heart attacks had increased from 367 in 1975 to 526 in 1979, and in response the criteria were made more restrictive (Napier 1981, p. 4). The claimant must prove that injury or death was produced by the work effort or strain in excess of the wear and tear of the claimant's daily living (N.J.S.A. 34:15-8.3). The previous criterion was that whenever the required exertion was too great for the person undertaking the work, whatever the degree of the exertion or the condition of the workplace, the heart attack was compensable.[2]

Also, under the new law, New Jersey has moved to a type of apportionment statute. Pre-existing disabilities due to the deterioration of a tissue, organ, or part of the body through the natural aging process are not to be compensated and are to be deducted from the overall disability (N.J.S.A. 34:15-31(b)).

As a *quid pro quo* for the tightening of these criteria for permanent partial disability benefits, the compensation rates were substantially increased. Prior to the amendments, the New Jersey maximum weekly benefit was $40 a week for permanent partial disability awards. Under the new law, the weekly maximums for permanent partial disability increase with the severity of the disability. Thus, the maximum weekly compensation available for the first 90 weeks of allowable compensation is set at 20 percent of the statewide average weekly wage. For those awards that range from 421 to 600 weeks (the maximum number of weeks), the maximum weekly benefit is 75 percent of the state average weekly wage. Thus as the duration of the permanent partial disability benefits increases, whether by reason of a scheduled or an unscheduled award, the maximum weekly compensation goes up. The same nominal percentage of lost earnings is paid for temporary total disability as for permanent partial and permanent total disability, namely 70 percent of the worker's preinjury wage. For temporary and permanent total disability, the maximum weekly benefit is 75 percent of the state average weekly wage, regardless of the duration of the disability.

In a separate piece of legislation, Senate Bill S. 3362, the legislature for the first time enacted an occupational hearing loss statute. It adopted criteria for the extent of the noise hazard necessary to produce a sensory neuro-hearing loss, and provided a formula for the calculation of the level of hearing impairments intended to cut back on many of the claims held compensable before the new law. (In years prior to 1980, an average of 1,500 awards per year were made for occupational hearing loss.) Standards were included for audiometric testing, and preexisting hearing impairments were deducted from the overall impairment in assessing compensable disability.

Perhaps the 1979 amendments are significant as much for what they did not do as for what they did. Although benefit levels were increased and disability definitions were changed, there was no fundamental change in the philosophy about which consequences of injuries justify compensation. Nor was additional guidance provided to the parties as to how to evaluate permanent partial disability. Nothing in the new statutes necessarily changes the procedures in the old law (which are discussed below).

In contrast, the 1973 Commission, which delved deeply into the permanent partial problem, recommended a four-step procedure for evaluating and awarding benefits for injuries and diseases with permanent consequences. The first step was the payment of temporary total benefits during the healing period. The second was a waiting period—which exists in the current law—of six months after maximum healing has been reached before permanent partial benefits could be paid. The third step was the award of benefits based on the extent of permanent impairments as established by the AMA *Guides* in multiples of 1 percent. The Commission recognized that such changes logically required the elimination of the schedule in the law, and they recommended its abolition except in cases of absolute incapacity limited to paraplegia, total loss of bilateral vision, and total loss of use of both hands, both feet, both arms, or any two thereof. These conditions led to a conclusive presumption of permanent total disability, and benefits would be payable for life without regard to the possibility of rehabilitation or actual earnings.

The fourth step was a wage-loss benefit. If impairment at the initial evaluation step were 20 percent or higher, the Commission recommended that the worker be considered for additional benefits after the expiration of the period during which he received his impairment benefits. These would be conditioned upon the showing of actual loss of wages suffered by the worker. The hearing officer would be directed to determine causation, that is, whether the wage loss was caused by the impairment in relation to such factors as rehabilitation success, age, occupational training or work experience, attitude, formal education, and capacity for competing in the open labor market. Employee wages earned before the injury would be contrasted to the wages earned after the injury, giving consideration to changes in wage rates and labor conditions. These benefits would be paid for the duration of the wage loss. The purpose of these recommendations was to encourage rehabilitation or return to some form of work, and to encourage employers to rehire injured workers.

The concern in the 1979 amendments seems to have been narrower, with an attempt to substitute statutory language for decisions that had evolved over the years. The apparent goals of the amendments were to reduce the numbers and costs of permanent partial disability cases, and in particular the dominance of minor permanent partial awards. The available evidence suggests that these goals were only partially achieved. Between 1978 and 1982 (the latest year with available data as of 1986), the number of all permanent disability cases as a share of all cases dropped in New Jersey (table 3.9), and this is true for the three types of permanent disability cases: permanent total, major permanent partial, and minor permanent partial (tables 3.6 to 3.8). Nonetheless, as of 1982, the New Jersey shares of all cases accounted for by minor permanent partial cases (table 3.8) and by all permanent disability cases (table 3.9) were more than 200 percent of the national average shares.

The average costs of all New Jersey permanent disability cases increased between 1978 and 1982 relative to the U.S. averages (table 3.13), and this was also true for each of the three types of permanent disability cases (tables 3.10 to 3.12). Nonetheless, because of the numerical dominance of minor permanent partial cases in New Jersey, as of 1982 the average cost of all permanent disability cases in the state was only about 57 percent of the national average (table 3.13).

A significant measure of the developments in New Jersey since 1978 is the share of all cash benefits accounted for by permanent disability benefits, a statistic that reflects the declining importance of New Jersey permanent disability cases as well as the increasing average costs of those cases. The data show that the share of all costs represented by permanent disability cases in New Jersey was relatively stable between 1978 and 1982, increasing from 110 to 113 percent of the national average (table 3.17). It is surprising, in light of the intended purpose of the 1979 New Jersey legislation, that the increasing overall share of costs was primarily due to the increased importance of minor permanent partial disability cases between 1978 and 1982. By 1982, these minor cases accounted for 49 percent of all cash benefits in New Jersey, more than twice the importance of such cases nationally (table 3.16).

The increasing share of all cash benefits accounted for by permanent disability benefits between 1978 and 1982 would have been expected to increase the employers' costs of workers' compensation in New Jersey between 1978 and 1984 according to our analysis in chapter 3. The data in table 3.18, however, indicate that New Jersey insurance costs dropped from about 20 percent above the national average in 1978 to about 10 percent below in 1984. We do not have a full explanation of the contrary movements in New Jersey between shares of costs accounted for by permanent disability benefits and the employers' costs of workers' compensation. Burton and Krueger (1986, pp. 179-97) examined cost developments in New Jersey, New York, and Connecticut between 1972 and 1983 and argued that one explanation of the developments was the movement of maximum weekly benefits for total disability. New Jersey's maximum for total disability compared to the state's average weekly wage has lagged behind the maximum in other jurisdictions in the last decade. As of 1986, for example, the New Jersey weekly maximum for temporary total disability benefits was $284, which represented 79 percent of the state's average weekly wage—a record exceeded by 34 other jurisdictions (U.S. Dept. of Labor, *State Compliance,* 1987).

The reductions in the New Jersey employers' costs of workers' compensation insurance between 1978 and 1984 thus appear to be in spite of, rather than because of, the attempted reforms of permanent partial disability benefits in 1979. The legislation does appear to have reduced somewhat the numerical importance of permanent partial cases, but not the significance of such cases in terms of share of costs. The lesson may be that meaningful changes in the New Jersey approach to permanent partial disability benefits may require reforms as fundamental as those endorsed by the 1973 Study Commission.

Procedure for Permanent Partial Cases

Few changes were made at the procedural level in the 1979 law. What follows is a review of the procedures that prevailed at the time of our field investigation.

Administratively, New Jersey classified itself as a direct payment state, one in which compensation is initiated and paid by employers and carriers, who notify the Division of Workers' Compensation as to when and how much compensation is being paid. In the law (N.J.S.A. 34:15-50), the system is referred to as an agreement system, although in practice no signed agreement between the employee and the employer (carrier) is necessary before compensation is paid. The so-called direct or voluntary payments are important for cases involving temporary disability benefits only, since permanent partial cases usually end up at a more advanced stage in the procedure.

An employee, his employer, the carrier, or the Division itself may request an informal hearing at a regional office before a hearing officer. Serious disability cases and questions of liability go directly to a formal hearing, but all minor permanent partial cases, if contested, must go through the informal process. The worker may or may not be represented by an attorney at the informal stage. The hearing official may propose a settlement based upon the medical evidence. If the suggestion is accepted by both parties, the case ends. If the suggestion is not accepted, or if none is made—perhaps because there is serious question of liability—the parties are notified of their rights and the burden for initiating a formal hearing rests on the employee.

The number of cases heard by the judge in one session varies. In a session in which minor permanent partial awards are made for fingers and minor injuries to the hand resulting in disability ratings of less than 5 percent, it is not unusual to process 25 cases in a morning session. In these cases, the outcome depends not only on the physician's findings, but also on an informal bargaining process between the carrier's representative and the petitioner's lawyer, with the hearing officer closely involved, making suggestions based on his observation of the claimant and the condition of his fingers or hands.

If the informal process does not result in an agreement, a formal hearing is initiated by the filing of the claim petition with the Division. If it appears that the issues are simple, possibly with only a narrow difference between the parties as to the extent and nature of the permanent partial disability, the claim may be scheduled for an accelerated award proceeding in which a binding decision is made by the judge based upon his review of the medical reports submitted. The matter may, however, go before a pretrial conference in which an attempt is made to list the legal, medical, and factual issues to be tried, the witnesses to be used at the time of trial, and so on.

Before the 1979 amendments, there was no provision in the New Jersey statute for compromise and release settlements. In practice, at the pretrial conference the judge would try to reach a compromise agreement acceptable to both sides. With the parties' agreement, the judge would issue an order in accordance with the settlement as an outcome of formal proceedings. It became a formal award, but such a compromise did not operate as a release. If the petitioner's physical condition changed, he could come in for review or modification of the award, so long as he did so within the statute of limitations.

The 1979 amendments specifically provided for compromise and release settlements for the first time. Under the new law, the judge of compensation, with the consent of the parties, after considering the testimony of the petitioner and other witnesses together with any stipulations of the parties, and after determining that it is fair and just under all the circumstances, may enter "an order approving settlement." That order has the force and effect of a conclusive dismissal of the claim petition. It is a complete surrender of any rights to compensation or other benefits arising out of such claim, both for the employee and for the employee's dependents, under the statute.

The petitioner has to be represented by an attorney and it has to be shown that the issue involves questions of jurisdiction, liability, causal relationship, or dependency of the petitioner. Any payment made under these procedures is to be recognized as a payment of workers' compensation benefits for insurance rating purposes only, and not as an admission of liability for workers' compensation benefits (N.J.S.A. 34:15-20).

Determining the Disability Rating

Settlement Procedures. In informal hearings, the percentage of disability is usually the percentage suggested by the hearing officer to the parties. In pretrial conferences in which a settlement is reached, a compromise figure, usually between the percentages stated by the respective parties' doctors, is worked out among the attorneys and the hearing officer. In a formal trial, however, the percentage of disability must be decided by the judge, based upon the evidence before him derived, for the most part, from the testimony of physicians. The skill and experience of the physicians, and the skill and experience of the attorneys in eliciting the appropriate answers from the physicians, become crucially important in such a process. At the formal trial there will be at least two reports, one from each of the parties' physicians, and, in addition, each of these physicians may testify. In a complicated case, more than one specialist (for example, a neurologist as well as an orthopedic specialist) may testify, each of them evaluating the percentage of disability.

It is important to note that the physician will almost always include a percentage rating in his report. This need not be a pure impairment rating, because he may also include his evaluation of the importance of nonmedical factors such as a patient's age and occupational status. Under the old law he could also note and evaluate subjective complaints. The 1979 amendments changed this, since "demonstrable objective medical evidence" is necessary to sustain a finding of "disability permanent in quality and partial in character" (N.J.S.A. 34:15-36).

Each of the physicians testifying at the formal hearing is retained by one of the parties. It would cause great shock if the petitioner's physician came in with a percentage rating of disability that was less than that of the respondent's. Such an event is rendered highly unlikely by the discovery procedures at the pretrial conference, which give each side a fairly good idea of the other's position.

It has been argued that judges of compensation have abdicated the responsibility for the evaluation of disability to the physicians. The accusation is not entirely fair, since final responsibility rests with the judges. Yet the physician's role is important, and for the most part, the physicians exercise discretion without any agency guidance as to how to evaluate the consequences of injuries. New Jersey does not provide what we have termed in the procedures chapter "evaluation" guidance as to the normal accepted ratings or the range of ratings for particular types of impairments, functional limitations, or even disabilities. As a result, the physicians have developed evaluation techniques governed not only by medical considerations, but by other considerations with which only they, as a corps of experts, are familiar.

A Physician's View. Saul B. Lieb, a physician experienced in workers' compensation matters, notes that the question of the amount of disability in nonscheduled cases does not lend itself to any easy practical guides. In the case of lost members of the body, there are statutory provisions in terms of weeks of compensation. "Otherwise the law is silent, assuming that the judge of compensation will make an award guided by expert medical testimony" (Lieb 1975, p. 62). In his view, the expert's estimates of disability are guided by:

> functional and anatomical impairment as determined by a medical examination; examiner's personality; petitioner's or respondent's viewpoint; prognosis (medical outlook for the future); social adaptability; impact on economic future; and examiner's experience as to awards in prior cases. (Lieb 1975, p. 65)

These criteria allow for idiosyncratic factors and economic or "disability" factors in terms of our typology. Lieb also recognizes that the examining physician's knowledge of what awards have been made in similar cases will necessarily have an impact on his estimate. In Lieb's view, the expert is one who knows how much has been awarded in similar cases.

Lieb recognizes that the legal merits of the case have a great deal to do with the eventual disability rating. Where there is a serious legal question about notice, or the facts of exposure, or the authenticity of an alleged accidental occurrence, the case may be disposed of with a markedly diminished disability rating (Lieb 1975, p. 71). We are presented here with a traditional type of problem in estimating benefit amounts. A 10 percent rating may be awarded, not so much because a man has an impairment of 10 percent of total, but because there is only a 10 percent chance that he has any disability, or only 1 chance in 10 that the impairment is the result of an occupational exposure or trauma.

An instance of how the system of rating operated in New Jersey before the 1979 amendments, and one that illustrates the shortcomings that provoked demands for change, is the way disability ratings were given for fractures. The theories discussed up to now dealt with physical impairment, such as loss of limb; functional limitations, defined as restrictions of motion or ability to make particular movements; and work disability, which is the effect that functional limitations can have on a worker's job chances. Where does a completely healed fracture that leaves no impairment, functional limitation, or apparent disability fit? Saul Lieb contends that fractures have been a tremendous part of the injuries seen in workers' compensation; note that the reference is to an "injury," not to any permanent impairment. A fracture of the wrist (Colle's fracture) has been evaluated at 25 to 35 percent of a hand; a simple fracture of the finger has been evaluated at 25 to 35 percent of the finger (Lieb 1975, p. 83). The 1979 amendments were designed to change the old practices. They explicitly stated that injuries such as minor lacerations, minor contusions, and minor sprains do not constitute permanent disability (N.J.S.A. 34:15-36). Under the new law, it has become more difficult to collect awards in the absence of a showing of a permanent impairment that restricts function and affects an employee's working ability.

Lieb concludes his presentation with an admonition to lawyers that the only way for the lawyer to become familiar with compensation practice is to apply himself, keeping up with the latest developments, refreshing his knowledge by constant reading and study in textbooks concerning anatomy, physiology, and pathology. He advises lawyers to be guided by the judges of compensation, who have developed a great deal of knowledge concerning the medical status of compensation cases.

Field interviews with lawyers and experts for both sides yield the same conclusion—most judges of compensation do become expert in rating. They are not products of any formal training program; their expertise is derived from a layman's exposure to physicians' reports over the years. From the treating physician's reports, the judge gets an idea of the type of injury sustained and the range within which the disability rating will fall. The judge is informed by the petitioner about complaints, and his evaluation of these complaints may well influence where, in the range, the decision will be. Such complaints may well involve the claimant's evaluation of his poor employment prospects. The judge may evaluate such information in light of the petitioner's age, occupation, and possibly even the effects of the injury on the nonwork activities of the claimant. But no criteria for weighting these complaints are set down. The judge decides a percentage based on his opinion of the medical evidence and his evaluation of the importance and severity of the complaints. Interviews with the staff of the division indicate that they would not be surprised if two judges gave different percentage awards for the same case, but they would expect the differences to be rather small. Of course, such a system works, but inevitably at the expense of extensive litigation.

New Jersey's 1979 amendments are the product of a compromise. It is significant that those amendments did not adopt a theory of permanent partial disability any different from the traditional one in that state. The path to improvement taken by the 1979 law was to redefine, or define for the first time, the concept of impairments. To be sure, these were not the only changes. Benefits were liberalized substantially, and in return not only was the definition of permanent disability tightened, but employers were allowed credits for preexisting disabilities to employees in the determination of awards for permanent partial and permanent total disability claims. Rules dealing with compensation for heart attacks changed. The basic change was the statutory definition of a permanent disability requiring a demonstration of objective medical evidence and a diminution of the claimant's work ability. The medical evidence, according to the explanatory note attached to the bill, is understood to mean evidence exceeding the subjective statement of the petitioner.

Still other changes, which ought not to be ignored, were made. The amendments limit the base upon which the attorney's fees are to be paid. Fees are assessed only at the amount awarded beyond an employer's offer, provided that offer is made within designated time frames. But nothing in the new law strengthens administrative procedures. Nothing in the amendments provides for evaluation or monitoring in the sense we have talked about.

The long-run effects of these changes on the equity, efficiency, and adequacy of the New Jersey statute cannot be evaluated yet. The initial impact does not seem too promising, as indicated by our discussion of the changes between 1978 and 1982 in the distribution of the benefit dollars. Surely, one of the primary objectives of the 1979 amendments was to move a larger part of the compensation dollar from the minor permanent partial awards, where no wage loss was suffered, to those workers with more serious injuries, and the evidence indicates that this objective has not been met.

Nevada

Nevada's Changing Organizational Structure

Until 1982, the Nevada Industrial Commission (NIC) operated the exclusive state fund and administered the workers' compensation act. There were three commissioners. One was selected from lists submitted to the governor by the AFL-CIO, one was appointed from lists submitted by employer groups, and the third was the chairman, who was required to have at least five years of actuarial experience and a master's degree in business administration or its equivalent. The chairman at the time of our field visits (1975-76), John Reiser, concentrated on the administrative aspects of the system, and hearings were conducted by the two other members.

The NIC acted as both the state workers' compensation agency and the state fund administrator. It determined insurance classifications and rates, made investments, directed the rehabilitation program, and administered the safety program and the State Inspector of Mines offices. It supervised the initial adjudication of claims and also functioned as the appellate board for the first level of appeal beyond the claims department. A separate appeals officer (not an NIC employee, but with functions and duties provided for under the workers' compensation statute, NRS 616.542) heard appeals from decisions of the NIC.

A complaint about the operations of the NIC was that the same commissioners were supervising the insurance function, administering claims, and adjudicating disputes. The 1981 legislation changed the organization so as to separate these functions and, for the first time, allow for self-insurance for qualified employers.

Effective July 1, 1982, the Nevada Industrial Commission was replaced by a new organization, the State Industrial Insurance System (SIIS), with a seven-member board of directors and a general manager designated as operating chief. The insurance regulation responsibilities rest with a newly formed Division of Insurance Regulation under the Department of Industrial Relations headed by a director and with a seven-person advisory board.

The Department of Industrial Relations also includes the Division of Mines Inspection and the Division of Occupational Safety and Health. The Department of Industrial Relations is responsible for regulation of all aspects of workers' compensation insurance, such as the certification of self-insurers and the establishment of rates, as well as for occupational safety and health. The appeals function remains with the hearings and appeals officers in the Department of Administration.

The SIIS's board of directors has three representatives of policyholders, three representatives of organized labor, and one public member. The SIIS is the exclusive fund insurer in the state, covering all employers except those who are qualified as self-insurers. Within the SIIS, the division of regional operations is responsible for most field services and has the most direct contacts with claimants and policy-holders. SIIS also includes the benefits services department with its medical advisors and benefit delivery sections in which the disability prevention teams and counseling specialists are housed. The Rehabilitation Center at Las Vegas is a separate division of SIIS.

Changing Methods of Evaluating Permanent Partial Disabilities

Nevada is an interesting state to examine because of the changes through time in the criteria for permanent partial disability benefits. Four periods of development can be distinguished: the years before 1972; 1972-73; the period from the 1973 amendments to the organizational changes of 1981; and from 1981 forward. Certain of the organizational changes did not become effective until July 1, 1982.

Before 1972, Nevada's statute contained a fairly comprehensive schedule. Scheduled awards, or, in terms of the Nevada law, awards for "specified injuries" (NRS 616.590), were listed in terms of number of months of benefits. Amputations of the arm at the shoulder, for example, called for an award of 60 months of benefits, payable at the rate of 50 percent of the worker's average monthly wage subject to a minimum and a maximum.

The second section of this statute provided that if the specific injuries

> result in a residual physical disability to parts of the body other than the members affected, the commission may consider and award additional compensation taking into consideration, among other things:
>
> (1) Any previous disability;
> (2) The occupation of the injured employee;
> (3) The nature of the physical injury;
> (4) The age of the employee, and
> (5) Such other factors as may be compatible with the injury incurred.

Thus, if an award were made solely on the basis of the schedule, the number of weeks awarded would be as specified in the statute and nothing additional would be paid for the permanent partial disability. A leg was valued at 50 months and entitled the worker to 50 percent of his wages (subject to the maximum) for 50 months. But if it were found that there were "residual physical disability to parts of the body other than the members affected'' the commission could take these other factors into account and make an award on the "body" basis.

In cases of permanent partial disability not specified in the schedule, that is, nonscheduled injuries, the NIC was directed by the statute to determine the percentage of disability and each percent was to be paid one month at 50 percent of the worker's wage, subject to a maximum slightly lower than that allowed for scheduled awards. In determining the percentage of disability, the commission was to consider among other things the exact list of ''other factors'' as specified in the scheduled section.

During this period, the NIC made some use of the AMA *Guides* to determine the extent of impairment, but there were no rules, directives, or guides for the application of the other factors, nor for when the specified or nonspecified ratings were to be made. In seeking objectivity, Nevada in 1972 turned to the example of its neighboring state and adopted a modified form of California's schedule to be used in place of the rater's subjective evaluation of the ''other factors.'' The system was to be used only if it resulted in an increase in the award to the worker.

These changes proved to be unsatisfactory, and following a number of studies, the law was amended with changes that became effective July 1, 1973. Under the new law (NRS 616.605), disability and impairment of the whole man were declared to be equivalent terms. The law then went on to state:

> The percentage of disability shall be determined by the physician designated by the Commission, or board of physicians, in accordance with the current American Medical Association publication, *Guides to the Evaluation of Permanent Impairment.*

Further, ''No factors other than the degree of physical impairment of the whole man shall be considered in calculating the entitlement to permanent partial disability compensation.'' These provisions from the 1973 amendments continue substantially unchanged in the law that became effective July 1, 1982.

The 1973 statute provided that each 1 percent of impairment of the whole man was to be compensated by a monthly payment of one-half of 1 percent of the claimant's average monthly wage prior to injury. Effective July 1, 1981, that was changed to six-tenths of 1 percent. Liability for payments is to begin on the day of injury, or the day after the last payment of temporary disability compensation, whichever is later. Payments are to continue on a monthly basis for a minimum of five years or until the 70th birthday of the claimant, whichever is later.

Compensation benefits are usually paid on a monthly basis, but may be paid annually to claimants who are receiving benefits of less than $100 a month. Claimants may receive up to $10,000, or one-quarter of the present value of their award, whichever is greater, in a lump sum.

Under the Nevada law, the maximum weekly wage used to calculate permanent partial benefits is 150 percent of the state's average weekly wage. The maximum monthly wage as of July 1985 was $2,159.33. Six-tenths of 1 percent of $2,159.33 is $12.96. Assuming that a worker entitled to the maximum monthly benefit had a 10 percent permanent partial award, he would be entitled to $129.56 per month. The same high-wage worker with a 60 percent award would receive $777.36 per month.

The monthly dollar amount of these awards for a 65-year-old worker and a 35-year-old worker with the same rating and earning the same wage would be exactly the same. However, the 65-year-old worker would receive these payments for 5 years, until age 70, whereas the 35-year-old worker would receive them for 35 years. The theory obviously is that wage-earning capacity has been impaired and compensation should be paid for the span over which wages would have been earned. Thus, the duration is for the rest of the worker's normal working life, which is presumed to end when he attains the age of 70.

Since Nevada's benefits are so crucially dependent on age, they are difficult to compare with those in other states. Obviously, the younger the worker, the greater the total amount received. The present value of the 60 percent award for the 35-year-old worker at maximum wages would be $136,433 discounted at 6 percent; for the 65-year-old worker, it would be $40,296. The latter's benefits would be received over five years, the minimum duration no matter what the age of the worker.

Lump-Sum Payments

When Nevada's law was amended in 1973, lump-sum payments were permitted only under specific conditions. If the total rating was 12 percent or less, a lump-sum payment was made on demand of the worker. For cases in which ratings totalled 13 percent or more, lump sums were to be allowed only "upon demonstration of a need which is substantiated by a comprehensive evaluation of possible rehabilitation." Effective July 1, 1979, a provision was added that up to one-quarter of a rating of 13 percent or more could be paid in a lump sum on demand. The practice has been to pay a lump sum, regardless of the percent rating, any time the value of the lump sum, which is a discounted figure that takes into account mortality rates, exceeds the total amount that would be due in installments. This occurs when the claimant's age is 56 years, 8 months or older.

When the law was again amended in 1981, the lump-sum provisions were further liberalized. Claimants injured after July 1, 1981, may receive up to $10,000 or one-quarter of the present value of their award (whichever is greater) as a lump sum without limitations on the percentage rating.

Permanent Total Disability Awards

Nevada uses a different and more usual method for calculating benefits for workers whose disability is adjudged as permanent total. The law (NRS 616.575) provides that certain specified injuries, in the absence of proof to the contrary, are deemed to be total and permanent: for example, the loss of sight of both eyes, the loss of two major limbs, an injury to the spine resulting in complete paralysis, and an injury to the skull resulting in incurable imbecility or insanity. The enumeration is not meant to be inclusive, and all other cases are to be determined in accordance with the facts presented. The permanent total benefit is calculated at two-thirds of the worker's preinjury wage, subject to a maximum weekly benefit of $332.46 as of January 1986 (U.S. Dept. of Labor, *State Laws,* 1986). This amount is payable for life, although the employee is required to file a report on any of his earnings on an annual basis, and presumably they would be deducted.

Hearing Procedure

Just as the law has changed to provide different methods of paying benefits, so has it changed in regard to hearing procedures. Before 1973, the NIC examined claims, decided on the benefits to be paid, and heard appeals of decisions of its own claims examiners. In 1973, the law added an appeals officer from the Department of Administration to hear appeals from Commission decision. In 1978, claimants could seek the services of the office of the State Industrial Insurance System attorney, and in 1979 the NIC was no longer authorized to hold any hearings on claims.

Under the law effective in 1982, claims examiners of SIIS investigate claims and, if there is no dispute, pay claims and close cases without any outside interference. Should a dispute arise, a hearing may be requested before a hearing officer of the Department of Administration, who will conduct a formal hearing at which the claimant may be represented by an attorney. From there, appeals may be made to the appeals officer (who is also from the Department of Administration), and thereafter to the court system.

Rehabilitation

At the time of our field visits in 1975 and 1976, there was great enthusiasm among the commissioner, staff, and representatives of interest groups about rehabilitation. It was seen as an NIC function that was just as important as the payment of benefits.

The chairman of the Commission at that time, John Reiser, was the most enthusiastic advocate of rehabilitation, and spoke of negotiations with employers to promote the possibility of rehabilitation for seriously injured workers. He argued that the claims person or the rehabilitation counselor could point out to the employer the reserves for medical and cash benefits that would have to be established and would eventually be reflected in the employer's insurance costs if workers were adjudged to be permanently and totally disabled, and could contrast these sums with the lesser sums involved in a rehabilitation program, which would be successful if employers agreed to take seriously injured workers back.

There can be no quarrel with the idea that return to the job is a primary goal of a workers' compensation program, but it is also true that rehabilitation programs are invariably beset by practical difficulties. These difficulties are apparent in Nevada, where experience has tempered initial enthusiasm. It has been difficult to select eligible candidates for rehabilitation, to decide on a program, to set limits on rehabilitation expenditures, and to motivate employees and employers.

The statutory provisions relating to rehabilitation have not changed in substance since 1973. NRS 616.222 provides:

> To aid in getting the injured workman back to work, to assist in lessening or removing any resulting handicap, the insurer may order counseling, training, or rehabilitation   services for the injured worker regardless of the date on which such workman first became entitled to compensation.

Before services can be ordered, the worker and his physician must be consulted, and if the services involve a change in vocation, the consultation must include the employer and a rehabilitation counselor. Compensation benefits may be withheld if a worker rejects counseling, training, or other rehabilitation services offered by the insurer.

NRS 616.223 provides authority for cooperative agreements between SIIS and the rehabilitation division of the Department of Human Resources as well as other public and private entities. To avoid reliance on other agencies, SIIS employed rehabilitation counselors and nurses. In 1976, it completed the building of a rehabilitation center in Las Vegas with accommodations for 250 outpatients daily. The rehabilitation center is one of the four operating divisions of the SIIS.

The changes in the regulations tell a part of the story of the changes in rehabilitation practices. In its original form, under regulation 13 of the NIC, rehabilitation was defined to encompass a very broad range of services, from guidance to transportation allowances. Regulation 14.1020 charged the Commission with establishing "a program of rehabilitation for each industrially injured worker in need of and capable of benefiting from such service."

Although some latitude is still in place, later regulations sought ways to limit services, perhaps recognizing that "need" is insufficient guidance in light of the finiteness of resources allocated for rehabilitation. Regulation 14.004 states that rehabilitation means "assisting in the return of an injured worker to gainful employment, *at a justifiable cost,* within a reasonable time after he is injured or contracts an occupational disease" (emphasis added).

Section 14.015, dealing with eligibility for rehabilitation services, stipulates that in order to receive services a worker must be physically unable to return to his former job, and that if he is released by his physician without any job restrictions he is not eligible for services. Neither is he eligible solely on the grounds that the job he performed before his injury is no longer available.

Section 14.045 lists in order of priority the options for returning the disabled worker to gainful employment. The first is to place him in the job he held before injury; the second, to place him with the former employer in a job that accommodates his limitations; and third, to place him with another employer in a job that utilizes his existing skills. Last on the list is assisting in initiating self-employment or other means of employment. Only if these are not possible will training be considered.

In general, the regulations require the counselors to approach formal training and educational programs with caution. Rehabilitation services are to cease when the employer offers a job whose demands do not exceed any limitations defined by a treating or examining physician.

The thrust of the regulations is to provide services that will return the worker to a job and not necessarily to develop his fullest potential. The counselor is to provide a written rehabilitation plan to be explained to the worker, and a copy is to be sent to the worker's previous employer. The plan is to include a budget together with a justification for the expenses.

The rehabilitation programs are administered by a staff of rehabilitation counselors stationed in Las Vegas and in the northern part of the state. Ideally, each counselor works with a nurse employed by the SIIS and with a claims examiner. This three-person team functions as a so-called disability prevention team.

If the worker receives compensation for more than 42 days, the file is examined by the team to determine if services are needed. If necessary, the nurse or counselor confers with the attending physician or the claimant. If the medical advisor deems it beneficial, the claimant might be sent to the Las Vegas center for evaluation. If a case is accepted for rehabilitation, the individual written rehabilitation plan will be worked out by the counselor and approved by the supervisor.

The Lessons from Nevada

Nevada's example is interesting for three reasons. First and foremost, it clearly illustrates some of the difficulties likely to be encountered in trying to operationalize criteria for permanent partial disability benefits. Before 1972, Nevada drew the conventional distinction between scheduled and nonscheduled injuries. Scheduled injuries were rated strictly on an impairment basis. Nonscheduled injuries (and scheduled injuries that affected other parts of the body) were evaluated essentially on the basis of the loss of earning capacity, with the rating depending on factors that included the worker's age and occupation. The determination of the extent of loss of earning capacity was done on a case-by-case basis, which produced controversies and inefficiencies. From the next phase in Nevada, a brief one (1972-73), one innovation has survived: the distinction between scheduled injuries (those specifically enumerated in the statute) and nonscheduled injuries was dropped. Another innovation from that period, namely the use of a formula approach *a la* California to evaluate all injuries in terms of the extent of loss of earning capacity, was soon abandoned. (The California model is discussed at length in the next chapter.)

The approach used in Nevada since 1973 to pay permanent partial disability benefits is unique among jurisdictions we have examined. There is no distinction between scheduled and nonscheduled injuries. Rather, all injuries are rated on the basis of the extent of impairment or functional limitations as spelled out in the AMA *Guides to the Evaluation of Permanent Impairment.* These ratings are then turned into weekly benefit amounts by a formula. (The 1973 formula was slightly modified in 1981.) The ratings and the weekly benefit amounts pay no attention to disability factors, such as age, education, or occupation. Only two aspects of the Nevada scheme make it something other than a "pure" impairment approach: the weekly benefits are related to the worker's preinjury wage, and the benefits terminate when the worker reaches age 70.

Because these permanent partial benefits are paid for the "working lifetime," it is possible to see their purpose as being to compensate for loss of earning capacity: a presumably permanent loss calls for compensation to be paid on a regular basis throughout the injured person's entire working life. But such a goal gives way before the practicalities of administration and the desires of the parties. The worker anxious for immediate benefits, the attorney eager for his fee, and the administrator who wants to minimize his record keeping—all combine to press for lump sums. The 1981 amendments made these easier to obtain, so that today, for some workers, such as those who receive a lump sum and then die before age 70, the relationship between their benefits and the extent of their work disability is muted. The lump-sum practice moves Nevada closer to a "pure" impairment approach for permanent partial disability benefits, and away from an approach that compensates work disability.

The second interesting aspect of the Nevada experience is the state's changing rehabilitation program. The enthusiasm with which rehabilitation was embraced as a panacea has gradually dimmed with the recognition that rehabilitation, in common with many other purposes, is subject to economic constraints. Not all injured workers can benefit from rehabilitation, and the SIIS, like others concerned with these problems, faces the task of choosing those who can be motivated to complete programs devised in light of cost-effective priorities.

One reason why a more free-wheeling system of rehabilitation—with claims persons bargaining with, cajoling, and threatening employers to take back workers—is not possible leads to the third interesting aspect of Nevada's experience. In 1973, the NIC was the exclusive insurer, the insurance rate fixer, the initial determiner of benefits, and the appellant level. These functions, in the interest of due process and equity, have been separated. This diffusion of authority since 1973 has made it more difficult in Nevada to mount a whole-hearted campaign to pursue any goal, including the promotion of rehabilitation.

Perhaps when all is said and done, the importance of Nevada lies in its unique method of assessing permanent partial disability. The state should continue to be monitored to determine if an objective AMA *Guides* type of evaluation can, despite the obstacles and difficulties outlined above, succeed in providing an efficient and equitable method of awarding permanent partial benefits.

Ohio[3]

Introduction

Ohio is an exclusive-fund state with a large number of self-insured employers. The Ohio Industrial Commission—a three-member panel appointed by the governor, with one member representing employees, another employers, and the third, the public—supervises the district hearing officers, the Regional Boards of Review, and the so-called "C-92 Section," which handles applications for percentage ratings of permanent disability. Most administrative functions are the responsibility of a separate unit, the Bureau of Workers' Compensation, which is headed by an administrator. The Bureau is responsible for claims and disbursements from the state fund and supervision of claims from the self-insured sector. It maintains claims records and rates employers for premium purposes for policies issued by the state fund.

The time span of our research encompasses two periods of major upheaval in the Ohio Workers' Compensation Program. The first culminated in action by the governor and the legislature in 1976 that largely affected administrative structure and procedure. The second resulted in wholesale statutory changes in 1986 that, *inter alia,* changed the type of benefits available to workers with permanent partial disabilities. As discussed below, the significance of the 1986 benefit changes is not yet clear, and for that reason we concentrate on the benefit scheme in effect before the latest set of changes.

Organizational Change

Our field work in Ohio was conducted in 1975 and 1976 at a time when the administration of the law was under investigation and scandals were threatening the stability of the workers' compensation program. One lengthy study, the *Report of the Joint Select Committee on Workmen's Compensation,* recommended several basic reforms of the program. One of these was redirection of the role of the medical practitioner toward objective evaluation of impairment and sound medical treatment. The report criticized the administration of the act and the absence of published policies and operating guidelines.

At the time of our field work, responsibility for the rather complex administration of the Ohio law was divided between the Commission and the Bureau. In the evaluation of permanent partial disability the medical unit played a crucial role, and we noted that the Bureau's and the Commission's shared control of that unit caused some tension. We also commented that beyond the great confusion induced by the apparently complex organization and the investigations, the process of determining the disability ratings was not guided by any well-known rules, regulations, or standards. "The agency's physicians make determinations in a manner that is apparently understood by them and some of the examining physicians, but that understanding is not widely disseminated. There are no extensive statistical data published as to the results and very little information as to the consistency of the awards that are made" (Berkowitz, Burton, and Vroman 1979, p. 234).

Because of allegations of abuse and fraud, the chairman of the Ohio Industrial Commission was removed by the governor in 1976. This action was followed by over 200 indictments and many subsequent convictions. A legislative investigation culminated in the passage of S.B. 545, which mandated specific management reforms at the Bureau and the Commission. These have since been carried out.

Overlapping responsibilities of the Bureau and the Commission were eliminated. The Bureau is the administrative body and the Industrial Commission is the adjudicative and policy-making body. Each agency has control over its own personnel, physical space, and budget. The reforms were designed to strengthen the political independence of the Bureau personnel and the commissioners. The Bureau's administrator, who formerly served at the pleasure of the governor, was given a fixed six-year term. The Industrial Commission members were limited to two terms in office. Employees of the Bureau of Workers' Compensation were placed under the classified civil service system.

Rules, procedures, and decisions of both the Bureau and the Commission were formalized and opened for public review and comment. Managerial improvements such as the introduction of electronic data processing and systematized rules and operating procedures were made. We note some of these changes below, and will discuss the evaluation guidance now given physicians to aid them in assessing the percentage of permanent partial impairments.

Procedures

For employers insured under the state fund, the Bureau of Workers' Compensation makes the initial determination on all uncontested claims. The Bureau, which also monitors self-insurers, has a central office in Columbus, and 16 district offices. The central office's claims section maintains the claims file and sets hearings for contested claims.

There are five Regional Boards of Review (O.R.C. 4123.14), each composed of three members: a representative of employers, a representative of employees, and a chairman who must be admitted to the practice of law in Ohio. The regional boards are under the jurisdiction of the Industrial Commission and are to follow uniform rules of procedure established by the Commission. The Industrial Commission determines appeals from the regional boards, and also determines applications for permanent partial awards.

If a claim is contested, the hearing on the matter is conducted by the district hearing officer, who is an employee of the Industrial Commission. Appeals from the orders of the district hearing officer may be taken by either party, and if the employee was unrepresented at the hearing, the administrator may appeal to the Commission. The Commission then assigns an appeal to a Regional Board of Review, which holds an informal hearing. New evidence, not presented to the District Hearing Officer, is allowed; the administrator is represented at the hearing.

Regional boards are given 60 days to decide the case or demonstrate reasonable grounds for delay to the Commission. Any dissatisfied party, or the administrator, can file an appeal with the Industrial Commission, which is given sole discretion to decide whether to accept the appeal. Most cases are accepted. When the appeal is not accepted, the regional board's order becomes a final order and may be appealed directly to the Court of Common Pleas (O.R.C. 4123.51a).

In addition to the appeals function, the Industrial Commission has original jurisdiction over settlements, permanent total cases, and safety violation awards. Staff hearing officers may hear such matters of original jurisdiction with an appeal of right directly to the Industrial Commission.

Types of Permanent Partial Disability Benefits[4]

There were three types of benefits available to workers with permanent partial disabilities in Ohio prior to the 1986 statutory amendments. The new law eliminated one type of benefit and created another, which "appears to be a substitute for the [type of benefit] the bill eliminates."[5]

Scheduled permanent partial benefits were retained by the 1986 amendments with some modifications. Previously these were provided by Sec. 4123.57 division C. The "old" benefits were for durations that depended on the nature and severity of injury (such as 60 weeks for a loss of a thumb), with the weekly benefit set at 66 2/3 percent of the worker's preinjury wage, subject to maximum and minimum weekly benefit amounts of 50 percent and 25 percent of the state's average weekly wage. These "old" scheduled benefits were in effect as of January 1986 and thus are the Ohio entries in the tables in chapter 5. The "new" Ohio scheduled benefits are moved to division B of Sec. 4123.57 and the maximum and minimum weekly benefit amounts are 100 percent and 40 percent of the state's average weekly wage. The durations of the scheduled benefits were not changed.

A second type of benefit was also retained by the 1986 amendments with some modifications. Previously these were provided by division B of Sec. 4123.57, and were sometimes referred to as "paragraph B awards." Under the new law, the benefits are moved to division A; in order to reduce confusion, we will refer to them as "C-92 awards" or "permanent partial awards," which are terms commonly used in Ohio. Previously the weekly benefit was 66 2/3 percent of the worker's preinjury wage subject to a maximum weekly benefit of 33 1/3 percent of the state's average weekly wage. The duration was a percentage of 200 weeks, with the percentage determined by the extent of the worker's disability. None of these provisions were changed by the 1986 law, although, as discussed below, the relationship between permanent partial awards and other types of benefits was modified. The permanent partial (or C-92) awards are essentially based on the extent of the worker's permanent impairment or functional limitations, and are the primary concern of the balance of this chapter.

The third type of benefit has changed as a result of the 1986 amendments. The old law provided in division A of Sec. 4123.57 a type of wage-loss benefit that the employee would choose instead of the C-92 or permanent partial awards; these benefits were commonly referred to as "temporary partial" disability benefits, although that term was not in the statute. The 1986 amendments eliminated these temporary partial disability benefits and added a new type of wage-loss benefit in division B of Sec. 4123.56. The new wage-loss benefits are not an alternative to a C-92 or permanent partial award; rather, the worker cannot receive a permanent partial award until 40 weeks after the termination of the new wage-loss benefit. Because both the old and new version of the third type of benefit are types of wage-loss benefits, we defer extended discussion until chapter 8.

Permanent Partial or C-92 Awards. Division A (previously division B) of Sec. 4123.57 provides that the Commission "shall determine the percentage of the employee's permanent disability . . . based upon that condition of the employee resulting from the injury or occupational disease and causing permanent impairment evidenced by medical or clinical findings reasonably demonstrable." Note that the Commission is to fix the *disability* percentage based upon the *impairment* that results from the condition, which in turn is the result of the injury. Although the terms are not used exactly as we have developed and defined them in chapter 1, they are quite similar, as will be seen from the evaluation guidance provided to physicians by the Commission.

The provision that established the "permanent partial award" (old division B) came into the law in 1941 in response to dissatisfaction with the "temporary partial" awards (old division A). Apparently, it became difficult to disassociate wage losses due to the conditions of the labor market from those due to the employee's medical condition. The complaint was that workers abused the provision. Employers sought some alternative, and employee groups were willing to accept percentage awards based on physical impairment because they eliminated the requirement to file periodic wage statements and undergo periodic medical examinations. In time, the impairment method became the prevailing method of assessing permanent partial disability in Ohio.

Applicants may file for permanent partial awards 40 weeks after last payment of temporary total benefits or 40 weeks after date of injury, whichever is later.[6] The claims are filed on Form C-92, hence the common name for these awards.

When a C-92 application is filed, the claimant is examined by an Industrial Commission physician, whose report becomes part of the file. The rules provide that the employer may have the claimant examined at the employer's expense. Self-insurers are likely to do this, and in such cases three physician reports may be presented at the hearing—the report from the physician of the Industrial Commission and reports from physicians retained by the employee and the employer.

The C-92 unit processes the claim. When there is substantial disparity (defined as 15 percent or more) among physicians' reports, a party may request a deposition from the physician. This is done at the expense of the requesting party, under the supervision of an attorney designated by the Industrial Commission's legal director.

If there is agreement on the percentage of permanent partial disability it is possible to waive a hearing, although this is not usual. Hearings are conducted by a district hearing officer in the various District Offices. The hearing is informal, and the only issue is the percentage of impairment. Physicians usually do not appear, but the hearing officer listens to arguments based on the medical evidence in the record. If there is substantial disparity among ratings, the hearing officer may refer the claimant to a specialist for examination. No payment is made until there is a final order.

The determination of permanent partial disability is exclusively within the Commissioner's jurisdiction. The Commission's decision may not be appealed to court (O.R.C. 4123.51a). It can be challenged only by a party filing a writ of mandamus, which requires the Commission to perform its legal duty to make or not make the percentage award. The Commission's decision will be upheld by the Court if there is some evidence to support the decision.[7]

Permanent Total Disability

Ohio's statute (O.R.C. 4123.58) provides for a scheduled type of permanent and total disability for "loss or loss of use of both hands or both arms, or both feet or both legs, or both eyes, or any two thereof." The award is to be paid in addition to any scheduled award for permanent partial disability. The statute does not otherwise define permanent and total disability, but provides that in cases of permanent and total disability, benefits based on 66 2/3 percent of preinjury wages, subject to the maximum of 100 percent of the state's average weekly wage, are payable for life. As of January 1986, the maximum was $365 per week.

"Nonscheduled" permanent total claims (those not involving the specified losses of body parts, such as both hands) are evaluated only after 200 weeks of temporary total compensation have been paid. The evaluation process is similar to that followed for permanent partial awards, with a great deal of reliance on medical findings. The final decision rests with the Industrial Commission, which must decide if the impairment has caused the worker to be unfit for sustained remunerative employment.

Providing Evaluation Guidance

At the time of our field work investigations, we observed that physicians who evaluated physical impairments in order to aid the hearing officers in fixing the physical disability rating were provided with little or no evaluation guidance. The 1976 reforms specifically provided that the Industrial Commission's medical section was to "issue a manual of Commission policy so as to increase consistency of medical reports" (O.R.C. 4121.38). The Ohio *Medical Examination Manual* (1981) defines terms commonly used in determining impairment ratings, examines the role of the examining physician in workers' compensation law, and, in general, provides guidance to the physician in the evaluation of permanent partial impairments.

The manual makes clear that the examining physician will be asked to perform two types of examination. In one, the physician is asked whether a particular condition is related to an identifiable occupational injury or occupational exposure. For the second type of examination, the physician is asked to state the percentage of impairment caused by the allowed injury or disease.

The Ohio *Medical Examination Manual* (1981, pp. 1-2) points out that the terms *disability* and *impairment* are not synonymous:

> "Impairment" is a medical term measuring the amount of the claimant's anatomical and/or mental loss of function as a result of the allowed injury/occupational disease. The examining physician evaluates impairment.

> "Disability" is a legal term indicating the effect that the medical impairment has on the claimant's ability to work. Disability is determined by the Industrial Commission and its hearing officer.

The Commission's definition of impairment combines our concepts of impairment and functional limitations, but its definition of disability is similar to ours in emphasizing the ability to work. The Commission stresses that disability is a legal concept and not a medical concept.

Physicians are told that they may choose any established guide, such as the AMA *Guides* (1984) or McBride's *Disability Evaluation* (1942), to decide on the percentage of impairment. They are asked to indicate which guide was used.

The opinion is to be expressed both as a degree and as a percentage of the entire body. The degree ranges from minimal (which is equivalent to 0-10 percent) through low, low moderate, high moderate, high, and maximum (which is rated at 85-100 percent).

The manual also discusses the physician's role in evaluating schedule losses. If there is an amputation, the loss is to be stated in definite anatomical terms and specifically noted as a scheduled loss. The physician is also asked to determine, however, if the claimant has a permanent partial impairment over and above the scheduled loss. The example cited in the Ohio *Medical Examination Manual* (1981, p. 8) is that of a claimant who has totally lost the vision in one eye due to an injury: "That would be a scheduled loss. If he/she suffers from a constant 'tearing' of that eye, he/she may have permanent partial impairment over and above the scheduled loss."

The issuance of such a medical rating manual shows a commendable willingness to assume the responsibility for providing evaluation guidance. Of course, no approach will satisfy everyone. The Ohio AFL-CIO's *Workers' Compensation Manual* (Jaffy and Smith 1981), for example, remains critical of the physician's rating of impairment, noting that different doctors use different approaches to evaluate disability and that doctors who do a great deal of disability evaluation are the ones familiar with the methods used. But the range of disagreement is probably lessened given the changes in Ohio's law.

Summary

There is little doubt that Ohio's permanent partial awards (C-92 awards) belong squarely in our category I. But despite the clear directives to physicians to this effect and supporting legal opinion,[8] some important ambiguity remains. An unanswered question is whether the district hearing officers are to take into account the "other factors" that, combined with the impairment, may result in the disability. Presumably they may, although no guidelines are offered. Interestingly enough, the AFL-CIO's *Manual* instructs the union representative that if there is some dispute over the amount of the award, it will be helpful to have the injured worker present at the C-92 hearing. The representative is advised that the hearing officer will ask whether the claimant is working regularly and whether he is earning the same amount as before, or less, or more (Jaffy and Smith 1981, p. 82). This question pertains to the extent of dissability,not just the extent of impairment. On the other hand, it is significant that the union representatives are advised to seek a medical specialist's examination in the event of a dispute; they are not advised to hire vocational experts.

Perhaps the Ohio handling of permanent partial awards only proves that impairment evaluation is an oblique way to operationalize a desire to compensate for actual or putative wage loss, and that even if the process begins by measuring the extent of the physical impairment, factors relevant for determining the extent of disability slip into the evaluation process.

Procedurally, Ohio does not go as far as California, which has a separate rating bureau, but it combines aspects of a rating bureau with aspects of New York's hearing system. Although a hearing can be waived, almost all C-92 cases come before a hearing officer. If there is no medical dispute, the hearing may be perfunctory. The advantage of such a procedure is that, combined with the examination by the Industrial Commission's doctor, it could bring about uniformity in evaluation, with a consequent improvement in equity. The banning of appeals concerning the extent of disability shows promise of promoting efficiency. What is necessary to make such a system truly equitable and efficient is detailed evaluation guidance. The physician's manual disseminated following the 1976 amendments is a step in the right direction. More detailed evaluation guidance should allow Ohio to improve further the efficiency of the program.

NOTES

1. New Jersey's law was approved April 4, 1911, to become effective on July 4, 1911. Three states enacted laws before New Jersey—Kansas and Washington on March 14, 1911, and Nevada on March 23, 1911—but of these laws, only Nevada's became effective before New Jersey's, since it went into effect on July 1 of that year. Nevada's act, however, applied only to specific employments, and it was superseded by another act in 1913. To complicate matters further, Wisconsin, which passed its act after New Jersey, put its statute into effect immediately upon adoption. New Jersey's law is, at any rate, the oldest statute from point of enactment that has remained in effect (Berkowitz 1960, p. 3).

2. *Dwyer v. Ford Motor Company,* 36 N.J. 487 (1962).

3. We are indebted to Richard J. Levine, attorney to the administrator, for providing information and useful insights.

4. The material in this subsection is based in part on material from Young (1984), sections 7.4.1 and 7.11-7.7.17.

5. The passage is from an analysis of S.B. 307 prepared by the Ohio Legislative Service Commission staff. The lack of certainty about the role of the new benefit suggests that a clear understanding of the new Ohio benefit scheme must await time and court interpretations.

6. Under the 1986 amendments, there is also a minimum of 40 weeks between the last payment of the Section 4123.56 wage-loss benefits and eligibility for permanent partial awards under Section 4123.57 division A.

7. *State, ex rel. Manley v. Industrial Commission,* 66 Ohio St. 2d 40, 417 NE 2d 1375 (1981).

8. "Permanent partial awards differ from most other types of compensation in that they are not a substitute for wages or an award for impairment of earnings capacity. Like scheduled loss-of-member awards this award is designed as a 'general damage' type of compensation, aiming to compensate a worker for loss of physical or mental function" (Nackley 1985, sec. 14:5).

Chapter 7
Nonscheduled Benefits in Loss of Wage-Earning Capacity (Category II) States

In this chapter we consider California, the District of Columbia, and Wisconsin, jurisdictions in which the basis for nonscheduled permanent partial awards is the loss of wage-earning capacity. These jurisdictions differ considerably in their approaches. California is particularly notable because it does not make the conventional distinction between scheduled and nonscheduled injuries (a feature that was examined in chapter 5).

California

Types and Levels of Benefits

Cash benefits in California fall into the classifications of temporary total, temporary partial, permanent partial, permanent total, and death benefits. In addition, medical care and rehabilitation services are provided. For our purposes, the temporary and permanent disability benefits are most relevant.

(a) Temporary disability benefits. Temporary disability benefits are paid during the recovery period following an injury or onset of a disease. Benefits do not begin in California until four days after the employee leaves work, although the waiting period is eliminated if the employee is hospitalized. Benefits for the waiting period are paid retroactively if the period of disability is at least 22 days. A worker eligible for temporary total disability benefits normally receives two-thirds of his preinjury average earnings, subject to minimum and maximum benefit rates that were $112 and $224 per week as of January 1986. This maximum was only 62 percent of the state's average weekly wage; only six other states had maximum weekly benefits that were as low relative to their average weekly wages (U.S. Dept. of Labor, *State Laws Compared,* Forthcoming 1987).

159

(b) Permanent partial disability benefits. A worker who experiences a permanent impairment as a result of a work-related injury or disease is eligible for permanent disability benefits. An impairment is considered permanent when it persists after the worker has reached maximum improvement, or when his condition has been stationary for a reasonable period of time. Permanent disability benefits are paid in addition to temporary benefits.

In determining the percentages of permanent disability, *Labor Code* Section 4660 provides that "account shall be taken of the nature of the physical injury or disfigurement, the occupation of the injured employee, and his age at the time of such injury, consideration being given to the diminished ability of such injured employee to compete in an open labor market." The section also provides that a schedule shall be adopted for determining the extent of permanent disabilities, and that the schedule shall be *prima facie* evidence of the percentage of disability.

The schedule is used to evaluate the extent of the injury, providing what roughly amounts to an impairment rating, and then to modify the rating by the worker's age and occupation. These factors are introduced to reflect the varying impact of a particular injury on the future ability to compete in the open labor market among workers who differ in age and occupation. As will be discussed later, there is more to the determination of the extent of permanent disability in California than a mechanical application of the schedule. The complexities result from the presence of discretion in the application of the schedule; the fact that the disability rating is only *prima facie* evidence, which can sometimes be successfully challenged; and the ability of the parties to avoid the use of the schedule in the determination of permanent disability benefits.

A worker with a permanent disability rating between 1 and 99.75 percent is eligible for permanent partial disability benefits. The worker receives progressively more weeks of benefits as the size of the rating increases, according to a formula in *Labor Code* Section 4658, shown in table 7.1.

The cumulative number of weeks increases with the severity of the disability, as shown in table 7.2. The benefits are based on two-thirds of the worker's wage, subject to a weekly minimum and maximum that were $70 and $140 in January 1986.

Table 7.1
Duration of Permanent Partial Benefits in California

Percentage range of disability rating	Number of weeks of benefits for each 1 percent of disability in range
Under 10	3
10–19.75	4
20–29.75	5
30–39.75	6
50–69.75	7
70–99.75	8

Table 7.2
Cumulative Duration of Permanent Partial Benefits in California

Percentage of permanent disability incurred	Cumulative number of benefit weeks	Percentage of permanent disability incurred	Cumulative number of benefit weeks
5	15.00	55	276.00
10	30.25	60	311.00
15	50.25	65	346.00
20	70.50	70	381.25
25	95.50	75	421.25
30	120.75	80	461.25
35	150.75	85	501.25
40	180.75	90	541.25
45	210.75	95	581.25
50	241.00		

Workers whose disabilities rate 70-99 percent receive a life pension at the end of the permanent partial benefit period. The pension is computed at 1.5 percent of average weekly earnings for each percent of rating above 60 percent. Thus a worker with an 99 percent rating would receive 39 x 1.5 or 58.5 percent of his wage, subject to a weekly maximum of $64.21 in January 1986. (The maximum of $64.21 could only be received by a worker with a 99 percent rating. Workers with lower ratings receive lower benefits.)

(c) Permanent total disability. Total permanent disability benefits are to be paid for life. The loss of both eyes, or the sight thereof, the loss of use of both hands, an injury resulting in "practically total paralysis," and an injury to the brain resulting in incurable imbecility or insanity are conclusively presumed to be total in character. All other cases are to be determined individually. As shown in table 3.6, permanent total cases are relatively uncommon in California compared to other states.

Permanent and total disability benefits are based on two-thirds of the worker's wage with a maximum as of January 1986 of $224 per week, the same as in the case of temporary total disabilities.

The Delivery System for Workers' Compensation

The California workers' compensation program is a direct-payment system, which means that a worker eligible for the benefits can receive the benefits without prior approval by the state workers' compensation agency.

Although the obligation to provide workers' compensation benefits is on the employer, most employers secure this obligation by purchasing insurance from a carrier that assumes much of the employer's administrative responsibility. In California, insurance can be purchased from the State Compensation Insurance Fund (the largest state fund in the country) or from private insurance carriers. Employers can self-insure if they obtain a certificate of self-insurance, and many of the state's largest employers have qualified. Public agencies are also permitted to administer their own workers' compensation programs.

Administrative Organizations. The primary responsibility for administering the California workers' compensation program lies with the Division of Industrial Accidents, which includes the Workers' Compensation Appeals Board. The Department of Industrial Relations, in which the Division of Industrial Accidents is included, also houses the

Division of Labor Statistics and Research, which is responsible for the collection and analysis of the employers' and doctors' first reports of work injuries. The administrative director of the Division of Industrial Accidents and the members (commissioners) of the Workers' Compensation Appeals Board are appointed by the governor and are subject to senate confirmation. The director serves at the pleasure of the governor, and the members of the Appeals Board have four-year terms.

The director of the Division of Industrial Accidents appoints all personnel in the division except the seven members of the Appeals Board. Among the most important appointments are the workers' compensation judges, who make the initial decisions in contested claims. There are 125 workers' compensation judges staffing 21 offices of the Workers' Compensation Appeals Board (U.S. Dept. of Labor, *Administration Profiles, 1985*).

The director also appoints the chief of the Disability Evaluation Bureau, the medical director, the chief of the Rehabilitation Bureau, and the chief of the Information & Assistance (I & A) Bureau. The Disability Evaluation Bureau employs disability evaluation specialists throughout the state who serve the offices of the Workers' Compensation Appeals Board. These disability evaluation specialists prepare formal permanent disability ratings in litigated cases and also, when requested by the employer or carrier and the injured employee, informal consultative evaluations. The I & A Bureau has responsibility for the Benefit Notice Program, which prepares a statistical analysis of such matters as promptness of payment of workers' compensation benefits. The Medical Bureau provides medical examinations of injured employees—either by staff physicians or by "independent medical examiners"—at the request of the judges and commissioners of the Workers' Compensation Appeals Board.

The Workers' Compensation Appeals Board is part of the Division of Industrial Accidents, but is independent of the administrative director of the Division in its judicial functions. The initial hearings in disputed cases are held in the 21 district offices of the Board. The appellate level of the Workers' Compensation Appeals Board is located in San Francisco. The Appeals Board consists of seven members, known as commissioners, of whom five must be attorneys. One member of the Appeals Board is appointed chairman by the governor.

Administrative Procedures. A worker who suffers a work-related injury is supposed to serve written notice on the employer within 30 days after the occurrence of the injury in order to maintain a claim for compensation (*Labor Code* Section 5400). However, a formal notice is not required from the employee when the employer has knowledge of the injury. In the normal case, the employer, or a foreman, or some other person in authority will be aware that the employee has been injured or has claimed an injury, and therefore the employee's obligation to provide written notice is not applicable (Swezey 1985, sec. 4.5).

The 30-day period for a notice has been held to start running only when the employee knows, or should know, that he has suffered an injury of industrial origin. In occupational disease and cumulative injury claims, the "date of injury" is that on which disability is first suffered and the employee had knowledge, or by the exercise of reasonable diligence should have had knowledge, that the disability was work-related (Swezey 1985, sec. 4.3).

Although an employer is not required to provide notice to state agencies of minor injuries to his employees, any injury that requires medical services other than ordinary first aid treatment or causes absence from work for a full day or beyond the shift of the day of the injury must be reported to the Division of Labor Statistics and Research. The first reports do not, however, become part of the records of litigated workers' compensation cases.

Physicians are also required to report instances of initial treatment—both medical-only and time-loss cases—to the insurer or self-insured employer. A copy of each report is then sent to the Division of Labor Statistics and Research.

In cases of work injuries that result in more than three days of lost time or that require hospitalization, the employer is required to submit a notice of commencement of benefits, or a notice explaining why benefits have not been paid, to the Division of Industrial Accidents under the Benefit Notice Program.

In the vast majority of cases involving a work injury that results in more than three days of lost time, requires hospitalization, or results in death, the employer accepts liability for cash benefits. The employer must file a First Notice of Work Injury with the Division of Labor Statistics and Research, and a notice of commencement (and subsequently a notice of termination) of benefits with the Benefit Notice Program in the Division of Industrial Accidents.

In disputed cases, a party files with the Board an application for adjudication, an original compromise and release agreement, or a stipulation with request for award. Each requires action by a workers' compensation judge.

Litigation normally is initiated with the filing of the application, usually by a worker or his representative, with the appropriate office of the Workers' Compensation Appeals Board. In the application, the party seeks a judicial determination of his rights under the law. The application is often filed before the case is ready to go to hearing. For example, an application may be filed for a worker who is severely injured shortly after the date of injury, requesting permanent disability benefits. (Often—in some years in more than 50 percent of the filings—the worker's application is the employer/insurer's first notice of injury.[1]) The determination of the extent of the disability cannot be made, however, until the injury is permanent and stationary, and therefore a hearing would be premature. An application for adjudication is not moved toward a hearing stage unless a form is also filed indicating that the case is ready to proceed to the hearing. A case may proceed to a hearing immediately after filing because a "declaration of readiness to proceed" is filed with the application, or the application may first be put on an inactive status and then moved to the hearing stage after a declaration of readiness.

After the parties are ready to proceed to a hearing, the Appeals Board usually holds some sort of pretrial conference to determine whether in fact a dispute exists, and, if so, whether the parties are ready to try the dispute or are willing to resolve it by voluntary agreement. If the parties do not resolve the issue voluntarily, the matter is set for a hearing before a workers' compensation judge. Although hearings do not adhere to all of the technical rules of evidence used in the court system, they nonetheless are formal and all parties are usually represented by attorneys.[2] The hearings usually rely on written medical reports, although the parties have a right to present medical evidence during the hearing and to cross-examine doctors who have filed written reports. Following the hearing, if the extent of permanent disability is an issue in the case, the workers' compensation judge may obtain a formal rating from the Disability Evaluation Bureau. The judge also may refer the case to an independent medical examiner (IME) or to an agreed medical examiner (AME), selected by the parties and approved by the judge; this examiner provides additional medical evidence to assist the judge in resolving conflicting evidence. The judge, after the hearing and after receipt of any additional medical evidence, issues a decision. Unless it is appealed by one of the parties, this decision is the final step in the case.

Formal cases that begin with an application for adjudication and result in a hearing and decision by a workers' compensation judge represent the clearest example of litigation. There are, however, other types of formal cases considered litigated because they involve a workers' compensation judge. For example, the parties may file an original compromise and release, which represents a complete agreement between the parties on all issues. The compromise and release, which releases the employer from any further liability in exchange for the benefits provided in the settlement, is normally approved by the workers' compensation judge without a hearing.

Another type of formal case, also counted as a litigated case, is one with stipulated findings and award. When an application has been filed and the parties feel that a hearing is not necessary to resolve the issues, a stipulated statement of facts may be filed, signed by all parties in interest, giving consent to the immediate issuance of an award. The Board then makes its findings and award based on the stipulation, or sets the matter for a hearing to take testimony, or conducts a further investigation into the matter (Swezey 1985, sec. 5.41). Ordinarily, stipulations are used when the parties agree on all or most facts, but disagree on the amount of permanent disability award, or prefer to avoid a contested hearing for reasons of economy or convenience.

Any party to a workers' compensation case may appeal the decision of a workers' compensation judge to the Workers' Compensation Appeals Board by filing a petition for reconsideration within 20 days of the issuance of award. When a party files a petition for reconsideration, the workers' compensation judge who issued the decision has 15 days in which to prepare a report and make a recommendation on the petition (Swezey 1985, sec. 10.37). After the judge has prepared the report, the file is forwarded to the Workers' Compensation Appeals Board, where it is assigned on an automatic-rotation basis to three members of the Appeals Board for consideration. The Appeals Board has 30 days from the date of the filing of the petition to act, although one 30-day extension is permitted. The three members of the Appeals Board may grant reconsideration and receive additional evidence, or grant reconsideration and issue an immediate decision based on the evidence in the case file, or deny reconsideration. The majority of petitions for reconsideration are denied at this stage. In addition, sometimes the Appeals Board grants reconsideration of a case but then upholds the decision made by the workers' compensation judge.

After the decision of the Workers' Compensation Appeals Board, the parties have 45 days to file a petition for review with an appropriate appellate court. These petitions for review have numbered about 600 annually in recent years, although there was a drop to 522 in 1985.[3] The court of appeals may grant the petition and set the matter for oral argument, which was done in 61 cases in 1985, or deny the petition without opinion. If the petition is granted, the awards are sometimes annulled.

The final step in the appellate procedure involves a petition for a hearing by the California Supreme Court, of which there were 153 in 1986. Petitions must be filed within 10 days after the opinion of the court of appeal becomes final, and are likely to be unsuccessful: only nine were granted in 1985.

Procedures for Permanent Disability Benefits—Voluntary Cases. Until the late 1960s, an employer could decide the appropriate amount of permanent partial disability benefits on the basis of medical evidence in its files, and the Division of Industrial Accidents (DIA) did not have to approve the amount of the payments or otherwise become involved in the case. This procedure was known as self-rating. The current procedure for voluntary cases requires that the Disability Evaluation Bureau of the Division of Industrial Accidents prepare an informal rating for every case. After the worker's injury becomes permanent and stationary, the employer sends him a Form 200, which asks the employee to describe the effect of the injury on his work. This form is returned to the employer, who submits it along with Form 201 (the employer or carrier request for an informal rating) and all medical evidence in the employer's file to the Disability Evaluation Bureau.

A disability evaluation specialist in the Bureau examines the forms and medical records and, if these are adequate, prepares a description of the disability and a rating of the extent of disability. If either party is dissatisfied with the rating, the Evaluation Bureau will reconsider the rating on request, or suggest that an application be filed for a hearing (Swezey 1985, sec. 16.43). If the informal rating is acceptable to both parties, the payment of compensation due under the rating is made directly to the employee.

Informal ratings are primarily used for minor injuries. Cases with serious injuries that began with informal ratings typically are later converted into litigated (or formal) cases. Even in informal cases, however, an attorney may be involved, and when this occurs, the informal rating is sent to a judge to "endorse" a reasonable attorney's fee (Swezey 1985, sec. 16.45).

Procedures for Permanent Disability Benefits—Litigated Cases. A litigated case begins with the filing of an application for adjudication (Form 1) by the claimant, which states the basis for the benefits claimed and the nature of the disagreement. When the claimant is ready to move forward on the case, a Declaration of Readiness to Proceed (Form 9) is filed.[4] A party can request a hearing on one of three calendars: conference pretrial, rating pretrial, or regular. The presiding workers' compensation judge in the Appeals Board office having jurisdiction over the case decides whether the case is ready to be placed on a calendar and, if so, on which calendar (Swezey 1985, secs. 6.17, 6.25).

The conference calendar is used for cases that the presiding workers' compensation judge does not believe should be directly sent to a hearing. In cases that are in a preliminary stage, the judge uses the conference to define the issue, to get an exchange of medical reports, or otherwise to move the case along. In cases in which the judge feels a resolution of the issues is imminent, the conference is used to try to reach an agreement. If that effort is unsuccessful, the case is sent to a regular hearing.

The rating pretrial calendar is often used when the extent of permanent disability is the primary issue. A disability evaluation specialist in the Disability Evaluation Bureau reviews the medical records and estimates the extent of disability. The rating (or often ratings, since the medical records obtained by both the employee and employer are rated) is prepared in advance by the disability evaluation specialist (Swezey 1985, sec. 6.6).

A number of outcomes of a conference pretrial hearing or a rating pretrial hearing are possible. The parties may reach a complete agreement and sign a compromise and release agreement (subject to the judge's approval), or they may reach a partial agreement and submit stipulated findings and a request for award to the judge for his resolution of remaining issues. If the parties do not reach an agreement, the case proceeds to regular hearing. A regular hearing may either follow a pretrial hearing or be the first hearing in the case. In either event the case is assigned to a workers' compensation judge, who assumes the roles of finder of fact and decider of legal issues.

The judge prepares a full description of the disability, basing the description on the medical evidence in the record and on the worker's testimony at the hearing. The judge's description of the disability is sent to the Disability Evaluation Bureau. A disability evaluation specialist prepares a rating of the disability and computes the number of weeks of disability payments, the weekly rate of compensation, and the total sum of payments due (Swezey 1985, secs. 16.50-16.55).

The disability evaluation specialist is required to make a recommendation solely on the information provided by the judge. The specialist can neither consider factors that are not included in the instructions nor disregard factors that are included. The recommendation is based on the specialist's independent judgment, the rating schedule, and published guidelines developed by the Evaluation Bureau (Swezey 1985, sec. 16.54).

The report of the disability evaluation specialist is evidence but not a conclusive finding of fact; therefore, it is not binding on the judge. The judge, however, will rarely disregard the percentage of disability recommended by the specialist. If the judge feels the rating is inappropriate, he may revise his instructions and ask the disability evaluation specialist to prepare a new rating for the case.

The specialist's report is returned to the judge and served on the parties. Any corrections or appeals of the rating must be pursued within seven days. If any party is dissatisfied with the recommended rating, several remedies are available.

When the dissatisfaction with the recommended rating stems from the judge's description of the factors of permanent disability in the instructions to the Evaluation Bureau, the dissatisfied party may do one of two things. He may write to the judge indicating his specific disagreements with the description and requesting that the matter be referred again to the disability evaluation specialist with amended instruction; or he may file a motion to strike the recommended rating, again indicating his specific disagreements with the judge's instructions. If the judge does not amend the instructions or approve the motion to strike, after a decision is issued in the case, it can be appealed by the dissatisfied party.

If the party is satisfied that the judge has properly described the factors of permanent disability, but dissatisfied with the percentage disability as calculated by the disability evaluation specialist, he then files a request to cross-examine the specialist and to submit rebuttal evidence. A party has a right to this cross-examination, but the subject matter of the cross-examination is carefully prescribed. The disability evaluation specialist may only be cross-examined about the procedure used to rate the factors included in the judge's description, and cannot be asked whether the judge's description is appropriate on the basis of the information in the medical records.

After receiving the rating from the Disability Evaluation Bureau and disposing of any objections to the rating, the judge issues findings and award. The written decision specifies the award and includes the reasons for the decision. This is the final determination of the case, unless one or both parties files a petition for reconsideration within 20 days, in which case the appellate procedure previously described becomes applicable.

Other Dispositions. The previous subsection discussed formal cases (cases in which a regular hearing is held). This section discusses two other types of dispositions that require involvement by a judge: stipulated findings and awards and compromise and release agreements. Use of a stipulated findings and award or a compromise and release agreement, either as the initial filing or as the resolution of a case that originated with an application for adjudication, accounts for the great bulk of the California formal cases.

The compromise and release agreement is used when the parties are in agreement about the disposition of the case. The parties complete a form that indicates the salient facts and the agreed settlement of the case. The form is submitted to the Workers' Compensation Appeals Board for approval. A judge reviews the proposed settlement and normally approves the parties' agreement. When the claimant is represented by an attorney (as is almost always the pattern in compromise and release cases), the judge is particularly likely to accept an agreement between the parties. Occasionally, the judge will use the Disability Evaluation Bureau to rate the permanent disability on the basis of medical evidence in the file.[5]

The consequences of a compromise and release agreement are twofold: The claimant receives his benefits in a lump sum, and the employer is released from any future liability for medical care and compensation for the work-related injury or disease. There are exceptions to that rule, but they are limited. Occasionally, the lump sum paid by the employer to terminate his liability is not immediately paid to the employee, but placed in a trust that pays the amount to the employee over an extended period. Also, occasionally a case is appealed or reopened after the compromise and release agreement is approved. The possibilities for reopening or appeal are for the most part limited, however, to situations involving fraud, duress, or mistakes of law or fact (Swezey 1985, secs. 13.52, 13.55).[6] As a practical matter, a compromise and release agreement reached by the parties is very likely to be found acceptable by the judge, and once it is approved by a judge it is very unlikely to be disturbed thereafter.

The stipulated findings and award is commonly used by the parties in one of two situations. The parties may be in complete agreement on the facts and issues, but may not want to terminate the possibility of future benefits. Thus, they may agree to the amount of temporary total and permanent disability benefits to be paid, and, in addition to stipulating those amounts, provide that future medical benefits will be paid as appropriate. The stipulated findings and award is also used when the parties agree on most issues and do not believe a regular hearing is necessary to resolve the remaining issues. For example, the parties may themselves resolve all issues except the extent of permanent disability, and agree that the judge should refer that issue to the Disability Evaluation Bureau for a rating. The judge will then issue a decision on the permanent disability issue based on the disability evaluation specialist's report.

The consequences of the stipulated findings and award are somewhat different from those of the compromise and release agreement. As with the compromise and release, the employee may receive his benefits in a lump sum or periodic payments. Unlike the compromise and release agreement, however, the stipulated findings and award does not preclude future benefits for the case. This is obviously the result in a stipulated findings and award that provides for future medical benefits. Less obvious, however, is that the stipulated findings and award (as well as the findings and award issued in a litigated case) is subject to reopening for additional cash benefits if the injury results in new and further disability within five years of the original injury.

Criteria for Permanent Disability Benefits in California

The California criteria are complex and their history is tangled; they are only summarized here.[7]

The California approach to determining the extent of disability is unique among American workers' compensation jurisdictions. For one thing, the California workers' compensation statute does not include a traditional schedule. Instead, the statute gives the administrative director of the Division of Industrial Accidents the authority to adopt a schedule for the determination of the percentage of permanent disabilities. The California schedule is also unusual because it considers factors other than the nature of the injury in determining the degree of disability. These factors, the procedure for adopting the schedule, and the significance of the schedule are included in statutory language that has been virtually unchanged since 1917, when the original statute effective in 1914 was amended to require consideration of the worker's diminished ability to compete in an open labor market when determining the percentage of permanent disability.[8]

> Section 4660. (a) In determining the percentages of permanent disability, account shall be taken of the nature of the physical injury or disfigurement, the occupation of the injured employee, and his age at the time of such injury, consideration being given to the diminished ability of such injured employee to compete in an open labor market.
>
> (b) The administrative director may prepare, adopt, and from time to time amend, a schedule for the determination of the percentage of permanent disabilities in accordance with this section. Such schedule shall be available for public inspection, and without formal introduction in evidence shall be *prima facie* evidence of the percentage of permanent disability to be attributed to each injury covered by the schedule.

The 1914 California schedule used a hypothetical "standard man" as a reference point for the occupational and age adjustments made to the standard rating of the injury. The standard occupation was a ditch digger. For the standard age, the 1910 census in California was used. After certain actuarial adjustments were made, the average worker was found to be 39 years old. Thus the standard man used in the 1914 schedule was a 39-year-old ditch digger (laborer).

The 1914 schedule contained 52 occupational classifications. The standard rating was increased or decreased depending on whether the physical demands for each occupation were relatively greater or less than those for the standard man for the part of the body involved. Similarly, if a worker were over 39, the disability rating was increased, and if under 39, the rating was decreased. Thus the 1914 schedule determined for each case a permanent disability rating based on the nature of the worker's injury, the particular occupation, and age at the time of injury.

The basic approach adopted in the 1914 schedule has remained largely intact to the present day. Minor amendments were made before World War II.[9] After World War II, because of concern that the schedule might have become outdated, an extensive review of the California permanent disability rating system and of alternative rating procedures was conducted and a report was submitted to the Industrial Accident Commission (the predecessor of the Workers' Compensation Appeals Board) in 1947. The 1950 revision that resulted did not disturb the basic concepts found in the 1914 schedule. The standard man, on whom the occupational adjustments are based, had been a laborer in the original schedule, but this specific occupation was abandoned in favor of a standard man who was in a generalized occupation, with average physical demands on all parts of the body. The age of 39 was retained for the standard man, as was the original plan of increasing the rating for older workers and decreasing it for younger workers, and there were some revisions in the standard ratings for injuries "in the light of analysis and Mr. Haggard's [superintendent of the Permanent Disability Rating Bureau] experience" (Welch 1964, p. 18).

The 1950 schedule is still in use. There have been some amendments, but the 1986 schedule is still essentially the 1950 schedule, which, in turn, is an obvious descendant of the 1914 schedule.

The current edition of the schedule, published by the administrative director in 1978, is 82 pages long. It is supplemented by a rule of the director (Sec. 9725) that the objective factors of disability be rated by methods described in a standard text (discussed below). The schedule also incorporates "work capacity guidelines" for the evaluation of troublesome injuries (such as back, heart, and pulmonary cases). Use of these various materials allows every injury and disease to be rated.

Each injury is given a standard rating based on the medical factors. For example, the loss of one leg at or above the ankle but below the knee receives a standard disability rating of 50 percent.[10] If the worker is a carpenter, his rating is increased to 62 percent because the schedule is based on the assumption that an amputation of the leg of a carpenter is more disabling than the same loss for an average worker. Standard ratings are increased for workers over 39 and decreased for workers under 39 on the assumption that older workers require more time to adjust to handicaps, or, if necessary, to find new employment. If the carpenter is 45 years old when injured, his rating is increased to 64 percent. The standard rating, modified by the occupational and age adjustments, is used to determine the amount of permanent disability benefits the carpenter receives.

Determination of the standard rating is often more difficult than the carpenter example suggests, in part because there are three sets of standards or criteria used to rate permanent disabilities in California: objective factors, subjective factors, and work-capacity guidelines (Swezey 1985, secs. 16.21-16.24).

Objective Factors. The measurement of objective factors is governed by Section 9725 of the Rules issued by the administrative director of the Division of Industrial Accidents.

> Section 9725. *Method of Measurement.* The method of measuring physical elements of a disability should follow the Report of the Joint Committee of the California Medical Association and Industrial Accident Commission, as contained in *Evaluation of Industrial Disability* edited by Packard Thurber, Second Edition, Oxford University Press, New York, 1960.

The Thurber volume resulted from an effort in 1940 to establish some uniformity in the measurement of impairments. It had become obvious by then that doctors were arriving at widely varying assessments of the extent of impairment for similar or identical injuries, resulting in widely varying standard disability ratings for identical or similar injuries.

A committee chaired by Dr. Packard Thurber, with representatives from the California Medical Association, the Industrial Accident Commission, and other agencies, prepared the guidelines for evaluation. The committee based its work on several principles: that the guidelines should be brief and not unduly complicated; that the evaluation procedures already used by the Industrial Accident Commission should be followed as much as possible; and that the relevant concept for determining restricted motion was the worker's remaining active (or functional) motion, not his passive motion.

The Thurber volume differs from the AMA *Guides to the Evaluation of Permanent Impairment* in several ways. The Thurber volume is confined to assessment of injuries to the musculoskeletal system, whereas the AMA Guides deal with all body systems, including the cardiovascular and digestive systems. For the musculoskeletal system, the Thurber approach is roughly the same as the AMA approach; they both concentrate on the objective manifestations of impairment, such as restricted motion or ankylosis.

Subjective Factors. The California permanent disability rating standards also consider subjective manifestations of impairment. These are known in California as "subjective factors" (Swezey 1985, sec. 16.23) and are explained in Section 9727 of the Rules issued by the administrative director of the Division of Industrial Accidents.

Section 9727. *Subjective Disability.* Subjective Disability should be identified by:
1. A description of the activity which produces disability.
2. The duration of the disability.
3. The activities which are precluded and those which can be performed with the disability.
4. The means necessary for relief.

The terms shown below are presumed to mean the following:
1. A *severe* pain would preclude the activity precipitating the pain.
2. A *moderate* pain could be tolerated, but would cause marked handicap in the performance of the activity precipitating the pain.
3. A *slight* pain could be tolerated, but would cause some handicap in the performance of the activity precipitating the pain.
4. A *minimal* (mild) pain would constitute an annoyance, but causing no handicap in the performance of the particular activity, would be considered as nonratable permanent disability.

The California *Schedule for Rating Permanent Disabilities* lists a number of injuries evaluated on the basis of subjective factors. The range of standard disability ratings for the injuries evaluated on this basis can be considerable: several injuries receive 20 percent ratings for "slight" disability and 100 percent for "severe" disability. Despite the language of Section 9727, the schedule does not confine consideration of the subjective factors to pain, nor are the only ratable categories "slight, moderate, and severe." Thus headaches receive a standard rating of

5 percent if slight; a 15 percent rating if moderate; 60 percent if severe; and 100 percent if pronounced. Neurosis adds the category "very slight," which receives a standard rating of 10 percent. Epilepsy contains the category "slight to moderate," which receives a standard rating of 50 percent. A "moderate" epilepsy receives a standard rating of 75 percent, and since a rating may be increased or decreased from the scheduled ratings when the degree of impairment so warrants, an epilepsy more serious than "slight to moderate" but less serious than "moderate" might be rated as a 60 percent or 65 percent disability.

There appears to be a potential for inconsistent ratings of similar injuries in this California schedule, especially when the disability evaluation specialist must rely on descriptions in the reports from doctors (or the instructions from the workers' compensation judges) that may not correspond, in an unambiguous fashion, to terms like "moderate" or "slight." The potential for inconsistency was probably greater prior to the development of the work-capacity guidelines described below. These guidelines are at least partial substitutes for the "minimal-slight-moderate-severe" approach for several important types of injuries such as back injuries.

Part of the impetus for the use of work-capacity guidelines in place of the subjective disability approach was a 1953 report of the California Senate Interim Committee. The report contains a section entitled "Incredible Inconsistencies in Rating Specialists' Computations."

> The claim by the rating specialists of the commission that ratings are consistent, one with another, is pure fiction. Called upon separately by us to rate a set of hypothetical cases, two specialists arrived at amazingly different rates. The test cases included twelve (12) disabilities of varying degrees of severity, each case to be rated for four (4) different occupations and all cases at age 39 years. For not one of these forty-eight (48) cases did the specialists arrive at the same rating. . . .
> For the forty-eight (48) cases, the average difference between ratings is 12.05 percent; the average difference in payment periods, 48 weeks; and in terms of cash benefits, the average difference between cases (at $30 per week) is $1,440. (1953, pp. 60-62)

The Senate Committee also selected 24 actual ratings from case files. These 24 cases were resubmitted to the same rating specialist who made the original computations. Three of the cases showed the same percentage on rerating as indicated on the original rating, but six reratings were higher than the original rating and eleven were lower. (The other four cases showed ranges on the original rating or the rerating, and all four cases involved some change between the original rating and the rerating.)

Although the Senate Committee did not confine its criticism to ratings involving subjective disability, it was obviously concerned about the subjective rating system,[11] and the committee's criticism was probably an important factor in the development of the work-capacity guidelines.

The subjective factors can be considered examples of subjective manifestations of impairment, as those terms were defined in chapter 1. They carry the California criteria for evaluating permanent disability beyond the factors considered by the AMA *Guides* or the factors covered in the Thurber volume. There is, however, no published guide to aid in the evaluation of the subjective factors other than the descriptions "severe," "moderate," "slight," and "minimal" contained in Section 9727 of the rules. Thus the Permanent Disability Rating Bureau's *Fundamentals for Applying the California Schedule for Rating Permanent Disabilities* (1967) contains rather detailed instructions for rating objective factors, but for subjective factors contains only general statements such as "if subjective factors were present, a percentage would be added to the rating for objective factors. The amount to be added would depend on the nature and effect of the subjective factors, consideration being given to scheduled ratings." The only other assistance to the rating of subjective factors is the verbatim reproduction of Section 9727 of the Rules defining pain.

Work-Capacity Guidelines. "In the 1950s, work-capacity guidelines were developed by the Rating Bureau to overcome a lack of uniformity and consistency in ratings" (Swezey 1985, sec. 16.24). As an example of the ratings problems the guidelines were designed to deal with, the discussion from Welch is instructive. "Initially the schedule provided only three ratings for the spine: slight (30%), moderate (50%), and severe (100%). It did not define these levels, and obviously all spinal disabilities could not be rated on only these three points. The guidelines were evolved to permit more precise ratings on spinal disabilities, and the definitions of work capacity were developed in relation to spinal disabilities only" (Welch 1973, sec. 15.17). The work-capacity guidelines since have been extended to other types of injuries, but their origin as a method to rate spinal disabilities is evident.

The Rating Bureau's work-capacity guidelines have eight levels, or "plateaus," of disability. Four of the plateaus are described below:

(a) *"Disability precluding very heavy lifting*—contemplates the individual has lost approximately one-quarter of his pre-injury capacity for lifting." This receives a standard rating of 10 percent. A note to this guideline elaborates: "A statement 'inability to lift 50 pounds' is not meaningful. The total lifting effort, including weight, distance, endurance, frequency, body position and similar factors should be considered with reference to the particular individual."

(e) *"Disability precluding heavy work*—contemplates the individual has lost approximately half of his pre-injury capacity for performing such activities as bending, stooping, lifting, pushing, pulling and climbing or other activities involving comparable physical effort." This receives a standard rating of 30 percent.

(g) *"Disability resulting in limitation to semi-sedentary work*—contemplates the individual can do work approximately one half the time in a sitting position, and approximately one half the time in a standing or walking position, with a minimum of demands for physical effort whether standing, walking or sitting." This receives a standard rating of 60 percent.

(h) *"Disability resulting in limitation to sedentary work*—contemplates that the individual can do work predominantly in a sitting position at a bench, desk or table with a minimum of demands for physical effort and with some degree of walking and standing being permitted." This receives a standard rating of 70 percent.

The predecessors to these current guidelines were used informally from the 1950s by the Disability Evaluation Bureau, first to rate spinal injuries, later to rate a few additional categories of injuries. The guidelines were formally incorporated into the *Schedule for Rating Permanent Disabilities* for injuries occurring on and after January 1, 1970, for chronic infections of the pulmonary tissues, heart disability, spinal disabilities, and abdominal weakness. Following an appellate court decision, the two most severe plateaus (g and h above) were added to the schedule as a basis for evaluating injuries to the lower extremities that occurred on or after January 1, 1973.

Several aspects of the work-capacity guidelines do not displace, but only supplement or complement, the subjective rating factors in the *Schedule for Rating Permanent Disabilities*. For example, the guideline for disability number 18 (neck, spine, or pelvis) provides alternative methods to obtain a standard rating of 10 percent: either a work-capacity rating of "disability precluding very heavy lifting" or a subjective factor rating of "constant slight pain." Moreover, disability number 18.1 (impaired function of the neck, spine, or pelvis) has a standard rating of 100 percent for a subjective factor rating of severe, "and this rating can be given even though the maximum plateau in the work-capacity guidelines is a 70 percent standard rating."

Second, aside from the use of the subjective factors as an alternative to the work-capacity guidelines, the guidelines themselves can be approached in two ways: in terms of the work restrictions named by the plateau designations (e.g., *disability precluding heavy work*) or in terms of the activities that the worker can still do after the injury or can no longer do because of the injury ("contemplates the individual has lost approximately half of his pre-injury capacity for performing such activities as bending, stooping, lifting, ...").

Finally, what is being evaluated by the work-capacity guidelines? Using the terminology of chapter 1, we consider the "objective factors" in California to be objective manifestations of impairment. The work-capacity guidelines are not so easy to classify. Certain of the guidelines' descriptions of the precluded activity correspond to functional limitations, that is, limitations in generalized (or nonwork-specific) activities such as walking, climbing, and bending. However, most of the plateau designations (for example, *disability resulting in limitation to semi-sedentary work*) and some of the guidelines' descriptions (for example, the descriptions of plateaus g and h quoted above) correspond to work disability. Thus the quest for more consistency in evaluating injuries as a result of the criticism of the use of subjective factors had led to more categories (eight plateaus in place of the three levels of subjective disability included in Section 9727 of the Rules) and the use of criteria that consider the consequences of injury further downstream in the injury-impairment-functional limitation-disability sequence shown in chart 1.2.

Final Elaborations. A few additional elaborations on the rating of permanent disabilities are needed. First, it should be stressed that "objective factors," "subjective factors," and "work-capacity guidelines" are not mutually exclusive categories. Rather it is quite common for an injury to have rating factors from more than one category, such as an injury to the wrist that causes restriction of motion and loss of grip. (See Swezey 1985, sec. 16.30, for such an example.)

Second, the discussion of the use of the schedule indicated some opportunities for the exercise of discretion in the rating of injuries. To a much more limited extent, a disability evaluation specialist has some discretion in the choice of the occupation to be used in adjusting the standard rating. This opportunity is more likely to arise if the worker has an occupation that does not fall on the list of occupations included in the *Schedule for Rating Permanent Disabilities.* The specialist can then turn for guidance to the "Outline of Occupational Groupings," a 16-page document published by the Division of Industrial Accidents but not a part of the schedule.

Preliminary Observations on the Criteria for Permanent Disability Benefits in California

Several observations can be made about the criteria for permanent disability benefits in California. One is that it has been some time since the schedule has been carefully reviewed to determine if it provides a meaningful guide to the evaluation of permanent disabilities. The last thorough review took place in the 1940s, and culminated in a schedule that celebrated its 35th anniversary in 1985. The schedule has had some revisions since 1950, including changes in the occupational adjustments in the 1960s and the introduction of the work-capacity guidelines in the 1970s. Nonetheless, the basic approach and most age and occupational adjustments have not been carefully scrutinized recently.[12] In light of such significant labor force developments in the last 30 plus years as the reduction in retirement age, the increasing participation of women in the labor force, and the shift from blue-collar to white-collar jobs, many of the age and occupational adjustment factors may be obsolete. Indeed, the starting point for the age and occupational adjustments—a 39-year-old worker with average physical demands on all parts of the body—may no longer be appropriate.

Another observation is that the California rating system for permanent disabilities is complex and difficult to learn. The same injury may be rated on more than one factor (for example, an injury to the wrist may have objective and subjective factors). Moreover, a worker may have multiple injuries, and there are rules for combining the ratings of injuries to the same extremities (see Swezey 1985, sec. 16.34) and of injuries to different parts of the body (see Swezey 1985, sec. 16.35). The rules are designed to avoid "pyramiding"—straight addition of the ratings for multiple injuries to an extremity, which could result in a permanent disability rating in excess of the rating for the amputation of the member even when the extremity maintains substantial function.

There are also special rules to deal with overlapping. "One disability is said to 'overlap' another when it does not reduce the employee's ability to compete in an open labor market beyond the limitation that resulted from the other disability. If the disabilities do not completely overlap, then additional compensation is payable to the extent that the second disability further restricts his ability to compete" (Swezey 1985, sec. 16.40).

Another set of rules is used for apportionment. Apportionment is used when a worker with a preexisting disability experiences a work-related injury or disease; California permanent disability benefits are paid only for the increased extent of disability due to the new injury or disease. (See Swezey 1985, secs. 16.38-16.39.)

Given these complexities, it is no surprise that considerable time and effort must be invested in order to learn the rating system. Disability evaluation specialists in the Disability Evaluation Bureau are given six months of training and need still more time to master the intricacies of the system. Representatives of all the interest groups interviewed in California for this project (including workers' compensation judges, Workers' Compensation Appeals Board commissioners, plaintiffs' attorneys, defense attorneys, and employers) expressed doubts about whether the other parties in the system really understood the intricacies of the rating system. Most admitted they themselves did not understand all the details of the system.[13]

Another observation on the California criteria for rating of permanent disabilities is that the rating procedure is not mechanical, but leaves considerable room for the exercise of discretion with no objective criteria. The greatest potential for discretionary handling is in deciding what factors are to be rated. For example, in a case with conflicting medical evidence and testimony about the extent of an injury to the spine, someone must decide whether the evidence supports a conclusion that the pain is "constant slight to moderate" or "constant moderate." That decision is worth 20 percentage points on a standard rating and (depending on the worker's age and occupation) about 120 weeks of benefits. The work-capacity guidelines, introduced to overcome a lack of consistency in rating such injuries, may provide some assistance to the person who must evaluate the conflicting evidence. Still, the difference between standard ratings of 30 percent and 50 percent reduces to a decision whether the injury results in limitations to "light work" or to "semi-sedentary work." The workers' compensation judge, faced with a typical file in a soft tissue back injury case, replete with conflicting and ambiguous medical evidence and with a record of a hearing with testimony that is less than totally persuasive, not only *can* exercise his discretion to decide whether the disability is to be described by factors that rate at 30 percent or 50 percent (or even a higher or lower figure), he *must* exercise that discretion.[14]

Although the exercise of discretion is most obvious in the decision about which factors are to be rated, other kinds of discretion are also possible in applying the schedule. The rules for rating multiple injuries, or subjective factors, for example, are not mechanical. Moreover, most injuries are not precisely on the schedule, and the disability evaluation specialist must exercise his discretion in rating these injuries or diseases.[15]

Another observation concerns the difference between the California schedule and the American Medical Association's *Guides to the Evaluation of Permanent Impairment.* The AMA *Guides* are concerned primarily with objective manifestations of impairment, but the California schedule considers subjective manifestations of impairment (the "subjective factors") and functional limitations and work disabilities (the "work-capacity guidelines"). In this sense, the California criteria for rating permanent disabilities are much more extensive than those of the AMA *Guides.* However, the AMA *Guides* are at least as broad, if not broader, in terms of the number of body systems covered. The objective factors in California are largely confined to the musculoskeletal system; coverage of body systems other than the musculoskeletal system is often cursory or incomplete, compared to the AMA *Guides.*[16] The *Guides,* for example, devote chapters to the digestive system and the reproductive and urinary systems; those systems are not even covered by the California schedule. In practice, injuries or diseases that affect these body systems may be compensable in California as nonscheduled disabilities. But the *Schedule for Rating Permanent Disabilities* by itself is a limited guide to the evaluation of permanent impairment compared with the AMA version.

The Lessons from California

California provides a unique answer to the question of what criteria should be used to provide permanent partial disability benefits. The conventional distinction between scheduled and nonscheduled injuries has never been used in California. Instead, all injuries are evaluated by use of a comprehensive schedule that purports to measure the loss of earning capacity by a formula, that incorporates information on the nature and severity of the injury plus the worker's age and occupation.

The use of a formula approach to determine the extent of loss of earning capacity might be expected to reduce the extent of litigation and to keep costs of permanent disability benefits under control. The lower costs should result because there appears to be less room to exercise discretion and bend the rules in a way to help an especially deserving worker when the benefits are calculated using an "objective" formula. The control of permanent disability benefit costs seems especially likely in California, since the maximum weekly permanent partial disability benefit was only $70 from 1972 to 1982, was $130 until the end of 1983, and then reached its current level of $140 in January 1984. Not only might permanent disability benefits be expected to be relatively inexpensive, but the cost of the entire program could be expected to be low because of the generally meager cash benefits. The maximum weekly benefit of $224 for total disability that has been in effect since 1984 represents only 62 percent of the state's average weekly wage.

The record in California largely contradicts these expectations. Almost all permanent partial disability cases involve litigation, in the sense of lawyers being used to help determine the amount of benefits. The legal assistance does not come cheap: a survey of carriers indicated that the total cost of litigating a claim in California was $3521 per case in 1984, which amounted to 43 percent of the $8137 average payment in disputed cases that year. These litigation expenses included attorneys' fees for both parties, the cost of forensic medical reports or testimony, and related costs, such as depositions. The study provided a "rough estimate" that "litigation in California's no-fault workers' compensation system is—conservatively—a $600 million-plus annual industry."[17] Although not all of these cases involve permanent partial disabilities, such claims are the most common since 59 percent of the litigated cases involved the application of the work capacity guidelines to back, heart, and psychiatric injuries.

Another dashed expectation is that California has contained the costs of permanent partial cases. Despite a relatively low share of all costs accounted for by permanent total cases (table 3.14), the high costs of permanent partial cases in 1982 made the California share of all costs accounted for by permanent disability cases the highest among the eight states with comparable data that we are intensively examining (table 3.17 and graph 3.1). California has been edged from this top position among the eight jurisdictions only once since 1958 (table 3.17). Moreover, as of 1982, all permanent disability cases (including permanent total, major permanent partial, and minor permanent partial) accounted for 82.11 percent of all cash benefits in California, a figure exceeded only in Rhode Island (84.21); below this odd couple were 43 jurisdictions (table 3.5).

The expectation of low costs of workers' compensation for employers is also contradicted by the data. From 1958 to 1984, the costs of workers' compensation insurance in California have consistently been above the national average; in the latter year, California ranked first among the 10 jurisdictions we are examining, with insurance costs more than 40 percent above the national average (table 3.18).

With all this litigation, a high share of benefits going to permanent disability cases, and substantial workers' compensation insurance costs, one would at least expect the benefits to be adequate and equitable for workers who are permanently disabled. However, this expectation is also contradicted by the results from our "wage-loss study" and by a recent study by the California Workers' Compensation Institute, discussed in chapters 10 and 11, respectively.

What explains these results, such as the extensive litigation and the high cost of permanent partial disability benefits in California? One factor may be the litigious environment that characterizes the state, especially the Los Angeles area: workers' compensation is only one example of the pervasive reliance on the law suit to solve disputes. This tendency is reinforced by the passive nature of the workers' compensation agency. As noted by Tebb (1986, p. 46), traditionally most of the agency resources have been devoted to providing the parties a forum to resolve their disputes, rather than administering a system that has as its *raison d'etre* the prevention of disputes. The total budget of the agency is only $37 million (table 4.1), only about 6 percent of the estimated $600 million cost for litigation. Moreover, most of the budget pays for the administrative law judge teams located throughout the state (Tebb 1986, p. 46), rather than the record keeping, monitoring, and evaluation functions central to an active workers' compensation agency. California is the very model of myopic efficiency described in chapter 2.

Still another explanation of California's record is that the "objective" formula used to determine the amount of permanent partial disability benefits is not all that objective. As this chapter has documented, there is considerable room for the exercise of discretion in application of the schedule. Where money is at stake in the exercise of discretion, there shall ye find lawyers.

The procedures and criteria for permanent disability benefits are not the only factors that explain the high costs of workers' compensation insurance in California. Vocational rehabilitation expenses increased 228 percent over the most recent five-year period with available data, and exceeded $115 million in 1983.[18] Medical benefits were estimated to account for 28.8 percent of net premiums in 1986, and their cost "has increased significantly and steadily since 1970" (California Study Committee Staff *Report* [hereafter CSCS *Report*], 1986, pp. 20-21). But even though these other factors are significant, permanent disability benefits are a major source of concern in California and have been a central part of recent reform efforts.

The most recent significant change in the California workers' compensation program occurred in 1982, when the maximum weekly benefit for permanent partial disability was increased from $70 to $140. This change and others were estimated to increase costs to employers by nearly $1 billion and may represent "the largest benefit increase in the history of workers' compensation" (Tebb 1986, p. 47). Nonetheless, with minor exceptions, "the 1982 amendments did little to make the California compensation program more equitable, effective, or efficient" (Tebb 1986, p. 45). The central features of the 1982 amendments were a buttressing of the exclusive remedy doctrine to protect employers from tort suits; in exchange, benefits were increased, with 90 percent of the new benefit dollars allocated to permanent partial disability, "leaving maximum weekly benefits for total disability, both temporary and permanent, woefully inadequate. . . . The 1982 benefit increases magnify the maldistribution of California workers' compensation benefits" (Tebb 1986, p. 47).

The concern over maldistribution of benefits and the high costs of the program led the Division of Industrial Accidents in early 1985 to propose a wage-replacement approach in place of the present criteria for permanent partial disability benefits (13 *CWCR* 57, April 1985). By September of 1985, the wage-replacement approach (nee the wage-loss approach discussed in chapters 8 and 9) was incorporated into a proposal sponsored by the Californians for Compensation Reforms (CCR), a coalition of employers and carriers. But there were outspoken objections to the CCR proposal, and the bill died in an assembly committee in January 1986 (14 *CWCR* 1, Feb. 1986).

The next month (February 1986), a significant examination of workers' compensation was issued as a staff report by the Joint Study Committee on Workers' Compensation (*CSCS* Report 1986).[19] The report examined the cost of workers' compensation in California, as well as the extent of litigation, the history of permanent disability benefits, and the current criteria and procedures for permanent disability benefits. The present approach was criticized in many respects, and issues and recommendations for reform were presented using the framework included in chapter 10 of this study.[20] Compensation for both work disability and nonwork disability ("personal loss") was endorsed in principle, which led to a recommendation for a dual system of permanent benefits. Operationally, the *Report* (p. 78) recommended that "work disability should be compensated directly by providing benefits when there are actual wage losses," while the separate benefit for the other consequences "should be based on the nature and extent of the permanent impairment or limitations."

The CSCS *Report* was criticized by some, including the California Applicants' Attorneys Association (14 *CWCR* 167, July 1986), but served as an input to a bill introduced by State Senator Bill Greene, chairman of the Senate Committee on Industrial Relations in Summer 1986. The Greene proposal (SB 1617) did not substitute wage-loss benefits for the current permanent partial disability benefits, but provided a "supplemental PD benefit" for seriously injured workers who experience actual wage loss after their benefits expire (14 *CWCR* 143, June 1986). This is a variant of the hybrid benefits found in New York (discussed in chapter 8 and endorsed in chapter 12). SB 1617 died in the Senate Committee on Industrial Relations in August 1986, but is expected to be the basis for a new legislative proposal in 1987.

District of Columbia

The principal employer in the District of Columbia is, of course, the federal government, whose employees are covered by the Federal Employees' Compensation Act. Until 1982, the private sector employees in the District were covered by the Longshoremen's and Harbor Workers' Compensation Act, a federal statute that remains in effect for employees throughout the nation who are engaged in longshoring and related activities, or who are working on the outer continental shelf or certain defense bases. The council of the District of Columbia, under the home rule provisions granted to the District by Congress, passed the "District of Columbia Workers' Compensation Act of 1979" (Act 3-88) to replace the Longshoremen's Act for private sector employees in the District and the District government's own employees. Although the District of Columbia Act was passed on May 14, 1980, because of court challenges it did not become effective until July 26, 1982.

We will examine some of the factors that led to the enactment of the District's new law, and note some of the differences between it and the Longshoremen's Act. We also provide a brief review of some of the initial consequences of the new law.

The Dynamics of Change

Some of the factors that explain the emergence of the new law in the District of Columbia are beyond the scope of this study—for example, the residents' increasing interest in self-governance and Congress's increased willingness to cede some of its traditional control over the capital. But some of the factors are internal to the workers' compensation program itself, and deserve a brief examination.

One part of the story concerns the surging importance of permanent disability benefits, and especially major permanent partial disability benefits, after 1968. In that year, major permanent partial cases accounted for only 3.43 percent of all cases in the District, less than the national average share of 4.38 percent. Then for 20 years, the jurisdiction's major permanent partial cases billowed, so that by 1978 they accounted for 13.75 percent of all cases in the District—a share that was more than 2 1/2 times the national average share of 5.14 percent for these cases. (All data from table 3.7.)

Superimposed on this explosion in the number of major permanent partial disability cases was an equally dramatic change in benefit levels. As previously noted, until 1982 the District of Columbia was covered by the provisions of the Longshoremen's and Harbor Workers' Act. In 1972, as a result of an agreement among various parties in the maritime industry, the benefits under the Longshoremen's Act were substantially increased in exchange for limits on employers' liability from suits outside the workers' compensation law. The private sector employers in the District of Columbia were "beneficiaries" of the reform agreement, even though the problem of suits outside the workers' compensation law did not involve them. As an example of the benefit increases that resulted from the 1972 legislative package, the maximum weekly benefits for total and partial disability in the District of Columbia went from $70.00 in January 1972 to $167.00 a year later and to $318.38 by 1976. Because the maximums automatically increase as wages increase, the weekly maximums reached $426.40 by 1980.

The higher maximums translated into higher average costs for permanent disability cases in the District. In 1968, before the increase in maximums resulting from the 1972 legislation, major permanent partial cases cost an average $11,987, about 20 percent above the national average. By 1973 the average for major cases was $17,242, some 30 percent above the national average. By 1978 the District average of $38,266 for major permanent partial cases was 78 percent above the national average (table 3.11). Because, as noted above, major permanent partial cases were becoming numerically more prevalent during the 1968 to 1978 period in the District, the average costs for all permanent disability cases spiraled. In 1968, the average cost of all permanent disability cases in the District was $4,707, some 39 percent above the national average; by 1973, the average of $10,711 in the District was more than twice the national average of $4,599; by 1978, the District average was more than three times the national average—$24,933 vs. $8,178 (table 3.13).

Two consequences of these developments concerning the numbers and average costs of permanent disability cases are worth noting. By 1978, permanent disability costs accounted for 81.73 percent of all cash benefits in the District of Columbia, a figure exceeded only by Alaska. Not only did permanent disability benefits account for a goodly share of the pie, the pie had grown through time. One measure of the cost of the workers' compensation program in the District of Columbia is the percentage of payroll devoted to workers' compensation insurance premiums by a representative sample of employers. In 1972 the premiums for District of Columbia employers were 0.737 percent. By 1978, the U.S. average cost of workers' compensation insurance was 1.420 percent, but District of Columbia employers were paying 3.502 percent of payroll for premiums, the highest rate in the nation (table 3.18).

The pressures for change that arose from these developments led the District of Columbia to enact its own workers' compensation law.

Comparisons of the Old and New Laws

Maximum Benefit Levels. The Longshoremen's Act provides a maximum weekly benefit rate fixed at 200 percent of the national average weekly wage. As of 1980, the maximum amounted to $426.40 per week; the 1986 maximum under the Longshoremen's Act is $595.24. The new District of Columbia Act reduces that maximum to 100 percent of the average weekly wage of insured employees in the District, which made the maximum $431.70 in 1986. That maximum applies to all benefits for disability and death, including permanent partial disability.

Scheduled Permanent Partial Benefits. Scheduled benefits under both statutes are essentially the same. Both include a basic schedule listing the extremities and sensory organs. For the most part the number of weeks of benefits is the same under the two laws. The weekly benefit is 66 2/3 percent of the worker's preinjury wage under both laws.

The new D.C. Act does tighten the hearing loss provisions. Employees must wait for a period of at least six months after they leave the work environment before loss of hearing can be tested if the claim results from nontraumatic causes in that environment. The employee is not prevented from filing for temporary partial benefits during that waiting period, however.

In the disfigurement section, both the D.C. and Longshoremen's Acts limit claims to $3,500 "for serious disfigurement of the face, neck or other normally exposed bodily areas," but the Longshoremen's Act and not the D.C. Act adds the modifying phrase "likely to handicap the employee in securing or maintaining employment."

Nonscheduled Benefits. The Longshoremen's Act tracks the language of New York State's statute almost exactly in nonscheduled benefits denominated as "other cases" (Sec. 8[c][21] of the Longshoremen's Act and Sec. 15[w] in the N.Y. Act):

> In all other cases in this class of disability, the compensation shall be sixty six and two-thirds per centum of the difference between his average weekly wages and his wage-earning capacity, thereafter in the same employment or otherwise, payable during the continuance of such partial disability, but subject to reconsideration of the degree of such impairment by the [board] [deputy commissioner] or [its] [his] motion or upon application of any party in interest.

As the law was interpreted in the District under the Longshoremen's Act, the test administered in nonscheduled permanent partial cases was that of impairment of wage-earning capacity. In theory, the extent of impairment of wage-earning capacity depended first on the physician's evaluation of the impairment, and second on the worker's wage after the injury as compared to his wage before. At the time of our field work, however, we observed that the physicians were the primary evaluators of impairment and that in many cases their ratings appeared to be the only information considered in closing the case. The physicians operated without any evaluation guidance from the deputy commissioner either through published works or through any other means. Although the practice at the informal level did not require evidence of actual wage loss, the decisions at the appeal levels held that reemployment of a worker at prior wages would preclude an award on the nonscheduled basis (*Kendal v. Bethlehem* [12 BRBS 150]) unless there was some reason to believe that the wages actually received were not what he could earn in the open labor market (*Silverstein v. Service Printing Company, Inc.* [2 BRBS 143]).

The new District Act charges the statutory provision for nonscheduled cases, presumably eliminating any doubts about its meaning. It does not use the term "earning capacity" but speaks instead of "wage loss." D.C. Code 36-508 Section 9 (a)(22), still denominated as the "other cases," provides:

> In this class of disability the compensation shall be sixty-six and two-thirds (66 2/3) percent of the employee's *wage loss,* payable during the continuance of such disability. Wage loss shall be the difference between the employee's average weekly wage before becoming disabled and the employee's actual wage after becoming disabled. If the employee voluntarily limits his income or fails to accept employment commensurate with his abilities, then his wages after becoming disabled shall be deemed to be the amount he would earn if he did not voluntarily limit his income or did accept employment commensurate with his abilities. [emphasis added]

Certainly, the intent of the statute is to provide an actual wage-loss test, which inevitably must test whether the postinjury wages are those a normally motivated worker might reasonably earn in the open competitive labor market. If this intent is carried out in practice, the District of Columbia will have to be reclassified as a category III jurisdiction.

Given the extensive schedule, it is likely that most permanent partial cases will be decided on the scheduled basis. At the time of our field study we could not locate any comprehensive statistics, but found a study made by Popkin (1975) of a sample of 811 cases handled by Administrative Law Judges over a three-month period. Of these, 491 involved a permanent disability issue. Four hundred and thirty-two of these, or 88 percent, were scheduled cases, and 45, or 9 percent, were nonscheduled cases. The remaining 3 percent could not be classified. Popkin concluded that most of the cases were decided on the scheduled basis if it was at all possible because resolution of these cases did not require proof of loss of wage-earning capacity. Since the new D.C. Act contemplates a sterner test of wage loss for nonscheduled cases, it is likely that the majority of cases will still be decided on the scheduled basis. Under the old law, as will probably be the practice under the new, the cases decided on the nonscheduled basis tended to be more serious and hence more costly. Benefits under the nonscheduled category can continue for life or for as long as the decrease in wage-earning capacity or wage loss remains.

Temporary Partial Benefits. Temporary partial disability benefits are paid when an injured worker returns to work before his medical condition has fully stabilized, and his wages are lower than prior to the injury. The Longshoremen's Act uses the same language relating to wage-earning capacity in its provision for temporary partial benefits as it does in its provision for the nonscheduled cases. The new D.C. Act also has a temporary partial benefit provision, which makes the same change as for nonscheduled injuries and thus speaks of wage loss and not loss of wage-earning capacity. Under both laws, the benefits are limited to a period of five years.

Lump-Sum Payments. Our finding at the time of the field work investigations was that lump-sum payments were not encouraged in the District under the Longshoremen's Act. Official settlements acted as a release under the Longshoremen's Act Sec. 8 (i)(A) if approved by the deputy commissioner. Apparently informal settlements were reached that did not come before the deputy commissioner, since the workers merely withdrew their claims.

A provision of the new D.C. Code (36-508 Sec. 9[h]) makes it clear that "such settlements are to be complete and final dispositions of a case and once approved require no further action by the mayor."

Permanent Total Disability. The Longshoremen's Act provided a presumption of permanent and total disability in the event of the loss of two major members. Also, "In all other cases permanent total disability shall be determined in accordance with the facts" (Sec. 8 [a]).

The new D.C. Act, in keeping with its attempt to foster a wage-loss orientation, provides for the same presumptions in regard to the loss of major members, but then goes on to state: "In all other cases permanent total disability shall be determined only if, as a result of the injury, the employee is unable to earn any wages in the same or other employment" (Sec. 9 [a]).

Administration. Under the old act, the District of Columbia was one of the geographical districts under the U.S. Department of Labor's unit that administered the Longshoremen's Act; a deputy commissioner and his or her assistant supervised the processing of claims. Claims examiners monitored claims and conducted some of the informal conferences. Contested claims were heard by the deputy commissioner and decisions could be appealed to an administrative law judge. Further appeals were to the Benefits Review Board established under the Longshoremen's Act and from there to the Circuit Court of Appeals.

The new act is to be administered by the mayor, who is empowered to make the necessary rules and regulations. The statute contemplates a direct payment system (Sec. 16 [a]) with the first installment due 14 days after the employer has received notice of injury. Penalties are provided in the event payment is not made promptly. The administrator is empowered in all cases, controverted and noncontroverted, to investigate, cause medical examinations to be made, hold hearings, and take any further action to properly protect the rights of all parties (Sec. 16[h]).

A system of hearings within the agency is provided for (Secs. 21 and 26), as is a system for review (Sec. 23). Any party adversely affected by a final decision may petition for a review of the decision by the District of Columbia Court of Appeals.

Initial Impact of the New Law

The new law did not become effective until July 26, 1982, and so little data are available to assess its impact. The 1982 data on the numbers and costs of permanent disability cases contained in chapter 3 cover a policy period that ran from February 1982 to January 1983, and so include about half a year of experience under the new law. The 1982 data show a drop from 1978 in the share of all costs accounted for by major permanent partial cases (from 193 percent to 154 percent of the national average share; table 3.15) and in the share of all costs accounted for by all permanent disability cases (from 121 to 113 percent of the national average share; table 3.16). The drop in the latter statistic moved the District from first to third place among the eight jurisdictions with comparable data that we are examining.

Even more dramatic evidence of the apparent impact of the new law is reflected in the data on the employers' costs of workers' compensation insurance shown in table 3.18. In 1978, District employers were expending 3.502 percent of payroll on insurance, a figure that was 247 percent of the national average. By 1984, these employers were spending 1.909 percent of payroll on insurance, only about 40 percent above the national average.

To the extent the purpose of the new workers' compensation law in the District of Columbia was to lower the employers' costs of the program, it must be judged a resounding success. The primary cause probably was the lowering of the maximum weekly benefits compared to the levels in the Longshoremen's Act; but the shift to new criteria for nonscheduled permanent partial disability benefits may also be a significant factor, since this would help explain the decline between 1978 and 1982 in the proportions of all cases accounted for by permanent partial disability cases (tables 3.7 and 3.8).

Wisconsin

The Wisconsin workers' compensation law was enacted in 1911 and was "the first law to become and remain effective."[21] The Wisconsin program is not only the oldest, but it is generally regarded as one of the best, particularly in terms of quality of administration. Nonetheless, Wisconsin criteria and procedures for permanent disability benefits are not without problems, as evidenced by the recent establishment of a Study Commission to examine *inter alia* permanent partial disability.

Criteria for Permanent Disability Benefits

The original Wisconsin law of 1911 based compensation on the loss of wages, but by the next year the Industrial Commission called for a restructuring:[22]

Compensation under the Wisconsin law is based on loss of wage. Theoretically this is the correct principle, but in order to secure a simpler administration, it may be well to adopt the New Jersey plan for certain definable injuries. For instance, the New Jersey law provides as compensation for the loss of a great toe, 50 percent of the daily wage during thirty weeks; for the loss of an eye, 50 percent of the daily wage during 100 weeks, and so on through a complete list of definite injuries. This provision makes it easy for the employee and employer definitely to ascertain the compensation without reference to the administering board. We suggest that both employers and employees consider this matter with the view of possible amendment to our law.

The Wisconsin law was amended in 1913 to provide the approach found in most states: first, a statutory schedule of injuries constituting permanent partial disability; second, a provision for nonscheduled permanent partial injuries; and third, a provision for permanent total disability. Although the statute has been amended since 1913, the three-way division of permanent disabilities is still found in the current act.

The schedule (Secs. 102.52 to 102.56), with some 43 entries, is more detailed than most. The list is lengthy because there are multiple entries for each of the fingers and toes, indicating the exact number of weeks of compensation to be paid for a loss at the specified joints.

For the "loss of use cases," the statute (Sec. 102.55[3]) provides:

For all other injuries to the members of the body or its faculties which are specified in this schedule resulting in permanent disability, though the member be not actually severed or the faculty totally lost, compensation shall bear such relation to that named in this schedule as disabilities bear to the disabilities named in this schedule.

For injuries that cannot be scheduled, the statute (Sec. 102.44[3]) provides that "the aggregate number of weeks of indemnity shall bear such relationship to 1000 weeks as the nature of the injury bears to one causing permanent total disability." And for permanent total disability, the statute provides:

Total impairment for industrial use of both eyes, or the loss of both arms at or near the shoulder or of both legs at or near the hip, or of one arm at the shoulder and one leg at the hip, constitutes permanent total disability. This enumeration is not exclusive, but in other cases the department shall find the facts. (Sec. 102.44[2])

The potential durations and weekly benefit amounts vary considerably among the three types of permanent disability benefits. As of 1986, permanent total disability benefits were 66 2/3 percent of the worker's preinjury wage, subject to a maximum weekly benefit of $329; the benefits were payable for life. Scheduled permanent partial disability benefits were 66 2/3 percent of the state's average weekly wage, subject to a maximum weekly benefit of $112, which was the fifth lowest in the country. Thus, even though the scheduled duration of 500 weeks for loss of an arm was the longest in the country, the maximum amount of benefits for loss of an arm in Wisconsin ($56,000) was less than in six other jurisdictions in our 10-state study (table 5.3). The same disparity between low weekly amount and long potential duration of benefits is also found for Wisconsin nonscheduled permanent partial disability benefits: the weekly benefit of 66 2/3 percent of preinjury wages was subject to a maximum of $112, while the potential duration of 1000 weeks was exceeded only by nine jurisdictions in the U.S.[23]

Basis for Nonscheduled Permanent Partial Awards. The statutory language for nonscheduled permanent partial disability (quoted above) is subject to various interpretations. Until the 1970s, the Workers' Compensation Division primarily relied on evaluations of impairment—the medical consequences of the work injury—to determine the number of weeks of benefits, even though decisions of the Wisconsin Supreme Court since 1947 had at least implicitly endorsed the notion that ratings for nonscheduled permanent partial disability should be based on loss of earning capacity.[24]

The movement towards the loss of earning capacity approach received substantial impetus from the court's 1968 holding in *Kurschner v. ILHR Department*, 40 Wis. 2d 10. The court held that a nonscheduled injury should be evaluated in comparison with permanent total disability for industrial purposes. It based its reasoning on the statutory provision for permanent total disability that speaks of "total impairment for industrial use," and the provision for nonscheduled injuries under which the number of weeks of benefits paid bears the same relationship to

1,000 weeks "as the nature of the injury bears to one causing permanent total disability." Thus, nonscheduled permanent partial injuries,
the court concluded (at 18), "are to be compared medically with injuries that would render a person permanently totally disabled for industrial purposes . . . and *not* to injuries that would totally disable a
person functionally without regard to loss of earning capacity."

Despite this 1968 decision supporting the evaluation of loss of earning capacity as the basis for nonscheduled permanent partial disability
awards, the operational basis for benefits remained the evaluation of
the extent of impairment or functional limitations. Only the terminology
was changed to bring practice into superficial conformity with the court's
edict. According to Neal, (1983 at p. 45),

> Attorneys (and examiners) became careful to have the
> physician express his percentage estimate (which almost
> always remained a functional estimate) in acceptable terms,
> such as "permanent disability for industrial purposes," "as
> compared to permanent, total disability" and the like. Most
> physicians went along with the game . . . . The use of the
> "magic words" by physicians was routinely held sufficient
> by the Supreme and Circuit Courts.

The *de facto* reliance on impairment as the basis for nonscheduled
permanent partial ratings despite the *de jure* adherence to disability (loss
of earning capacity) is the situation that existed when we conducted our
field work in 1975-76, and explains why we classified Wisconsin as
a category I (impairment) state in the *NSF Report* (Berkowitz, Burton,
and Vroman 1979). Subsequent court decisions and changes in agency
practices have now clearly moved Wisconsin into category II, among
jurisdictions that base nonscheduled benefits on loss of earning capacity.

A significant case in this transformation of Wisconsin was *Balczewski
v. ILHR Department,* 76 Wis. 2d 487 (1977). The claimant was found
to be 55 percent permanently disabled as a result of the work injury,
with the rating based on the physician's estimate of the extent of impairment (apparently phrased in the "correct" terms enumerated above
by Neal). A guidance counselor who was an expert in industrial employment testified that the claimant was not qualified for any industrial
employment by reason of her condition, age, and lack of education.
The court invoked the "odd lot doctrine," which is a rule of evidence
that when a claimant has been injured in an industrial accident and cannot, because of her "injury, age, education and capacity," secure a

job, there is a *prima facie* case showing of permanent total disability, and the burden of showing that jobs do exist for the claimant shifts to the employer. The court concluded that the odd-lot doctrine was part of Wisconsin law, but since it had not been recognized as part of the law by the examiner, or the department on review, the case was remanded for further consideration.

The *Balczewski* decision was interpreted by many, according to Neal (1983, p. 45), "as a signal that physicians were no longer competent to estimate loss of wage earning capacity, whatever language was used to express the estimate." In short, the Supreme Court was insisting that the practice converge to the legal norms it had established.

Any doubts that the Supreme Court meant that loss of earning capacity was the basis for all nonscheduled awards (and not just in the conversion of a serious nonscheduled rating into a permanent total award, as in *Balczewski*) were removed with the decision in *Pfister & Vogel Tanning Co. v. DILHR,* 86 Wis. 2d 522 (1979). Two physicians had rated the claimant at 5 percent disabled; another physician had reported the permanent partial disability at about 15 percent; and the hearing examiner found that the claimant had a 20 percent permanent disability. However, the lower court that initially reviewed the agency's decision found that none of these ratings had considered the economic loss of earning capacity resulting from the injury. The Supreme Court was adamant in rejecting this agency approach in *Pfister*. The court (at p. 529) distinguished functional or medical impairment from impairment with regard to earning capacity, and concluded that it was the latter impairment that should be measured in assessing nonscheduled injury:

> In *Kurschner* we held that the Industrial Commission erred in adopting the finding of the examiner who determined permanent partial disability by comparing the employee's injuries to those of a hypothetical person totally disabled functionally and not to one totally disabled as to loss of earning capacity. Workers' compensation disability is not the same as functional disability. In a number of cases we have said that a finding of permanent partial disability by the Industrial Commission must be based on a consideration of both factors—loss of bodily function and loss of earning capacity. Consideration of both factors is necessary to implement the objective of the Workers' Compensation Act, namely to "compensate in some measure injured workmen for *loss of wage-earning power* sustained in the industry."

Three consequences of the court's clear mandate to use loss of earning capacity rather than impairment (''loss of bodily function'') warrant attention. First, the law was amended in 1980 to require nonscheduled injuries to be rated solely on the basis of physical limitations without regard to loss of earning capacity when the worker returns to work for the same employer as at the time of injury at a wage loss of less than 15 percent (Sec. 102.44). A good faith offer of employment refused by the worker without reasonable cause has the same effect as actual reemployment. A case closed under this provision can be reopened if within 12 years there is a termination of employment or wage loss of 15 percent or more. The result of this amendment is to give Wisconsin a distinctive set of rules for determining the ratings for nonscheduled injuries with permanent consequences: (1) a minimum rating is based on the extent of impairment; (2) the minimum rating cannot be increased or decreased if the worker has actual wage loss of less than 15 percent of preinjury wages; and (3) if actual wage loss exceeds 15 percent, the minimum rating can be increased (but not decreased) based on the extent of loss of earning capacity.

The second consequence of the court's decision was a capitulation by the workers' compensation agency (DILHR) to the view that nonscheduled permanent partial disability cases (other than those just discussed involving minimal actual wage loss) should be rated on the basis of loss of earning capacity. By a rule (Ind. 80.34) effective October 1982 all departmental determinations as to loss of earning capacity for nonscheduled permanent partial disability and permanent total disability are to:

> take into account the effect of the injured employee's permanent physical and mental limitations resulting from the injury upon present and potential earnings in view of the following factors: (a) Age; (b) Education; (c) Training; (d) Previous work experience; (e) Previous earnings; (f) Present occupation and earnings; (g) Likelihood of future suitable occupational change; (h) Efforts to obtain suitable employment; (i) Willingness to make reasonable change in a residence to secure suitable employment; (j) Success of and willingness to participate in reasonable physical and vocational rehabilitation program; and (k) Other pertinent evidence.

A third notable consequence of the shift from impairment to loss of earning capacity as a basis for nonscheduled permanent partial disability is a change in the professions relied upon for ratings. In the period before the *Kurschner* decision in 1968, physicians were dominant because ratings were based on impairment. The initial impact of the *Kurschner* decision, as previously discussed, was to change the language of the reports (so terms such as "permanent disability for industrial purposes" were used), but to continue to rely on physicians for the reports. But the court's continuing insistence on loss of earning capacity as the basis for ratings eventually forced a change, as discussed by Neal (1983, pp. 45-46):

> *Balczewski's* rejection of the physician's estimate (apparently phrased in the "correct" terms) . . . was perceived by many as a signal that physicians were no longer competent to estimate loss of wage earning capacity, whatever language was used to express the estimate. And applicant's attorneys soon learned that the vocational expert's opinion was much more favorable to the client than the physician's.
>
> The trend toward the use of vocational experts has since grown steadily. . . .
>
> What is the law and practice today? Most applicants' attorneys use vocational experts because the estimates are higher. Some also voice fear of malpractice suit if they do not. The Labor and Industry Review Commission, in reaction to *Pfister,* has been remanding some awards where a permanent disability finding is based on medical testimony only.

Administration of the Wisconsin Program

Processing workers' compensation cases is a responsibility of the Workers' Compensation Division of the Department of Industry, Labor and Human Relations (DILHR). The administrator of the division oversees the hearing examiners and, in general, actively administers the act. Reviews of examiners' decisions are made by a commission within the department.

The division is active in communicating with the parties and seeing to it that procedures are followed and payments made in a timely fashion. As discussed in chapter 4, Wisconsin provides evaluation guidance to the parties so they know the amounts to be paid in permanent partial disability cases.

The active administrative stance of the administrator of the workers' compensation system extends to legislative concerns. Workers' compensation legislation, by tradition and by statute (Sec. 102.14), originates with an advisory council on workers' compensation, consisting of five representatives from labor and five from industry, chaired by the administrator of the Workers' Compensation Division. Three representatives of the insurance industry attend meetings of the council, but do not have a vote. Once the legislative issues are thrashed out by the advisory council, the division takes the responsibility for putting the council's recommendations into final form. The tradition has been to submit an agreed-upon bill to the legislature with the understanding that the members of the advisory council will support the agreed-upon bill and oppose all others.

Processing Permanent Partial Disability Cases

The active role of the administration in communicating with the parties and in providing guidance in the evaluation of permanent partial disabilities is illustrated by the procedures involved in the processing of cases.

Wisconsin is the epitome of the direct payment state. The employer is required to file a first report of injury or disease (Form WC-12) and, 11 days after the accident or the beginning of disability, a supplemental report (WC-13). The latter form indicates the amount of compensation paid or the reason compensation was not paid. The same form is used to let the division know of a final payment, and may be used in case of a suspension of payments.

Insurance carriers and self-insured employers are expected to pay claims promptly. The division's standard is that 80 percent of cases be mailed or delivered within 14 days after injuries are reported. The Workers' Compensation Division has monitored first payment performance since 1921, either by correspondence or by personal visits. The division releases periodic reports detailing the promptness records of individual carriers. In 1985, local government self-insurers, on the average, met the standard, but 22.3 percent of payments from nongovernmental self-insurers and 26.9 percent of payments from insurance carriers were not made within the 14-day period (Gmeinder and Tatarsky 1986, p. 30). Insurers and self-insurers who do not meet the standard are asked to explain why.

The division requires a physician's report if the disability lasts more than three weeks or if there is any permanent disability. The physician is asked to estimate the amount of permanent disability resulting from the injury. Such estimates are influenced by the guidelines established by rule of the division. If there is some controversy about the extent of disability, the carrier is expected to pay the minimal amount conceded without any order from the division. Failure to do so may subject the carrier to a 10 percent penalty. There are, of course, cases in which employers or carriers dispute liability completely; when they do so, they are expected to notify the division.

In some states, such notification, or any dissatisfaction by the division with some action of the carrier, results in the case being scheduled before a hearing officer. In Wisconsin, much is accomplished by correspondence between the division and the parties. For example, if compensation payments are not being made, the agency may send a form letter to the carrier with the following message: "More than 30 days have elapsed since compensation payment was due in this case. You have had more than enough time to complete a necessary investigation, unless unusual circumstances prevail" (Guide Letter #6). If the injured worker complains about not receiving compensation, the agency sends a letter to the worker informing him that the agency has notified the employer's insurance carrier of the complaint and has requested an explanation.

If the carrier does not respond, one of the administrative staff will attempt to find out whether the cause of delay is a genuine dispute or perhaps confused communications. If the problem, for example, is that the doctor has not filed the necessary medical reports, the worker may be asked to contact the doctor to urge him to send in the necessary report. The division has made arrangements to invoke the aid of the Wisconsin Medical Society in securing these reports. In short, the division does not hesitate to intervene actively by correspondence or by phone call to one party or the other.

Of course, cases of serious dispute concerning liability or extent of disability result in applications for hearings, but even at this stage the employer is advised to pay the compensation that is admittedly due and accrued.

The case may go directly to a hearing, or may be set down for a pretrial conference to establish the issues in dispute, although before that stage is reached the administrative personnel of the agency will make sure that the file is complete and that the physician's forms are in. The administrator may give a good deal of assistance to the claimant in filling out forms, because it is not automatically assumed that the claimant needs an attorney.

At the pretrial conference, the examiner attempts to get the parties to agree about the issues, or, if that is not possible, to determine whether a formal hearing is necessary. Some compromises are reached at this stage, although these do not necessarily involve a release of the employer's obligation for further medical care or even for future cash benefits should the employee's condition worsen. The parties are urged to stipulate to as many mutually accepted facts as possible at the pretrial conference.

A 1980 amendment (Sec. 102.18 [1][c]) provided for a tie-breaking procedure for cases in which two or more examiners have conducted hearings and are unable to agree within a range of 5 percent of the highest or lowest estimate of permanent partial disability. An additional examiner may be appointed for findings of fact, and an order of award may then be issued by a majority of the examiners. Also, these same amendments provided that any award that falls within a range of 5 percent of the highest or lowest estimate of permanent partial disability is presumed to be a reasonable award "provided it is not higher than the highest or lower than the lowest estimate in evidence" (Sec. 102.18 [1][d]).

Evaluation Rules

Wisconsin has issued a series of rules to guide physicians who rate the permanent consequences of injuries. Rule 80.32 covers "percentages of loss of use or losses of motion as compared with amputations at the involved joints." It also includes injuries to the back. As the rule states in paragraph 1:

> The disabilities set forth in this section are the minimums for the described conditions. However, findings of additional disabling elements shall result in an estimate higher than the minimum. The minimum also assumes that the member, the back, etc., was previously without disability. Appropriate reduction shall be made for any preexisting disability.

> Note: An example would be where in addition to a described loss of motion, pain and circulatory disturbance further

limits the use of an arm or a leg. The removal of a semi-
lunar cartilage in a knee with less than a good result would
call for an estimate higher than 5% loss of use of the leg
at the knee. The same principle would apply to laminectomies
or spinal fusions. The schedule of minimum disabilities contained in this section was adopted upon the advice of the orthopedic advisory committee.

Thus the general guides provide for minimum ratings that may be
supplemented if there is a finding of additional disabling factors. Further, the physician has the discretion to determine whether pain or a
circulatory disturbance contributes to the restriction for practical purposes of the use of an extremity.

The guides provide fairly detailed instruction for rating amputation
of the upper and lower extremities and sensory loss to the digits, hands,
portions of the arms, and so on. Some (though less) guidance is provided for rating back injuries and loss of hearing and vision.

The deputy administrator has prepared a guide for physicians and carriers showing comparisons between evaluations of disability as expected
under Wisconsin's Workmen's Compensation Act and those listed in
the AMA *Guides to the Evaluation of Permanent Impairment.* Some
of the conditions listed are impairments by AMA standards, but would
not be compensable under Wisconsin's workers' compensation standards.

Not only are Wisconsin's statutory provisions relating to permanent
partial disabilities quite detailed, but the division has issued rules and
regulations supplementing the statute that provide further guidance to
the parties in making their evaluations. In addition, the administrators
provide guidance on an informal basis, so that the physician has some
way to translate his findings into percentage ratings acceptable to the
administrators. Finally, the administrator actively communicates the division's policies to the parties and is perfectly willing to instruct physicians as to whether they are meeting the guidelines.

Cases and Work Load

Wisconsin has been widely esteemed as a state that has succeeded
in keeping litigation within reasonable bounds. This remains largely
true, although litigation has increased, in part because the number of
cases has increased. In 1970, the state received 39,841 first reports of
accidents that were likely indemnity cases. By 1979, the number of cases
had increased to 82,352—more than doubling the number of reported

cases in less than a decade. Then the case load dropped—to 54,579 cases reported in 1983—and then partially rebounded—to 65,679 in 1985 (Gmeinder and Tatarsky 1986, p. 3).

Application for hearing is one measure of litigation. From 1970 to 1979, the number of applications almost doubled (from 2,069 to 3,822), roughly matching the increase in first reports of injuries, so that the "litigation rate" (number of applications per 100 first reports) hovered around 5 in the 1970s. Then as the number of reported cases dropped in the 1980s, the applications for hearing did not. In 1984 there were 4,989 applications for hearing out of 61,588 reported cases, for a 8.1 percent litigation rate. In 1985, applications exceeded 5000 for the first time (at 5,133), but the number of reported cases increased to 65,679 and so the litigation rate dropped to 7.8 percent (Gmeinder and Tatarsky 1986, p. 31)—still high by Wisconsin's historical standards.

Other measures of litigation are the numbers of informal hearings (pretrial conferences) and of formal hearings, and these also show increasing litigiousness in Wisconsin. To be sure, formal hearings have not expanded—from 1,478 in 1970 to 1,093 in 1980 to 1,463 in 1985. But pretrial conferences have spurted—from 1,360 to 3,019 to 4,255 in these same years (Gmeinder and Tatarsky 1986, p. 33).

One "solution" to disputed cases in most states is a compromise and release agreement, in which the worker typically receives a lump-sum settlement in exchange for a release of the employer's further liability. Compromise agreements in Wisconsin are discouraged. Every compromise may be reviewed and set aside or modified within one year after the filing of the agreement. Also the act clearly specifies that a stipulation of settlement is not a compromise agreement and it does not bar future claims. The claimant, for example, may be entitled to future medical benefits. As a result, compromise agreements are uncommon in Wisconsin, with the 1,614 in 1985 accounting for only 3 percent of the 52,088 cases initially closed that year.

Lessons from Wisconsin

The experience in Wisconsin illustrates the difficulties of meeting all three criteria presented in chapter 2: adequacy, equity, and efficiency. The tension between equity and efficiency is particularly evident.

Wisconsin's record on efficiency is outstanding using several measures of performance. The employers' costs of workers' compensation insurance in Wisconsin have been consistently below the national average since 1958, with a representative sample of employers paying only 62 percent of the national average in 1984 (table 3.18). Moreover, the record has not been achieved by paying parsimonious benefits. Rather, among the seven Great Lakes states with comparable data (all but Ohio), Wisconsin in 1984 had the highest ratio of benefits received by workers to insurance premiums paid by employers (Burton and Partridge 1985, p. 62).

The Wisconsin workers' compensation agency also appears to be a model of efficiency. The data in table 4.1 indicate that the size of the budget and workforce in Wisconsin are relatively low compared to the other jurisdictions we are intensively examining. If anything, the comparisons are "stacked" against Wisconsin since its agency performs the full set of administrative functions described in chapter 4, including monitoring and evaluation, while some of the other states' agencies are essentially passive, doing little more than adjudicating disputed claims.

The reasons for the efficiency in Wisconsin, as reflected in the employers' costs of insurance and the agency operations, include several factors previously discussed. The share of all cash benefits accounted for by permanent disability cases is generally related to the employers' costs of workers' compensation insurance (graph 3.2), and Wisconsin has consistently kept its permanent disability benefits share at or below the national average (table 3.17). The agency efficiency results in part from its aggressive stance in promoting voluntary settlements and avoiding litigation. Among 13 states with data available from the National Council on Compensation Insurance, Wisconsin and Pennsylvania had the lowest percentage (2 percent) of cases where claimants were represented by attorneys; the average for all 13 states was 8 percent (NCCI *Claims Characteristics,* 1984, p. 3). The quality performance of the Wisconsin agency also appears to reflect the general reputation of Wisconsin as a "good government" state, in which government employment is a career rather than a way-stop. The long-standing support of the Wisconsin program by the Advisory Council is also a factor that helps explain the quality of the agency.

The record of the Wisconsin workers' compensation program is not unsullied, however. There is cause for concern about the adequacy of the permanent partial disability benefits because of the low weekly maximum. As documented in chapter 10, Wisconsin workers who were injured in 1968 and received permanent partial disability awards did receive adequate benefits. However, between 1968 and 1986 the maximum for permanent partial disability benefits increased 136 percent (from $47.50

to $112), less than the 182 percent increase in average wages in the state over the latest comparable period.[25] Wisconsin benefits for permanently disabled workers may, therefore, no longer be adequate.

Even if Wisconsin is at least arguably satisfying the adequacy criterion for permanent disability benefits, there is strong evidence that the benefits are inequitable. The essence of equity is that workers with equal losses of income due to work injuries receive equal benefits (horizonal equity), while workers with different amounts of income losses receive benefits proportional to their losses (vertical equity). The data in chapter 10 for Wisconsin workers injured in 1968 show numerous violations of horizonal and vertical equity. Similar results were found by Ginnold (1979), who also studied workers injured in 1968. He found, for example (p. 85), that workers with scheduled permanent partial ratings averaging 13 percent were on average experiencing no earnings losses in 1973, but by then the workers with nonscheduled ratings averaging 11 percent were experiencing 25 percent earnings losses.

A concern for equity in the Wisconsin workers' compensation program is reflected in the Wisconsin Supreme Court's decisions about the basis for nonscheduled permanent partial disability benefits. The court in effect recognized that if the purpose of workers' compensation benefits is primarily to compensate workers for work disability—an economic consequence of the injury—then an operational approach that only examines the workers' impairments ("functional disabilities") is unlikely to produce benefits that serve the primary purpose well. Following that reasoning, the court (in conjunction with the legislature) in a quest for equity ruled that nonscheduled benefits should be based not only on impairment but on a combination of impairment, loss of earning capacity, and even a strain of actual wage loss.

The transformation of the basis for nonscheduled benefits can be considered a trade-off of efficiency for equity. For whatever are the defects of ratings based on impairment, they are relatively objective and thus less prone to disagreement and litigation than ratings based on loss of earning capacity. Surely even reasonable men and women would disagree about the application of the factors enumerated in agency rule Ind. 80.34 (quoted earlier) that are used in determining the loss of earning capacity.

The tension between equity and efficiency reflected in the transformed basis for nonscheduled benefits is a tension present in the determination of all permanent disability benefits in Wisconsin (and indeed in all states). How can equity be promoted without reducing efficiency? The problem must be carefully stated, because as we have argued in chapter 2, it is easy to achieve a myopic version of efficiency in which the only concern is for low costs of the delivery system (and in particular low costs of the state workers' compensation agency) without regard to the quality of the program, as measured by the equity and adequacy of benefits. A more appropriate version of equity—which we have termed panoramic efficiency—is concerned simultaneously with the costs of the delivery system and the quality of the program.

The proper view of efficiency will not consider a larger budget for a state agency or even more litigation as necessarily inefficient if these are necessary to achieve greater adequacy or equity of benefits. We hasten to add, however, that the evidence from other states that will be reviewed in chapter 11 provides no support for the notion that greater litigation necessarily promotes equity or adequacy. And we particularly doubt that greater litigation resulting from the use of loss of earning capacity as a basis for permanent disability benefits is likely to promote adequacy or equity. We are therefore concerned that the recent change in the basis for nonscheduled permanent partial disability benefits in Wisconsin has been accompanied by increased litigation. We realize that other factors—including, perhaps, a trend towards greater tolerance of litigation—may partly explain the increased litigation in Wisconsin. We view the recent change of job title in the Wisconsin workers' compensation program from "hearing examiner" to "administrative law judge" as a disturbing evidence of such a trend. But regardless of the influence of these other factors, we believe that use of loss of earning capacity as a basis for nonscheduled benefits will almost inevitably increase litigation, and we are skeptical of the view that improvements in equity will result.

One of the challenges for the new Wisconsin Study Commission is to figure out a better way to improve equity than by changing the basis for permanent disability benefits to loss of earning capacity. One problem with the recent developments in Wisconsin is that ratings for scheduled permanent partial disability benefits are still based strictly on an assessment of impairment. Thus, even if a case can be made that the transformation of the basis for nonscheduled benefits has been beneficial, the majority of workers in Wisconsin with permanent disabilities must still rely on scheduled benefits that are demonstrably inequitable.

NOTES

1. During the second quarter of 1986, 39 percent of all new original filings of applications for adjudication contained the insurer's first notice of the injury, down from the 1977 record of 53 percent (California Workers' Compensation Institute *Bulletin* [hereafter CWCI *Bulletin*], No. 85-8, Oct. 2, 1985 and CWCI *Bulletin* No. 86-7, Aug. 14, 1986).

2. In 90-95 percent of cases involving an application for adjudication, the worker is represented by an attorney (U.S. Dept. of Labor, *Administration Profiles*, 1985, p. 29).

3. The data on the activity in the Courts of Appeal and Supreme Court are from 14 *California Workers' Compensation Reporter* (hereafter *CWCR*) 63, April 1986.

4. An employer, his carrier, or the Board can also initiate movement in a case by filing a Declaration of Readiness to Proceed.

5. In some cases involving a request for approval of a compromise and release, the case has already had an informal or formal disability rating prepared by the Disability Evaluation Bureau, and that could be considered by the judge in determining the appropriateness of the proposed compromise and release settlement.

6. The order of the judge approving a compromise and release agreement is subject to a petition for reconsideration or a writ of review, and the Workers' Compensation Appeals Board may on its own motion reconsider a compromise and release agreement approved by a judge (Swezey 1985, sec. 13.52). The latter procedure is rarely used.

7. More extensive discussions can be found in the chapter "Permanent Disability Evaluation" (Welch 1973), and in the June 4, 1964, "Presentation on Permanent Disability Ratings" to the Workmen's Compensation Study Commission ("Moss Commission"), both by Eli P. Welch, chief of the Permanent Disability Rating Bureau; and in the California Senate Interim Committee's *Report on Workmen's Compensation Benefits* (Part I, 1953). These items were relied on for much of the material in this chapter. Welch's "Permanent Disability Evaluation" chapter is similar to chapter 16 in Swezey (1985).

8. The only other change in the language was made in 1966, when authority to prepare, adopt, and amend the schedule was transferred from the Industrial Accident Commission (the predecessor of the Workers' Compensation Appeals Board) to the administrative director of the Division of Industrial Accidents.

9. There were 14 amendments by 1939, according to Welch (1964, p. 16).

10. The example is from Swezey (1985, sec. 16.29).

11. "Actually, 'slight,' 'moderate,' and 'severe' have different meanings to different persons involved in the judicial process of the commission. What may be 'slight,' 'moderate,' or 'severe' as the case may be, to litigants and referees alike, may prove to be something different to the rating specialist although presumably the latter also functions under the same legislative formula and rules of evidence" (Senate Interim Committee 1953, p. 42).

12. A May 20, 1986 letter from Barry F. Carmody, acting administrative director of the Division of Industrial Accidents, to All Interested Parties indicated that the Division is renewing the *Schedule for Rating Permanent Disabilities* in order to provide "more equitable permanent disability determinations." A request was made for a list of occupations not currently in the schedule that should be included.

13. Nor do we.

14. To be sure, the workers' compensation judge can use an independent medical examiner or an agreed medical examiner to assess the extent of injury, but ultimately the judge must decide whether to accept the medical opinion from these sources, and that decision is an act of discretion.

15. These injuries or diseases are described in California as nonscheduled (see quotation below). This use of the term "nonscheduled," however, differs from the term's use in most states, where all cases that cannot be rated by reference to the list of injuries in the statute are considered nonscheduled and are evaluated on the basis of a general standard. In California, the procedure in "nonscheduled" cases is roughly comparable to the process used in most states to evaluate loss of use cases for scheduled injuries. As described by Welch (1973, sec. 15.22), in California "a disability rating (sometimes referred to as a judgment rating) is one for which the disability is not precisely described in the schedule, or the occupation is not specifically listed. Most ratings are nonscheduled. The schedule can be applied to nonscheduled disabilities in three ways: (1) by comparison with the most similar scheduled disability, or (2) by analogy to a scheduled disability, or (3) by comparison with the entire scheme of relative severity of disability."

16. The California schedule for mental deterioration, for example, consists of four levels—slight, moderate, severe, and pronounced—with no description of what these levels involve. The AMA *Guides* devote a chapter to mental illness.

17. CWCI *Bulletin* No. 85-6, July 10, 1985. The CWCI estimate of $600 million plus has been challenged by the California Applicants' Attorneys Association (CAAA) in "Litigation Costs in California's Workers' Compensation System," a three-page, undated memorandum. The CAAA estimates the costs as only $243 million. This figure, however, excludes $110 million of applicants' attorneys fees and $27 million for the costs of the WCAB because these "costs are not paid by employers as a part of their workers' compensation costs." As we have defined costs of the delivery system in chapter 2, however, these costs should be included, and doing so would make the total costs of litigation some $380 million annually in California. Obviously the difference between the CWCI estimate of $600 million and the $380 million figure is substantial, but even the lower figure indicates that the cost of the litigation process in California is considerably greater than the budget of the workers' compensation agency for its nonadjudicatory functions.

18. CWCI *Bulletin* No. 86-3, April 24, 1986.

19. The Study Committee was created in 1983 and directed to report by November 1984. "The joint committee did not meet this deadline, the chairman retired from the Legislature, and the committee was not extended" (CSCS *Report,* 1986, p. 1). Under these apparently beneficial conditions, the staff produced an excellent 279-page report.

20. The committee staff relied on an earlier version of portions of chapter 10 of this study published by Burton and Vroman (1979).

21. National Commission on State Workmen's Compensation Laws, *Compendium on Workers' Compensation* (1973, p. 18). The 1910 law in New York was held unconstitutional by the Court of Appeals of New York, thus allowing Wisconsin its honor.

22. The passage is from the *Bulletin* of the Industrial Commission of Wisconsin, Vol. 1, No. 3 (July 20, 1912), as quoted in Gmeinder (1983, p. 12).

23. Nine jurisdictions (Arizona, the District of Columbia, Maine, Maryland, Michigan, New Hampshire, New York, Rhode Island, and South Dakota) pay nonscheduled permanent partial disability benefits for the duration of the disability without limits on the total amount of payments. Data for this note and the text are from U.S. Dept. of Labor, *State Laws* (1986).

24. In *Northern States Power Co. v. Industrial Comm.*, 252 Wis. 70 (1947) at Note 2, p. 76, the court stated that "since an award for permanent disability is to be made for all time . . . it must be based upon some sort of prediction as to impairment of earning capacity."

25. The latest data for the average weekly wage of workers covered by the Wisconsin unemployment insurance program are for 1984. In order to match the 18-year period over which benefits are compared in the text, wage data from 1966 were used to estimate the 182 percent increase in average weekly wages in the state (from $115.55 to $325.57). Wage data are from U.S. Dept. of Labor, Employment and Training Administration, *Handbook of Unemployment Insurance Financial Data, 1938-1976*, as supplemented by a 1986 release from U.S. Dept. of Labor, Bureau of Labor Statistics.

Chapter 8
Nonscheduled Benefits in Wage-Loss (Category III) States

We now consider nonscheduled permanent partial disability cases in the wage-loss states in our sample. Prominent among these is Florida, which is examined individually in chapter 9 because of its widely heralded 1979 wage-loss statute. But aspects of the wage-loss approach are also present in Pennsylvania, Michigan, New York, and Ohio, the states discussed in this chapter.

Definition of the Wage-Loss Approach

The definition of a "pure" wage-loss approach that follows is elaborate. Nonetheless, all of the dimensions of a wage-loss approach represented by the five traits we name must be recognized in order to accurately capture the differences among the states using the wage-loss approach.

Trait One. The wage-loss approach applies to the period after the date of maximum medical improvement (MMI), not to the period between the date of injury and the date of MMI. (See graph 2.1 in chapter 2.) In our terminology, the period between the date of injury and the date of MMI is the temporary disability period, and the period after the date of MMI is the permanent disability period.

Most states do not use this precise terminology in distinguishing between the temporary and permanent disability periods. Indeed, some states do not explicitly distinguish between temporary disability and permanent disability. Nonetheless, each state has to decide how to compensate workers after their medical conditions are stable whether they explicitly recognize that date or not, and we examine whatever approach each state uses to compensate workers after the healing period.

Trait Two. The wage-loss approach requires that as of the date of MMI, there is some remaining impairment or functional limitation that was caused by the work-related injury or disease. This requirement is true for all three categories of nonscheduled permanent partial disability benefits, but needs emphasis here. It means that most workers' compensation cases cannot qualify for wage-loss benefits (or any type of permanent disability benefits), since the medical problems are temporary.

Trait Three. After the date of MMI, the worker's postinjury potential earnings are determined by projecting the preinjury wage into the period of permanent disability with adjustments to reflect what would have happened to the wage had the worker not been injured. These potential earnings (line BC in graph 2.1) are compared to his actual earnings (line FG) and the difference, which is defined as "true" wage loss due to injury, serves as the basis for the wage-loss benefits. Two outcomes are possible: (a) if the worker has no wage loss after the date of MMI, then *no* permanent disability benefits are paid; however, (b) if the worker does have wage loss after the date of MMI, then permanent disability benefits are paid that are related to the amount of wage loss (for example, the benefits could be 66 2/3 percent of the "true" wage loss).

Trait Four. Even in a pure wage-loss approach, it is recognized that some workers will voluntarily restrict the amount of their actual earnings after the date of MMI. It would be unfair to require the employer to pay benefits because of the worker's voluntary limitation of work activity. Therefore, even in a pure wage-loss approach the employer has the right to establish that the worker's earning capacity after the date of MMI is greater than the worker's actual earnings. This means that the compensable wage loss is the lesser of: (a) the worker's potential earnings minus the worker's actual earnings; or (b) the worker's potential earnings minus the worker's earning capacity.

Bringing in the notion of earning capacity makes this sound like the category II approach. But there is a crucial difference. In the category II approach, only the difference between potential earnings and earning capacity is considered in determining benefits; as a result, a worker can receive permanent disability benefits even if there is no actual wage loss so long as a decision is made that he has experienced a loss of earning capacity. A worker in the same situation receives no benefits under the wage-loss approach.

Trait Five. Under a pure wage-loss approach, a worker would be eligible for wage-loss benefits any time between the date of MMI and the worker's retirement age that the worker experiences true wage loss. Further, this extended period would not be limited by statute (for example, by a maximum duration on permanent partial disability benefits that could terminate benefits for some workers before their normal retirement age) or by agreements between the parties to limit the period of eligibility (for example, by compromise and release agreements).

The preceding discussion of the wage-loss approach provides a "pure" version that no state altogether meets, although each of the traits is met (or at least approached) by one or more states. We are not suggesting that "pure" is best. We offer the definition only because it provides a model to which the laws in Pennsylvania, Michigan, New York, Ohio, and Florida can be compared.

Following are some of the ways that state laws deviate from the pure approach (these will be elaborated in subsequent sections).

1. The law does not measure "true" wage loss but "restricted" wage loss, as those terms are defined in graph 2.1. "True" wage loss requires that preinjury wages be escalated through time to simulate what the worker would have earned had the injury never occurred. In contrast, "restricted" wage loss takes the worker's wage as of the date of injury and projects this wage into the postinjury period without escalation. This deviation from the "pure" wage-loss approach characterizes most states.

2. The law considers only wage loss above a certain minimum amount to be compensable. Florida, for example, only compensates wage loss in excess of 15 percent of potential earnings.

3. The law restricts the eligibility period for wage-loss benefits. For example, the statute may terminate benefits for some workers before their normal retirement age even though their wage loss is continuing. Or the statute may require workers to establish their eligibility for wage-loss benefits within a certain period after the date of MMI.

4. The eligibility period may be restricted by private agreements beween the parties. A common example is the compromise and release agreement (variously known as a redemption, washout, or "C & R"), whereby the worker receives a lump-sum payment and the employer is released from any further liability for the particular injury. Under such an agreement, the worker is obviously no longer eligible for wage-loss benefits even if actual wage loss occurs after the date of the agreement; this violates trait five of the "pure" wage-loss approach. Also, the lump-sum part of the settlement means that some workers receive benefits even though they experience no actual loss of earnings after the date of MMI—a

violation of trait three. Moreover, since the size of the lump-sum settlement is likely to reflect an estimate of future wage loss, the agreement essentially converts a *de jure* wage loss approach (category III) into a *de facto* loss of earning capacity approach (category II).

5. Finally, a "pure" wage-loss approach pays benefits only because of actual loss of earnings, not, for example, because of the mere existence of an impairment or functional limitation. A state may deviate from the pure wage-loss by awarding benefits above and beyond wage-loss benefits for certain injuries, such as amputations.

With this catalogue of traits and deviations in mind, we now turn to a review of the jurisdictions that have at least some elements of a wage-loss approach in their workers' compensation statutes.

Pennsylvania

Types and Levels of Benefits

In Pennsylvania, a worker who is out of work due to the consequences of an injury may receive what are termed "total disability" benefits for the duration of his total disability. As in other states, these benefits are calculated at two-thirds of the employee's preinjury weekly wage, subject to the statutory maximum ($347.00 on January 1, 1986). There is no stated number of weeks after which such total disability payments automatically cease. The law simply provides that "nothing in this clause should require payments of compensation after disability shall cease" (Section 306). If disability continues for the worker's entire life, the payments also continue. There is no distinction in Pennsylvania's law between "temporary total" and "permanent total" benefits, except for the statutory presumption that certain combinations of scheduled injuries constitute total disability. The statute provides, "Unless the Board shall otherwise determine, the loss of both hands or both arms or both feet or both legs or both eyes shall constitute total disability" (Section 306[b] [23]).

If, as a consequence of the injury, the worker suffers a permanent impairment that is included on the schedule (say the loss of a hand), he receives, as an exclusive remedy, 66 2/3 percent of his wage during the stipulated period (335 weeks for one hand, for example) plus his total disability payments during a healing period defined by law. (The scheduled benefits are subject to a $347.00 per week maximum.) The law provides that he is to receive, in addition to his scheduled award, payments during any period of disability ''necessary and required as a healing period.'' The healing period ends either when the claimant returns to work without impairment in earnings or on the last day of the period specified in the schedule, whichever comes first. Thus, for the loss of a hand he would receive the benefits for 335 weeks as indicated, plus a maximum of 20 weeks for the healing period if he were out of work for that long.

There are three restrictive aspects of the schedule in Pennsylvania that are relevant for an understanding of the relationship between scheduled and nonscheduled cases. First, the schedule provides compensation only for total, not for partial, loss of most body members included in the list. In other states' schedules, by contrast, partial loss of the listed body members results in awards that are proportional to the extent of loss. (For example, in most states if the loss of the hand resulted in an award of 335 weeks, then loss of two-thirds of a hand would result in an award of 223 weeks. In Pennsylvania, partial loss of a hand is only evaluated in terms of the scheduled awards for loss of the fingers.) Second, the Pennsylvania schedule is largely confined to physical loss of the listed body members, and loss of use is not compensable as in most states' schedules. (Pennsylvania does allow loss of use to be compensated when there is a permanent loss of use of two or more body members.) These two restrictive aspects of the Pennsylvania schedule mean that a relatively large proportion of injuries with permanent consequences are not encompassed by the schedule and will receive permanent disability benefits only if they qualify for nonscheduled permanent partial (or permanent total) disability benefits. The third restrictive aspect of the Pennsylvania schedule is the limitation found in most statutes, namely the exclusiveness of scheduled benefits in the sense that an injury that qualifies for scheduled benefits cannot qualify for any other type of permanent disability benefits.

In the nonscheduled cases, if, in the words of the law, the ''disability [is] partial in character'' (Section 306 a), the worker is entitled to 66 2/3 percent of the difference between his preinjury wages and his ''earning power'' thereafter paid ''during the period of his partial disability . . . but for not more than 500 weeks'' (Section 306 b). If a period of total disability is followed by partial disability, the 500 weeks maximum period of partial disability is not reduced. The nonscheduled benefits were also subject to a $347.00-per-week maximum on January 1, 1986.

The administrative problems in Pennsylvania for nonscheduled cases revolve around determining when the period of total disability should end, and in determining the employee's earning power. The statute offers no guidance as to the former, but does for the latter. First, earning power "shall in no case be less than the weekly amount which the employee receives after the injury." "Further, the combined compensation and wage received are to be no more than the amount received by a fellow employee in employment similar to that in which the injured employee was engaged at the time of the injury" (Section 306 b).

The first condition—that of taking the actual wages as a floor to establish earning power—came as a result of a 1939 amendment. Before 1939, earning power could be less than actual postinjury wages if the worker could show that the reason for his higher wage was inflation, promotion, or some other reason not connected with his permanent injury. Today, if a worker who earned $200 a week before his accident returned after his period of total disability to a job that paid $110 a week,[1] he would be entitled upon showing the necessary proof to a benefit of $60, which is two-thirds of the difference between his wage before his injury, $200, and his present wage of $110.

If his wage remained at $110, he would continue to receive the $60 a week benefit for the maximum duration of 500 weeks. If, however, his wage gradually increaseed, his benefits would correspondingly decrease and, once his earnings reached $200, cease. The termination of benefits occurs regardless of the reason for the increase in wages.

As noted by a judge of the Court of Common Pleas, "It seems paradoxical that, while statutory changes to benefit employees and to account for inflationary forces have been repeatedly enacted by the legislature since 1939, this post-injury disadvantage to partially disabled employees has remained unchanged since 1939 and throughout most inflationary times" (Barbieri 1975, pp. 46-47).

Obviously, for those employees who return to a job, the establishment of actual wages as an indicator of earning power, however unfair, does simplify the administrative task of determining "earning power." The problems become more complicated for an employee who does not return to a job. The difficulty is in assessing whether his loss of earnings results from his injury. Although his actual earnings are zero, his earning power may be a good deal more. The employer or the insurance carrier is likely to claim that his lack of a job has nothing to do with the work-related injury.

Procedures

In Pennsylvania, within 21 days after an insurance carrier is notified of an injury, it must submit a form indicating acceptance or denial of the claim. If the carrier accepts the claim, it is supposed to begin payments of total disability benefits promptly. Any change in the status of the claim, including a stoppage of payments because the employee returned to work or because the carrier believes that he is capable of returning to work, requires notice to the claimant and to the agency. Once total disability benefits begin, they normally continue until the employee recovers and is back to work. The carrier then files a final receipt of compensation form that requires the signature of the employee. If the employee refuses to sign, say on grounds that he continues to be totally disabled, the carrier must then petition the agency to terminate or modify the benefit payments.

If an employer's petition to stop or modify payments alleges either that the employee has returned to work at the same or higher wages or that he is fully recovered as attested to by a physician's affidavit, the carrier may stop or modify the payments and await a final determination by a referee. Provisions may be made for an expedited hearing to determine the issue. If the employee has not returned to work, the burden of proof for establishing his employability at a certain wage falls on the employer. As in those states where the criteria center around impairment or measures of functional limitation, the controversy centers around conflicting medical evidence and physicians' estimates of the employee's ability to work. The referee is called upon to make a decision based on the medical and lay testimony before him.

When the extent of impairment is not resolved but the employee is not suffering any current wage loss, the referee can order a suspension of benefits. The suspension in effect imposes a 500-week rather than a three-year time limit within which the case can be reopened if actual wage loss occurs. This is a common procedure in back cases.

Of course the parties may agree as to the nature and extent of the impairment or functional limitation and disagree about the significance of that condition for the employee's chances in the labor market. Conflicting medical testimony is usually supplemented by employment experts' testimony as to the availability of jobs within a reasonable distance from the employee's home for workers with the claimant's impairment and functional limitation. The referee must decide on the basis of the evidence before him whether it is reasonable to conclude that the claim-

ant could return to some job. In some instances, the hearing is adjourned to give the claimant an opportunity to test the labor market, although
the referee's decision will not always turn on the actual results of that
job search. Of course, if the employee does get a job that pays as much
as his former wage, that eliminates his claim for wage-loss benefits.
In general, however, in Pennsylvania, if the claimant's physician testifies,
based on some reasonable evidence, that his patient is unable to return
to work, the employer's task of proving otherwise is a difficult and time-
consuming one.

Although statistics on litigation are difficult to interpret on a comparative basis, they do suggest that Pennsylvania is not an overly litigious
state. There are 13 states with data on attorney representation available
from the National Council on Compensation Insurance (*Claims
Characteristics* 1984, p. 3). For all types of claims, 2 percent of all
claimants are represented by attorneys in Pennsylvania (a record
matched only by Wisconsin), well below the 13-state average of 8 percent. For permanent partial claims, Pennsylvania has the lowest percentage of attorney representation—7 percent, compared to the 13-state
average of 23 percent.

Compromise and Release Settlements

In spite of a wage-loss statute under which claims remain open for
an indefinite period of time, Pennsylvania is not plagued with a rash
of compromise and release settlements.

The director of the Bureau and the attorney general have interpreted
Section 407 of the statute as constituting a complete bar to compromise
and release settlements. Section 407 states (in part):

> the employer or insurer and employee or his dependents may
> agree upon the compensation payable to the employee or his
> dependents under this act, but any agreement . . . permit-
> ting a computation of a payment contrary to the provision
> of this act, or varying the amount to be paid or the period
> during which compensation shall be payable . . . shall be
> wholly null and void. . .

A referee (Stander 1976) has pointed out that the "tortured syntax"
of the section makes possible interpretations other than the prevailing
one, which bars any compromise and release settlements. The rationale
for such settlements is eroded due to the provisions that allow reopenings in cases where settlements have been reached. In a 1975 case,

General v. Roseman and Company, 343 A. 2d 683, the claimant was awarded compensation beyond that stipulated in a prior settlement to which he had agreed. The amount of the settlement was credited against the compensation benefits the court found appropriate.

The formal ban on compromises has not eliminated all settlements. They still can be implemented by agreeing to stipulations to dismiss or withdraw pending petitions, which can be done without disclosing any details of the settlement. The incentive for the carrier or employer to enter into such settlements is dulled, however, by the knowledge that such settlements are not accompanied by binding releases. The claimant can file a petition any time within the statute of limitations and reopen the matter for adjudication and determination.

Experience with Permanent Disability Benefits in Pennsylvania

Pennsylvania's experiences with permanent total disability cases and with permanent partial disability cases contrast sharply. Throughout 1958-82, the number of permanent total cases as a share of all cash benefit cases was relatively high in Pennsylvania (table 3.6). In 1982, for example, the state had 173 permanent total cases, a number exceeded in only two other jurisdictions for which the National Council on Compensation Insurance collects data.[2] These cases accounted for 0.31 percent of all Pennsylvania cash benefit cases, which was 209 percent of the national average share for permanent total cases that year (table 3.6). Not only were these cases numerous, they were expensive. In 1982, for example, the average cost of a permanent total case in Pennsylvania was $180,187, which was 96 percent above the national average of $92,055 for permanent total cases that year (table 3.10). Altogether, Pennsylvania's 1982 permanent total cases cost $31.172 million, which represented 11.27 percent of all cash benefits that year—the second largest share of cash benefits accounted for by permanent total disability cases among the 45 jurisdictions included in table 3.5.

Pennsylvania's experience with permanent partial disability benefits is quite different. Although the average costs of both major and minor permanent partial cases have been relatively high since 1973—as of 1982, major cases had average costs of $78,575, which was 313 percent of the national average (table 3.11), while minor permanent partial cases averaged $9,176, some 185 percent of the U.S. average (table 3.12)—the numbers of permanent partial cases in Pennsylvania have been relatively low. In 1982, for example, major permanent partial cases accounted for only 1.40 percent of all cash benefit cases in Pennsylvania, a share that was only 21 percent of the U.S. average share for such cases (table 3.7). Similarly, minor permanent partial cases accounted for only 9.86 percent of all cash benefit cases in Pennsylvania, which was 57 percent of the national average share for minor permanent partial cases (table 3.8). The relatively low number of permanent partial cases more than offset the high average costs of those cases, resulting in a total cost that, as a share of all costs for cash benefits, was relatively low; in 1982, the Pennsylvania share of all costs for major cases was only 52 percent of the national average share (table 3.15), while the state's share of all costs for minor cases was only 82 percent of the national average share (table 3.16).

The data just cited, which are from the National Council on Compensation Insurance, do not distinguish between scheduled and nonscheduled permanent partial cases, and any conclusions drawn from them must be somewhat speculative. It appears that the relatively restrictive schedule in Pennsylvania, plus the requirement that nonscheduled cases be paid only when there is actual wage loss, substantially limit the number of cases that qualify for benefits, while those cases that do qualify involve serious wage loss and thus the average costs are high. In short, one possible outcome of a limited schedule plus a wage-loss approach for nonscheduled benefits is to channel most of the permanent disability benefits to a relatively small number of workers, with the overall cost of the permanent disability benefits in the state below the costs in most jurisdictions. This is true in Pennsylvania even when the relatively expensive permanent total disability benefits are added to the costs of the major and minor permanent partial benefits: all three types of permanent disability cases accounted for only 51.64 percent of all cash benefits in the state in 1982, a share that was only 75 percent of the national average share for permanent disability cases that year (table 3.17) and that was the lowest share among the eight jurisdictions with comparable data that we are intensely examining (graph 3.1).

Pennsylvania's record of a low share of all cash benefits accounted for by permanent disability cases has persisted since 1958, compared to the national average (table 3.17) and the rest of the eight states (graph 3.1). The cost of workers' compensation insurance in Pennsylvania has also been consistently below the national average since 1958 (table 3.18). Pennsylvania's experience thus supports the general relationship shown in graph 3.2—employers' costs of workers' compensation insurance tend to be lower in jurisdictions with a lower share of cash benefits accounted for by permanent disability cases.

Michigan

Workers' compensation in Michigan has experienced recurrent turmoil and criticism for decades. A continuing complaint of employers has been the high cost of workers' compensation in Michigan, a charge that changed from ill-founded to accurate between 1958 and 1978 (table 3.18). Three separate study commissions were appointed in the 1960s and 1970s with little success. Then a series of amendments were enacted in 1980 and 1981 that made significant changes in the criteria and procedures for permanent disability benefits. In January 1983 open competition for workers' compensation insurance rates became effective. Despite these significant changes, which will be reviewed in this section, pressures for additional amendments did not completely dissipate. Partly in response to these pressures, in 1983 Governor Blanchard appointed Theodore J. St. Antoine as Special Counselor on Workers' Compensation. St. Antoine in his report (1984, p. 21) concluded that "it is entirely too soon to seek further major amendments affecting the substantive rights of employers or employees," but he did recommend significant changes in administrative structure and procedure. Many of St. Antoine's recommendations were included in 1985 legislation, which is discussed below. The legislature only partially heeded St. Antoine's advice to delay further amendments to the substantive criteria for benefits: no changes were enacted in 1985 but crucial sections dealing with wage-loss benefits are subject to a May 15, 1987, sunset provision. Whether that date will be extended or substantive amendments made before then is unclear as of early 1987, when this chapter was completed.

Throughout these decades of strife, the wage-loss approach for workers with permanent disabilities has been one focus of attention. The Michigan approach was cited with favor by the National Commission on State Workmen's Compensation Laws (1972, p. 69), but subsequently was described as "a sullied wage-loss approach at best" by the National Commission's former chairman (Burton 1983, p. 26). Michigan's problems with wage-loss benefits primarily relate to the fourth and fifth traits of the approach provided earlier in this chapter: the ability of the employer to establish that the worker's earning capacity is greater than his actual earnings, and the use of redemptions (compromise and release agreements) to terminate eligibility for benefits for subsequent wage loss.

Administrative Structure and Procedures

Michigan is a direct payment state. The employer is required to file a report in all compensable cases. When the carrier begins payment, it sends the Bureau a notice to that effect. The Bureau is the administrative body located within the Department of Labor. It is headed by a director who is appointed by the governor with the advice and consent of the Senate for a period of three years.

The "old" administration. Many of the administrative features will be affected by the 1985 amendments. There is a two-tier structure for decisionmaking in contested cases. Initial hearings are conducted by a hearing referee, who must be an attorney and who is almost always referred to as an administrative law judge (ALJ). In recent years, there have been about 30 ALJs, who are Civil Service personnel appointed by the director of the Bureau.

Parties have the right to appeal the ALJ's decision to the Workers' Compensation Appeal Board, which consists of 15 members, a majority of whom are required to be attorneys-at-law. Five members are representatives of employee interests, five of employer interests, and five of the general public. The chairperson of the Board is designated by, and serves at the pleasure of, the governor. Matters pending in review are assigned to a panel of three members of the Board for disposition, with each panel consisting of one representative from each of the interest groups.

St. Antoine (1984, pp. 67-78) documented several problems with the procedures. For the last two decades, the average time from application for a hearing to the actual hearing ranged from about a year to 15 months. Once the ALJ decisions were made, they routinely were carried to the Appeal board—indeed, between 75 and 85 percent of all ALJ awards were appealed in the last decade. This had caused the Board's backlog "to mushroom from a mere 2,000 cases in 1976 to almost 7,000 as of November 1984 . . . which is the equivalent of about five or six years' output by the Appeals Board" (St. Antoine 1984, p. 68).

St. Antoine termed the delay "simply intolerable." One major explanation in his view was that the reviews by the Appeal Board were *de novo,* with both determinations of fact and law subject to a "whole fresh look." Even though the ALJs were affirmed in about 75 percent of the cases, "the very notion of *de novo* review . . . is an open invitation to disappointed litigants and their lawyers to retry the case from scratch'' (St. Antoine 1984, p. 69).

St. Antoine recommended that findings of facts by ALJs be conclusive if supported by competent, material, and substantial evidence on the whole record. He also recommended that the selection procedure for ALJs be modified by use of a bipartisan ALJ Qualifications Advisory Committee. Further, he recommended that a new five- or possibly seven-member Appeal Board be created to replace the old 15-member Board, with members all to be lawyers screened by a Qualifications Advisory Committee before appointment.

The "new" administration. The essence of St. Antoine's recommendations were enacted by the legislature in 1985. The first level of decisions were to be by magistrates, of whom 30 may be appointed by the governor with prior recommendation from the qualifications advisory committee. A seven-member appellate commission was established, again with all members to be lawyers screened before appointment by the Qualifications Advisory Committee. Effective October 1, 1986, the finding of fact made by a magistrate was to be considered conclusive by the appellate commission "if supported by competent, material, and substantial evidence on the whole record" (Sec. 861a[3]), thus ending *de novo* reviews.

The 1985 legislation provided for the position of hearing referees to be abolished as of March 31, 1987, with the initial magistrates to be appointed no later than March 31, 1986, and there were overlapping provisions for other aspects of the old and new administrative procedures. One feature of the 1985 law challenged by the Civil Service Commission and the ALJs was the switch to a system of magistrates appointed by the governor. After a circuit court decision ruled against the provision, the Supreme Court upheld its constitutionality in March 1986.[3] Because of the delays caused by the legal challenge, the new magistrates could not be appointed before late 1986. Thus the new administrative process began with almost a year's backlog of cases by the time it became operative.

Types and Levels of Benefits

Total Disability Benefits. Effective January 1, 1982, Michigan discarded 66 2/3 percent of preinjury wages as the basis for the weekly amount of total disability benefits in favor of a formula that calculates benefits as 80 percent of the employee's after-tax average weekly wage, subject to a maximum of 90 percent of the state's average weekly wage. The maximum weekly benefit in January 1986 was $375.00. "After tax" wages are defined as gross weekly wages reduced by federal and state income taxes and the Federal Insurance Contributions Act tax (social security contribution), using the standard deductions and the exemptions calculated according to the number of the employee's dependents.

Michigan's act provides for permanent total disability when the worker experiences a loss of two major members; or permanent and complete paralysis of both legs or both arms or one leg and one arm; or incurable insanity or imbecility; or permanent and total loss of industrial use of both legs or both hands or both arms, or one leg and one arm. The statute provides that the conclusive presumption of total and permanent disability shall not extend beyond 800 weeks from the date of injury, and "thereafter the question of permanent and total disability shall be determined in accordance with the fact, as the fact may be at that time" (Sec. 351).

Scheduled Benefits. Michigan has a schedule in its law that lists the extremities normally covered, such as arms, hands, and fingers. The law provides (Section 361) that the disability "shall be considered to continue for the period specified" in this schedule and during that time the employee is to be paid compensation at 80 percent of his after-tax average weekly wages, subject to the minimum and maximum weekly benefits ($104.05 and $375.00, respectively, as of January 1986).

The Michigan schedule is rather restrictive because it applies only to physical loss of the listed body members, not loss of use, as in most states' schedules. Also, the schedule provides compensation only for total loss, not partial loss, of most body members included in the list. These aspects of the Michigan schedule are at least as restrictive as the corresponding provisions in the Pennsylvania schedule. (The Pennsylvania law does compensate for loss of use when multiple body members are involved.) Unlike the Pennsylvania schedule, however, the Michigan schedule is not exclusive, because workers who experience continuing wage loss after periods specified in the schedule are eligible for further benefits based on the wage-loss approach.

Partial Disability Benefits. The Michigan statute (Sec. 361) does not distinguish between temporary and permanent partial disability. In either case, weekly benefits are 80 percent of the difference between the worker's after-tax average weekly wage before the personal injury and the after-tax average weekly wage "which the employee is able to earn after the personal injury,'' subject to a maximum benefit that is 90 percent of the state's average weekly wage ($375.00 in January 1986). The benefits are paid for the duration of the disability. The partial disability benefits represent a form of wage-loss benefits potentially payable for life.

The legal requirements for these wage-loss benefits are extraordinarily complex and the impact of the 1980, 1981, and 1985 amendments is unclear; we attempt a brief overview relying in large part on St. Antoine (1984, pp. 23-35).

The definition of the wage-loss approach provided earlier in this chapter involved several requirements, including: (1) there must be some remaining permanent impairment or functional limitation at the date of MMI; (2) there must be actual wage loss after the date of MMI, which is calculated by subtracting postinjury actual wages from postinjury potential earnings; (3) wage-loss benefits are calculated by subtracting postinjury earning capacity from postinjury potential earnings when postinjury earning capacity exceeds postinjury actual wages.

Michigan has, in effect, added an additional requirement, namely: (1B) the impairment or functional limitation must cause a disability, which means a loss of earning capacity by the employee. Earning capacity thus appears in two of the Michigan requirements: (1B), where the employee must show that the injury caused some loss of earning capacity, and (3), where the employer must show that earning capacity is greater than postinjury actual wages.

Michigan requirement (1B) has a history that Arthur Larson has described as "sheer freakishness."[4] The courts defined disability as the loss of earning capacity in the work the employee was doing at the time of injury. Moreover, a distinction was drawn between a skilled worker—who was considered totally disabled if he could not resume his former job—and an unskilled worker—who was considered only partially disabled so long as he could perform some job in the field of common labor. The 1981 amendments added a definition of disability (Sec. 301[4]), namely, "a limitation of an employee's wage earning capacity in the employee's general field of employment resulting from a personal injury or work related disease." The apparent intent was to remove the distinction between skilled and unskilled workers and to generally make it more difficult for a worker to establish that he is disabled. St. Antoine (1984, p. 25) has expressed doubt, however, that the new 1981 definition of disability will have much impact.

One reason for St. Antoine's skepticism about the practical impact of the change in definition of disability is that once any degree of disability is established—however slight—the worker may qualify for full wage-loss benefits (St. Antoine 1984, p. 26). To restate in terms of our framework, a 1 percent or greater permanent impairment will fully satisfy requirement (1) for wage-loss benefits; and, in Michigan, a 1 percent or greater disability will fully satisfy requirement (1B).

The second requirement for wage-loss benefits—that actual wage loss exists after subtracting actual postinjury earnings from postinjury potential earnings—is encompassed in several sections of the Michigan statute (St. Antoine 1984, p. 26).

Michigan's most noteworthy contribution to the quest for an operational wage-loss approach involves the handling of requirement (3): employers can reduce their liability for wage-loss benefits by demonstrating that postinjury earnings capacity is greater than postinjury actual wages. There are a number of elements to the Michigan scheme. Since the 1981 amendments, if the employee refuses a bona fide offer of reasonable employment without good and reasonable cause (Sec. 301.[5][a]), the worker is not entitled to wage-loss benefits during the period of refusal. In effect, there is a conclusive presumption that the refusal of a reasonable job means that postinjury earning capacity is equal to postinjury potential earnings.

The most difficult aspect of requirement (3) involves the question: if the worker is employed after the injury, do the earnings from that job establish a postinjury earnings capacity that will continue to be used to calculate wage-loss benefits if the worker subsequently loses his job? A simple example may help: a worker earns $500 a week in 1986; is injured in 1987 and has no earnings that year and receives benefits based on $500 of earnings loss; returns to work at $300 per week in 1988 and receives wage-loss benefits based on the $200 of actual wage loss; and then has no earnings in 1989. Question: are the wage-loss benefits in 1989 based on $200 or $500 of earning loss?

The Michigan answer is: it depends! Prior to 1981, a distinction was drawn between "favored work," which was essentially a temporary position that made limited demands on the worker because of his injury, and "recognized regular employment." The former did not establish a postinjury earning capacity, whereas the latter did. Unfortunately, this distinction was overlaid with a concern about why the postinjury job was terminated—if the employee was responsible, he would be treated as having established a postinjury earning capacity; otherwise, he would not (St. Antoine 1984, pp. 30-31).

The Legislature dealt with the issue of how postinjury earning capacity is established in 1981. Sec. 301(5)(e) provides that if the postinjury employment period is less than 100 weeks and the employee "loses his or her job for whatever reason," then (in effect) postinjury earning capacity is zero for the period subsequent to the job loss. As noted by St. Antoine (1984, p. 33), this appears to be more favorable to the employee than the law prior to 1981, since an employee who voluntarily quits during the 100 weeks can take advantage of the provision. St. Antoine recommended that the defect be remedied, which was not accomplished in 1985. Sec. 301(5)(d) provides that if the postinjury employment period is between 100 and 249 weeks and the employee loses his job "through no fault of the employee" and the employee exhausts his unemployment benefit eligibility, then (in effect) postinjury earning capacity, *if any,* will be determined by the worker's compensation magistrate or hearing referee. That postinjury earning capacity apparently is "the normal and customary wages paid to those persons performing the same or similar employment" as the injured worker was performing in the postinjury period. Unfortunately, the language of Sec. 301(5)(d) is sufficiently confusing that other interpretations are possible, but we agree with St. Antoine (1984 at p. 34) that this is the most reasonable interpretation of the legislature's intent for those workers with 100-249 weeks of postinjury employment. As for the worker with 250 or more weeks of postinjury employment who then becomes unemployed for any reason, Sec. 301(5)(d) provides that "there is a presumption of wage earning capacity established." This means the magistrate or referee must find a postinjury earning capacity equal to "the normal and customary wages paid to those persons performing the same or similar employment" as the worker was performing after the date of injury.

The 1981 amendments have not received extensive interpretations and their ultimate significance is thus hard to assess. St. Antoine (1984, p. 35) suggests that, compared to previous case law, they seem to make disabled workers better off during the first two years on a postinjury job, to make little difference for the next three years, and to treat injured workers with five years of postinjury employment no better than other workers. He concluded that, while the statute could stand some clarifying amendments, the underlying rationale for the 1981 amendments is sufficiently defensible to justify an extended trial period before additional significant changes are made in the wage-loss provisions of the statute. Whether St. Antoine's advice will be heeded remains to be seen. In any case, his trenchant analysis of the evolution of the wage-loss approach in Michigan provides valuable guidance to those in other jurisdictions. One possible "lesson" we draw is that the parameters of the wage-loss approach may require detailed legislation rather than reliance on the courts to flesh out the operational details. Although the 1981 amendments are not free of ambiguity, the effort to delineate in a statute the meaning of postinjury earning capacity seems preferable to relying on sporadic court pronouncements.

Retirees

The recent amendments also dealt with the problem of retirees. Michigan was awarding a large portion of its compensation dollars to individuals who voluntarily retired and then filed for benefits alleging wage loss as a result of a prior injury or exposure.

The problem had its origin in 1956, when some of the United Automobile Workers' agreements eliminated pension benefit offset against workers' compensation. Under the newly negotiated provision, the worker could receive both a workers' compensation benefit and his full pension benefit. In 1960, court decisions liberalized the statute of limitations for the notice required of a worker to an employer of a work-related injury. Claimants and their attorneys, taking advantage of these developments, began to file claims on behalf of retired workers alleging wage loss due to some prior injury. These began as contested claims, since no initial report of injury or notice of beginnings of payment had been filed. The argument made to justify benefits was that the retired worker could not find another job because of a work-related injury. Many of the earlier cases were filed by foundry workers with impairments of the lungs, heart, or back. The incentives to file such claims grew after 1965 amendments removed the duration limits for total disability payments.

A single attorney could represent a large number of clients and negotiate a bulk settlement with representatives of the automobile companies. Hundreds of these cases were redeemed in a type of class action. Employees received some predetermined amounts, and the employers disposed of a number of claims in the least expensive way, given the interpretation of the law.

Some UAW representatives interviewed at the time of our 1976-77 field work indicated they were anxious to find some solution to the retiree problem, since it held back reform of other aspects of the law. With possibly some understandable exaggeration, they spoke of workers inquiring about their pensions and workers' compensation benefits at one and the same time; a workers' compensation settlement became a form of retirement bonus.

One ingredient that complicated the problem in Michigan was the early retirement plan in the automobile industry. Many retirees were in their fifties and looked forward to another job, if only on some part-time basis. If they could not find that job, for example because of a failure to pass a physical examination due to a bad back or decreased lung capacity, they had the basis for a workers' compensation claim on a wage-loss basis. Because court interpretations had lessened the need to show the occurrence of an accident, it was more difficult for the employer to demonstrate that the pre-retirement job was not the proximate cause of the worker's condition. The worker's case was strengthened because the employer could not demonstrate the employee's fitness by offering him a job, since the labor contract had provisions that made it difficult to rehire a retired and pensioned worker. Such a case was ripe for redemption, and that was the path followed in Michigan.

The retiree problem is not inherent in the wage-loss approach but grew out of conditions peculiar to Michigan. The ingredients were (1) a low retirement age in the principal industry, (2) the relaxed requirement for showing the occurrence of an accident and liberal interpretations of the statute of limitations, and (3) the practice of redeeming wage-loss cases in order for the employer to avoid potential liability of an uncertain amount and duration.

The 1980 and 1981 amendments contained a frontal attack on the retiree problem. Section 373 of the Act provides that an employee who has terminated active employment and is receiving either a governmental or a private pension paid by an employer from whom workers' compensation benefits are sought is presumed not to have suffered a loss of earnings or earning capacity as a result of a compensable injury or disease. The presumption may be rebutted by a preponderance of evidence that the employee is unable to perform work suited to his qualifications because of the work-related disability.

The retirement problem came about because of liberal interpretations of the notice of accident requirement. Under the recent amendments, notice of accident must be given within 90 days and claims for compensation must be made within two years of the date of injury or, in the case of occupational disease, within two years of the time the employee knows or should have known of the disability and its work-relatedness.

A "coordination of benefits" provision, another recent amendment, will also affect the amount of workers' compensation benefits received by retirees. Effective March 31, 1982, benefits are reduced by the amounts received from a private pension or disability insurance plan. In addition, 50 percent of an old age insurance benefit from Social Security is to be deducted from the net workers' compensation benefits. If an employee is eligible to receive such an old age retirement benefit from Social Security at his normal retirement age, he is obligated to apply for that benefit. A controversial Michigan Supreme Court decision, *Franks v. White Pine Copper Div.*, 422 Mich. 636, 375 N.W.2d 715 (1985), held that the coordination provision applies not only to workers injured after March 31, 1982, but to workers injured before that date. The decision was estimated to affect as many as 40,000 workers, in some instances completely eliminating their workers' compensation benefits,[5] and efforts to amend the law so as to remove the retroactive application of the benefits coordination provision have been mounted, without success as of early 1987.

The retirement problem will also be affected by Sections 301(2) and 401 (2), under which conditions of the aging process are deemed to be compensable only if they are contributed to, aggravated by, or accelerated by the employment in a significant manner. These provisions of the act should go a long way toward eliminating simultaneous receipt of retirement pensions and workers' compensation benefits.

Redemptions

We include Michigan in this chapter devoted to jurisdictions that use the wage-loss approach, and the National Commission *Report* (1972, p. 69) so described the state. Whether this is an accurate characterization depends in large part on the importance attached to compliance with trait five of a wage-loss approach (provided earlier in this chapter), which requires an extended period of eligibility for the wage-loss benefits.

The problem has been succinctly stated by St. Antoine (1984, p. 58):

Under the Michigan "wage loss" theory, one might expect that the standard award would require the payment of weekly benefits during the period of an employee's disability and continuing lack of work. In fact . . . more than half the total dispositions in contested workers' compensation cases have consisted for many years of compromises or so-called "redemptions," usually in the form of lump-sum settlements. Typically, a redemption terminates all further employer liability for income maintenance, medical benefits, and vocational rehabilitation. The practical effect is to transform the Michigan wage loss system, in many cases, into a modified impairment rating system.

The problems with redemptions have long been recognized in Michigan. During our field work for the NSF report (Berkowitz, Burton, and Vroman 1979) almost a decade ago, criticism was received from several quarters. The labor representatives we interviewed felt that the law should be amended to limit redemptions because of the risks for the worker who redeemed all future benefits. Concerns were expressed that these redemptions could be very disadvantageous to the worker in the long run, especially to workers who face the prospect of continuing medical care expenses. Insurance representatives were not happy with the high number of redemptions, but felt that in light of the way the law was administered, it was financially prudent to close out cases as rapidly and as inexpensively as possible.

The 1981 legislature stared down the problem. Section 836, to be effective January 1, 1984, consisted of a single sentence: "For any petition filed after the effective date of this section, entitlement to workers' compensation benefits under this act shall not be redeemed."

The 1983 legislature blinked. Section 836 was repealed and redemptions were again authorized, subject, however, to a new and stricter system for approval. Hearing referees are required to consider a variety of factors, including the intended use of the proceeds, before approving the agreement as being in the "best interests of the injured employee" (Sec. 836), and each party to the agreement must pay a $100 fee to the bureau (Sec. 835). Nonetheless, the discount rate used to commute the future payments to their present worth for determining the amount of the lump-sum settlement is 12 percent—a rate unlikely to severely dampen the employer or carrier interest in a redemption settlement.

The new procedures for redemptions became effective on January 1, 1984, and assessment of the effect is premature, although St. Antoine (1984, p. 58) reported that redemptions represented 54.4 percent of dispositions in the first nine months of 1984—only marginally better than in the previous five years. Nonetheless, St. Antoine concluded that further stringent restrictions on redemptions were unfeasible at this time because of the enormous backlog of cases. He was also encouraged by the close scrutiny being given by ALJs to proposed agreements under the new act. His ultimate advice (p. 59) bears repeating: "This whole area has enough potential for abuse, however, that it calls for continuing surveillance."

Experience with Permanent Disability Benefits in Michigan

The costs of workers' compensation in Michigan have been of concern to employers and others in the state for decades. Indeed, one of the authors of this study became involved in workers' compensation research because of a fear expressed in the early 1960s that high workers' compensation costs were affecting plant location decisions in Michigan. His earlier study (Burton 1966, p. 73) concluded that "the actual magnitude of the interstate differentials in employers' costs of workmen's compensation should not influence plant location decisions." This conclusion seemed particularly appropriate for Michigan at the time, because Michigan's workers' compensation costs were not out of line with those in other states. One measure of the cost of the workers' compensation program is the percentage of payroll devoted to workers' compensation premiums by a representative sample of employers. In 1965, the premiums for Michigan employers were equivalent to 0.715 percent of payroll, below the average cost of 0.791 percent of payroll in the 28 states for which comparable data are available (table 3.18).

This relatively sanguine situation for Michigan employers did not last, however. By 1972, insurance premiums for workers' compensation represented 0.914 percent of payroll in Michigan, which was 17 percent above the average (0.783) in the 28 jurisdictions. Costs continued to escalate rapidly in Michigan, and by 1978 Michigan employers were expending 1.890 percent of payroll on workers' compensation premiums, compared to the 28-jurisdiction average of 1.460 percent. Thus by 1978 Michigan employers were spending 33 percent more on workers' compensation than comparable employers in the other jurisdictions.

The rapid increase in Michigan workers' compensation costs between 1972 and 1978 is particularly interesting because the benefit levels prescribed by the Michigan law lagged during this period. For example, in terms of the maximum weekly benefit for temporary total disability, as of 1972, when one state (Arizona) had a maximum that was at least 100 percent of the state's average weekly wage, Michigan's maximum for temporary total of $79.00 was 50 percent of the state's average weekly wage. By 1978, Michigan's temporary total maximum had increased to $171.00, which was 64 percent of the state's average weekly wage, but by then 24 jurisdictions had increased their maximums for temporary total disability benefits to at least 100 percent of the state's average weekly wage (U.S. Dept. of Labor, *State Compliance,* 1982). The relatively slow increase in maximum benefits in Michigan during this period is explained in part by the employers' reactions to the escalating costs of the program, which in turn they related to "abuses" of permanent disability benefits, such as the retiree problem.

The magnitude of Michigan workers' compensation costs during the 1970s do appear to be largely due to permanent disability benefits. Surprisingly, at one level it is hard to identify an adverse trend in Michigan's experience with permanent disability benefits during this period. For example, the share of all cash benefits accounted for by all types of permanent disability benefits in Michigan was consistently below the national average share for such cases from 1968 to 1978 (table 3.17).

Michigan's problems with permanent disability benefits become more apparent as the data are disaggregated, however. The pattern over time of permanent total disability benefits, for example, helps to explain why Michigan had a deserved reputation as a problem state. Michigan was the only state that failed to meet recommendation R3.11 of the National Commission on State Workmen's Compensation Laws, which limited permanent total disability benefits to those workers who did not retain substantial earning capacity. By 1978, 0.45 percent of all Michigan cases were permanent total cases, which was 331 percent of the national average share and the highest share of the eight states intensively analyzed in chapter 3. (See table 3.6.)

The problems with permanent partial disability benefits in Michigan are less obvious than the permanent total problem. A few comparisons with Pennsylvania will help to put the problem in relief. Because Michigan has a restrictive schedule roughly comparable to that in Pennsylvania, and both states have a statute that purports to base nonscheduled benefits on a wage-loss approach, a comparable experience with permanent partial cases in the two jurisdictions could be expected. In fact, there was a significant difference in 1978 in the share of all cash benefits accounted for by permanent partial disability cases (major and minor) in the two jurisdictions: 39.45 percent in Pennsylvania and 60.40 percent in Michigan (tables 3.15 and 3.16).

How is it that two states with similar statutory approaches to permanent disability benefits had such different experiences with the numbers and costs of these benefits? The answer in large part appears to be that whereas the theory and practice of wage-loss benefits are largely congruent in Pennsylvania, in Michigan the practice often deviates from the theory. In theory, except for those few cases handled entirely by paying scheduled benefits, permanent partial disability benefits in Michigan were supposed to be paid only when the worker experiences an actual loss of earnings because of the work injury, and those benefits are supposed to continue for the duration of the wage loss and cease when wage loss ends.

The practice in Michigan was captured by Hunt's study (1982) of Michigan workers' compensation cases closed in 1978. Hunt found that some cases were in fact handled as the theory dictates, with benefits paid over an extended period, but many were not. The cases typically were litigated and ended in redemptions, with the employer released from further liability and the worker given a settlement with the amount related, at least loosely, to the extent of loss of earning capacity.[6] The redemption settlement was not conditioned upon the worker showing an actual loss of wages due to the injury, with the most extreme example being the redemptions for retirees.

How significant are these interrelated phenomena of litigation and redemption settlements? Hunt found (p. 183) that nearly three-fourths of all Michigan claims were voluntarily paid by the insurers. Among serious injury cases, however, litigation and redemption settlements are the dominant approach. Overall, Hunt found (at p. 189) that *"60 percent* of all the compensation paid over the lifetime of these closed cases was paid in lump sums rather than weekly payments." Thus, even though, as Hunt observes (p. 184), "in a theoretical context, the wage-loss principle and lump-sum settlements are generally regarded as mutually exclusive," the practice in Michigan clearly was dominated by these lump-sum settlements. Moreover, Hunt estimated that from 25 to 35 percent of all litigated cases in Michigan were filed by retirees, and that they received a minimum of 18 percent of all the indemnity payments reported in the study.

The litigation-redemption-lump-sum nexus took a particularly heavy toll on the theory that permanent partial benefits in Michigan were paid on a wage-loss basis. Whatever the theory, and however the statute reads, the practice in Michigan had converted the permanent partial benefit scheme into a perverse variant of a loss of wage-earning capacity approach.

What needs to be stressed is that the fate of the wage-loss approach in Michigan was not inevitable. Stretching the wage-loss concept to compensate retirees for earnings they never would have earned even if they had never been injured is an aberration of the wage-loss approach, as the Pennsylvania experience demonstrates.

The failings of the Michigan workers' compensation program as of 1978 precipitated a number of reforms described, in large part, earlier in this section. There were multiple strategies and purposes, including the tightening of the definition of disability in order to reduce the number of total disability cases, the introduction of open competition for insurance rates in order to reduce costs, and the elaboration of the criteria for redemptions in order to discourage their use. These changes are still working their way through the system in an interactive fashion and it is too early to provide a definitive evaluation of their impact. Some preliminary evidence is available, however.

One result that is particularly compelling is that the cost of workers' compensation insurance fell sharply between 1978, when Michigan costs were 33 percent above the U.S. average, and 1984, when costs were 6 percent below the U.S. average (table 3.18). Burton, Hunt, and Krueger (1985, p. 135) attempted to disentangle the sources of the reduced insurance costs between 1978 and 1984 and concluded that open competition reduced insurance rates by 30.2 percent and the 1983-84 benefit changes resulting from the statutory changes in the preceding years reduced rates an additional 6.2 percent. There were other developments, such as higher medical benefits, that partially offset the impact of open competition and the 1983-84 benefit changes. In combination, all these factors produced a cumulative reduction of 31.8 percent in insurance rates between 1978 and 1984. The estimated savings to Michigan employers in 1983 and 1984 from open competition and the 1983-84 benefit changes were $502 million (Burton, Hunt, and Krueger 1985, p. 137).

The data from the National Council on Compensation Insurance (NCCI) analyzed in chapter 3 do not extend beyond 1982 policy year experience, and so the impact of the recent amendments is only partially reflected. The data in table 3.6 are suggestive of the potential impact: Michigan's share of all cases that were permanent total cases dropped from 331 percent of the national average in 1978 to 130 percent in 1982. Supplemental data through 1983 injuries were provided by the NCCI and analyzed by Burton and Partridge (1985, p. 46), who found that permanent partial cases as a percentage of all claims had dropped about 20-30 percent in 1982-83 compared to 1979-81.

The supplemental NCCI data also indicate that other facets of the Michigan program are changing subsequent to the 1980-81 amendments. The percentage of permanent partial cases closed by lump sums was almost halved from 1979-81 to 1982-83,[7] and the percentage of all permanent partial claims accounted for by workers 50 years or older was also down about 15 percent between the two periods (Burton and Partridge 1985, pp. 48-49).[8]

Changes in workers' compensation criteria and procedures for permanent disability benefits inevitably take time to have their full impact on the program, especially when, as in Michigan, court interpretations of key provisions are needed. To be sure, as St. Antoine concluded (1984, p. 19), the preliminary data are consistent with the view that the 1980 and 1981 amendments are having significant effects on several aspects of the program. We believe the salutary effects include a reduction in the use of redemption settlements and in the use of the program by retirees, which move Michigan closer to a "true" wage-loss approach. We can easily draw up a list of further changes that would hasten the convergence of practice and theory of wage-loss in Michigan. But given the magnitude of the recent amendments, we are persuaded by St. Antoine's "one fundamental conclusion: It is entirely too soon to seek further major amendments affecting the substantive rights of employers or employees" (1984, p. 21).

New York

Administrative Structure and Procedure

Administrative Structure. The New York workers' compensation law is administered by the Workers' Compensation Board, headed by a chairman and consisting of 13 members. The members are appointed by the governor for seven-year terms. The chairman is the administrative head of the agency that processes claims and also the chairman of the Appeals Board.

One of the principal divisions under the chairman's authority is the Operations Division. Under the Operations Division are several units including the Claims Bureau, the Judges Bureau, the Review Bureau, the Medical Bureau, the Disability Benefits Bureau, the Health Provider Practices Bureau, and the Rehabilitation Bureau. Altogether, the Board has a staff of 1,627, which is the highest in terms of absolute members and, among states without exclusive state funds, the highest per million covered workers of the jurisdictions we are intensively examining (table 4.1).

The Claims Bureau processes and monitors the claims for workers' compensation: at the appropriate stage, the Bureau schedules the cases for hearings before the administrative law judges.

There are 28 hearing rooms, or parts, in New York City and an equal number of workers' compensation law judges staffing these parts, under direction of a supervisor. The six district offices outside of New York City have their own law judges, who conduct hearings at about 70 designated hearings points throughout their respective districts. Each district office has a small staff whose primary responsibility is to set up the calendar for the hearings in that district. They also have their own claims examiners, medical examiners, rehabilitation counselors, and statistical clerks.

The Board is authorized to hear cases on review in panels of three, which are formed on a rotating basis. Unlike the law judges, the Board panels hold their hearings only in the seven district offices.

The Office of the General Counsel occupies a strategic place in the work of the Board. It enforces the insurance provisions of the act, including supervision of all cancellations and renewals; it administers the Uninsured Employers' Fund and obtains and collects judgments from defaulting employers. It drafts legislative proposals and helps to steer them through the legislature, following clearance with the governor's office. It has the responsibility of assuring that the law judge and Board decisions are in conformity with the law; of preparing digests of the law and its amendments, and of Board decisions and administrative rulings; and of answering inquiries about the act and conducting investigations.

The Review Bureau has the responsibility to get cases ready for Board review, when an appeal has been filed from a law judge's decision. This involves screening cases for reviewability, digesting and summarizing the facts and issues in the cases, and preparing the Board panel members for the review. This may include preparation of a memorandum for the Board members that analyzes the significant points in the case, the evidence on both sides, and the summarizer's opinion on the case.

The Basic Procedure: Indexing and Hearings. All work-related injuries and diseases resulting in a loss of time beyond the working day or shift on which the accident occurred that require medical treatment beyond ordinary first aid must be reported to the Workers' Compensation Board, which reviews the reports and indexes all cases appearing to involve more than seven days' lost time or the likelihood of permanent disability. All cases that have been indexed can be closed only after a hearing before a law judge. The claims examiner with responsibility for monitoring a case that has been indexed must schedule a case for hearing at some appropriate time, depending on the seriousness of the injury, controversion of the case, termination or reduction of benefits, or other factors. This mandatory hearing is unique to the New York workers' compensation program, and helps explain the size of the staff.

The Motion Calendar. When the examiner determines that no award of scheduled or other permanent disability benefits will be made or required, the case may be set for the "motion calendar." The parties are notified of the hearing but are not necessarily expected to appear. A law judge conducts the hearings on the motion calendar and automatically closes a case unless the claimant requests a regular hearing. If no parties appear, the case may be closed without a substantive review.

The motion calendar provides a procedure to permit the case to be closed by a law judge in fulfillment of the statutory requirement; it also allows a claimant to request a regular hearing when his claim has been set for the motion calendar. Only 18 percent of all cases closed are actually processed on the motion calendar (New York Temporary Commission 1986, p. 63). Efforts are being made to have more claims processed on the motion calendar, in order to enable the law judges to devote more of their time to the more difficult cases.

The Trial Calendar. The trial calendar includes cases requiring an immediate hearing either because the case is being controverted or because benefits have been terminated by the carrier; such cases are put on a "preference calendar" and usually set for hearing within six weeks. More routine cases, such as those in which all bills and benefits have been paid but which involve some permanent impairment, are set for a hearing usually six months or one year after the date of injury, depending on the severity of the injury.

When a case is called at a regular hearing, the law judge checks to see that all necessary information required for the case is in the case folder and that all the participants who should be present are actually available. If all is not ready, the case may be adjourned, with notices being sent to the parties to tell them what they should do before the next hearing.

An important part of the procedure in permanent disability cases is an examination by a board doctor for a Final Adjustment. At this time the claimant is given a finding of disability.

The judge develops the record by having the witnesses for both sides testify. After all evidence is submitted by both sides, the judge usually makes an award or states his decision immediately. Notice of the decision is sent to all parties by the Board, since the decisions of the judges are considered official actions of the Board.

If a particular case is not yet ready for a Final Adjustment (for example, if the claimant is still temporarily disabled), the judge may make a temporary reduced earnings (TRE) award, if appropriate, and abey the case for another few months. The abeyance will continue until the case is ready for final adjustment.

Board Action on Lump-Sum Adjustments. A decision to close a case by making a "lump-sum adjustment" must be made by a member of the Board (prior to October 1984, approval of a three-member panel was required). The Review Bureau has a special unit called the Lump-Sum Unit that reviews applications for lump-sum adjustments. After reviewing the case, an examiner in this unit may make a recommendation and pass the case on to the Board office that schedules Board hearings.

Reopenings. Generally, reopening a case that has once been closed requires evidence of a change in the medical condition of the claimant. A case can be opened only upon the signature of a Board member. Then the case is scheduled for hearing before a law judge, under generally the same procedure as for a new case.

Upon reopening a case, the Board may make such modifications or changes in its previous findings or awards as it considers to be in the interest of justice. The modifications may be made on a change in condition or proof of an erroneous wage rate, or on a showing of a mistake in facts, errors of law, or newly discovered evidence.

The provisions relating to reopening of cases and continuing jurisdiction of the Board are given a broad, liberal interpretation. This relative liberality, as compared with most other United States jurisdictions, is made possible by the presence of a Special Fund for Reopened Cases which relieves carriers and self-insurers of liability in certain "stale" cases. To be reopened under this section, the claim must have been originally closed on its merits, but there does not necessarily have to be a change in condition. Even the "reopened case fund" is relieved of possible liability after a lapse of 18 years from the date of the original injury and eight years since the last payment of compensation for the injury. When a claim is disallowed after a hearing on the merits, or the case is closed without award (after notice and opportunity to be heard), the carrier is relieved of all liability after a lapse of seven years from the date of injury or death, but the claimant may still be compensated from the reopened case fund if the claim is filed within the time limitations mentioned above.

A defender of the fund for reopened cases, to protect the fund from unwarranted claims, is appointed by the chairman of the Board, who has to approve payments out of the fund.

Appeals to the Board. Any party to a hearing may appeal a decision or award of a law judge by making written application to the Board within 30 days after the notice of decision or award has been filed. Administrative review of the decision is made by a three-member panel of the Board. The panel has the authority to weigh the evidence in the record of the case and make its determination based on the facts as well as the law. If the panel deems it necessary, it may send the case back to the law judge for further development, that is, for the purpose of getting more testimony. Panel decisions may be appealed to the full Board, which must hear the case if one panel member has dissented.

Appeals to the Courts. From the Board a further appeal may be made within 30 days to the Appellate Division of the Supreme Court, third department. An appeal to the courts from a Board decision can be made only on questions of law, not on questions of fact. The final step in the appellate process is an appeal to the Court of Appeals, within 30 days of the decision of the appellate division.

During the time the case is on appeal to the courts, any benefits awarded by the Board must be paid to the claimant. If the award is reversed, the claimant does not need to return the money he or she may have received up to that time; instead, the carrier is reimbursed from the Board's budget.

Representation at Hearings. Either party to a claim before a workers' compensation law judge or before the Board may be represented by an attorney admitted to practice in the state or by a layman licensed by the Board. (Carriers or self-insurers may be represented by their own regular employees even though they are not licensed.)

According to statistics on compensated cases closed in 1982,[9] only 19 percent of the cases involved legal fees, and the average fee was $445. The total amount of legal fees ($10.5 million) amounted to 3.0 percent of the total compensation awarded in the cases where the claimant had legal representation, or 2.0 percent of compensation awarded in all cases. The legal fee allowed "generally varies inversely with the amount of compensation. For the 3,455 cases in which the compensation award was under $1,000, legal fees amounted to 12 percent of the awards, but for the 5,917 cases in which the award was $10,000 or over, legal fees amounted to only 2 percent of the awards."

The Relationship between Temporary Total Disability Benefits and Scheduled Permanent Partial Awards

If the injury is a scheduled one, the doctor at the hearing will state a specified percentage of partial loss. The percentage rating is used in conjunction with the statutory schedule to determine the nominal duration of the permanent partial disability benefits. Thus a 100 percent loss of a leg results in a nominal duration of 288 weeks; a 50 percent loss of a leg produces a nominal duration of 144 weeks, etc. In New York, the period of temporary total benefits is deducted from the nominal duration of the scheduled award, subject to certain limits on the deduction as determined by the prescribed healing periods. These limits, as provided in the statute, range from a low of eight weeks for the loss of a toe (other than the great toe) or for the loss of the third or fourth finger, to a high of 40 weeks for the loss of a leg (Sec. 15, subd. 4-a).

If a worker lost a leg and was out on temporary total benefits for exactly the 40 weeks prescribed in the healing period, he would be paid for 40 weeks at the temporary total rate, which was a maximum of $300 a week in 1986. That 40 weeks would be deducted from the 288 weeks of benefits allowed by the schedule, and the worker would receive 248 weeks at the permanent partial rate, which was a maximum of $150 a week in 1986. If, however, the worker were out for 48 weeks, the additional eight weeks of "protracted temporary total" would not be subtracted from the scheduled award. The worker would receive 48 weeks of temporary total benefits and 248 weeks (288–40) of permanent partial benefits.

When the number of weeks the worker is out on temporary total (or the specified healing period, if that is less than the actual period of temporary disability) is greater than the scheduled award, he receives no permanent partial benefits. (This is known as disability exceeds schedule, or DES.) For example, a worker with a 30 week healing period and a nominal scheduled award of 28.8 weeks for the loss of 10 percent of the leg will actually receive no permanent partial benefits. Of 30,118 scheduled permanent partial cases closed in 1983, there were 1,694 DES cases in which the injured worker received no permanent disability benefits.[10]

New York's method of relating temporary total disability benefits to permanent partial scheduled benefits is unique among U.S. jurisdictions (Burton, Larson, and Moran 1980, p. 258). One purported advantage is that the provision provides an incentive to return to work as soon as possible, since each extra week of healing period benefits reduces the scheduled award by a week. The incentive argument is undermined, however, since the temporary total weekly benefit rate is higher than the permanent partial rate, and consequently the worker receives more benefits in total with an additional week off work. The incentive argument does nonetheless have some merit when the New York provision is compared with the approach used in most jurisdictions, where a worker who extends the duration of his healing period by one week receives an additional week of temporary total benefits and no reduction in his permanent partial award.

One disadvantage of the approach is the confusing relationship between temporary disability benefits and scheduled awards. The statute provides in Sec. 15, subd. 4-a:

> In any case resulting in loss or partial loss of use of arm, leg, hand, foot, ear, eye, thumb, finger or toe, where the temporary total disability does not extend beyond the periods above mentioned for such injury, compensation shall be limited to the schedule contained in subdivision three.

It seems unlikely that a worker would understand this language to mean that the longer the period of temporary total disability benefits, the smaller the scheduled award. Even if this provision were clarified and workers were fully appraised of its impact, there would remain other disadvantages. One is that the provision has administrative complexities. Workers with temporary partial disability benefits must have these benefits translated into an equivalent duration of temporary total benefits in order to determine how many weeks to subtract from the scheduled award, and this multistep process invites errors and confusion.

The most compelling argument against the healing period provision is the effect of the provision on workers with extended and brief healing periods. Workers with the longest healing periods experience the most drastic reductions in their permanent disability benefits, which makes sense only if it is assumed that the workers generally have control over the duration of their healing periods.

The Relative Importance of Scheduled and Nonscheduled Awards

In 1982, 121,028 cases were closed with $526 million in cash benefits. Over 40 percent of these were permanent partial disability cases. Of these permanent partial disability cases, 89.6 percent (or 36.4 percent of all cases) were scheduled cases, but the 10.4 percent of the permanent partial disability cases (or 4.2 percent of all cases) that were nonscheduled accounted for 52.4 percent of all compensation awarded.[11] Thus by far most cases in the permanent partial disability category are decided on a scheduled rather than on a nonscheduled basis, and the nonscheduled cases are obviously much more expensive.

The numerical dominance in New York of scheduled permanent partial cases compared to nonscheduled cases is due in large part to the expansive nature of the schedule. The New York schedule applies to partial as well as total losses of the body members included in the schedule, not just to total losses as in Michigan and Pennsylvania. Also, unlike the schedules in the other two states, the New York schedules apply to losses of use as well as physical losses of the scheduled members. Only if the injury cannot be scheduled does it fall under Sec. 15, subd. 3-(w), the so-called "other cases" category, which deals with nonscheduled permanent partial cases and involves consideration of wage loss. These nonscheduled cases typically involve injuries to the back or other parts of the trunk.

Nonscheduled Benefits: the Legal Requirements

Benefits for nonscheduled permanent partial disabilities in New York State are 66 2/3 percent of the difference between the wages earned before the injury and the wages the worker is earning, or is able to earn, after the injury. The benefits are subject to a maximum of $150 a week and a minimum of $30 a week (or actual wages, if less). Most state laws limit the total amount of the award or the number of weeks of payment for nonscheduled benefits. New York's law is one of the few that provide for the payment of such benefits for the full period of disability; however, the Board has the authority to modify the degree of disability upon a showing of change in condition or earning capacity.

The statutory criteria for nonscheduled permanent partial benefits warrant elaboration. The law bases benefits on the difference between the claimant's average weekly wages before the injury and the "wage-earning *capacity* thereafter in the same employment *or otherwise,* payable during the continuance of such partial disability, but subject to reconsideration of the degree of such impairment by the board" (Sec. 15, subd. 3-[w]; emphasis supplied). The statute also provides that the wage-earning capacity of the claimant in such cases shall be determined by his actual earnings, if any. If, however, the employee has no actual earnings, the Board has the authority to fix the wage-earning capacity "having due regard to the nature of his injury and his physical impairment." The capacity cannot be determined to be in excess of 75 percent of the worker's preinjury earnings (Sec. 15, subd. 5-a).

Application of these statutory criteria results in three types of nonscheduled permanent partial disability cases: cases in which benefits are paid because of continuing wage loss; nonscheduled lump-sum adjustments, which can be approved by the Board in cases where continuance of disability and of future earning capacity cannot be made with reasonable certainty; and cases in which there is no present loss of earnings and payments consequently may never begin or may be discontinued (upon notice to the Board and a hearing).

Continuing Compensation Payments (CCP) Cases. In order for a worker to receive nonscheduled benefits, there must be affirmative answers to three questions. First, are the worker's actual earnings in the period after the medical condition is stabilized less than the worker's earnings before the date of injury? If the answer is no, then no benefits can be paid. In short, unlike in the case of scheduled awards, there can be no compensation for nonscheduled awards in New York except upon a showing of actual wage loss. Second, if there is a wage loss, can this be attributed at least in part to the permanent consequences of the work-related injury? If the answer is no, then no benefits can be paid. If the answer is yes, then normally the nonscheduled benefits are a specified portion (66 2/3 percent) of the actual wage loss. If the worker has no actual earnings in the period after the medical condition is stabilized, however, a third question must be asked, namely, does the worker have any wage-earning capacity? If the answer is no, the worker qualifies for permanent total, not permanent partial, disability benefits. If the answer is yes, then the nonscheduled benefits are a specified portion of the difference between the worker's preinjury wages and the postinjury earning capacity determined by the Board. The second and third questions deserve further elaboration.

Second, can the wage loss be attributed to the injury? In some situations, there is a question as to whether the claimant's reduction of earnings is attributable to a compensable injury or to other factors, such as economic conditions or voluntary withdrawal from the labor force.

(1) Retirement. In a number of cases, claimants have gone into retirement after beginning to receive permanent disability benefits. In *Yamonaco v. Union Carbide Corp.*, 42 A.D. 2d 1014, 348 N.Y.S. 2d 196 (1973), and other cases the court has outlined the standards to be used: if reduced earnings are due solely to voluntary withdrawal from the labor market, old age, economic conditions, or other factors unconnected with the disability, no compensation is payable. If there is substantial proof that the claimant's disability is at least a contributing factor to the reduced earnings, however, an award is warranted.

In *Mazziotto v. Brookfield Construction*, 40 A.D. 2d 704, 338 N.Y.S. 2d 1001 (1972), the claimant received benefits for three separate accidents. He went into retirement as a result of a union rule regarding work over age 65. The Appellate Division overruled the Board and denied benefits because the claimant failed to show efforts to seek work.

In *Hyars v. Wells Fuel Oil Co.*, 46 A.D. 2d 704, 360 N.Y.S. 2d 94 (1974), the claimant elected retirement but was awarded benefits based upon a showing that he was limited to light, sedentary work as a result of a nonscheduled injury. Evidence that a claimant had sought and received part-time employment was sufficient to sustain a claim in another retirement case: *Mulpagano v. Crucible Steel*, 53 A.D. 2d 930, 385 N.Y.S. 2d 193 (1976). In *Hartman v. W. H. Dunne Company*, 50 A.D. 2d 643, 374 N.Y.S. 2d 166 (1975), the claimant had sustained a compensable back injury in 1948, and had received benefits until 1972. After her retirement in 1973, the claimant attempted to find work but was unsuccessful. Thereupon the Board made an award, which the Appellate Division upheld.

(2) Return to School. The Yamonaco standard of voluntary withdrawal also applies here. In *Larke v. Bell Aerosystems,* 50 A.D. 2d 649, 374 N.Y.S. 2d 455 (1975), the claimant sustained a compensable back injury, looked for employment, and then returned to school full-time. With one justice dissenting, the court affirmed the Board's decision in finding that reduced earnings were due in part to disc protrusion. Similarly, in *Dooley v. NYS Bronx Children's Hospital,* 56 A.D. 2d 680, 391 N.Y.S. 2d 526 (1977), inability to perform prior duties as a registered nurse and subsequent enrollment in school as a full-time student were found not to constitute voluntary retirement.

(3) Rehabilitation and the effect of economic conditions. What if a claimant is trained for a new occupation under a rehabilitation program and then laid off? In *Boyle v. G. J. Gatti,* 40 A.D. 2d 1063, 339 N.Y.S. 2d 65 (1972), the claimant suffered a compensable permanent partial disability back injury as a mason in 1960. He received rehabilitation as an engineering administrator, and was laid off in 1970. Here the court would only allow the claim if it could be shown that the back injury was a limiting factor in the claimant's search for employment. The matter was remitted to the Board. Similarly, in *Topf v. American Character Doll and Toy Co.,* 62 A.D. 2d 1111, 404 N.Y.S. 2d 451 (1976), the claimant sustained an injury in 1961, was rehabilitated as an accountant, and was laid off in 1974. Here the court found that economic conditions were the sole cause of the layoff and denied benefits.

(4) Other factors. In another case involving a change of occupation, a telephone installer suffered a compensable back injury and took a desk job. Three years later, his earnings were reduced as a result of a strike, and the Board made an award. The court regarded as "speculative" the Board's finding that the disability was a limiting factor for employment purposes, and reversed the Board's ruling. (*Colletti v. New York Telephone Company,* 48 A.D. 2d 491, 370 N.Y.S. 2d 212 [1975].)

Finally, one need not retire or return to school to be able to collect benefits. In *Miller v. Pan American World Airways,* 46 A.D. 2d 718, 360 N.Y.S. 2d 293 (1974), the claimant, a stewardess, sustained a permanent partial disability and subsequently married and had children. On appeal by the employer, the Appellate Division found that the wage loss was not solely related to factors other than the disability, and affirmed the award.

These various cases suggest that the general answer to the second question is: so long as the permanent consequences of the work-related injury are at least a partial cause of the wage loss, nonscheduled benefits can be paid. When, however, there are no earnings after the medical condition has stabilized, then the third question must be asked.

The third question is: does the worker have any wage-earning capacity? If so, then benefits are based on the difference between preinjury actual earnings and postinjury earning capacity. For example, if a worker earned $200 a week before he was injured and (despite his lack of actual earnings) he is considered by the Board to maintain 75 percent of his earning capacity, then his nonscheduled permanent partial benefits are $33.33 per week (66 2/3 percent of $50.00).

Determining the earning capacity of a worker with no actual earnings is a formidable challenge. A tremendous share of the responsibility falls on the Board's doctors, who conduct the examination at the time of the final adjustment. They usually limit their evaluations of disability in the nonscheduled cases to mild, moderate, or marked (basically equivalent to 25, 50 or 75 percent of total disability, respectively). The doctor makes his report on a Form C-210 and may be called to testify on his report if either party requests it. That medical report is then considered by a law judge, who determines the extent of loss of earning capacity. The ultimate responsibility for determining the extent of disability rests with the judge rather than the doctor, subject, of course, to possible Board and court review. This is because the payment of benefits is contingent upon a showing that the physical impairment sustained is responsible for a reduction in wage-earning capacity, and the doctor's opinion is supposed to be directed toward medical aspects only. The statutes specifically indicate that the nature of an injury and the impairments resulting from it can be taken into account in determining the extent of loss of wage-earning capacity.

In general, the Board appears to defer to medical findings in determining the extent of earning capacity, and in turn the courts generally defer to the determinations made by the Board. For example, in *Smith v. GAF Corporation*, 44 A.D. 2d 864, 355 N.Y.S. 2d 484 (1974), the Appellate Division affirmed a Workers' Compensation Board finding of a 25 percent nonscheduled, permanent partial disability, which was based on an orthopedist's testimony that the claimant could only perform light work. "The sole question presented in this appeal is whether there was substantial evidence to support the board's determination, and we find that there was." The test is whether the Board has "substantial evidence to support its determination." *Sansome v. Maislin Transport Ltd.*, 72 A.D. 2d 644, 421 N.Y.S. 2d 137 (1979). When the evidence is not deemed to be sufficient, the court can remand the matter for further evidence.

Another case shows the extent of deference to medical testimony by the Board and the courts. In *Walsh v. New York Telephone*, 55 A.D. 2d 765, 389 N.Y.S. 2d 463 (1976), the claimant sustained nonscheduled injuries to her back and leg as a result of a fall. The Board in this case based its award on the testimony of a neurological specialist, who accepted the claimant's description of her continuing pain. The Appellate Division affirmed.

On the other hand, the court does not always affirm the Board. In *Grossman v. Posture Line Shops, Inc. et al.*, 28 A.D. 2d 1149, 284 N.Y.S. 2d 242 (1967), the court reversed, stating that "[T]here is lacking any qualified opinion testimony as to the exact cause of the claimant's neurological condition . . . The board's determination . . . is unsupported by substantial evidence."

Nonscheduled Adjustments (Lump-Sum Settlements). Nonscheduled adjustments through the payment of a lump sum may be approved by a Board member upon a showing that several conditions have been met. Some of these conditions are statutory and some are the result of rules or practice.

Lump-sum settlements, or nonscheduled adjustments, in New York State cannot be easily compared to the so-called "compromise and release agreements," which form a substantial part of the claims-closing process in many other states. One difference is that in the other states permitting redemption of the employer's liability by a compromise, the agreement may involve not only extent of disability but other matters, such as the issue of compensability itself. Under the New York provision adjustments are permitted only if both the carrier and employee agree to a settlement, and then only under certain carefully defined conditions. At least three conditions must be met before a lump-sum adjustment is allowed: the right to compensation has been established and compensation has been paid for at least 13 weeks, the case involves a nonscheduled permanent partial disability, and the continuance of disability and of future earning capacity is uncertain. In addition, there must be no outstanding payments or bills for either cash benefits or medical treatment; the general rule is that there must have been no medical treatment required within the past three months. Other rules of thumb concern the claimant's working status, his purpose in wishing to settle the case, and his psychological condition. Generally there is a medical report indicating that the settlement would be of "therapeutic" value to the claimant, presumably because he would no longer worry about the case and would be encouraged to return to gainful employment. The Board normally will not approve a settlement for a claimant who is not working unless he has voluntarily withdrawn himself from the labor market.

Another thing that distinguishes the New York lump-sum adjustment system is that the claimant has the opportunity to later reopen the case upon a showing of change in medical condition. For this reason the procedure is not as appealing to carriers or employers as are compromise and release agreements, which operate as an absolute release of the claimant's right to further benefits.

No Present Loss of Earnings. As indicated previously, no compensation is payable for nonscheduled permanent partial disability unless actual wage loss can be shown. The injured worker will of course receive necessary medical treatment and payment of cash benefits for temporary total or temporary partial disability. If the medical evidence shows that there is a permanent residual impairment even in the absence of wage loss, the judge will indicate a classification of "permanent partial disability" with no present loss of earnings, and close the case without prejudice; it can later be reopened if the claimant's condition or status changes.

The Relative Importance of the Three Types of Nonscheduled Awards

Although data on the prevalence of the three types of nonscheduled awards are not routinely published by the Workers' Compensation Board, information on several years is presented in table 8.1. In 1970, cases with continuing compensation payments (CCP) and cases with lump-sum payments each accounted for about 44 percent of nonscheduled awards, while nonscheduled cases closed without permanent disability benefits because of no present loss of earnings accounted for about 12 percent of nonscheduled awards. By 1982, the CCP cases dominated, accounting for 60 percent of all cases, while lump-sum awards were made in 31 percent of the cases, and cases closed without nonschedul-

Table 8.1

Numbers of Cases and Costs of Compensation for Three Types
of Nonscheduled Permanent Partial Disability Cases, as a Percentage
of All Nonscheduled Permanent Partial Disability Cases, Selected Years, 1970–82

Year	Lump sum		No present loss of earnings		Payments to continue	
	Number of cases	Amount of compensation	Number of cases	Amount of compensation	Number of cases	Amount of compensation
1970	44.9	25.0	11.8	2.4	43.4	72.6
1973	35.4	19.4	13.7	2.6	50.9	78.0
1977	26.1	12.8	8.5	1.3	65.4	85.9
1980	28.9	14.9	8.3	1.2	62.8	83.9
1982	31.3	17.4	8.6	1.4	60.1	81.2

SOURCE: Special tabulation provided by Research and Statistical Department, State of New York Workers' Compensation Board.

ed benefits because of no present loss of earnings accounted for about 9 percent of the cases. The predominant place that the payments-to-continue awards had achieved by 1982 is even more strikingly shown in the table by a breakdown of the amount of compensation awarded by the three categories of award.

The data showing that cases closed with payments to continue are the dominant type of nonscheduled permanent partial disability case must be used with caution. In a recent study of cases involving 1972 injuries that resulted in nonscheduled permanent partial disability benefits, Burton, Partridge, and Thomason (1986, pp. 65-66) found that 29.7 percent were originally closed with lump-sum settlements (a statistic comparable to the figures in table 8.1); however, many cases originally closed with no present loss of earnings or with payment to continue were reopened and reclosed with lump-sum settlements, so 51.1 percent of the 1972 injury cases had been ultimately resolved with lump-sum settlements by 1983. Unfortunately, comparable data for other years are unavailable, but the results strongly suggest that the use of lump sums to terminate eligibility for the New York wage-loss benefits is much more prevalent than data published by the Board suggest.

Major Member Continuing Disability Benefits

New York, in 1970, added Sec. 15, subd. 3-(v), calling for additional payments beyond the period specified in the schedule in a case where there is 50 percent or more loss or loss of use of certain major members (arm, leg, hand, or foot) and where there is actual wage loss at the end of the scheduled period of benefits, provided the impairment of earning capacity is due solely to such physical loss and provided the worker participates in a Board-approved rehabilitation program. The injured worker must make application for such continuing disability payments and the benefits are subject to an offset of 50 percent of social security disability benefits.

There are relatively few cases involving 50 percent or more loss or loss of use of a major member. Of 30,118 cases involving scheduled injuries that were closed in 1983, only 227 (or 0.75 percent) met the criteria for Sec. 15(3)(v) benefits.[12] Moreover, a special analysis of claims involving such loss resulting from injuries occurring in 1972 showed that, at least partly owing to the restrictions written into the law, very few 50 percent major member losses have actually qualified for continuing disability benefits under this provision (Burton, Larson, and Moran 1980, pp. 139-40 and chapter 11).

Permanent Total Benefits

Benefits: Weekly Amounts and Duration. Benefits for permanent total disability in New York are now payable at two-thirds of the employee's average weekly wage, subject to a maximum weekly rate of $300 and a minimum of $20, or actual wages, if less, for life or the duration of the disability. If the injured worker, though classified as permanently and totally disabled, is able to work for some wages, the compensation payable may be partially offset by the worker's actual earnings, so that compensation plus the earnings shall not exceed the wage base on which the maximum weekly benefit is computed under the law in effect at the time of such earnings. No deduction from the compensation payable takes place, however, if the permanent total disability was due to the loss or loss of use of both eyes; or both hands, arms, legs, or feet; or of any two thereof. There are two categories of permanent total disabilities: the scheduled type, covering these impairments mentioned in the previous sentence, and the non-presumptive type, which is assessed in accordance with the facts. The scheduled cases are presumed to be permanent and total "in the absence of conclusive proof to the contrary."

Experience with Permanent Disability Benefits. Permanent total disability cases have been relatively rare in New York, never accounting for as much as 0.1 percent of all cases with cash benefits during the 1958 to 1982 period (table 3.6). As of 1982, the share of all cases represented by permanent total cases was only 34 percent of the national average share for such cases (table 3.6). Nor have these cases been particularly expensive. In 1982, for example, the average permanent total case in New York involved $60,789 of cash benefits, only 66 percent of the national average figure of $92,055 (table 3.10). As a result, cash benefits for permanent total cases accounted for slightly less than 1 percent of all cash benefits in New York in 1982, about one-fourth of the national average share of costs accounted for by such cases (table 3.14).

Permanent partial disability cases are also relatively inexpensive in New York compared to other jurisdictions, although the facts concerning them are somewhat more complex. The schedule is relatively comprehensive in New York, especially in comparison with Pennsylvania and Michigan, and thus a relatively large number of permanent partial cases are compensated in New York. As of 1982, permanent partial cases (major and minor) accounted for 27.81 percent of all New York cases, above the average of 22.05 percent for the eight states intensively examined in chapter 3 (see tables 3.7 and 3.8). Among the eight states, only in California (29.9 percent), with its comprehensive schedule, and New Jersey (45.18 percent), with its aberrant legal doctrines, did permanent partial cases represent a higher percentage of all cases than in New York.

Although permanent partial cases were relatively common in New York, their costs were relatively low as of 1982. In 1958, the average cost of major permanent partial disability cases in New York was $8,897, which was 129 percent of the national average for that year. However, by 1982, the New York average of $19,730 was only 78 percent of the national average ($25,139) (table 3.11). Similarly, the average cost in New York for minor permanent partial cases was $1,044 in 1958, or 80 percent of the national average, whereas in 1982 it was $2,619, or only 53 percent of the national average of $4,953 (table 3.12).

The total costs of permanent partial cases in New York were also relatively low. Reflecting the below average cost per case, in 1982 the major permanent partial cases accounted for 36.71 percent of all cash benefits in New York, which was only 86 percent of the average share for such cases nationally (table 3.15). Although minor permanent partial cases were relatively common in New York, because of their low average cost their total cost in 1978 was 18.26 percent of all cash benefits, only 82 percent of the national average share for minor permanent partial cases (table 3.16).

If the total costs of all types of permanent disability cases (permanent total, major permanent partial, and minor permanent partial) are considered, New York devotes a relatively low share of all cash benefits to such cases. As of 1982, 55.95 percent of all cash benefits were spent on permanent disability cases in New York; among the eight jurisdictions intensively examined in chapter 3, only Pennsylvania, with its restrictive schedule, had a lower percentage (51.64; see table 3.17). Indeed, among the 45 jurisdictions for which data are presented in table 3.5, only Arizona (40.59 percent), Indiana (55.81 percent), Missouri (50.25 percent), and Pennsylvania (51.64 percent) devoted lower percentages of their cash benefits to permanent disability benefits than did New York (55.95 percent).

The rather tranquil picture of permanent disability benefits in New York conveyed by those data may, however, be somewhat misleading in terms of the dynamics of permanent partial disability benefits in New York. One reason is that the data in chapter 3, which are based on information from the National Council on Compensation Insurance, have a serious deficiency for purposes of analyzing the New York experience. The NCCI data separate permanent partial cases into major and minor categories depending on the seriousness of the injury. In New York, however, the more significant distinction is between scheduled and nonscheduled injuries, and unfortunately benefits for both types of injuries are included in both the major and minor permanent partial categories of the NCCI.

As discussed earlier, in New York, scheduled injuries are rated primarily on the basis of impairment and functional limitations, whereas nonscheduled injuries are rated on the basis of loss of wage-earning capacity, which is operationalized through measurement of actual wage loss. The worker must actually be out of work or earning less than his preinjury wages before he is judged to have lost wage-earning capacity.

The result is that there is a sharp distinction in New York between scheduled and nonscheduled injuries. It is not simply a matter of scheduled injuries being assessed on the basis of the number of weeks listed for a particular extremity and nonscheduled being based on the number of weeks that represents the "whole person," as in our category II states analyzed in chapter 7. It is not a difference in base, it is a difference in concept.

One data source that does distinguish between the scheduled and nonscheduled benefits in New York is the information published by the State of New York Workers' Compensation Board on compensated cases closed. In particular, there is an annual publication showing, *inter alia,* the number and costs of cases closed in the year. Table 8.2 provides data for selected years between 1960 and 1983, the most recent data available. Scheduled cases have accounted for about 35 percent of all cases throughout the period, whereas their share of all costs has declined from about 35 percent to about 25 percent. Nonscheduled cases have represented about 2.5 to 4.5 percent of all cases, whereas their share of all costs has increased from about 32 percent to over 50 percent; virtually all of the increased costs occurred during the 1970s. In short, this disaggregation of data reveals that scheduled awards have declined in importance while nonscheduled awards have grown in importance.

Of particular interest here is the rapid escalation in the numbers and costs of nonscheduled permanent partial benefits during the 1970s. Burton (1983) has examined this issue in a separate study. He made a statistical analysis of the determinants of the number and costs of workers' compensation cases in New York from 1959 to 1979, and used the results to help explain developments in the 1970s in nonscheduled permanent partial benefits. The number of nonscheduled cases per thousand employees was up 54.6 percent during the 1970s; the average cost of the cases (in constant dollars) was up 23.5 percent; the total costs (in constant dollars) of nonscheduled cases per thousand employees was up 91.0 percent. Burton found that over half of the increases during the 1970s in these three measures of nonscheduled permanent partial benefits was associated with increases in the unemployment rate. He also found that there was no statistically significant relationship between labor market conditions and the number of costs of scheduled permanent partial disability benefits in New York from 1959 to 1979. The difference between scheduled and nonscheduled benefits in their sensitivity to labor market conditions was consistent with Burton's expectations for New York, since the scheduled benefits are paid regardless of wage loss, while a precondition for the nonscheduled benefits is actual losses of earnings. In a labor market as slack as New York's in the 1970s, when the unemployment rate almost doubled (from 2.5 to 4.9 percent), it is reasonable to expect that more injured workers with nonscheduled injuries will experience actual wage loss and thus qualify for benefits.

Table 8.2
Number of Cases and Cost of Compensation
for Scheduled and Nonscheduled Permanent Partial Disability,
as a Percentage of All Cases, Selected Years, 1960–83

	Scheduled awards		Nonscheduled awards	
Year	Number of cases	Amount of compensation	Number of cases	Amount of compensation
1960	34.1	35.0	3.0	32.2
1965	38.9	34.8	2.6	34.8
1970	37.9	35.7	2.6	34.5
1975	37.3	30.0	3.1	44.7
1980	35.6	24.0	3.8	50.9
1983	34.8	23.0	4.4	52.1

SOURCE: *Compensated Cases Closed,* Workers' Compensation Board, State of New York, for years shown. The figures for 1983 are preliminary.

In light of the rapidly increasing costs of nonscheduled benefits during the 1970s, it is somewhat surprising that the overall costs of workers' compensation did not increase particularly fast in New York in that decade. In 1972, insurance premiums for workers' compensation represented 0.864 percent of payroll in New York, which was 10.3 percent above the average figure of 0.783 percent in the 28 jurisdictions (table 3.18). By 1978, New York employers were expending 1.770 percent of payroll on workers' compensation, which was 24.6 percent above the U.S. average of 1.420 percent. Thus over the 1972 to 1978 period for which data are available, New York's costs increased only somewhat more rapidly than costs elsewhere, despite the escalating cost of the nonscheduled permanent partial disability benefits. Moreover, by 1984 insurance rates in New York had been sharply reduced, and New York employers were spending about 21 percent less on workers' compensation than were employers elsewhere, on average (table 3.18).

Several factors help explain these favorable insurance cost developments in New York during a period when the costs of nonscheduled permanent partial cases rapidly escalated. One is the relatively slow pace of benefit increases. In 1972, for example, the maximum weekly benefit for temporary total disability benefits was $95.00 in New York, which was 63 percent of the state's average weekly wage, and New York ranked well above the median for the 52 jurisdictions for which data are available. By January 1986, the maximum was $300.00, which represented 80 percent of the state's average weekly wage. However, as of that date, 32 of 52 jurisdictions had maximums for temporary total disability that were at least 100 percent of the state's average weekly wage, and only 16 jurisdictions had maximums that were lower relative to their average weekly wages than the 80 percent figure for New York (U.S. Dept. of Labor, State Compliance, 1987).

Permanent partial disability benefits have also declined relatively in New York during the last decade. As of 1972, the maximum for permanent partial was $80.00 per week, which was 53 percent of the state's average weekly wage. The maximum in January 1986 was $150.00, which represented only 40 percent of the state's average weekly wage. The relatively slow increase in maximum weekly benefits helps explain how overall workers' compensation costs in New York have increased rather slowly despite the surge in nonscheduled benefits (Burton and Krueger 1986).

New York is not usually thought of as a wage-loss state, and yet with the exception that preinjury earnings are not escalated through time as a basis for calculating wage loss, the New York nonscheduled benefits are probably the most pristine version of a "pure" wage-loss approach found in the country. The reason is that the New York wage-loss benefits, unlike those of Pennsylvania and Florida, for example, can be paid for as long as wage loss continues. Compromise and release agreements and other devices to limit the potential duration of wage-loss benefits are a threat to the wage-loss approach in New York, however, although the problem is not as severe as in Michigan.

The reason that New York wage-loss benefits are less conspicuous than those of the other jurisdictions is that the New York schedule encompasses a high proportion of all injuries with permanent consequences, leaving only a relatively few nonscheduled cases. Approximately 90 percent of permanent partial cases are rated on the basis of the schedule, leaving only 10 percent to be compensated on the nonscheduled wage-loss basis. In contrast, the scope of injuries covered by the Pennsylvania schedule is quite limited, leaving most cases to be handled by the wage-loss approach, and the 1979 Florida statute makes wage-loss benefits potentially available to all workers with permanent disabilities (including those workers who also receive scheduled or 'impairment' benefits). In Michigan, the schedule is used extensively, but workers who suffer continuing wage loss may qualify for wage-loss benefits as well as scheduled awards.

The wage-loss benefits in New York, although inconspicuous, provide valuable lessons. They demonstrate that wage-loss benefits can be expensive, particularly in a slack labor market. The legal decisions from New York also provide valuable guidance on issues that are inherent in a wage-loss approach, as will be evident in the next chapter when we review the legal controversies concerning the Florida wage-loss provision.

The Temporary State Commission

An extensive examination of the New York workers' compensation program was completed in 1986 by the Temporary State Commission on Workers' Compensation and Disability Benefits. Although the Final Report considered a variety of topics, ranging from rehabilitation to third-party suits for employer contribution, considerable attention was devoted to "eleven issues relating to the adequacy and equity of disability benefits" (New York Temporary Commission 1986, p. 29).

One issue concerned the statutory maximum for partial disability, which at $150 per week is only half of the maximum for total disability; the Commission recommended that the maximum for partial disability should be increased so that in no more than three years there would be a single maximum for total and partial disability. Another issue involved the subtraction of temporary total benefits from the scheduled awards, which the Commission would eliminate. Lump-sum settlements were examined, and the Commission (at p. 46) raised the "troublesome possibility that lump sums in some, and perhaps many, cases are the product of desperation" by claimants. The Commmission (at pp. 165-66) "concluded that additional limitations and safeguards on lump sum settlements are warranted," such as prohibitions on any lump-sum settlement that impairs the claimant's right to medical benefits.

The most fundamental reform proposed by the Temporary Commission would eliminate the current provisions for permanent total, scheduled permanent partial, and nonscheduled permanent partial benefits. Instead, all workers with injuries that had permanent consequences would receive benefits in three stages. During a worker's healing period, the worker would receive temporary disability benefits as under the current law. When the worker reaches maximum medical improvement, he would be rated using a comprehensive rating system to evaluate the extent of impairment, such as the American Medical Association *Guides* (1984). If the worker had an impairment rating above a minimum threshold, he would receive presumed disability benefits, with the duration determined by the size of the impairment rating. The presumed disability benefits would be paid regardless of the worker's labor market experience. At the expiration of the presumed disability benefits (or six months after the date of maximum medical improvement, whichever is later) a worker with an impairment rating above a continuing disability threshold could qualify for continuing disability benefits if he were then experiencing actual wage-loss due to the work injury.

This hybrid system of benefits was unanimously endorsed in principle by all members of the broad-based Temporary Commission, although specific aspects, such as the exact benefit formula for the continuing disability benefits, were left for the legislature to decide. A bill incorporating the Commission's restructuring of permanent disability benefits is expected to be introduced in 1987. The proposed reform is consistent with our views of desirable reform, as discussed in chapter 12.

Ohio

Several types of benefits have been or are payable to Ohio workers with nonscheduled permanent partial disabilities. One type, known as permanent partial or C-92 award, relates the amount of benefits to the seriousness of the worker's permanent impairment. This choice was discussed in chapter 6, which also provided information on the structure and procedures used to provide permanent disability benefits in Ohio. Until 1986, the worker also had the choice of a form of wage-loss benefit instead of the permanent partial (C-92) award. The 1986 amendments removed the choice and made a form of wage-loss benefits a prerequisite to the granting of the C-92 award. We review first the pre-1986 optional form of wage-loss benefits and then briefly summarize the new provision.

The "Old" Wage-Loss Benefit

The alternative approach to compensating permanent partial disabilities was included in paragraph (A) of Section 4123.57:

> In case of injury or occupational disease resulting in partial disability other than [the scheduled benefits], the employee shall receive per week sixty-six and two-thirds per cent of the impairment of his earning capacity . . . during the continuance thereof. . . .

These benefits were subject to a weekly maximum of 100 percent of the state's average weekly wage and a maximum aggregate amount of $17,000. It is not immediately obvious that the paragraph (A) benefits belonged in our category III approach to nonscheduled permanent partial disability benefits, that is, the wage-loss approach. One reason is that paragraph (A) did not confine itself to permanent disability, as opposed to temporary disability. Indeed, the paragraph (A) awards were commonly referred to in Ohio as "temporary partial" awards, even though the statute contains no such terminology. Despite this usage in Ohio, we consider the paragraph (A) awards in at least some cases as benefits paid for permanent partial disabilities. As we understand the Ohio provision, workers could qualify for paragraph (A) awards even if they had reached maximum medical rehabilitation, and for these workers, the benefits could be classified as permanent partial disability benefits.

The language of paragraph (A) also seems to be inconsistent with our characterization of the approach as wage-loss, since it refers to "the impairment of his earning capacity." This sounds like our category II approach (chapter 7). Using the definition of wage-loss approach elaborated early in this chapter, however, we believe our classification of the paragraph (A) benefits is correct. Specifically, trait four indicated that in a wage-loss approach, the definition of compensable wage loss is "the lesser of: (a) the worker's potential earnings minus the worker's actual earnings; or (b) the worker's potential earnings minus the worker's earning capacity."

The application of paragraph (A), as described by Young (1971), the former administrator of the Ohio Bureau of Workmen's Compensation, appears generally to follow this definition. Potential earnings for paragraph (A) awards are calculated as "the average weekly wage for the year prior to the injury" (p. 126). No provision is made for escalation of the wages after the date of injury, which is one of the deviations from the pure wage-loss approach in Ohio. As to earning capacity, Young (1971, p. 135) indicates the term "is not defined in the statutes. It involves all of the factors relative to the ability to earn. The wages actually lost are evidence of impairment in earning capacity although such an impairment can exist without any actual loss in wages. *Industrial Commission v. Royer,* 122 Ohio St. 271, 171 NE 337 (1930)." This passage suggests that loss of earning capacity by itself will result in benefits. However, Young (at p. 136) then provides examples that clarify the use of the earning capacity measurement in Ohio.

One example involves a worker who had a $100 average weekly wage before he was injured, which by the Ohio approach means the post-injury potential earnings are $100. As a result of the injury, the worker "suffered a twenty-five percent physical disability," which means the worker retains 75 percent of his earning capacity. This means the worker's potential earnings minus the worker's earning capacity is $25. The worker does not automatically get benefits based on the loss of earning capacity, however, as he would in a category II state, because benefits are based in part on actual earnings. If the worker actually earns $70 after the injury and the wage loss is due to the injury, then the benefits under paragraph (A) are two-thirds of the actual wage loss of $30, or $20. Young then adds (p. 136) that the "twenty dollars per week . . . would be within the twenty-five dollar maximum that had been set and, therefore, payable to the employee." Clearly, in this example the benefits paid are less than the amount suggested by the loss of earning capacity, because the compensable portion of the actual wage loss was a smaller amount.

Young also provides an example in which the potential earnings were $100 and the loss of earning capacity was 10 percent. This means the worker's potential earnings minus the worker's earning capacity is $10. If this worker then has actual earnings of $70 after the injury, two-thirds of the actual wage loss is $20, but the worker only receives a benefit of $10 since the loss of earning capacity is less than the compensable portion of the actual wage loss.

The "New" Wage-Loss Benefit

Despite the apparent lack of utilization of and enthusiasm for the optional wage-loss benefits, the 1986 legislature added a mandatory form of wage-loss benefit that replaces the former paragraph A benefits. Sec. 4123.56 (B) now provides that when an employee

> suffers a wage loss as a result of returning to employment other than his former position of employment or as a result of being unable to find employment consistent with [his] physical capabilities, he shall receive compensation at sixty-six and two-thirds [sic] of his weekly wage loss not to exceed the statewide average weekly wage for a period not to exceed two hundred weeks.

The wage-loss approach to permanent partial disability benefits found in paragraph (A) of Section 4123.57 was the only choice available to workers until 1941. At that time, according to Young (pp. 144-45), the approach was "advantageous to an injured employee" because of the adverse economic conditions. Presumably, Young means that because of the high unemployment of the era, many workers experienced actual wage loss and therefore received benefits under the provision. The paragraph (B) option was then added with the "fundamental purpose . . . to encourage injured workers to return to work." The feature of the impairment benefits under paragraph (B) that would encourage such efforts to find jobs is that the benefits "could be received even though the employee had returned to work and was earning wages." Also, under the paragraph (B) approach, the worker was relieved of the burden of periodic wage reports and periodic physical examinations.

In addition to these factors identified by Young as to why the paragraph (B) benefits might be preferred, another feature attractive to workers was that benefits of a known amount could be received with certainty, whereas the paragraph (A) awards depended on uncertain subsequent evaluations of actual wage loss and of loss of earning capacity. For risk-averse workers, the wage-loss benefits would be unattractive because of the risk they entail, even if they have the theoretical advantage of providing a better match between lost earnings and benefits paid.

Whatever the reasons—and we may have overlooked some—paragraph (B) benefits were much more attractive to workers than were the wage-loss benefits under paragraph (A). Young reports (p. 145) that the paragraph (B) benefits accounted for 19 percent of the benefits paid by the State Insurance Fund, compared to only 3 percent for the paragraph (A) wage-loss benefits.

The 1986 amendments also provide that the permanent partial (C-92) award or scheduled permanent partial benefits cannot be paid until at least 40 weeks after the termination of temporary total disability or wage-loss benefits under Sec. 4123.56 (B). This obviously can lead to a gap in the benefits provided to workers with permanent disabilities. The Ohio benefits scheme is also questionable because the wage-loss benefits precede the benefits based on the extent of impairment. We argue in chapter 12 that the preferable order is presumed disability benefits followed by wage-loss benefits. As experience develops under the Ohio provision, we will be able to assess the consequences of a policy that is the inverse of our best judgment of how benefits should be structured.

NOTES

1. If he returned to work at the $200 wage and if he could show an impairment as a result of his injury, he could still receive an award, but payments could be suspended until actual earnings loss occurred. *Benedict v. Fox,* 192 Pa. Super. 197,159 A.2d 756,758 (1960), cited by Larson (1986), Sec. 57.12.

2. National Council on Compensation Insurance, "Countrywide Workers' Compensation Experience Including Certain Competitive State Funds—1st Report Basis," Exhibit dated June 1986. On an ultimate report basis, Pennsylvania had 496 permanent total cases in 1982, the largest number of any jurisdiction. As explained in chapter 3, we concentrate on the first report data in order to provide historical comparability.

3. *Civil Service Commission v. Dept. of Labor,* 424 Mich. 571, –N.W.2d– (1986).

4. As cited by St. Antoine (1984. p. 23).

5. *Detroit Free Press,* 5 Jan. 1986, p. 1.

6. Although, as Hunt notes, the conclusions involving the determinants of the size of the lump-sum payments "must be regarded as somewhat tentative," the evidence does show a "positive relationship between the size of the lump-sum and previous repeated spells of disability, a record of hospitalization, or a claim of a back injury." (Hunt 1982, p. 191.) These are the kinds of factors that affect estimates of the extent of loss of earnings capacity in states that use that approach.

7. These NCCI data showing a decline in lump-sum settlements are not entirely consistent with the data presented by St. Antoine (1984, p. 58), which shows only a modest decline in redemptions as a percentage of dispositions from 63.8 percent in 1981 to 54.4 percent in the first nine months of 1984.

8. Additional data showing a decline in the percentage of claims filed by retirees are provided by St.Antoine (1984, pp. 60-62).

9. All data on 1982 legal fees are from New York Workers' Compensation Board (1984), pp. 13-14 and tables 1 and 16.

10. The 30,118 scheduled permanent partial cases closed in 1983 were analyzed by Burton and Thomason (1986), Appendix I. Not all scheduled cases closed that year were included in the study; two reasons are (1) only 1979-1982 injuries were included because maximum benefits for total and partial disability did not change in this interval, and (2) certain cases involving 1979-1982 injuries were excluded because of apparent errors on the data tape provided by the Workers' Compensation Board.

11. The data are from New York Workers' Compensation Board (1984), table 2. Board data are based on information collected at the time of initial closing of the cases, which includes estimates of the present value of future benefits for those cases in which benefits were still being paid as of the date of closing.

12. The data are from Burton and Thomason (1986), discussed supra note 10.

13. The unemployment rate is the insured unemployment rate lagged two years for reasons explained in Burton (1983).

Chapter 9
The Transformation of Florida
to a Wage-Loss State

Florida's population in 1980 was 9,747,197, the seventh largest among the states. That population had grown by more than 2.9 million during the 1970s, a figure surpassed only by California and Texas.

As the population grew in Florida during the 1970s, so did the workforce and the size of the workers' compensation program. There were about two million workers covered in 1970; by the end of the decade, the number had grown to over three million.[1] More important than the change in the size of the program was the significant change in the approach to compensating permanent partial disability benefits that resulted from legislation enacted in 1979. At that time, Florida abandoned an unusual, if not unique, approach that allowed the worker to have his nonscheduled permanent partial injury evaluated on the basis of the extent of impairment (our category I approach) or on the basis of the loss of earning capacity (our category II approach). The 1979 law, probably the most widely discussed reform in workers' compensation in the last decade, essentially dropped the distinction between scheduled and nonscheduled permanent partial injuries, and established the wage-loss approach as the primary basis for compensating permanent disabilities.

The first section examines the approach used before the 1979 reforms.[2] Such a review is important because the unique choice of criteria approach for nonscheduled benefits needs to be documented for the edification of policy makers who may some day reinvent the approach. The pre-1979 situation also needs to be examined in order to understand the forces that led to the enactment of the wage-loss approach. In addition, the pre-1979 legislation provided the benefits paid to the workers examined in the study of Florida workers reviewed in part III of this volume. Even though the Florida law has been drastically changed since 1979, its essence—the determination of the amount of permanent partial disability benefits on an *ex ante* basis—is still the approach used in most jurisdictions, and therefore an understanding of how the prior

Florida law operated provides information relevant for reform efforts nationally.

The second section will examine the nature of the 1979 reforms, together with several changes made in 1978 that are also reflected in the current statutory scheme in Florida. The third section reviews data on the experience with the wage-loss approach, and the last section provides some evaluation of the 1979 reforms.

Florida Before Wage-Loss

Statutory Criteria for Permanent Partial Disability Benefits

Before 1979, permanent partial disability was covered by paragraph (3) of Section 440.15 of the Florida Workmen's Compensation Law. The weekly amount was 60 percent of the worker's average weekly wage prior to the date of injury. For scheduled injuries, the durations specified in the statute ranged from 200 weeks for the loss of an arm to 15 weeks for the loss of the fourth finger, plus additional provisions for loss of hearing, loss of vision, and disfigurement. The schedule was typical, covering most body extremities and providing for total or partial loss and for total or partial loss of use. It was also typical in that not much guidance was provided to the parties as to how the schedule was to be applied.

The determination of the duration of nonscheduled permanent partial benefits was provided for in a relatively brief paragraph, as follows:[3]

> In all other cases in this class of disability the compensation shall be 60 percent of the injured employee's average weekly wage for such number of weeks as the injured employee's percentage of disability is of 350 weeks; provided, however, that for purposes of this paragraph "disability" means either physical impairment or diminution of wage earning capacity, whichever is greater.

The statute provided no guidance as to how physical impairment or diminution of wage-earning capacity was to be determined.

The statute in effect in Florida before 1979 thus relied on the normal distinction between scheduled and nonscheduled benefits, with the durations for both types of permanent partial disability benefits determined on an *ex ante* basis. That is, as soon as the medical condition was stable (when the date of "maximum medical improvement" was reached), the permanent consequences of the worker's injury were evaluated and the rating was used to determine the duration of the permanent partial disability benefits.

Criteria for Nonscheduled Permanent Partial Disability Benefits[4]

The statute, as quoted above, offered the worker with a nonscheduled injury the choice of having the permanent consequences rated in terms of the physical impairment or in terms of the diminution of wage-earning capacity. In general, workers preferred to use the loss of wage-earning capacity approach because usually there were some factors pertaining to age, education, and so forth that could be relied on to increase the rating beyond that based strictly on the evaluation of the worker's physical impairment.

Neither the statute nor the Bureau of Workmen's Compensation had published guidelines or instructions for measuring diminution of wage-earning capacity. As a result, the Florida courts spelled out the factors to be considered in determining the extent of loss of earning capacity. In *Walker v. Electronic Products & Engineering Company,* 248 So. 2d 161,163 (Fla. 1971), for example, the Florida Supreme Court listed eight factors, including: inability to obtain work of a type which claimant can perform; wages actually earned after injury (a factor entitled to great weight); and "ability to compete in the open labor market the remainder of his life, including the burden of pain, or the inability to perform the required labor."

This list makes clear that actual wage loss was a factor in determining the extent of loss of earning capacity. There is, however, a crucial difference between this approach and an actual wage loss approach. In an actual wage-loss approach, if the worker earns more after the date of maximum medical improvement than before the date of injury, then the employer has no liability for permanent partial disability benefits,[5] whereas in a loss of earning capacity approach, the fact that there is no actual loss of earnings will not necessarily preclude a finding of a loss of earning capacity. Thus, in *Woodward v. Dade County Board of Public Instruction,* 278 So. 2d 620 (Fla. 1973), the court reinstated the order of the Judge of Industrial Claims for an award of 20 percent of loss of earning capacity even though the worker had returned to the same employer and was earning the same wages as before the injury. In this case, the physical impairment had been rated at only 5 percent of the whole man, and the worker's other characteristics had been used to justify the 20 percent loss of earning capacity judgment.

The *Woodward* case is a good illustration of how workers with nonscheduled injuries often benefited from having their cases rated on the basis of diminution of wage-earning capacity rather than on the extent of physical impairment. There were, however, a few obstacles to the use of loss of earning capacity as a basis for compensation:[6] the claimant had to make a good faith job search,[7] and determination of loss of earning capacity was constrained by several requirements (the loss of earning capacity rating had to be based on facts existing at the time of the award, not on predictions about the claimant's future loss of earning capacity because of the delayed effects of the injury;[8] and the deputy commissioner could not take judicial notice of employment opportunities in the area when assessing the loss of earning capacity rating, but must rely on evidence in the record).[9] But in most cases, compensation was greater than it would have been if it had been based strictly on physical impairment. The reason is that most cases were handled by lawyers who tried to circumvent the agency and the courts by concluding compromise and release settlements (known as "washouts" in Florida). In practice, the rule of thumb, according to plaintiffs' lawyers interviewed during our field work under the pre-1979 law, was that the percentage rating for loss of wage-earning capacity was about double the physical impairment rating.

At the time of our field work, there was widespread unhappiness in Florida with the high incidence of washouts, and a sense that workers with serious injuries were being undercompensated and those with minor injuries overcompensated. Legislation enacted in July 1978 provided that the number of weeks of benefits to be multiplied by the percentage of disability was to increase with the severity of the injury according to a new formula: a rating of 1 to 10 percent was multiplied by 175 weeks; a rating of 11 to 50 percent, by 350 weeks; and a rating of 50 to 99 percent, by 525 weeks. This provision very likely did have the effect of redirecting benefits away from minor injuries and toward major injuries, but the approach still relied on the evaluation of physical impairment and diminution of earning capacity. That is, it remained an *ex ante* approach to benefits. Moreover, because of poor draftsmanship, the amendment produced anomalies: a worker with a 10 percent rating received 17.5 weeks of benefits, while a worker with an 11 percent rating received benefits for 38.5 weeks.

Procedure for Permanent Partial Disability Benefits

Before the 1979 reform legislation, the administrative posture in Florida was essentially one of allowing the employee to pursue his own interest. In practice, this usually meant retaining an attorney and filing a claim. Almost all permanent partial disabilities other than those delineated by the schedule involved the filing of a claim.

Florida had not issued any manual or other guide to assist the parties in evaluating cases. Each case that was contested depended on an individual determination based upon the presentation of the respective attorneys, as well as, sometimes, the respective bargaining power of the parties. Most cases involving permanent partial benefits were litigated, and a high percentage ended up in compromise and release settlements. One insurance claims examiner stated he did not offer to pay anything voluntarily in cases where a physician's evaluation of 5 percent permanent partial disability was made. His rationale was that if he agreed to 5 percent, the attorney would file a claim for 15 percent and the judge would compromise on 10 percent. On the other hand, if he offered nothing, the compromise figure might be 5 percent of permanent partial plus an attorney's fee. The probability of litigation was so high in these cases that carriers found it to their advantage to procrastinate and compromise only after litigation was well advanced. Carriers who paid some amount on the basis of physical impairment recognized that a higher rating would result when loss of wage-earning capacity was assessed.

The absence of an active workers' compensation agency and the vagueness of the criteria for evaluating nonscheduled cases resulted in considerable litigation. The number of awards issued by the judges of industrial claims increased from 14,076 in 1970 to 20,153 in 1974 to 25,381 in 1978. The time involved in processing a case from claim filing to judge's decision increased from 170 days in 1970 to 201 days in 1974. Most orders issued by judges were washouts. Of the 25,381 orders issued in 1978, 17,058 (or 67 percent) were in this category. This compares with 9,237 washouts out of 14,076 orders in 1970.[10]

Attorneys' fees were an important part of this litigious system. In 1972, for 9,720 awards by judges, the total attorneys' fees awarded were $8 million. In 1978, attorneys' fees were awarded in 15,883 cases and totaled $19.7 million.[11] Before amendments effective July 1, 1978, these fees were paid entirely by the employer or carrier and did not come out of the employee's portion of the award.[12]

Experience with Permanent Disability Benefits through 1978

Costs for major permanent partial disability cases were high. The average cost per case was only moderate (see table 3.11), but the number of such cases as a proportion of all cases paying cash benefits more than tripled between 1958 and 1978, when the numerical share was 131 percent of the national average (table 3.7). In terms of the share of dollars expended on cash benefits, major permanent partial disability benefits in Florida were 23 percent above the national average share by 1978 (table 3.15). The effect of the resulting high total cost for major permanent partial cases was to dominate the below-average costs (as a percentage of all cash benefits) of permanent total and minor permanent partial cases, so that the cost of all Florida permanent disability cases as a percentage of all cash benefits was 106 percent of the national average in 1978.

The economic pressures that led to the 1979 reforms in Florida involved more than the increasing frequency and total costs of permanent disability benefits as a share of all cash benefits. Not only had the permanent disability slice of the pie grown, but the entire pastry had swollen. One reason was the substantial increase in benefit levels during the 1970s. The maximum weekly benefit for total and partial disability was $56 as late as 1972 (46 percent of the state's average weekly wage), but then the maximums increased annually through 1978, at which time the maximum weekly benefit was $126, or 74 percent of the state's average weekly wage.[13] Total expenditures on workers' compensation in Florida, including cash benefits and medical expenses, went from $75 million in 1970 to $257 million in 1978.[14] The higher cost was due in part to the increased number of workers covered by the Florida workers' compensation program, but even the cost per employee increased rapidly during the 1970s. One figure that illustrates the high cost of the workers' compensation program as of 1978 is the average insurance premium for workers' compensation paid by a representative sample of employers. Florida employers were expending 2.641 percent of payroll on workers' compensation insurance in 1978, a figure well above the 28-jurisdiction average of 1.420 percent (table 3.18). Indeed, among 47 states with comparable data for 1978, Florida's percentage was exceeded only by the District of Columbia and Oregon (Hunt, Krueger, and Burton 1985).

The objective evidence thus indicates that Florida was facing a real problem with workers' compensation costs as of 1978, and that the problem was partly associated with the increasing numbers and costs of permanent partial disability cases. Particularly suspect were the nonscheduled permanent partial disability cases. As previously discussed, a choice of criteria could be used to determine benefits in these cases, which generally resulted in the duration being determined on the basis of the ill-defined diminution of earning capacity. The nonscheduled permanent partial disability provision was generating litigation and widespread reliance on washouts to resolve cases. The problems of administration were confounded by a relatively passive workers' compensation agency, which did little to assist workers or to reduce litigation by anticipating and solving problems. The system was perceived not only as expensive, litigious, and poorly administered, but as arbitrary in its treatment of workers—especially those with permanent partial disabilities for which the benefits awarded seemed to depend as much on the location in the state, the lawyer, and the judge of industrial claims as on the merits of the case.

By 1978, pressures for reform, or at least drastic change, were building in Florida. Some changes were made that year, such as a new formula for translating percentage ratings in nonscheduled permanent partial disability cases into weeks of benefits. But the critical enactment in 1978 was a sunset provision, declaring that the workers' compensation law would expire in 1979. This sunset provision was a strategic ploy designed to force a major overhaul of the workers' compensation program in 1979.

The Florida Wage-Loss Approach to Permanent Partial Disability Benefits

The wage-loss approach to permanent partial disability benefits adopted in Florida in 1979 has been described as a "bold experiment" that "has attracted national attention."[15] The factors that led to the enactment of the law, the features of the 1979 legislation and subsequent amendments, and the cases interpreting the law are provided in this section.[16]

The Economics and Politics of Change

The story of the forces and maneuvering that culminated in the enactment of the 1979 legislation is much too complex to recount in this chapter. Fortunately, there is an excellent study of the reform process, *The Circle Solution,* written by Jim Mintner, which was sponsored by the Florida Association of Insurance Agents and published in 1982.[17] Although not devoid of hyperbole and although clearly sympathetic to the wage-loss approach, the book is surprisingly frank and accurate, at least about those matters with which we are personally familiar.

As outlined in the previous section, workers' compensation costs had rapidly increased in Florida, to the point that its system was the third most expensive in the country. Moreover, the criteria for nonscheduled permanent partial disability benefits were ambiguous, the state workers' compensation agency was passive, and litigation and reliance on washouts to resolve cases were increasing. Other factors that made Florida a likely target for reform were the prominence of the state— large and rapidly growing—and the political environment. Unlike some other jurisdictions in which high cost had emerged as a problem, such as Michigan, the District of Columbia, and Oregon, Florida had a relatively conservative legislature. One reason was the low proportion of workers who were union members—the 11.7 percent of the nonagricultural labor force organized in 1978 ranked Florida 46th among the 50 jurisdictions in this respect (Gifford 1982, p. 68). Thus workers' compensation in Florida was an inviting target for reform efforts: pernicious, prominent, and pliable.

Although some reform of permanent partial disability in Florida was almost inevitable, the adoption of the wage-loss approach was not. That element in the reform picture was, to a large degree, a legacy of the National Commission on State Workmen's Compensation Laws. Although it did not explicitly endorse the wage-loss approach and made no pretense of having invented it, the National Commission in its *Report* (1972, p. 69) suggested that:

> Consideration should be given to the use of two types of benefits:
>
> *permanent partial impairment benefits,* paid to a worker solely because of a work-related impairment

permanent partial disability benefits, paid to a worker because he has both a work-related impairment and a resultant disability.

In addition to this tacit support for a wage-loss approach contained in the *Report,* the idea was examined in a Supplemental Study for the National Commission that was written by the commission's chief counsel. He criticized permanent partial disability benefits paid on the basis of impairment or loss of wage-earning capacity, and composed a paean to a wage-loss system (Lewis 1973).

The direct link between the National Commission and the Florida wage-loss approach was John Lewis, who, coincidentally, was both the general counsel of the National Commission and a Florida attorney who became the chairman of the Florida Workers' Compensation Advisory Committee. As the movement toward reform began in Florida in 1977, Lewis introduced the idea of the wage-loss approach at meetings of the committee. Then at a subcommittee meeting in January 1978, the preliminary results of the NSF study were presented by Wayne Vroman and a tentative proposal for reform of permanent partial disability benefits in Florida was provided by John Burton. The NSF study results are essentially those presented in part III of this volume, which document the serious problems of inequities and excessive litigation for Florida permanent partial disability cases under the law described in the previous section. The proposal for reform suggested *inter alia* that comprehensive guidelines be issued to rate impairments in all cases and that a dual benefit system be established. One part of the system was impairment benefits, to be paid to each worker with a permanent impairment rating of 1 percent or more. The other part was pure wage-loss benefits, paid according to what was termed the "80/80 plan." The wage-loss benefits were 80 percent of estimated wage loss, which in turn was defined as 80 percent of adjusted preinjury wages minus the actual wages after the date of maximum medical improvement.

The general ideas for the wage-loss approach discussed at the January 1978 meeting were then translated into draft legislation by John Lewis. The Lewis draft used the "80/80" formula for computing the wage-loss benefits and provided that any worker with a permanent impairment of at least 1 percent would receive a permanent impairment benefit, with the dollar amounts for the permanent impairment benefits being $100 for each percent rating from 1 to 10 percent, and higher amounts for more serious injuries.

As the wage-loss concept was thus being translated into a specific statutory proposal, the pressures for change were building. An important factor at this stage was the Florida Association of Insurance Agents (FAIA), which had been actively involved in an unsuccessful effort to amend the Florida workers' compensation law in 1977. To increase the influence of the insurance industry in subsequent legislative sessions, the FAIA and several national insurance companies had formed The Last Manifesto, a "multi-million dollar program" to reform the "state's Workers' Compensation mess."

In early April 1978, Lewis took his draft legislation to an FAIA meeting and explained the general idea of the wage-loss approach and the specific version of the concept included in his bill. Reactions were mixed at the meeting. A more serious obstacle arose when the National Council on Compensation Insurance prepared a cost estimate that indicated the bill at best would lead to a slight rate reduction. Regardless of the merits of the wage-loss bill, the likelihood that costs would not significantly drop made enactment of the Lewis bill unrealistic because of the resistance of the business community (Mintner 1982, p. 17).

The FAIA leadership, although unhappy with the specific variant of wage loss in the Lewis bill because of its costs, nonetheless was persuaded that the concept was sound. The FAIA then redrafted the Lewis bill to scale back the benefits and began to promote the idea. The wage-loss bill was not enacted in 1978 because of the short time available to educate the legislators and to muster support from all elements of the insurance industry. Furthermore, the Florida trial lawyers were a formidable opponent to the adoption of the wage-loss concept. So the 1978 session produced, instead, some limited changes in the workers' compensation statute and the enactment of a sunset provision that was designed, according to Senator MacKay, its sponsor, "to hold a gun to the Legislature's head" in 1979 (Mintner 1982, p. 21).

The wage-loss concept was further promoted and refined between the 1978 and 1979 legislative sessions. A drafting committee of The Last Manifesto rewrote the bill, and Fred Karl, general counsel of the FAIA, and other FAIA staff members met with various groups within Florida promoting the wage-loss approach.

By November 1978, Associated Industries of Florida also provided tentative support for a kind of wage loss. But the Associated Industries leadership also were unwilling to support the Lewis version of the wage-loss bill because of the expense involved. Consequently, Mary Ann

Stiles, the association's workers' compensation expert, started her own research on closed cases at the Bureau of Workers' Compensation in order to provide a basis for her own variant of wage loss.

The FAIA/Last Manifesto version of wage loss suffered a serious blow in January 1979 when the National Council on Compensation Insurance actuary appeared before the Florida legislature and presented figures suggesting that the "rate savings were minimal to nonexistent, while benefits might actually decrease" (Mintner 1982, p. 49). But even though the specific version of wage loss promoted by the FAIA was thus side-tracked next to the original Lewis proposal, nonetheless the general concept soon picked up more steam.

The impetus was provided by a Workmen's Compensation Conference on Wage Loss held January 16, 1979, that was sponsored by the FAIA. The conference, at which (according to *The Circle Solution*) "all the right buzz words were used," was held in the chambers of the Florida House of Representatives, and played to an audience of legislators, interest group representatives, and the media. Speakers included the new governor, Bob Graham, the insurance commissioner, who endorsed wage loss as a "bold, but brilliant" concept, the House speaker, the Senate president, and the chief executives of three of the Manifesto companies. John Lewis and John Burton also spoke.

The next day the Joint Legislative Committee on Workmen's Compensation voted 4-2 to endorse the general concept of wage loss. Moreover, the specific version of wage loss favored by the FAIA apparently was favored by the Joint Committee. By February, however, the FAIA proposal began to be dismantled by the Joint Committee. "At the urging of Associated Industries' Jon Shebel, the Joint Committee trimmed back impairments benefits to cover only amputation, blinding or disfigurement. Attorneys' fees would be paid 100% by the claimant, another of Shebel's proposals" (Mintner 1982, p. 70). As a result of the conflicting pressures,

> in early March, the Joint Committee adopted a comprehensive and massive wage-loss bill that promised to cut rates by 21%. It contained many fundamental changes in the way Comp would be administered, and there were amendments to the agents' original bill that made them and the companies unhappy. Still it was very close to their original proposal, and was "wage-loss at its finest," they maintained. (Mintner 1982, p. 73)

Then the bombshell was dropped. On March 14, the AFL-CIO and Associated Industries of Florida announced they were supporting a new workers' compensation reform package. One reason the AFL-CIO was willing to join this coalition is that the bill supported by the Joint Committee (which had its best chance for enactment in the Senate) would have almost entirely favored business by reducing benefits. Dan Miller, the AFL-CIO president, was convinced that some form of wage loss was going to pass, and he wanted to salvage something for labor (Mintner 1982, p. 75). What the Associated Industries got from the coalition was support of the AFL-CIO for a package that included a substantial curtailment of lawyers' role in the system. Shebel, president of Associated Industries, felt that the lawyers' chances of defeating reform would be weakened if labor's normal support for plaintiffs' attorneys could be neutralized.

The steps between the March announcement of the AFL-CIO and Associated Industries coalition and the eventual enactment of the workers' compensation statute in April are complicated, but the essence is that most of the provisions those parties sought were included in the statute. The statute made substantial changes in the structure of the workers' compensation delivery system, in the role of lawyers, and in the criteria for permanent partial disability benefits. It adopted a dual benefit system for permanent partial disability, with impairment benefits for certain types of injuries and wage-loss benefits for workers with actual wage loss after the date of MMI.

The dual benefit system can be traced back at least to the Lewis bill first proposed in 1978. The agents had modified the proposal, limiting the amount of benefits. The bill as enacted contained impairment benefits considerably more restricted than those in the Lewis bill, and a wage-loss formula that was considerably more generous than the Lewis version. This obviously was acceptable to labor and management, since they negotiated the provision, and it was accepted with some reservations by the Florida Association of Insurance Agents. An advisory committee appointed by the governor to evaluate the 1979 legislation, however, unanimously recommended that the law not be signed. (The chairman of the advisors, John Burton, was particularly concerned about the paltry impairment benefits and the unduly generous wage-loss formula.) Governor Graham ignored his advisors and signed the bill into law on May 11, 1979.

This abbreviated recounting of the enactment of the 1979 Florida legislation suggests several useful lessons. One is that enactment of wage-loss legislation—or any major overhaul of workers' compensation, for that matter—is likely to require a crisis environment. In the case of Florida, the crisis was the rapid escalation of the costs to employers of workers' compensation. The second lesson is that the process of reform is unpredictable and even erratic. The Lewis proposal for a dual benefits system in early 1978 had modest impairment and wage-loss benefits; the ultimate legislation had much more restrictive impairment benefits coupled with more generous wage-loss benefits. The path be-ween the starting and ending versions of the dual benefits system reflects political influences that at times were almost random. Indeed, FAIA, the organization that devoted the most resources over the 1977-79 period to the enactment of the wage-loss concept, almost lost control of the reform process at the end. The third lesson is that the reform outcome in a particular state is very much tied to the political power of the key interest groups in that state. In most states, organized labor and claimants' attorneys are natural allies in the struggle against the introduction of wage-loss benefits, and they usually are strong enough to prevail. In Florida, organized labor is relatively weak, and when it became ap-parent that the labor-lawyer alliance could not defeat wage loss, the AFL-CIO leadership threw in with management in order to salvage something for labor. As Dan Miller, the Florida AFL-CIO president, has observed, the 1979 wage-loss bill and the accompanying increase in maximum weekly benefits were of particular value to high-skilled workers in hazardous occupations, and it is among those types of workers that AFL-CIO strength is centered in Florida.[18] Thus the AFL-CIO sup-port for wage loss in Florida was the product of special circumstances not found in many states.

The forces that led to the enactment of wage-loss legislation in Florida are unlikely to be duplicated in many other jurisdictions. Whether the outcome deserves to be emulated in any case will be further examined in the final pages of this chapter.

Key Features of the 1979 Florida Workers' Compensation Reform

The 1979 legislation eliminated the previous approach to permanent partial disability benefits, which distinguished between scheduled and nonscheduled injuries and for the latter type offered the worker the choice of basing ratings on physical impairment or loss of earning capacity.

The new law established a dual benefit system with impairment benefits and wage-loss benefits.

Impairment Benefits. These benefits are provided in Section 440.15(3)(a). They are paid to workers with certain types of permanent impairments (amputations, loss of 80 percent or more of vision, or serious head or facial disfigurements) but are not paid to workers with other types of permanent impairments (such as total or partial loss of use of a body member). This is a restrictive schedule, since it excludes most permanent partial injuries which involve loss of use rather than amputation. The only change since 1979 in the injuries qualifying for impairment benefits is that in 1982 the law was amended to make clear that 80 percent of loss of vision in either eye qualifies for benefits.

The amounts of impairment benefits in the 1979 legislation were $50 for each percent of permanent impairment for ratings of 1 to 50 percent, and $100 for each percent over 50 percent. Thus a worker with a 60 percent impairment rating received $3,500 under the 1979 law. These amounts were increased, effective May 1, 1982, to $250 for each percent of permanent impairment for 1 to 10 percent ratings, and $500 for each percent over 10 percent. Thus a worker with a 60 percent impairment rating since that date receives $27,500. These impairment benefits can be paid in a lump sum as of the date of MMI.

Determination of the extent of the permanent impairment is governed by Section 440.15(3)(a)(3), which provides, in part, that

> the division shall establish and use a schedule. . .based on generally accepted medical standards for determining impairment and may incorporate all or part of any one or more generally accepted schedules used for such purpose . . . pending the adoption, by rule, or a permanent schedule, Guides to the Evaluation of Permanent Impairment . . . by the American Medical Association, shall be the temporary schedule. . . .

Wage-loss Benefits. Workers with permanent impairments are also eligible for wage-loss benefits as of the date of MMI if they suffer at least a 15 percent loss of earnings. Benefits are 95 percent of the earnings losses in excess of the 15 percent threshold. The maximum wage-loss benefit is the lesser of (a) 66 2/3 percent of the worker's preinjury wage, or (b) 100 percent of the state's average weekly wage. The maximum weekly benefit was $195 in 1979 and $318 as of January 1986. For wage-loss benefits that extend more than 25 months beyond the date of MMI, there is (in effect) a 5 percent per year escalation in potential earnings used to calculate wage loss.[19]

There are several important limitations on workers' eligibility for wage-loss benefits. One is that workers lose their eligibility for the benefits if they do not experience at least three consecutive months of compensable wage loss in each two-year period after the date of MMI. Other limitations concern the potential duration for wage-loss benefits once they commence. The 1979 statute provided that the maximum duration for the wage-loss benefit was 525 weeks (those injuries that occurred on or before July 1, 1980, had a maximum duration of 350 weeks) or age 65, whichever occurred first. The law was amended effective July 1, 1980, to provide that the benefits stop at age 65 only when the worker becomes eligible for Social Security Old Age Benefits. For workers age 62 who were actually receiving Social Security Old Age Benefits, the wage-loss benefits were reduced by the amount of the Old Age benefits, not to exceed 50 percent of those wage-loss benefits. In 1983, the provision was further amended to eliminate the termination of wage-loss benefits at age 65 if the worker is eligible for Old Age benefits. Effective June 30, 1983, Section 440.15(3)(b)(4) provided that when the worker is eligible for Old Age benefits (normally age 62), the wage-loss benefit is not terminated but the amount is reduced so that the sum of the Old Age and wage-loss benefits is equal to the amount of wage-loss benefits that would otherwise be payable. The 1983 legislation also provides that any month when no wage-loss benefit is paid because the Old Age benefit is greater than the wage-loss benefit nominally due counts toward the three consecutive months in each two-year period during which benefits must be payable in order for eligibility for wage-loss to continue.

The aspect of the wage-loss benefits that has provoked the most contention is the definition of earnings losses. Section 440.15(3)(b)(1) provides, in part, that wage-loss benefits "shall be based on actual wage-loss" and "shall be equal to 95 percent of the difference between 85 percent of the employee's average monthly wage [before the injury] and the salary, wages, and other remuneration the employee is *able to earn* after reaching maximum medical improvement as compared on a monthly basis" (emphasis added). As to what is meant by "able to earn," Section 440.15(3)(b)(2) of the 1979 statute provided:

> The amount determined to be the salary, wages, and other remunerations the employee is able to earn after reaching

the date of maximum medical improvement shall in no case be less than the sum actually being earned by the employee, including earnings from sheltered employment. In the event the employee voluntarily limits his or her income or fails to accept employment commensurate with his or her abilities, the salary, wages, and other remuneration the employee is able to earn after the date of maximum medical improvement shall be deemed to be the amount which would have been earned if the employee did not limit his or her income or accepted appropriate employment . . . the burden shall be on the employee to establish that any wage loss claimed is the result of the compensable injury.

This seemingly innocuous language has led to a series of significant decisions that will be reviewed at some length below. The decisions in turn have provoked a 1983 amendment to Section 440.15(3)(b)(2) that will be discussed in conjunction with those cases. As with these original statutory provisions, the amendment has generated controversy as to the legislative intent.

Other Benefits. In addition to the changes involving permanent partial disability benefits, there were also significant changes in the other types of benefits. For example, the nominal replacement rate for temporary total disability and permanent total disability benefits was increased from 60 percent of the worker's preinjury wage to 66 2/3 percent. In addition, the maximum for all types of benefits was increased from 66 2/3 percent of the state average weekly wage ($130 prior to July 1, 1979) to the lesser of (a) 100 percent of the state average weekly wage ($196 as of July 1, 1979, and $318 as of January 1, 1986) or (b) 66 2/3 percent of the worker's preinjury wage.

Administration. The 1979 legislation also included significant changes in the administrative structure and procedures of the workers' compensation program. The previous law had provided that disputed claims were first heard by judges of industrial claims, with appeals going to the Industrial Relations Commission and then by petition for writ of certiorari to the Florida Supreme Court. The 1979 law abolished the IRC and changed the nomenclature of the judges to deputy commissioners. Appeals from the deputy commissioners now go to the First District Court of Appeal (part of the regular court system in Florida) and then to the Florida Supreme Court by petition for writ of certiorari. In short, there is no longer an appellate level within the workers' compensation program that deals exclusively or primarily with workers' compensation cases.

The 1979 legislation also elevated the Bureau of Workmen's Compensation to the Division of Workers' Compensation and gave it greater authority and responsibility for administration. Section 440.44 provides that the Division is to "assume an active and forceful role in its administration of this act so as to ensure that the system operates efficiently and with maximum benefit to both employers and employees." The law attempts to ensure that injured workers are fully and promptly informed of the proper procedures and their legal rights. For example, injured workers are to be mailed information on the program, and those suffering injuries that might permanently disable them are to be contacted personally. Moreover, the Division is to become more actively involved in controverted claims, including the issuing of advisory opinions as to the benefits payable in each case.

Attorneys' fees were also affected by the 1979 law. Before July 1, 1978, attorneys' fees for claimants were entirely paid by the employer or carrier; in 1978, the worker was required to pay 25 percent of his own attorney's fee. The 1979 law requires the claimant (with several exceptions) to pay 100 percent of his own attorney's fee. All attorneys' fees have to be approved as reasonable by the deputy commissioner based on criteria included in the statute, such as the amount of time expended by the attorney. The statute was amended in 1980 to provide that in determining a reasonable attorney's fee, the deputy commissioner shall consider only those benefits the attorney is responsible for securing. In other words, those benefits voluntarily paid by the employer or carrier are not to be considered in determining the claimant's attorney's fee.

The widespread utilization of washouts (compromise and release agreements) to terminate cases was also affected by the 1979 statute. Section 440.20(12)(a) states that "it is in the best interests of the injured worker that he receive disability or wage-loss payments on a periodic basis." Washouts of future medical benefits are strictly prohibited. Settlements involving cash benefits are absolutely prohibited until six months after the date of MMI, and thereafter are permitted only in special circumstances, such as when the claimant can demonstrate that a lump-sum payment will definitely aid in the rehabilitation process or is otherwise clearly in the workers' best interest and that lump-sum payment will avoid undue expense or undue hardship to any party.

The 1983 legislation provides a limited exception to the general prohibition on washouts found in Section 440.20(12)(a). The new law allows washouts when the employer or carrier denies that a compensable injury occurs and the deputy commissioner "finds a justifiable controversy as to legal or medical compensability of the claimed injury or the alleged accident." Lump sums are not permitted under this exception if the employer or carrier initially accepts the case as compensable or provides any benefits.

These are by no means the only changes in the Florida Workers' Compensation program included in the 1979 statute and the subsequent amendments. Our focus for the balance of this section is primarily on those matters pertaining to permanent partial disability benefits. But it should be obvious that an overall assessment of the 1979 legislation in terms of its desirability to labor, management, carriers, workers, and the public is complicated because of the many aspects of the program that were affected.

Constitutionality of the 1979 Legislation

The Florida Supreme Court rejected a constitutional challenge to the permanent partial benefits provisions of the 1979 legislation in *Acton v. Fort Lauderdale Hospital,* 440 So.2d 1282 (Fla. 1983). Acton injured his knee at work and received medical care and temporary total disability benefits for five months, at which time he returned to work. Acton received a 25 percent permanent disability rating for the knee injury, which would have qualified him for permanent partial disability benefits under the Florida law in effect before the 1979 amendments. Under the new law, however, the deputy commissioner found that the injury did not qualify Acton for permanent impairment benefits, which are limited to amputations, 80 percent or more vision loss, or serious head or facial disfigurement, nor was Acton entitled to wage-loss benefits because he was earning more after the injury than before. Acton unsuccessfully argued that the 1979 legislation violated constitutional guarantees of equal protection and access to the courts.

While the courts in *Acton* and other cases have endorsed the constitutionality of the basic scheme for permanent disability benefits in the 1979 legislation, they have not hesitated to scrutinize and arguably even modify the statutory criteria for wage-loss benefits.

Wage-Loss Benefits: The Legal Requirements

It may be true that "wage-loss in concept is disarmingly simple" (Mintner 1982, p. 9). Nonetheless, in practice, wage-loss in Florida has complicated elements. This subsection examines some of the legal issues that have emerged as courts have interpreted the statute. We simplify the analysis by ignoring many of the issues that arise in a case in which a worker has filed a claim for wage-loss benefits, such as whether the worker experienced an injury arising out of and in the course of employment. We focus on three sets of requirements that must be met by a worker in order to qualify for wage-loss benefits: the permanent impairment requirements; the "objective" wage-loss requirements; and the "legally sufficient" wage-loss requirements. These three categories of requirements are our construct, designed to help in analyzing the Florida law. Within these three sets of requirements are subissues that may or may not be critical in a particular case.

The Permanent Impairment Requirements. First, has maximum medical improvement been reached? If the answer is no, then the worker is only potentially eligible for temporary total disability or temporary partial disability benefits, since the impairment is not yet permanent.

Second, does the worker have a permanent impairment using an acceptable rating system? The worker need not have a permanent impairment falling into one of the three categories that are prerequisites for permanent impairment benefits. But the worker must have a permanent impairment with a rating of at least 1 percent using an appropriate rating system before potentially qualifying for wage-loss benefits.

The statute designates the AMA *Guides* as the temporary schedule to be used in determining the existence and degree of permanent impairment. Initial interpretations of the 1979 statute suggested that workers would find it difficult to demonstrate they had permanent impairments not encompassed by the AMA *Guides*. Thus in *Rhaney v. Dobbs House, Inc.,* 415 So.2d 1277 (Fla. 1st DCA 1982), the claimant's allegation that she had a 5 to 10 percent impairment of the hand was denied by the deputy commissioner because under the AMA *Guides* there was no permanent impairment. The District Court of Appeals rejected a challenge to the exclusive reliance on the AMA *Guides* because there was "no evidence that claimant is not permanently impaired under the AMA *Guide* [sic] but is permanently impaired under some other standard." The reference to "some other standard" suggested that exclusive reliance on the AMA *Guides* might not suffice. The example offered by the Court, however—loss of an arm or a leg demonstrable to the deputy by his own observation—is encompassed by the AMA *Guides* and provided little solace to those hoping to avoid exclusive reliance on the *Guides*. The high-water mark for use of the AMA *Guides* as an exclusive rating system probably was *Mathis v. Kelley Construction Co.*, 417 So.2d 740 (Fla. 1st DCA 1982). Mathis had a knee injury that caused an excessive range of motion: the knee was unstable and would buckle unexpectedly. The AMA *Guides* rate only restrictions in motion of the knee, not excessive motion, and as a result Mathis was found to have no ratable permanent impairment and was denied wage-loss benefits.

The halcyon days were short lived for the doctrine denying wage-loss benefits unless the worker had a permanent impairment ratable by the AMA *Guides*. The Court was forced to deal with facts demonstrating the limits of the AMA *Guides* in *Trindade v. Abbey Road Beef 'N Booze*, 443 So.2d 1007 (Fla. 1st DCA 1983), decided *en banc* with all 12 judges concurring. Trindade experienced a knee injury that caused his knee to buckle on occasion, for which his physician recommended a knee cage to limit motion. The surgeon could not rate the injury using the AMA *Guides* because they dealt only with loss of range of motion in rating knees, while Trindade's knee had instability due to excessive range of motion. The physician rated the knee using the American Academy of Orthopedic Surgery *Manual* and found a 5 to 10 percent permanent impairment. The Court noted that its own efforts to give the AMA *Guides* exclusive effect in order to facilitate the goal of uniformity in determining the existence and extent of permanent impairment were undertaken in anticipation of the Division adopting a more comprehensive schedule. But four years had passed since the legislature imposed on the Division the duty of establishing a comprehensive guide and mandated the use of the AMA *Guides* as a temporary schedule. Meanwhile, the Court had found it increasingly difficult to justify the exclusion of certain injuries with permanent consequences because they did not meet the rating criteria in the AMA *Guides*. Moreover, the Division during the course of this case had indicated that ''it not only has been unable to produce a comprehensive schedule as mandated by the statute: It expresses doubt that a suitable schedule can be prepared, and it is anticipated that no such schedule will be forthcoming.'' The Court concluded that exclusive reliance on the AMA *Guides* under these circumstances would be inappropriate and indeed would be unconstitutional as a violation of due process because of the arbitrary distinction between covered and excluded impairments. The Court therefore held

> that for purposes of determining eligibility for wage loss benefits . . . the existence and degree of permanent impairment resulting from injury shall be determined pursuant to the [AMA] Guides, unless such permanent impairment cannot reasonably be determined under the criteria utilized in the Guides, in which event such permanent impairment may be established under other generally accepted medical criteria for determining impairment.

The Division's immediate reaction to the December 1983 *Trindade* decision was to adopt by rule the *Manual for Evaluation of Permanent Physical Impairment of the American Academy of Orthopedic Surgeons* for use in evaluating those conditions of the hip, knee, shoulder, and elbow not covered by the AMA *Guides*. In October 1984, the Division adopted by rule the 2nd edition of the AMA *Guides* to replace the 1971 edition that had been previously used.

The use of the *Manual* of the American Academy of Orthopedic Surgeons for certain conditions not encompassed in the AMA *Guides* is defensible. More problematical are the recent rulings concerning the use of subjective complaints as a basis for permanent impairment ratings. In *Maggard v. Simpson Motors,* 451 So.2d 529 (Fla. 1st DCA 1984), the Court affirmed a denial of wage-loss benefits when the impairment rating was based solely on subjective complaints. But because of a concern over lack of uniformity among the three-judge panels in the First District Court of Appeals, an *en banc* review was held in *Martin County School Board v. McDaniel,* 465 So.2d 1235 (Fla. 1st DCA 1985). The worker experienced a back injury and during the healing period there were objective findings, such as muscle spasm. The worker was given medication, used a prescribed back brace, and his activity was restricted. After the date of maximum medical improvement there was no objective evidence of a permanent impairment. The treating physician made a permanent impairment rating of 5 percent that did not rely on the rating criteria in the Orthopedic Surgeons' *Manual for Evaluation of Permanent Partial Impairment* but was made "in reference" to the methods in the *Manual* and his experience as an orthopedic surgeon who had treated many bad backs. The deputy commissioner found there was a permanent impairment, and the eight-member majority of the Court affirmed. The opinion noted that the doctor had monitored the claimant's chronic complaints of pain and stiffness over an extended period of two years and also noted that the program of medication and activity restriction were themselves responsible for the absence of objective signs after the date of MMI. The majority opinion distinguished the case from *Maggard,* where the permanent impairment rating was based on bare unverified subjective complaints. The four-judge dissent objected to the finding of permanent impairment because there was no objective evidence after the date of MMI, thus rendering "meaningless the standard of 'other generally accepted medical criteria for determining impairment' which we approved in Trindade."

While the *McDaniel* case involved a physician who at least made an oblique use of the Orthopedic Surgeons' *Manual,* a subsequent case abandoned even this extent of reliance on a published guide. In *United General Construction v. Cason,* 479 So.2d 833 (Fla. 1st DCA 1985), the permanent impairment rating was based primarily on a physician's "personal judgment of the claimant's history of subjective complaints of pain and specifically excluded consideration of the recognized medical reference guides." The award of wage-loss benefits by the deputy commission was affirmed by the Court, which noted that "the physician's opinion was particularly compelling due to the length of time spent in evaluating and monitoring the pattern of subjective symptoms." These recent decisions can only be viewed as a threat to the effort to restrict the eligibility for wage-loss benefits to those workers with readily verifiable permanent impairments.

The "Objective" Wage-Loss Requirements. First, are the actual earnings after the date of maximum medical improvement less than the earnings before the date of injury? If not, then the worker is not eligible for wage-loss benefits for the months in question. Two additional qualifications are necessary. First, for injuries occurring since July 1, 1980, the actual earnings in months that are more than two years after the date of MMI are discounted by a factor of 5 percent per year before they are compared to preinjury earnings. Second, the actual earnings in the month for which wage-loss benefits are claimed must be at least 15 percent below preinjury earnings before the worker qualifies for the benefits because of the threshold built into the statute.

Second, did the actual wage loss start soon and sustain sufficiently? The statute requires the actual wage loss to begin within two years from the date of MMI or the right to wage-loss benefits lapses. In addition, wage-loss benefits must be payable for at least three consecutive months during each 24-month period after the date of MMI.

Third, did the actual wage loss last too long or occur too late in life? For injuries that occurred after July 1, 1980, the maximum duration on wage-loss benefits is 525 weeks. Thus a worker with a permanent impairment who qualifies for wage-loss benefits at age 25 can in no case receive these benefits after age 35. Also, as a result of a 1980 amendment (further changed in 1983), wage-loss benefits terminated at age 65 if the worker was eligible for Old Age benefits from the Social Security program. The age 65 cutoff was challenged in *Sasso v. RAM Property Management*, 452 So. 2d 932 (Fla. 1984), appeal dismissed, 469 U.S. 1030 (1984). Sasso was age 78 at the time of his injury, and consequently the carrier denied wage-loss benefits. The Florida Supreme Court found that the age 65 cutoff provision did not violate constitutional guarantees of equal protection and access to the courts. The age 65 cutoff provision also was alleged to violate the Federal Age Discrimination and Employment Act of 1967 (ADEA), but the Florida Supreme Court held that the Florida law was not unconstitutional under the Federal Supremacy clause in *O'Neil v. Department of Transportation*, 468 So. 2d 904 (Fla. 1985), cert. denied, ____ U.S. ____, 106 S.Ct. 174 (1985). A similar allegation that the Florida statute violated the Federal Supremacy clause because it conflicted with the Social Security Act was rejected by the Florida Supreme Court in *Acosta v. Kraco, Inc.*, 471 So. 2d 24 (Fla. 1985), cert. denied, ____ U.S. ____, 106 S.Ct. 576 (1985). As discussed in the previous subsections, the termination of wage-loss benefits at age 65 for workers qualifying for Social Security Old Age benefits was eliminated in 1983, and in its place an offset provision was added that reduces wage-loss benefits for workers who are eligible for Old Age benefits.

The "Legally Sufficient" Wage-Loss Requirements. The two sets of requirements for wage-loss benefits described above only provide the background for the most interesting legal developments concerning wage-loss benefits. The portions of the statute that have given rise to the controversies are Section 440.15(3)(b)(1) and (2) (quoted earlier in this chapter).

At least five separate requirements have been used in one or another of the Florida cases that have decided whether a wage loss was "legally sufficient" to satisfy Section 440.15(3)(b). The five tests (with alternative versions of the fifth) are:

    (i)   There must be an interruption of employment because of the permanent impairment.

(ii)   There must be an adequate job search.

(iii) There must be no refusal of suitable work.

(iv)   There must be no voluntary limitation of income.

(va)   Even if tests (i)-(iv) are satisfied, the wage loss must be due *solely* to the worker's physical inability to perform work, and other factors, such as slack economic conditions, must play no part in the loss of wages.[20]

(vb)   The wage loss must be due at least *in part* to the physical consequences of the injury. Even if economic conditions also play a part in causing loss of earnings, the worker is not disqualified if tests (i)-(iv) are satisfied.

The law in Florida has evolved since 1979 concerning the use of these five tests because of both court cases and the 1983 amendments to the law.

Probably the test that has been involved in most cases concerns whether the job search was adequate. The Florida courts have provided some guidance on the requirement. The employee is excused from conducting a good-faith job search if the employer or carrier has failed to notify the claimant of the search requirement, *DeFrees v. Colt and Dumont/HIT Sales*, 483 So. 2d 848 (Fla. 1st DCA 1986). Similarly, in a case involving temporary total disability benefits but that is relevant for wage-loss benefits, a worker cannot be denied benefits because of a failure to search for work if "he neither knew nor should have known that he was medically released to work," *Davis v. Phillips & Jordan*, 483 So. 2d 534 (Fla. 1st DCA 1986). A job search is not adequate when the claimant misrepresented his medical limitations by telling prospective employers he was medically limited to working only four hours per day when his physician had imposed no such limit, *Snowdon v. Sambo's*, No. BG-442, slip op. (Fla. 1st DCA 1986). There are numerous similar cases interpreting the adequate job search requirement. Nonetheless, "it is impossible to find a single, definitive statement of what constitutes an 'adequate' job search," *Flesche v. Interstate Warehouse*, 411 So. 2d 919 (Fla. 1st DCA 1982).[21]

The fourth requirement for wage-loss benefits—no voluntary limitation of income—was involved in *Topeka Inn Management v. Pate*, 414 So. 2d 1184 (Fla. 1st DCA 1982). Pate was injured on August 2, 1979, while working as a waitress. Her back injury was rated as 5 percent permanent impairment with a date of MMI of February 18, 1980. From April to August 1980, she worked as a full-time secretary at the minimum wage, which was less than the wage she had earned as a waitress. From August to October 1980 she quit work to take care of her husband, who had suffered a heart attack. From October 1980 to January 1981, she worked full time as a nurse's aid, again at the minimum wage. The court agreed with the deputy commissioner that Pate was entitled to wage-loss benefits during the periods she was working as a secretary or as a nurse's aid, with the benefits replacing a portion of the difference between her pre-injury wage and her actual earnings. But what of the period in which she quit work?

The court opined:

> Strictly speaking, her wage loss during this period of time was not solely due to her compensable injury. That fact, however, does not preclude her entitlement to wage-loss benefits . . . Section 440.15(3)(b)(2) provides:

> . . . *In the event the employee voluntarily limits his or her income or fails to accept employment commensurate with his or her abilities, the salary, wages, and other remuneration the employee is able to earn after the date of maximum medical improvement shall be deemed to be the amount which would have been earned if the employee did not limit his or her income or accepted appropriate employment. . . .* [emphasis supplied in original]

> Considering the statute as a whole and applying it to these facts, we conclude that, by accepting employment as both a secretary and a nurse's aide, claimant has demonstrated the "salary, wages, and other remuneration (she) is able to earn after the date of maximum medical improvement." Therefore, the wage loss attributable to her injury for these months when she was caring for her ill husband is the difference between her former salary as a waitress and the prevailing minimum wage.

The relationship between the requirements of adequate job search (test ii) and no voluntary limitation of income (test iv) was involved in *Anderson v. S & S Diversified, Inc.*, 477 So. 2d 591 (Fla. 1st DCA 1985). The deputy commissioner used the deemed earnings provision to diminish the wage-loss award for the six months when the job search was "sporadic and ineffective." For an additional two months, the deputy denied any wage-loss benefits because of the lack of any job search. The District Court of Appeals affirmed the use of the deemed earnings provision for the six-months interval, but reversed the deputy's decision for the two-months period, holding that the deemed-earnings approach "applied equally to inadequate and absent search." In short, an adequate job search is not "a condition precedent to any consideration of the merits of a wage loss claim," but is only one factor to be used in determining the extent of wage-earning capacity.

Although the job search and voluntary limitation of income tests can in part be analyzed in isolation from the other tests that compose the "legally sufficient" requirements, the most interesting developments concern the combinations of the tests, which can be traced in a series of cases.

LeHigh Corp. v. Byrd, 397 So. 2d 1202 (Fla. 1st DCA 1981), involved a claim for temporary total disability benefits, but was cited in subsequent permanent partial disability cases. The claimant was injured in December 1979 and paid temporary total disability benefits. He returned to work for two weeks and then was discharged on February 23, 1980. Between then and June 27, 1980, there were two periods when Byrd was medically able to work but was unemployed. The deputy commissioner awarded temporary total disability benefits for these two periods. The District Court reversed and laid down these requirements for temporary total disability benefits:

> . . . the claimant must show that his work search was successful, but that he was unable to perform the work. Alternatively, he would have to show that his work search was unsuccessful due to his disability (rather than unavailability of work). . . . The claimant in this case has completely failed to establish any of the preceding elements. [citations omitted]

The District Court decision makes clear that Boyd did not make a conscientious job search during most of the time when temporary total disability benefits were controverted, and denying the benefits for these periods is consistent with earlier cases. By June 15, however, Byrd had made a conscientious search (according to the court), and yet he was denied temporary total disability benefits for June 15 to June 27 (when he started a new job) because, according to the court (at p. 1204), "the claimant did not establish that the work search was unsuccessful due to the disability."

The *LeHigh* test for temporary total disability benefits was adopted for wage-loss benefits under the permanent partial disability sections of the 1979 statute in *Lake County Commissioners v. Walburn,* 409 So. 2d 153 (Fla. 1st DCA 1982). Walburn was injured in November 1979 and reached maximum medical improvement on July 23, 1980. Between July 23 and October 1, 1980, Walburn had no earnings even though he made extensive job searches (averaging two or three inquiries per week with the State Employment Office, for example). The deputy commissioner awarded wage-loss benefits for this period, but the District Court reversed, holding that:

> Section 440.15(3)(b)2, Fla. Stat. (1979) . . . places the burden on the employee to establish that any wage loss benefit claimed is a result of the compensable injury. As claimant is qualified by training and experience for a number of jobs, including surveying, accounting and construction, the evidence is totally insufficient to prove that his work search was unsuccessful due to his disability (rather than because work was unavailable) and that he was entitled to wage loss benefits.

Judge Ervin dissented on the issue of Walburn's eligibility for wage-loss benefits, arguing that "The majority's interpretation of Section 440.15(3)(b)2, forcing a claimant to prove that his work search was unsuccessful due to his disability, rather than because of unavailability of work could place a well-nigh impossible burden on an injured claimant. . . ."

The decisions in *LeHigh* and *Walburn* represent a stringent view of the tests that must be satisfied before wage-loss benefits are paid. The cases form a backdrop for the landmark decision in *Regency Inn v. Johnson,* 422 So. 2d 870 (Fla. 1st DCA 1982). The claimant was injured in August 1979, only days after the legislation enacted that year took affect. She reached maximum medical improvement on August 4, 1980, and had a 5 percent permanent impairment due to the 1979 injury. Johnson remained unemployed after the date of MMI and filed for wage-loss benefits. Her claim for benefits for the period August 4, 1980 to December 10, 1980, was denied by the deputy commissioner because of the absence of a job search; this period was not an issue in the appeal. Thereafter, Johnson made an extensive job search that the deputy commissioner found was in good faith, but she was unsuccessful in obtaining employment. The deputy commissioner also found that the employer had not made Johnson a job offer for the period of wage loss after December 10, 1980.[22] The deputy commissioner therefore awarded her 100 percent wage-loss benefits for December 10, 1980, to April 10, 1981, and the employer filed an appeal concerning this period. The appeal was initially decided by a three-judge panel of the First District Court of Appeal, which upheld the award of wage-loss benefits for the December 1980 to April 1981 period. The court concluded that the *Lehigh* rule is inapplicable for the purpose of wage-loss benefits, and specifically endorsed the reasoning and authority set forth in the dissenting opinion in *Lake County Commissioners v. Walburn.* The court noted that the language pertaining to permanent total benefits was different from the language pertaining to wage-loss benefits. Specifically, for permanent total disability the statute provides:

> "the burden shall be upon the employee to establish that he is not able uninterruptedly to. . .work *due to physical limitations,*" and no compensation of that character shall be payable 'if the employee. . .is *physically capable* of. . .gainful employment.'' Section 440.15(1)(b), Florida statutes.

In contrast, the court notes, "For wage loss the statute provides simply for general causal relation by covering any such loss which 'is the result of the. . .injury.' ''

The three-judge panel concluded that the difference in statutory language for permanent total and wage-loss benefits made the *LeHigh* rule inapplicable for the latter type of benefits.

The decisions in *Walburn* and *Regency* obviously conflict, reflecting in part the different composition of the three-judge panels from the First District Court that rendered these decisions. To resolve the conflict between the cases, the *Regency* case was reheard *en banc,* and the First District Court of Appeal unanimously upheld the original decision in *Regency. The per curium* opinion reflects the diversity of arguments presented to the court.

One argument that was significant concerned the final sentence of Section 440.15(3)(b)2, which reads: "Whenever a wage-loss benefit as set forth in subparagraph 1. may be payable, the burden shall be on the employee to establish that any wage loss claimed is the result of the compensable injury.'' The employer/carrier argued that this sentence placed the burden of proof on the employee to show a causal relationship between the wage loss and the injury, and that this burden could not be satisfied merely by proving "economic dislocation'' or "job disruption" by reason of the compensable injury, as had been concluded by the panel that originally decided the case. The full court then restated the burden of proof provision to:

> require the employee to go forward with evidence showing a change in employment status due to the injury, and an adequate and good faith attempt to secure employment commensurate with his abilities so as to establish, prima facie, an economic loss and to show that he or she has not voluntarily limited his or her income or failed to accept employment commensurate with his or her abilities. Once this evidence has been presented by the employee, the burden of proving that the employee has refused work or voluntarily limited his or her income is on the employer.

But what if an employee who could meet the four elements of the burden of proof requirement, which corresponds to the first four tests for "legally sufficient wage loss" that were previously enumerated, still could not find a job, at least in part because suitable jobs were unavailable? The *en banc* opinion (at p. 879) could not have been more clear:

> We hold that the unavailability of jobs due to economic conditions does not preclude recovery of wage loss benefits, and, accordingly, it is not necessary for a wage loss claimant to present evidence that his refusal for employment was not due to unavailability of jobs resulting from economic conditions. Any other decision on this issue would convert wage loss hearings under the act into seminars on economics, requiring the gathering and presentation of complex information beyond the ken of all but the most schooled in the field of economics, and certainly beyond the resources and ability of the average worker to present or defend against. The sheer impracticability of burdening wage loss claim procedure with such evidence is obvious.

The decision in the *Regency* case surprised and dismayed some of the supporters of the 1979 legislation. For example, Mary Ann Stiles, then general counsel for the Associated Industries of Florida, wrote (1983) that in the *Regency* case,

> The Court failed to see that it shifted the burden of the unemployed from the unemployment rolls to the workers'

compensation rolls. What is accomplished in arguing that employers should rehabilitate and reemploy injured workers when there are no jobs available? That issue is not and never has been a workers' compensation issue in the State of Florida. The Court did not look at the real world when it decided *Regency*.

The adverse reaction to the *Regency* decision, exemplified by the Stiles statement, produced legislation in 1983. Of primary relevance for the "legally sufficient" wage-loss requirements is the sentence added to Section 440.15(3)(b)(2):

> It shall also be the burden of the employee to show that his inability to obtain employment or to earn as much as he earned at the time of his industrial accident, is due to physical limitation related to his accident and not because of economic conditions or the unavailability of employment.

The apparent intention of this amendment was to overrule the holding in the *Regency* case and require the injured worker to show that the only reason for the loss of wages was the physical limitations caused by the injury. This was the legal doctrine enunciated in *Lake County Commissioners v. Walburn* and then rejected in *Regency*. The First District Court of Appeal made a different interpretation of the 1983 amendment in *City of Clermont v. Rumph*, 450 So. 2d 573 (Fla. 1st DCA 1984), *petition for review denied*, 458 So. 2d 271 (Fla. 1984). The Court found that the first four tests for wage-loss benefits (enumerated above) were met, which then required the Court to choose between the (va) and (vb) versions of the fifth test. Rumph had made an extensive job search and testified that once prospective employers found out about his work injury, they would not hire him. The employer argued this was insufficient and that as a result of the 1983 amendments wage-loss benefits were precluded unless the "claimant establishes that economic conditions do not affect his employability." In short, the employer's position would have required the employee to demonstrate that the sole reason for the wage loss was the worker's permanent impairment. This interpretation was rejected by the Court because it would have so limited the workers' remedies as to "seriously imperil the constitutional validity of the workers' compensation law." The interpretation of the 1983 amendment that the Court found constitutional and therefore adopted was that wage-loss benefits were precluded "when predicated solely on economic considerations unrelated to a claimant's physical limitations by ordinary proximate cause standards.'' Although this interpretation seems to turn the apparent intent of the 1983 amendment on its head, the result indicates that sometimes two wrongs do make a right. The questionable decision nullified a dubious amendment that was intended to vitiate the essence of the wage-loss approach: to provide benefits to workers who experience actual loss of earnings because of work injuries.

Experience with the Wage-Loss Approach

This section examines the impact on various aspects of the Florida workers' compensation program of the 1979 reform of permanent partial disability benefits. Data are assembled from the National Council on Compensation Insurance, the Florida Division of Workers' Compensation, and various other sources.

Data from the National Council on Compensation Insurance

Chapter 3 presents extensive data from the National Council on Compensation Insurance on the numbers, average cost, and total cost of permanent partial disability cases in Florida between 1958 and 1982. Here we present additional data pertaining to the pre-1979 legislation era, which serves as a benchmark for evaluating the impact of the new law, plus more data on experience under the new law.

Table 9.1 presents data from the eight most recent policy years currently available. Three technical aspects of the data must be discussed before their significance can be assessed. First, a policy year in Florida involves all policies written between December 1 of one year and November 30 of the next year. Thus policy year 1974-75 includes policies sold between December 1974 and November 1975. Second, policies are in effect for 12 months. Thus the experience for policy year 1974-75 includes reports on some injuries that occurred as early as December 1974 and some that occurred as late as November 1976. Third, the first report basis as shown in table 9.1 reflects the actual experience of policies in the specified policy year based on reports submitted six months after the expiration of each policy sold during the year. The fifth report basis is a simulation of what the experience is expected to be after five years of development (and the ultimate report basis is the simulated ultimate cost), based on development factors derived from earlier policy years in Florida. The beginning point for the simulations is the actual data shown in the first reports, which are then

Table 9.1
Numbers and Costs of Permanent Partial Cases in Florida, 1974–79 as Reported by National Council on Compensation Insurance

Policy year	Major Permanent Partial			Minor Permanent Partial		
	Number of cases	Average cost	Total cost	Number of cases	Average cost	Total cost
Panel A: First Report Basis						
1974–75	2,973	17,454	51,890,505	8,108	3,661	29,680,722
1975–76	3,316	18,563	61,555,061	8,654	3,583	31,005,129
1976–77	3,094	19,691	60,923,728	8,762	3,676	32,207,949
1977–78	3,122	19,276	60,179,192	7,735	3,703	28,639,391
1978–79	2,289	20,403	46,702,989	4,421	3,769	16,661,384
1979–80	2,753	18,323	50,442,886	2,543	3,326	8,458,317
1980–81	2,201	26,675	58,711,198	3,187	4,925	15,697,131
1981–82	2,448	30,728	75,223,310	3,576	3,992	14,276,621
Panel B: Fifth Report Basis/Ultimate Report Basis Since 1979-80						
1974–75	4,468	21,323	95,270,967	7,824	3,414	26,712,650
1975–76	4,821	23,263	112,153,321	8,516	3,291	28,028,637
1976–77	3,967	24,326	96,503,185	8,306	3,447	28,632,867
1977–78	3,878	23,401	90,750,222	7,263	3,478	25,259,943
1978–79	2,891	24,749	71,548,979	4,333	3,484	15,095,214
1979–80	3,785	25,348	95,942,369	2,469	3,049	7,527,902
1980–81	(2,201)	50,373	110,870,696	2,884	4,811	13,876,264
1981–82	4,103	50,015	205,209,942	3,136	3,546	11,121,488

SOURCES: National Council on Compensation Insurance, *Countrywide Workers' Compensation Experience Including Certain Competitive State Funds*, *1st Report Basis* (Jan. 24, 1979, March 1980, March 1981, April 1982, March 1983, April 1984, June 1985, and June 1986); *5th Report Basis* (March 14, 1979, March 1980, March 1981, April 1982, and March 1983); *Ultimate Report Basis* (April 1984, June 1985, and June 1986).

NOTE: The number of major permanent partial cases on an ultimate report basis for 1980–81 apparently represents an error in the NCCI source, since it is identical to the number on a first report basis.

multiplied by the appropriate development factors. As can be seen by comparing panels A and B in table 9.1, case developments between the first report and fifth (or ultimate) report typically decrease the number, average cost, and total cost of minor permanent partial disability cases and increase the number, average cost, and total cost of major permanent partial disability cases. This reflects, in part, the conversion of some cases initially classified as minor permanent partial into major permanent partial as the costs of those cases increase through time.

With these technical aspects in mind, what "lessons" can the data in table 9.1 provide on the consequences of the 1979 reforms? Policy years 1974-75, 1975-76, and 1976-77 entirely involved experience under the old law, as did about 95 percent of the policy year 1977-78 experience,[23] and the data suggest a fairly stable pattern of about 11,000 to 12,000 permanent partial disability cases (major plus minor) per policy year on a first report basis and about 11,000 to 13,000 permanent partial disability cases per policy year on a fifth report basis. Average cost on the fifth report basis increased through time to about $25,000 for major permanent partial disabilities and were fairly stable during the period at about $3,400 for minor permanent partial disabilities. Total costs of both major and minor permanent partial disabilities on a fifth report basis were in the $115-$140 million range between policy year 1974-75 and policy year 1977-78.

Policy year 1978-79 contains policies that expired between December 1979 and November 1980, and about half of all injuries in that policy year occurred after the effective date of the 1979 legislation. In addition to the data from the 1978-79 transition year, there are data from policy years 1979-80 through 1981-82 that are entirely under the new law. Thus, in a rough sense, the first four policy years in table 9.1 can be considered "old law" experience and the last four policy years "new law" experience.

For minor permanent partial cases, the effect of the new law is consistent in both panels of table 9.1. Average costs have increased moderately under the new law, while the number and total costs have been cut in half. Thus the 1979 amendments have succeeded in eliminating many of the cases with minor injuries from the program.

The effects of the new law on major permanent partial cases are more complex. The numbers are clearly down on a first report basis, and there also is probably a decline in numbers on the fifth report/ultimate report basis. Average costs are up under the new law, especially on the ultimate report basis, and as a result total costs of major permanent partial cases are higher under the new law than they were prior to the 1979 amendments. The higher costs occurred in the last two policy years, when first the average cost and then the total cost doubled compared to the corresponding figures under the old law.

The higher cost estimates for permanent partial cases were a major factor in the increases in worker compensation insurance rates that began in 1982 (table 9.2). Concern over the increases led to the appointment of the Workers' Compensation Experience Review Committee, which reported in October 1984. The *Report* found that much of the explanation for the higher costs was the realization by carriers, employers, and the NCCI that wage-loss cases were more expensive than originally anticipated when the new law went into effect. In particular, the increase in estimated costs of the wage-loss cases between the first and ultimate reports (the incurred loss development factors) had to be substantially increased as actual experience under the new law became available. The finding that wage-loss cases have significant costs for many years after the year of injury is reinforced by data in the next subsection.

Table 9.2
Florida Workers' Compensation Insurance Rate Revisions, 1979–86

Effective date	Percentage change from previous rates	Cumulative change from January 1, 1978 rates
August 1, 1979	−15.0	−15.0
January 1, 1981	−5.1	−19.3
July 1, 1981	−15.6	−31.9
January 1, 1982	−6.5	−36.3
September 1, 1982	+10.0	−30.0
December 1, 1982	+10.7	−22.5
March 1, 1984	+10.1	−14.7
January 1, 1985	+18.7	+1.3
January 1, 1986	+11.8	+13.3

SOURCES: 1979–85 data from National Council on Compensation Insurance, *1986 Annual Statistical Bulletin*, p. 18. 1986 data from National Council on Compensation Insurance, *Memorandum FL-86-1* (Feb. 3, 1986).

Data from the Florida Division of Workers' Compensation

The data from the National Council on Compensation Insurance have some advantages, such as their rough consistency with data from other NCCI jurisdictions. There are also some disadvantages, however, such as the limitation of results to those employers who purchase insurance, thus omitting results for self-insuring employers. When there is a trend to greater self-insurance, as there has been in Florida during the last decade,[24] the NCCI data may provide misleading evidence on changes through time in the number and total cost of permanent partial disability cases. The data collected and published by the Florida Division of Workers' Compensation have the advantage of encompassing all employers, including self-insurers.[25] Unfortunately, most of the annual statistical reports published by the Division in recent years contain only one line of data on permanent partial disability cases that combines information on permanent impairment and wage-loss cases.[26] Fortunately, the Division has introduced a computerized data system in recent years that contains considerable valuable material. The tables in this subsection are based on unpublished tabulations provided by the Florida Division of Workers' Compensation.[27]

Table 9.3 presents information on the number of cases that have received permanent impairment benefits under Section 440.15(3)(a) or wage-loss benefits under Section 440.15(3)(b) between August 1979 and December 1985. The data are by year of injury and show a total of about 3 1/2 times as many wage-loss as permanent impairment cases in the first seven years of the new law. Several observations are warranted. An unknown number of cases appears twice because the workers received both types of benefits. The apparent decline in numbers of cases in recent years is misleading because there often is a considerable lag between the date of injury and the date when the worker first qualifies for permanent impairment or wage-loss benefits. This is particularly true for wage-loss benefits, because the worker must both reach the date of MMI and experience a subsequent period of wage-loss due to the work-injury.

The lag between date of injury and the initial payment of wage-loss benefits is documented in table 9.4. The first full year under the new law was 1980,[28] and by the end of that year (corresponding to 0 years after the year of injury) there were 235 cases involving 1980 injuries that had received wage-loss benefits. The peak year for new wage-loss cases involving 1980 injuries was 1981 (corresponding to 1 year after the year of injury), when 1,057 cases were established. Of interest is that five years after the 1980 date of injury, 68 new wage-loss cases were established. The data for 1981-83 in table 9.4 also show the pattern of new wage-loss cases peaking the year after the date of injury, with numerous additional cases initially qualifying for wage-loss benefits in subsequent years. The data in columns (1) and (2) of table 9.7 summarize the general relationship between time and numbers of wage-loss cases resulting from injuries in 1980-84. One hundred percent represents the number of wage-loss cases established by one year after the year of injury (by December 1981 for 1980 injuries, for example). By four years after the date of injury the percentage is 198, and by the end of year 5 it is 213 percent. In short, there is a long and thick tail to the number of wage-loss cases.

Table 9.3
Pernament Impairment and Wage-Loss Cases in Florida
1979–85 Injuries

Year of injury	Number of impairment cases established by December 1985	Number of wage-loss cases established by December 1985
1979 (Aug.–Dec.)	409	1,023
1980	1,095	2,755
1981	1,004	3,438
1982	870	3,348
1983	707	2,965
1984	492	2,233
1985	164	495
Total	4,741	16,257

SOURCE: Calculated from data in tables provided by Florida Department of Labor and Employment Security, Division of Workers' Compensation (August 1986).

The wage-loss cases once established tend to receive benefits over extended periods as well, as shown in table 9.5. For example, for 1980 injuries, 863 (or 42 percent) of the 1,059 cases established by the end of 1982 (two years after the year of injury) received benefits during the average month in 1982. During the average month in 1985, 439

Table 9.4

Number of New Wage-Loss Cases in Florida, by Year of Injury, for 1979–85 Injuries

No. of years after year of injury	1979 injuries (August–December)		1980 injuries		1981 injuries	
	Cases with 1st payment in year -1-	Cumulative total by end of year -2-	Cases with 1st payment in year -3-	Cumulative total by end of year -4-	Cases with 1st payment in year -5-	Cumulative total by end of year -6-
0	15	15	235	235	339	339
1	324	339	1,057	1,292	1,488	1,827
2	334	673	767	2,059	1,018	2,845
3	181	854	433	2,492	431	3,276
4	98	952	195	2,687	162	3,438
5	51	1,003	68	2,755		
6	20	1,023				

No. of years after year of injury	1982 injuries		1983 injuries		1984 injuries		1985 injuries	
	Cases with 1st payment in year -7-	Cumulative total by end of year -8-	Cases with 1st payment in year -9-	Cumulative total by end of year -10-	Cases with 1st payment in year -11-	Cumulative total by end of year -12-	Cases with 1st payment in year -13-	Cumulative total by end of year -14-
0	427	427	463	463	508	508	495	495
1	1,638	2,065	1,657	2,120	1,725	2,233		
2	959	3,024	845	2,965				
3	324	3,348						

Table 9.5
Number of New Wage-Loss Cases Receiving Benefits in Florida, by Year, for 1979–85 Injuries

No. of years after year of injury	1979 injuries (August–December)		1980 injuries		1981 injuries		1982 injuries		1983 injuries		1984 injuries		1985 injuries	
	Monthly average of cases receiving payment -1-	As percentage of all established cases -2-	Monthly average of cases receiving payment -3-	As percentage of all established cases -4-	Monthly average of cases receiving payment -5-	As percentage of all established cases -6-	Monthly average of cases receiving payment -7-	As percentage of all established cases -8-	Monthly average of cases receiving payment -9-	As percentage of all established cases -10-	Monthly average of cases receiving payment -11-	As percentage of all established cases -12-	Monthly average of cases receiving payment -13-	As percentage of all established cases -14-
0	5	33	49	21	72	21	98	23	107	23	113	22	132	27
1	101	30	486	38	748	41	836	40	808	38	1,004	45		
2	251	37	863	42	1,180	41	1,124	37	1,172	40				
3	293	34	836	34	972	30	943	28						
4	253	27	608	23	720	21								
5	178	18	439	16										
6	131	13												

(or 16 percent) of the 2,755 cases involving 1980 injuries received wage-loss benefits.

The lags between dates of injury and the initial payments of wage-loss benefits and the tendency for wage-loss cases to continue receiving benefits over extended periods of time help explain the patterns for total costs shown in table 9.6. For 1980 injuries, the wage-loss benefits cost $356,400 in 1980 (year 0); peaked at $6,424,780 in 1982 (year 2); and were still $3,093,330 in 1985 (year 5); with a cumulative cost through the end of 1985 of $23,400,290. The data in columns (3) and (4) of table 9.7 summarize the general relationship between time and total costs of wage-loss benefits involving 1980-84 injuries. One hundred percent represents the total costs of the wage-loss cases by one year after the date of injury (by December 1981 for 1980 injuries, for example). By five years after the date of injury, the percentage is 585.

The continuing increase in numbers of wage-loss cases and the explosive increase in costs of the cases for the five years after the year of injury are shown in graph 9.1, which uses the data from columns (2) and (4) of table 9.7. The results illustrate the finding of this and the previous subsection: that wage-loss cases have significant costs for many years after the years of injury. They also dramatize the benefits and costs of the wage-loss approach: benefits to workers in the form of long-term protection, but costs to employers and carriers in the form of extended periods of liability. One way to try to avoid these costs is to terminate future liability by use of compromise and release agreements—known as "washouts" in Florida.

Data on Washouts

As recounted earlier in this chapter, washouts—once widely used to terminate payments in permanent partial disability cases in Florida—were supposed to be greatly restricted by the 1979 law. Washouts of future medical benefits were strictly banned, and settlements of cash benefits were prohibited until at least six months after the date of maximum medical improvement and then only in special circumstances. In 1983, a limited exception to the general prohibition on washouts for all benefits (including medical) was provided: washouts are permissible when there is a legitimate controversy over compensability and the employer or carrier has provided no benefits.

The limitations on washouts contained in the 1979 legislation withstood constitutional challenges in *Johnson v. R. H. Donnelly Co.*, 402 So.

Table 9.6
Total Costs of Wage-Loss Cases in Florida, by Year, for 1979–85 Injuries
(thousands of dollars)

Number of years after year of injury	1979 injuries (August–December)		1980 injuries		1981 injuries	
	In year -1-	Cumulative -2-	In year -3-	Cumulative -4-	In year -5-	Cumulative -6-
0	9	9	356	356	980	980
1	653	661	3,641	3,998	5,565	6,546
2	2,102	2,764	6,425	10,422	8,637	15,182
3	1,732	4,496	5,730	16,152	7,273	22,455
4	1,539	6,035	4,155	20,307	5,526	27,982
5	1,069	7,103	3,093	23,400		
6	786	7,889				

	1982 injuries		1983 injuries		1984 injuries		1985 injuries	
	In year -7-	Cumulative -8-	In year -9-	Cumulative -10-	In year -11-	Cumulative -12-	In year -13-	Cumulative -14-
	694	694	730	730	809	809	967	967
	6,373	7,068	6,164	6,894	7,906	8,715		
	8,787	15,855	9,486	16,380				
	7,608	23,463						

Table 9.7
Developments by 1985 in Number and Cost
of Wage-Loss Cases in Florida, 1980–84 Injuries

Number of years after year of injury	New cases in year as percent of total number of cases established by end of year one	Cumulative total number of cases as percent of total number established by end of year one	Total cost in year as percent of total cost by end of year one	Cumulative total cost as percent of total cost by end of year one
0	20	20	11	11
1	80	100	89	100
2	50	150	139	239
3	24	178	121	360
4	12	198	94	468
5	5	213	77	585

NOTE: The percentages are the average for the available data for 1980–84 injuries shown in tables 9.4 and 9.6. Only 1980 injury year data are available for 5 years after the date of injury; only 1980 and 1981 injury year data are available for 4 years after the date of injury; etc.

Graph 9.1
Cumulative Total Number of Cases and Cumulative Total Cost of Wage-Loss Cases, 1980-84 Injuries

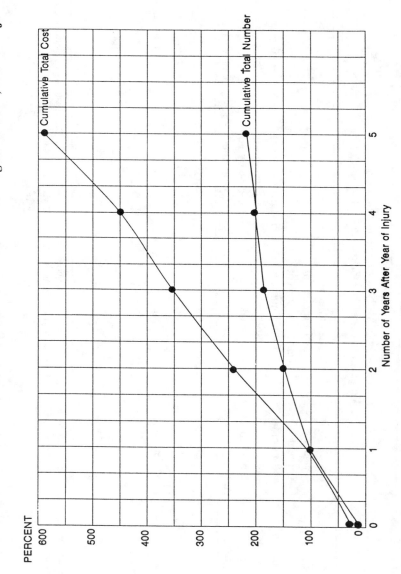

2d 518 (Fla. 1st DCA 1981). The absolute prohibition on washouts of medical benefits was challenged as unconstitutional because the provision denied the worker access to the courts, was an impairment of contract, and was an improper exercise of the state's police power. The court rejected all three arguments.

The essence of the washout is that in exchange for a lump-sum payment of benefits the employer or carrier is released from any further liability. Under the 1979 legislation, a practice arose that is not technically a washout, since there is no complete release from liability, but that has many attributes in common with washouts. This practice is the use of advances, whereby a specified period of future benefits is paid in a lump sum. The main distinction from a washout is that if the employee has actual disability beyond the period covered by the advance, payments can resume. But if the actual period of disability should turn out to be less than the period covered by the advance (perhaps because the injured worker died), the carrier or employer cannot as a practical matter recover any portion of the advance. In that sense, the use of an advance defeats one of the purposes of the 1979 legislation—namely, to limit benefit payments to times when the worker experiences actual wage loss.

Advances are generally involuntary in the sense that the carrier or employer opposes the settlement, while it is typically supported by the worker and his lawyer. In *Sanford v. Alachua County School Board*, 425 So. 2d 112 (Fla. 1st DCA 1983), the First District Court of Appeal rejected the argument that an advancement prejudiced the carrier because of the low discount rate (4 percent) used to calculate the lump-sum settlement and because basing the lump-sum calculations on the entire remaining life expectancy (21.5 years) would make it impossible to later challenge the claimant's status as permanently disabled if she were to regain her earning capacity or die.

The 1983 legislation provided relief on the advance problem. Section 44.20(12)(c) was amended to provide for an 8 percent interest rate to be used in discounting the future payments to their present value for purposes of making a lump-sum payment. Section 440.20(13)(d) was amended by adding a sentence limiting the advance to the greater of $7,500 or 26 weeks of benefits in any four-year period. The threat to the wage-loss approach posed by involuntary advancements may have been completely ended by the First Court of Appeal decision in *Murphree Bridge v. Brown*, 492 So. 2d 451 (Fla. 1st DCA 1986). The Court stated,

Since each month of wage-loss benefits constitutes a separate claim, it follows that the liability for payment of those benefits accrues monthly. Consequently, there is no identifiable indebtedness associated with the wage-loss provisions which could support an award of an advance payment which encompasses an amount more than the amount due as a monthly benefit.

If the problem of involuntary advances seems to be declining, the situation for voluntary washouts is not so clear. The percentage of permanent partial cases involving washouts has dropped from 34 percent under the old law to 27 percent under the new law, according to one comparison made by the National Council on Compensation Insurance (Workers' Compensation Experience Review Committee 1984, at p. 54).

This is progress, but hardly to the degree envisaged by Mary Ann Stiles, one of the architects of the 1979 law, when she wrote (1983 at p. 6):

Wash-outs have been all but virtually eliminated from the system. The basic reason for that is, of course, that if the Legislature allowed wash-outs under the wage loss system, we would again be guessing into an indefinite future what a person's loss of wages was going to be.

The extent of washouts under the 1979 law (together with the 1983 amendments facilitating washouts) has been monitored by the Workers' Compensation Command Post, an insurance industry effort, and reported in various issues of the *Command Post Briefing*. In an early issue (Vol. 1, No. 2, May 1981) the publication noted three ways the ban on washouts was being avoided:

The initial strategy seemed to be "let's *try* to wash out cases, including future medical; the Deputy Commissioner will probably approve them." They were right; some commissioners did approve them as a matter of course. It took Division intervention, in the form of "reminders" of the statutory mandate, to stop this practice.

A second method of "washing out" a client came to light in the *Baker* case. Baker filed a highly questionable claim. . . . Perhaps the carrier should have fought this "nuisance" claim. However, "rather than risk uncertainties attendant to litigation to this matter and incurring further costs," the parties agreed to a washout-type settlement of about $1,000. The method of circumventing the law? A signed statement by the claimant that *no accident occurred....*

The final "innovative" approach is just now coming to light. Claimants are signing stipulations agreeing to washout all compensation benefits. No mention is made to the claimant of his right to future medical. The letter of the law has been upheld, but the claimant, rarely reading the "legalese" of the final order, doesn't know he can claim additional medical, and therefore doesn't.

Subsequent to the 1983 amendments liberalizing the rules for washouts, the *Command Post Briefing* (Vol. 4, No. 3, Apr. 1984) found the number of washouts under the new provision growing rapidly. For all of 1984, there were 5,269 cases washed out for an average cost of $13,235. The *Command Post Briefing* (Vol. 5, No. 9, Nov. 1985) noted this was down from 17,058 washouts in 1978 that averaged $5,282, and concluded that it is hoped carriers and self-insurers would continue to show restraint and wash out "only the more serious cases." While we question the wisdom of this strategy, it is hard to disagree with the conclusion found in the *Command Post Briefing* (Vol. 3, No. 4, May 1983) that "washouts are flourishing despite the restrictive criteria" in the 1979 legislation.

Conclusions

The wage-loss approach to permanent partial disability benefits adopted in Florida in 1979 has been widely publicized and vigorously debated. How has the Florida experiment worked? This chapter has tried to assemble information that is at least reasonably reliable. There can be little doubt that the number of permanent partial disability cases has plummeted in Florida as a result of the 1979 legislation, which was one of the purposes of the law. There also is persuasive evidence that one of the other purposes of the law—to virtually eliminate washouts—has not been achieved. In addition, the review of case law in this chapter makes clear that the new approach to permanent partial benefits is not free of litigation and vexatious issues.

Most observers would probably accept the preceding conclusions. Other evaluations have been made that are more controversial, however, and some of these are worth reporting. Surely one of the most glowing accounts was included in *The Circle Solution* (Mintner 1982, p. 1):

> Since the effective date of the Wage-Loss statute, workers
> have been compensated fairly; the need for workers to hire
> and pay lawyers has diminished; insurance companies have
> become increasingly eager to sell their products in Florida,
> . . . and rates have been slashed by at least 50%.

Although this passage contains its share of hyperbole that is difficult to document or disprove, some of it can be evaluated. For example, the cost of workers' compensation insurance before and after the 1979 legislation can be measured. As shown in table 3.18, in 1978 a representative sample of Florida employers was expending 2.641 percent of payroll on workers' compensation insurance. This was 86 percent above the 28-jurisdiction average of 1.420 percent. Then a series of reductions took place in Florida rates, cumulating to a 36 percent decline by January 1982, followed by a series of rate increases thru 1986 (table 9.2). In 1984, partway through this cycle of rates, Florida employers was expending 1.552 percent of payroll on workers' compensation insurance premiums, only 14 percent above the 28-jurisdiction average of 1.368 percent. Thus as of 1984, Florida had improved its Florida workers' compensation rates relative to those in other states. Perhaps even more relevant, the National Council on Compensation Insurance estimated that those 1984 Florida rates would have been 62 percent higher if the wage-loss reforms of 1979 had never been enacted because of the inflationary pressures from higher weekly maximums and medical benefits. Thus there appears to be some merit to the 50 percent savings alleged by *The Circle Solution*.

This chapter has focused on the reduction in costs sought by employers in enactment of the 1979 legislation. But we would endorse the view expressed in the *Journal of American Insurance* article on the Florida law that ''wage loss would be viewed primarily as a means of improving equity, but not necessarily as a cost-saver.'' An evaluation in part III of this study shows that equity was lacking under the pre-1979 legislation in Florida. We are unaware of any effort under way to evaluate the equity of the new law. This would require a systematic effort to collect data on all workers with permanent impairments that would measure their benefits and their earnings before and after their injuries. At least some of the masses of data that are needed to evaluate a wage-loss system are available in the Division's files, but a major effort will have to be mounted to use the data in an analysis of equity.

Other evaluations of the 1979 legislation are not so favorable as those in *The Circle Solution*. As might be suspected, some of the criticism has come from those who initially opposed the law. But some of the original supporters have also been critical, and it is not evident which camp has raised the greatest outcry against the wage-loss approach.

The most consistently outspoken opponents of the wage-loss approach have been the claimants' attorneys. Any hopes that the objections raised to the 1979 legislation before its enactment might be overcome with time have been largely disappointed. One claimant's attorney wrote to one of us that:[29]

> To me, and for all the claimants I represent, wage loss as it is used and adopted in Florida is a miserable failure. The theory behind wage loss is very sound just as the theory of communism is sound. However, from a practical aspect, it will not work, cannot work, and represents a true rape of the working man in the State of Florida.

As remarked, some criticisms of the 1979 law also have been expressed by some of the original supporters, most notably representatives of the employer and insurance communities who are concerned about the case law that developed the criteria for wage-loss benefits. Certainly some of the toughest legal issues concern instances in which the employer or carrier feels that the worker's actual earnings in the period after the date of MMI are not truly reflective of the worker's earning capacity, or feels that the loss of actual earnings is due to factors other than the work-related injury. Above, we examined at some length the cases that led to the *Regency* case, which in turn led to amendments of the law in 1983 and the *Rumph* case.

The decisions and 1983 amendment can be placed in perspective by comparing Florida with New York, a state with a long history of wage-loss benefits. The comparisons cannot be made point by point because the particulars of the statutes differ, but some general comparisons can be made. The third set of requirements for wage-loss benefits in Florida was termed the "legally-sufficient" wage-loss requirements. These can be related to the second question posed for New York: Can the wage loss be attributed to the injury? In New York, the answer was, "So long as the permanent consequences of the work-related injury are at least a partial cause of the wage loss, nonscheduled benefits can be paid." The New York answer is thus similar to the holding of *Regency* and

Rumph, which have rejected the idea that wage-loss benefits can be paid only if the injury is the sole cause of the wage loss. Thus what is viewed by some as an aberration of the wage-loss approach in Florida is a long-standing legal doctrine in New York.

If this defense of *Regency* is correct, then we believe it is also correct to assert that the First District Court of Appeal interpretation of the 1983 amendments in Florida was appropriate in *Rumph.* This is not to say that every aspect of the Florida law is operating properly; for one thing, as previously discussed, the extensive reliance on washouts is disturbing. Nor is it to say that every component of the wage-loss section in the statute is ideal; for example, as discussed by Burton (1983, pp. 41-46), the benefit formula creates disincentives for workers to return to work. But what this analysis does suggest is that the *Rumph* decision, although in some respects disingenuous, is nonetheless compatible with the underlying philosophy of a wage-loss approach and with the case law for wage-loss cases in other jurisdictions.

NOTES

1. State of Florida, Department of Labor and Employment Security, Division of Workers' Compensation, *Analysis of Work Injuries Covered by Workers' Compensation, 1977-1978* [also titled *1977-1978 Cases Causes Costs,* and so cited hereafter], table V, p. 214, shows that the estimated number of workers covered by workers' compensation was 2,039,100 in 1970 and 3,008,800 in 1978.

2. The first section relies in part on field work conducted in Florida in 1975 by Katherine Hagerty.

3. The provision pertaining to the duration of nonscheduled permanent partial disability benefits was amended effective July 1, 1978, to provide that the specified number of weeks to be multiplied by the percentage of disability increased with the severity of the injury. The 1978 provision, discussed in the text *infra,* was effective only until 1979, when the wage-loss approach was adopted.

4. The discussion of Florida decisions in the balance of this section relies in part on Alpert and Murphy (1978).

5. More precisely, wage-loss benefits are paid only when actual earnings after the date of MMI are less than the worker's potential earnings. Generally, in workers' compensation, potential earnings are defined as preinjury earnings. See, however, a later section for a discussion of the Florida wage-loss approach adopted in 1979, in which potential earnings and preinjury earnings are not always identical.

6. See generally Stiles (1982), p. 44.

7. Compare *City of Hollywood v. Castora,* 380 so. 2d 1148 (Fla. 1st DCA 1980) (adequate job search before original hearing apparently required) with *Flesche v. Interstate Warehouse,* 411 So. 2d 919 (Fla. 1st DCA 1982) (adequate job search permitted after original hearing).

8. *Bill Bard Associates, Inc. v. Totten*, 418 So. 2d 418 (Fla. 1st DCA 1982).

9. *United States Sugar Corporation v. Hayes*, 407 So. 2d 1079 (Fla. 1st DCA 1982).

10. *1977-1978 Cases Causes Costs*, p. 23, earlier editions of *Cases Causes Costs*.

11. *1977-1978 Cases Causes Cost*, p. 23.

12. Section 440.34 of the Florida Workmen's Compensation Law effective July 1, 1978, provided that 75 percent of the claimant's attorney's fees on claims other than medical benefits were to be paid by the employer or carrier and 25 percent by the worker. If, however, the employer or carrier handled the claim in a negligent, arbitrary, or capricious manner, the employer or carrier was liable for 100 percent of the claimant's attorney fee. This provision was further modified in 1979, as will be discussed in the next section.

13. U.S. Department of Labor, *State Compliance* 1983.

14. *1977-1978 Cases Causes Costs*, p. 211.

15. "Florida's Bold Experiment in Cutting Worker (sic) Compensation Costs," *Journal of American Insurance* (Summer 1982), pp. 21-22.

16. At various stages of the process that led to the enactment of the 1979 law, the authors of this volume were participants. We do not want to exaggerate our roles, but we would be remiss if we did not mention them. A major reason for our involvement is that Florida is one of the states included in the NSF study that is the progenitor of this volume (Berkowitz, Burton, and Vroman 1979). The preliminary results from the NSF study became available just as the movement for reform took off in Florida, and as a result we played cameo roles in the Florida drama.

17. The balance of this subsection relies extensively on Mintner (1982). Citations are provided only for specific quotations.

18. Comments by Dan Miller to Conference on Workers' Compensation Co-sponsored by the AFL-CIO and the New York State School of Industrial and Labor Relations, Cornell University, at the George Meany Center, July 23, 1981.

19. Section 440.15(3)(b)(5) provides that for injuries occurring after July 1, 1980, the escalation factor is 5 percent per year or the annual rate of inflation measured by the National Consumer Price Index, whichever is less. Rather than escalating preinjury wages by 5 percent and comparing these earnings to actual earnings in the months when wage-loss benefits are paid, the Florida law provides that the actual earnings will be discounted by 5 percent and compared to preinjury earnings as a basis for the benefits. This discount procedure provides lower benefits than the escalation procedure would using the same percentage adjustment factor.

20. Some Florida decisions have considered the inability to find employment for reasons other than worker's physical limitations as evidence that the job search was inadequate (the second test), rather than viewing this fifth test as a separate requirement.

21. Although the decision in *Flesche* was in 1982, the law in effect before the 1979 amendments was involved. The job search test was similar under the old law, however, and so the decision is still useful. The Court in *Flesche*, note 11 at page 925, elaborated on the difficulty of defining "adequate" when it noted, "The condition of the economy and the locale in which the work search is conducted may create a wide disparity in the extent of the search that might be termed 'adequate' or 'inadequate.' What might be properly considered adequate in Clewiston might well be totally inadequate in Miami, for comparable claimants similarly injured."

22. Regency had made a job offer prior to the hearing before the deputy commissioner on the claim for wage-loss benefits for the August to December 1980 period, for which benefits were denied. According to the District Court, *Regency Inn v. Johnson,* 422 So. 2d 870, 880-81 (Fla. 1st DCA 1982), after the claim for the December 1980 to April 1981 period was filed, her attorney "repeatedly requested the Regency reemploy claimant, or that Regency and the carrier provide rehabilitation, retraining, or job placement counseling and assistance. The E/C 'stonewalled,' provided neither, and offered no explanation for their refusal."

23. Policy year 1977-78 contained a limited amount of experience under the new law (since policies written in August-November 1978 did not expire until August-November 1979, when the new law was in effect). Since about 95 percent of the policy year 1977-78 experience involved injuries under the old act, however, the experience can be considered essentially old law data.

24. In 1977, self-insurers accounted for 12.0 percent of all benefit payments in Florida (Price 1980, table 3, p. 8). In 1984, self-insurers accounted for 30.3 percent of all Florida payments (Price 1987, table 2).

25. For reasons unknown, however, the annual number of permanent partial cases reported by the National Council on Compensation Insurance (table 9.1) is greater than the number of permanent impairment and wage-loss cases recorded by the Florida Division of Workers' Compensation (table 9.3) even though the data from the Division include self-insurers.

26. State of Florida, *1984 Workers' Compensation Injuries,* table 9, p. 44, shows 1,210 permanent impairment cases involving 1984 injuries with a total of $14,656,356 of indemnity benefits. This apparently represents developments through June 30, 1985. The report also contains some information on cases involving 1982 and 1983 injuries with developments through June 30, 1985.

27. These data were provided with the assistance of several present or former members of the Division of Workers' Compensation, including J. Baxter Swing, Sheldon Kemp, Timothy Kearnes, and Pat Parmer. Robert Altvilla is the staff member who prepared the tables in response to our requests.

28. Tables 9.4 to 9.6 contain data on wage-loss cases resulting from 1979 injuries after the August effect date of the law, but because there is only five months' experience from 1979, the text and table 9.7 do not deal with the 1979 data.

29. Letter from a Sarasota, Florida attorney to John F. Burton, Jr., September 22, 1981.

Part III
The Wage-Loss Study

Chapter 10
The Wage-Loss Study
of
California, Florida, and Wisconsin

This chapter is based on a wage-loss study that examined the relationships among work-related injuries, earnings losses, and workers' compensation benefits for male workers who were injured in 1968 and who received permanent partial or permanent total disability benefits in Wisconsin, California, or Florida. The study was sponsored by the National Science Foundation, and considerable additional material on the wage-loss study is contained in the *NSF Report* (Berkowitz, Burton, and Vroman 1979) submitted at the end of the project.

Although the data analyzed in this chapter are for injuries that occurred 19 years ago, the findings warrant discussion for several reasons. One is that for any study to track workers for several years after the date of injury (in this case, six years), it must involve "old" injuries. Second, the methodology used to prepare the *NSF Report* has not been widely used in workers' compensation research, and the dissemination of the results may encourage others to conduct such studies. Third, and most important, the findings are relevant for understanding the approaches used currently in most states to compensate workers with permanent partial disabilities. As of 1968, Wisconsin based such benefits on the extent of impairment (category I), California based permanent partial benefits on the extent of loss of earning capacity (category II), and Florida offered workers the choice of the two approaches. At present, most jurisdictions pay permanent partial benefits by evaluating the extent of impairment or the extent of loss of earning capacity. Our findings can provide useful guidance about how these approaches are currently operating, since nothing fundamental has changed in the application of these approaches since 1968.

The Conceptual Framework

The conceptual framework was introduced in chapter 1 of this study (see, in particular, graph 1.1). The worker represented in graph 1.1

had wages increasing through time from A to B, corresponding to the worker's higher productivity and general increases in the price level. In the NSF study, such preinjury earnings data were available for 1966 and 1967. At point B, which is 1968 for the NSF study, the worker experienced a work-related injury that permanently reduced his earnings. If the worker had not been injured, his earnings would have continued to grow along the line B-C. Although these potential earnings cannot be observed, they can be estimated from information such as the worker's preinjury earnings and age. The worker's actual earnings normally are significantly affected if the injury results in the payment of permanent partial disability benefits; the line BDEFG in graph 1.1 traces such a result. In the NSF study, data on actual earnings were available for the 1968 to 1973 period. When the actual earnings in the six-year period are subtracted from the estimate of potential earnings for the same interval, the results are the estimates of the wage loss due to the injury. In graph 1.1, the "true" wage loss is potential earnings (line BC) minus actual earnings (line BDEFG). Many workers do not follow the pattern represented by graph 1.1, of course, but in all cases we defined wage loss as the difference between potential earnings and actual earnings between 1968 and 1973.

The workers' compensation benefits received by the workers between 1968 and 1973 were also measured in the NSF study. Between the date of injury and the date of MMI (maximum medical improvement) the worker is entitled to temporary disability benefits; afterward, he qualifies for permanent disability benefits. The date of MMI is not a term used in every state, but each has an equivalent date when the worker's medical condition is first considered ratable for purposes of permanent disability benefits. In the NSF study, much of the analysis involves comparisons between the total of all types of workers' compensation cash benefits received between 1968 and 1973 and the estimated loss of wages during this period. The ratio of benefits-to-wage loss is the replacement rate, which is a key variable in determining the adequacy and equity of the workers' compensation benefits in the state.

The Wage-Loss Study of Wisconsin

The Wisconsin Workers' Compensation Program[1]

In 1968, the year of injury for the workers in our sample, temporary total disability benefits were 70 percent of the worker's preinjury wage, subject to a maximum weekly benefit of $73.00 effective March 1, 1968 (the maximum was $68.00 for 1968 injuries that occurred before March 1) and subject to a minimum weekly benefit of $8.75. Permanent partial disability benefits were paid for up to 1,000 weeks depending on the severity of the injury, and the weekly benefit was 70 percent of the worker's weekly wage, subject to a maximum weekly benefit of $47.50 effective March 1, 1968 (the maximum was $46.00 for 1968 injuries that occurred before March 1) and subject to a minimum weekly benefit of $14.00. Permanent total disability benefits were paid for the duration of the disability at weekly amounts equivalent to the temporary total disability benefit amounts (except that the minimum weekly benefit for permanent total disability was $14.00).

The duration of the Wisconsin permanent partial disability benefits normally was based on the extent of the worker's impairment or functional limitations. Typical of most workers' compensation statutes, there was a schedule (or list) of certain impairments with a corresponding list of durations. For example, the loss of a hand resulted in 400 weeks of benefits, and the loss of a palm where the thumb remains was "worth" 275 weeks of benefits. The schedule primarily described amputations, and injuries that involved loss of use of the scheduled injuries were evaluated relative to the schedule. Thus, an injury that caused 50 percent loss of use of the hand resulted in 200 weeks of benefits. Finally, injuries not on the schedule or that could not be related to the schedule were rated on their seriousness relative to permanent total disability; in practice, such ratings generally were based on the degree of functional limitations or impairment compared to a whole man. Total disability for purposes of unscheduled permanent partial disability benefits was 1,000 weeks, and so a back injury rated as equivalent to 25 percent of total disability resulted in 250 weeks of benefits.

Presumably the purpose of the benefits in Wisconsin was (and is) to provide compensation for work disability, that is, loss of earning capacity or loss of actual earnings. Wisconsin had adopted the normal approach in workers' compensation, which is not to measure work disability, but to measure impairment or functional limitations and use these measures as a predictor of the resulting work disability.[2]

The procedure for providing permanent disability benefits in Wisconsin is unusual because of the extensive role played by the state workers' compensation agency. In most jurisdictions, the extent of the permanent disability usually is decided through litigation (often involving a hearing before the state workers' compensation agency) or through negotiations between attorneys representing the worker and the employer (often resulting in a compromise and release agreement). In the typical jurisdiction, the workers' compensation agency is less important than the private parties in determining the outcome of the case, but in Wisconsin the agency is an active participant in the determination of permanent partial disability benefits. Medical reports must be filed, and if the amount of permanent partial benefits proposed by the employer or carrier seems inappropriate, the state agency intervenes to protect the worker's interest. One consequence of this active involvement of the state agency in Wisconsin is that only a minority of cases in the NSF study required a hearing or resulted in a compromise and release agreement.

Methodology and Empirical Results for Wisconsin

This section briefly describes the methodology and empirical results for the Wisconsin sample.[3] The first step was to reconstruct a record of all cases involving 1968 injuries that resulted in permanent disability benefits, to eliminate certain cases from the sampling frame because they involved workers of the wrong age or with other disqualifying factors, and then to draw a sample that included all the workers with serious injuries and some of the workers with minor injuries. The second step was to collect data on the workers in our sample and to conduct some initial processing and tabulation of the data. The collection involved inspection of the case folders to verify certain data and to collect additional data needed for this study, such as the timing of benefits. The data were then key punched and a number of tabulations were prepared showing items such as total benefits payments to the workers in our sample. The third step was to have the Social Security Administration process the data and prepare tabulations. Social Security received finder cards that include *inter alia* each worker's social security number, age, sex, disability rating, and present value of workers' compensation benefits received between 1968 and 1973. Social Security then searched the Summary Earnings Records for 1966 to 1973 earnings, made estimates of total annual earnings when the taxable maximum was reached, performed various calculations, and provided us with tabulations.

The results from our two male samples in Wisconsin are presented in tables 10.1 and 10.2.[4] Most Wisconsin permanent partial disability cases paid benefits without litigation or use of compromise and release agreements, and these uncontested cases are shown in table 10.1. The male contested cases are shown in table 10.2. Both tables contain summary data (line 1) and data for the sample disaggregated by 10-year age categories (lines 2-5) and by the part of the body injured (lines 6-9). The permanent disability ratings were derived from the number of weeks of permanent disability benefits, with 10 weeks of benefits equivalent to a 1 percent rating.

Panel A of the tables presents the weighted counts for the workers in the sample. Table 10.1 indicates that the total sample of male un-contested cases was 1,685, with a mean rating of 3.70 percent (as shown in the next to last column of panel A). The sample of males who received their benefits in contested cases contains 284.5 workers (rounded to 285 workers for textual purposes), who had an average disability rating of 10.14 percent (table 10.2).

In both samples, the extent of disability is associated with age and location of injury. There is a slight tendency for disability ratings to increase with age, although 40-49-year-olds were an exception in both samples. Injuries to the trunk and "all other cases" are the two most serious categories and injuries to the upper extremities the least serious for both samples. When the A panels in the two tables are compared, there is clear-cut evidence of a positive association between severity of injury and probability of the case becoming contested. In the 1-2 percent rating interval, 95 percent of the cases are uncontested (941 of 981 cases), but of the cases with ratings of 16 percent or more, 51 percent are contested (50 of 98 cases). Also, controlling for severity, there is an association between injury location and controversion. For example, among cases with ratings of 16 percent or more, 20 of 31 extremity cases were uncontested, whereas all 19 trunk cases were contested.

Panel B shows mean potential earnings between 1968 and 1973, calculated by multiplying each worker's 1966-67 actual earnings (from the Summary Earnings Record) by his 1968-73 expected earnings growth ratio (EGR). The potential earnings are estimates of what the workers would have earned during the six years if they had not been injured on the job.

The expected growth ratio (EGR) was derived from the experience of workers in our control group, who were injured in 1968 and who received a 1-5 percent permanent disability rating in California. The actual earnings of these workers were increased to reflect their loss of earnings during their healing periods after their injuries. We assumed the workers with these minor disability ratings had no permanent loss of income beyond the healing period. Then for each worker in the con-

Table 10.1
Wisconsin Uncontested Permanent Partial Disability Cases for Men with 1968 Injuries

Classification of workers	Percent rating						Mean ratings	Total
	1–2	3–5	6–10	11–15	16–50	51–100		
Panel A								
	Weighted counts of workers and mean disability ratings							
1. Workers age 20–59	941	467	177	52	48		3.70	1,685
2. Workers age 20–29	294	105.5	36	15	14		3.54	464.5
3. Workers age 30–39	226	122	39.5	10	14		3.69	411.5
4. Workers age 40–49	219.5	140.5	53.5	11	13		3.68	437.5
5. Workers age 50–59	201.5	99	48	16	7		37.1	371.5
6. Upper extremities	785	192	82	20	20		2.80	1,099
7. Trunk cases	17	93	42	10	0		5.83	162
8. Lower extremities	120	150	34	9	4		3.76	317
9. All other cases	19	32	19	13	24		9.62	107
Panel B								
	Mean potential earnings (1968–73, in dollars)†							
1. Workers age 20–59	42,567	43,938	43,320	42,472	37,960			42,892
2. Workers age 20–29	40,144	44,412	38,743	41,693	32,671			40,829
3. Workers age 30–39	43,641	46,232	47,880	52,464	42,605			44,995
4. Workers age 40–49	45,298	44,383	48,995	48,364	41,628			45,414
5. Workers age 50–59	41,925	39,973	36,673	32,905	32,434			40,159
6. Upper extremities	42,740	44,084	41,644	39,699	35,516			42,706
7. Trunk cases	37,364	44,193	45,224	44,276	—			43,748
8. Lower extremities	42,497	43,123	43,355	37,036	37,720			42,670
9. All other cases	40,529	46,136	46,279	49,113	40,036			44,159

Panel C — Mean earnings losses (1968–73, in dollars)†

1. Workers age 20–59	1,554	2,759*	4,292*	7,175*	2,519*
2. Workers age 20–29	1,714	1,890	1,337	8,757*	2,096
3. Workers age 30–39	3,009	7,595*	6,399*	9,611*	5,162*
4. Workers age 40–49	2,822	954	4,647*	4,241	2,520*
5. Workers age 50–59	-1,694	287	4,379	4,586	117
6. Upper extremities	1,535	1,688	2,913	7,503*	1,838*
7. Trunk cases	4,583	5,417*	3,395	—	5,022*
8. Lower extremities	1,808	2,307	9,349*	1,984	3,137*
9. All other cases	-1,978	3,581	3,178	7,766*	3,889*

Panel D — Standard deviation of mean earnings losses (1968–73, in dollars)†

1. Workers age 20–59	860	1,150	1,138	2,046	662
2. Workers age 20–29	1,482	2,057	2,987	3,398	1,237
3. Workers age 30–39	2,194	2,449	2,272	3,059	1,559
4. Workers age 40–49	1,768	1,951	1,760	5,055	1,228
5. Workers age 50–59	1,294	2,596	2,248	4,129	1,213
6. Upper extremities	875	1,952	1,726	2,328	809
7. Trunk cases	4,430	1,364	2,132	—	1,115
8. Lower extremities	1,639	1,160	2,351	4,188	935
9. All other cases	2,613	3,354	3,767	3,436	1,596

Panel E — Proportional earnings losses

1. Workers age 20–59	.036	.063	.099	.189	.059
2. Workers age 20–29	.043	.043	.035	.268	.051
3. Workers age 30–39	.069	.164	.134	.226	.115
4. Workers age 40–49	.062	.021	.095	.102	.055
5. Workers age 50–59	-.040	.007	.119	.141	.003
6. Upper extremities	.036	.038	.070	.211	.043
7. Trunk cases	.123	.123	.075	—	.115
8. Lower extremities	.043	.053	.216	.053	.074
9. All other cases	-.049	.078	.069	.194	.088

Table 10.1 (continued)

Classification of workers	Percent rating						Mean ratings	Total
	1–2	3–5	6–10	11–15	16–50	51–100		
Panel F	Mean benefits net of legal fees (1968–73, in dollars)†							
1. Workers age 20–59	696	2,479	4,957	7,807	10,980			2,150
2. Workers age 20–29	742	2,316	5,078	8,388	12,846			2,047
3. Workers age 30–39	626	2,509	5,451	7,224	10,286			2,136
4. Workers age 40–49	706	2,316	4,999	7,360	10,327			2,201
5. Workers age 50–59	696	2,846	4,412	7,934	9,851			2,234
6. Upper extremities	593	2,057	4,503	6,716	11,641			1,453
7. Trunk cases	1,288	3,141	5,371	8,410	—			3,850
8. Lower extremities	1,261	2,636	5,803	10,254	13,537			2,809
9. All other cases	842	2,348	4,485	7,326	10,003			4,782
Panel G	Replacement rates: benefits as proportion of earnings losses							
1. Workers age 20–59	.45	.90	1.15	1.04	1.53			.85
2. Workers age 20–29	.43	1.23	3.80	1.27	1.47			.98
3. Workers age 30–39	.21	.33	.85	.55	1.07			.41
4. Workers age 40–49	.25	2.43	1.08	1.78	2.44			.87
5. Workers age 50–59	a	9.91	1.01	1.11	2.15			19.11
6. Upper extremities	.39	1.22	1.55	1.32	1.55			.79
7. Trunk cases	.28	.58	1.58	.94	—			.77
8. Lower extremities	.70	1.14	.62	.87	6.82			.90
9. All other cases	a	.66	1.41	1.03	1.29			1.23

*Significant at the .05 level.

†1968 present value dollars discounted at 6 percent.

a. The replacement rate is not shown because the mean earnings loss estimate is negative.

trol group, an actual EGR was calculated as the ratio of the worker's actual 1968-73 earnings divided by the worker's actual earnings in 1966-67. Regressions were run on the actual EGRs for the control group and the regression results were used to derive the expected EGRs for the workers not in the control group. Each worker in Wisconsin was assigned an expected EGR that was a function of the worker's sex, age in 1968, and level of actual earnings in 1966-67. These were factors that the regressions on the control group indicated were useful explanatory variables for the actual EGRs.[5]

Panel B of table 10.1 indicates that the 941 workers with 1-2 percent disability ratings could have expected on average to earn $42,567 from 1968 to 1973 (measured in 1968 present value dollars discounted at 6 percent, as are all dollar figures in tables 10.1 and 10.2). The mean potential earnings for the uncontested sample ($42,892) times the sample size (1,685) yields potential earnings of $72.273 million for the entire sample. For the contested males, panel B of table 10.2 indicates the potential earnings for the 285 workers were $11.478 million. The total potential earnings for both samples were thus $83.751 million.

For each worker, the actual 1968-73 earnings shown in the Social Security Summary Earnings Records were subtracted from that worker's potential earnings over the six-year period. Panel C shows the mean earnings losses for the workers in each cell, and panel D shows the standard deviation of the earnings losses for all workers in the particular cell. Asterisked figures in panel C are statistically significant earnings losses, as determined by comparing the cell mean to the cell standard deviation.

The earnings loss for the male uncontested sample was $2,519 per worker times 1,685 workers for a total of $4.244 million. For the contested male sample, the mean loss was $8,826, and with a sample of 285 the total loss was $2.511 million. The aggregate earnings loss for both samples was $6.755 million. That is, we estimate that the actual earnings between 1968 and 1973 of the 1,970 Wisconsin workers were $6.755 million less than they would have been if the workers had not been injured.

Panel E provides estimates of proportional earnings losses, which are calculated by dividing the mean earnings losses from panel C by the mean potential earnings from panel B. For the entire sample of male uncontested cases, the workers experienced an average 5.9 percent loss of potential earnings because of their injuries (table 10.1, panel E), and

Table 10.2
Wisconsin Contested Permanent Partial Disability Cases for Men with 1968 Injuries

Classification of workers	Percent rating						Mean ratings	Total
	1-2	3-5	6-10	11-15	16-50	51-100		
Panel A								
	Weighted counts of workers and mean disability ratings							
1. Workers age 20–59	40	79	88.5	27	46	4[b]	10.14	284.5
2. Workers age 20–29	8	24	19	6	8	—	8.57	65
3. Workers age 30–39	15	21	21	9	12	—	9.46	78
4. Workers age 40–49	10	20	27.5	8	15	—	9.11	80.5
5. Workers age 50–59	7	14	21	4	11	—	9.79	57
6. Upper extremities	22	29	25	0	11	0[b]	7.25	87
7. Trunk cases	3	19	32	17	15	4[b]	13.87	90
8. Lower extremities	0	20	16.5	3	4	0	7.99	43.5
9. All other cases	15	11	15	7	16	0	10.27	64
Panel B								
	Mean potential earnings (1968–73, in dollars)†							
1. Workers age 20–59	37,807	40,982	40,545	38,374	41,940	43,754		40,346
2. Workers age 20–29	32,384	38,100	36,117	40,797	40,150			37,318
3. Workers age 30–39	43,549	44,504	46,129	42,115	42,992			44,249
4. Workers age 40–49	39,767	40,778	39,879	34,925	43,285			40,231
5. Workers age 50–59	28,904	40,930	39,841	33,221	40,260			38,382
6. Upper extremities	38,954	43,106	37,340	—	40,635	—		40,087
7. Trunk cases	23,451	40,948	40,574	34,933	43,781	43,754		39,692
8. Lower extremities	—	39,475	41,921	40,925	39,052	—		40,464
9. All other cases	38,998	38,182	44,312	45,639	41,833	—		41,538

Panel C — Mean earnings losses (1968–73, in dollars)†

1. Workers age 20–59	4,318	6,847*	8,332*	13,558*	12,882*	25,363*	8,826*
2. Workers age 20–29	9,935	7,345*	6,180	17,599*	10,282		8,631*
3. Workers age 30–39	4,740	8,627*	4,773	11,670	12,598*		7,804*
4. Workers age 40–49	−1,429	3,487	12,328*	9,770	12,982*		8,290*
5. Workers age 50–59	5,205	8,123*	8,607	19,319*	14,947*		10,045*
6. Upper extremities	4,522	7,956*	8,981*	—	4,485		6,943*
7. Trunk cases	−968	7,703*	5,996	12,408*	20,846*	25,363*	10,671*
8. Lower extremities	—	4,450	6,663*	11,852*	19,092*		7,146*
9. All other cases	5,075	6,803	14,073*	17,081*	9,637*		9,935*

Panel D — Standard deviation of mean earnings losses (1968–73, in dollars)†

1. Workers age 20–59	2,549	1,581	2,240	2,410	2,207	11,052	1,029
2. Workers age 20–29	6,274	2,680	4,133	4,636	7,916		2,099
3. Workers age 30–39	5,126	2,778	3,334	2,705	3,265		1,650
4. Workers age 40–49	3,047	3,389	3,101	4,930	3,774		1,746
5. Workers age 50–59	4,164	3,957	6,747	7,649	3,467		2,896
6. Upper extremities	3,567	2,686	2,929	—	4,253		1,626
7. Trunk cases	7,177	3,169	4,586	3,276	3,381	11,052	2,137
8. Lower extremities	—	3,211	3,185	3,601	4,845		2,078
9. All other cases	4,078	3,702	6,246	4,285	3,492		2,170

Panel E — Proportional earnings losses

1. Workers age 20–59	.114	.167	.206	.353	.307	.580	.218
2. Workers age 20–29	.307	.193	.171	.431	.256		.231
3. Workers age 30–39	.109	.194	.103	.277	.293		.176
4. Workers age 40–49	−.036	.085	.309	.280	.300		.206
5. Workers age 50–59	.180	.198	.216	.582	.371		.262
6. Upper extremities	.116	.185	.241	—	.110		.173
7. Trunk cases	−.041	.188	.148	.355	.476	.580	.269
8. Lower extremities	—	.113	.159	.290	.489		.177
9. All other cases	.130	.178	.318	.374	.230		.239

Table 10.2 (continued)

Classification of workers	Percent rating						Mean ratings	Total
	1-2	3-5	6-10	11-15	16-50	51-100		
Panel F			Mean benefits net of legal fees (1968–73, in dollars)†					
1. Workers age 20-59	1,422	2,603	5,318	7,609	10,264	12,067		5,128
2. Workers age 20-29	1,070	2,427	5,332	8,027	11,904			4,792
3. Workers age 30-39	1,678	2,239	5,080	6,394	9,336			4,467
4. Workers age 40-49	1,439	2,754	5,816	8,520	9,878			5,537
5. Workers age 50-59	1,250	3,234	4,891	7,895	10,609			5,351
6. Upper extremities	1,113	2,230	4,771	—	11,555	—		3,857
7. Trunk cases	1,973	2,514	4,899	7,942	9,689	12,067		5,990
8. Lower extremities	—	3,341	7,275	7,097	11,920	—		5,881
9. All other cases	1,764	2,396	4,970	7,020	9,501	—		5,133
Panel G			Replacement rates: benefits as proportion of earnings losses					
1. Workers age 20-59	.33	.38	.64	.56	.80	.48		.58
2. Workers age 20-29	.11	.33	.86	.46	1.16			.56
3. Workers age 30-39	.35	.26	1.06	.55	.74			.57
4. Workers age 40-49	a	.79	.47	.87	.76			.67
5. Workers age 50-59	.24	.40	.57	.41	.71			.53
6. Upper extremities	.25	.28	.53	—	2.58			.56
7. Trunk cases	a	.33	.82	.64	.46	.48		.56
8. Lower extremities	—	.75	1.09	.60	.62	—		.82
9. All other cases	.35	.35	.35	.41	.99	—		.52

*Significant at the .05 level.

†1968 present value dollars discounted at 6 percent.

a. The replacement rate is not shown because the mean earnings loss estimate is negative.

b. Distribution of the four cases with 51–100 percent ratings among age categories is not possible because of confidentiality requirements.

the male contested sample experienced on average a 21.8 percent loss of potential earnings during the six-year period because of their work-related injuries (table 10.2, panel E).

The relationship between seriousness of injury and extent of earnings losses is emphasized by the results in line 1 of panel E, because the mean proportional earnings losses consistently increase as disability ratings increase. For the male uncontested cases (table 10.1), workers with a 1-2 percent rating experienced an earnings loss estimated to be 3.6 percent of potential earnings, whereas workers with 16-50 percent ratings experienced an average 18.9 percent loss of earnings. There is also a clear-cut monotonic relationship between average disability ratings and proportional earnings losses for the contested male sample (table 10.2). Losses in the 1-2 percent rating category average 11 percent of potential earnings, and increase to a maximum for the four cases with ratings in the 51-100 percent category, with average losses that are 58 percent of potential earnings. When the two samples are compared, it is evident that the wage losses are consistently larger in the contested cases. One demonstration of this fact is that for each disability rating category, the proportional earnings loss for the contested cases exceeds the loss for the uncontested cases. For example, for the rating category 6-10 percent, contested cases average a 20.6 percent earnings loss and uncontested cases a 9.9 percent earnings loss.

Panel F presents the mean benefits net of legal fees for the Wisconsin workers. For each worker in our sample, we determined the amount and the timing of all types of workers' compensation cash benefits received between 1968 and 1973. From these amounts, we subtracted attorneys' fees (which averaged about 2 percent of gross benefits for all Wisconsin cases, including contested and uncontested cases) to arrive at net benefits, and then calculated the present value of these benefits as of 1968. For the entire sample of uncontested cases, the average worker received $2,150 in benefits, which means the total net benefits received by the sample of 1,685 workers were $3.623 million. The mean benefits for the contested cases were $5,128 which means that the 285 workers in the sample received a total of $1.459 million in benefits. The grand total for both samples of male workers in Wisconsin was $5.082 million.

Panel G contains the replacement rates for the Wisconsin workers, which were calculated by dividing the mean benefits in panel F by the mean earnings losses in panel C. Overall, we estimate that benefits replaced 85 percent of earnings losses for the workers in the uncontested sample and 58 percent of the earnings losses for the workers in the contested sample.

The Wage-Loss Study of Florida

The Florida Workers' Compensation Program[6]

In 1968, the year of injury for the workers in our sample, temporary total disability benefits were 60 percent of the worker's preinjury wage, subject to a maximum weekly benefit of $49. Permanent partial disability benefits were paid for up to 350 weeks depending on the severity of the injury, with the weekly amount the same as the temporary total disability benefits. Permanent total disability benefits were paid for the duration of the disability at weekly amounts equivalent to the temporary total disability amounts.

As of 1968, the duration of the Florida permanent partial disability benefits was determined by one of several approaches, depending on the nature of the injury. The statute included a schedule of certain injuries with a corresponding list of durations. The schedule provided a fixed number of weeks for amputation or total loss of use of such members as hands, fingers, and feet, and provided that partial loss or partial loss of use of each member was compensated proportionally relative to total loss of the member. For injuries that could not be rated on the basis of the schedule, the statute provided for permanent disability benefits based on "either physical impairment or diminution of wage earning capacity, whichever is greater." The "physical impairment" ratings were based on the degree of functional limitations or impairments compared to a whole man. "Diminution of wage earning capacity" was not defined by statute, and court cases used factors such as extent of impairment, age, education, and ability to compete in the open labor market as factors relevant to the determination of the extent of diminution of earning capacity. The disability rating determined in a nonscheduled case was multiplied by 3.5 weeks per percentage point to determine the duration of the permanent partial disability benefits. If the worker was determined to be permanently and totally disabled because of the extent of his impairment or functional limitation and factors such as age, education, and ability to compete in the open labor market, benefits were paid for the duration of the disability.

The extent of permanent disability was usually determined by litigation or by negotiations between lawyers representing the parties. These negotiations often culminated in compromise and release agreements (known as washouts in Florida), which had to be approved by the industrial claims judges. However, these approvals were normally perfunctory, as evidenced by lack of information in many of the Bureau's case folders for washouts about how the judge assessed the extent of disability and the adequacy of the settlement.[7] The passive nature of the Florida workers' compensation agency was underlined by the unavailability to the judges of any procedure within the agency to evaluate the extent of permanent disability when this was a controverted issue.

Empirical Results for Florida

The methodology used for Florida was similar to that described for Wisconsin, consisting of drawing a sample from a tape record of 1968 injuries, collecting data on the sampled cases by examining Florida case folders, and then having the Social Security Administration process the data and prepare tabulations, which included the information in tables 10.3 and 10.4.[8] Male regular cases—those that paid benefits without litigation or use of a compromise and release agreement—are included in table 10.3 and constitute less than a third of all permanent partial disability cases. Male controverted cases are shown in table 10.4. The format of tables 10.3 and 10.4 is similar to that of tables 10.1 and 10.2, except that the percent rating intervals that define the columns differ between Florida and Wisconsin. (The lowest interval, for example, is 1-2 percent in Wisconsin and 1-5 percent in Florida.) Also, the Florida percent ratings were based not on the permanent disability ratings (as in Wisconsin) but on the lost time charges assigned to each case on the basis of the American National Standards Institute Z:16 lost time scale. This scale is an impairment rating scale that assigns to each permanent disability case a time charge of from 1 to 6,000 days (the latter for permanent total disability). Dividing each time charge by 60 yields a percent rating of from .02 to 100.[9]

Panel A presents the weighted counts for the workers in the sample. Table 10.3 indicates that the total sample of male regular cases was 1,665, with an average disability rating of 5.57 percent. The sample of those who received their benefits in controverted cases contains 3,937 workers, with an average disability rating of 15.29 percent (table 10.4).

In both samples, the disability rating is associated with age and with injury location. Disability ratings tend to increase with age, and of the four injury locations, the upper extremities have the lowest average ratings and the trunk the highest.

Table 10.3
Florida Regular Permanent Partial Disability Cases for Men with 1968 Injuries

Classification of workers	Percent rating						Mean ratings	Total
	1–2	3–5	6–10	11–15	16–50	51–100		
Panel A								
Weighted counts of workers and mean disability ratings								
1. Workers age 20–59	1,141	343	107	46	28		5.57	1,665
2. Workers age 20–29	267	54	17	12	7		5.04	357
3. Workers age 30–39	304	83	37	7	6		5.17	437
4. Workers age 40–49	319	112	32	17	9		6.22	489
5. Workers age 50–59	251	94	21	10	6		5.70	382
6. Upper extremities	745	147	42	24	11		4.30	969
7. Trunk cases	91	83	36	14	0		9.25	224
8. Lower extremities	259	86	24	8	6		5.90	383
9. All other cases	46	27	5	0	11		8.73	89
Panel B								
Mean potential earnings (1968–73, in dollars)†								
1. Workers age 20–59	36,560	37,957	38,038	38,577	38,048			37,023
2. Workers age 20–29	36,546	37,944	35,977	42,365	23,067			36,661
3. Workers age 30–39	39,150	42,659	40,102	33,785	46,622			39,914
4. Workers age 40–49	38,581	40,490	40,383	41,320	73,799			39,426
5. Workers age 50–59	30,869	30,796	32,494	32,720	30,224			30,979
6. Upper extremities	36,306	36,789	39,678	37,105	35,465			36,536
7. Trunk cases	40,383	36,848	39,384	42,155	—			39,024
8. Lower extremities	35,090	40,989	33,927	36,730	44,622			36,525
9. All other cases	41,380	38,070	34,292	—	37,044			39,442

Panel C

	Mean earnings losses (1968–73, in dollars)†					
1. Workers age 20–59	154	−466	1,601	290	4,124*	190
2. Workers age 20–29	4,807*	1,351	4,714	−1,863	529	3,972*
3. Workers age 30–39	−912	−3,536	149	2,938	5,886*	−1,166
4. Workers age 40–49	−633	−877	940	−2,998	2,979	−602
5. Workers age 50–59	−2,506	1,693	2,645	6,609	8,276	−782
6. Upper extremities	1,167	−546	−104	−1,626	4,619	822
7. Trunk cases	−380	563	1,461	3,714	—	521
8. Lower extremities	−2,130	1,505	3,553	43	7,851	−756
9. All other cases	−2,339	−9,464	7,549*	—	1,597	−3,459

Panel D

	Standard deviation of mean earnings losses (1968–73, in dollars)†					
1. Workers age 20–59	811	1,238	1,128	1,983	2,075	561
2. Workers age 20–29	1,548	2,453	4,269	2,901	3,581	1,137
3. Workers age 30–39	1,849	2,843	1,877	4,033	856	1,244
4. Workers age 40–49	1,305	2,240	1,690	3,351	3,922	934
5. Workers age 50–59	1,601	2,147	1,692	4,879	5,896	1,104
6. Upper extremities	1,134	2,050	1,543	2,156	3,323	924
7. Trunk cases	1,573	1,819	2,290	4,424	—	1,054
8. Lower extremities	1,474	1,806	2,229	4,932	6,080	1,144
9. All other cases	1,806	5,458	3,530	—	2,138	1,991

Panel E

	Proportional earnings losses					
1. Workers age 20–59	.004	−.012	.042	.008	.108	.005
2. Workers age 20–29	.131	.036	.131	−.044	.023	.108
3. Workers age 30–39	−.023	−.083	.004	.087	.126	−.029
4. Workers age 40–49	−.016	−.022	.023	−.073	.061	−.016
5. Workers age 50–59	−.081	.055	.081	.202	.274	−.025
6. Upper extremities	.032	−.015	−.003	−.044	.130	.022
7. Trunk cases	−.009	.015	.037	.088	—	.013
8. Lower extremities	−.061	.037	.105	.001	.176	−.021
9. All other cases	−.057	−.249	.220	—	.043	−.088

Table 10.3 (continued)

Classification of workers	Percent rating						Mean ratings	Total
	1–2	3–5	6–10	11–15	16–50	51–100		
Panel F								
	Mean benefits net of legal fees (1968–73, in dollars)†							
1. Workers age 20–59	864	1,803	2,966	4,015	6,399			1,372
2. Workers age 20–29	750	1,666	2,756	3,700	6,447			1,195
3. Workers age 30–39	856	1,896	3,138	3,980	5,040			1,355
4. Workers age 40–49	982	1,821	2,826	4,132	6,999			1,515
5. Workers age 50–59	843	1,779	3,049	4,217	6,800			1,376
6. Upper extremities	755	1,606	2,345	3,732	5,725			1,083
7. Trunk cases	1,186	2,051	3,152	4,191	–			2,010
8. Lower extremities	1,061	1,897	3,753	4,552	6,307			1,572
9. All other cases	881	1,819	3,072	–	7,123			2,060
Panel G								
	Replacement rates: benefits as proportion of earnings losses							
1. Workers age 20–59	5.63	a	1.85	13.85	1.55			7.24
2. Workers age 20–29	.16	1.23	.58	a	12.18			.30
3. Workers age 30–39	a	a	21.11	1.35	.86			a
4. Workers age 40–49	a	a	3.00	a	2.35			a
5. Workers age 50–59	a	1.05	1.15	.64	.82			a
6. Upper extremities	.65	a	a	a	1.24			1.32
7. Trunk cases	a	3.65	2.16	1.13	–			3.86
8. Lower extremities	a	1.26	1.06	105.57	.80			a
9. All other cases	a	a	.41	–	4.46			a

*Significant at the .05 level.

†1968 present value dollars discounted at 6 percent.

a. The replacement rate is not shown because the mean earnings loss estimate is negative.

Comparison of the A panels in tables 10.3 and 10.4 reveals a strong association between size of the disability rating and probability of controversion. Only about half of the cases with 1-5 percent ratings are controverted (1,308 of 2,449), but over nine-tenths of the cases with 26-50 percent ratings are controverted (430 of 458). Also, controlling for severity, there is an association between injury location and controversion. For example, among cases with 1-5 percent disability ratings, about one-third of upper extremity cases were controverted (408 of 1,153) whereas over four-fifths of trunk cases were controverted (393 of 484).

Panel B shows the mean potential earnings between 1968 and 1973 for workers in our sample. As shown in table 10.3, the mean potential earnings for all of the males in the regular sample were $37,023 (measured in 1968 present value dollars discounted at 6 percent, as are all dollar figures in tables 10.3 and 10.4). This amount times the sample size (1,665) yields potential earnings of $61.643 million for the entire sample of regular cases. For the controverted sample (table 10.4), the mean potential earnings for 1968-73 were $32,735, and thus the aggregate potential earnings for the 3,937 workers in the sample were $128.879 million. The total expected or potential earnings for both samples were $190.522 million.

Panel C shows the mean earnings losses for the workers, and panel D shows the standard deviation of the earnings losses for all workers in each cell. Statistically significant earnings losses in panel C are asterisked. The mean earnings loss between 1968 and 1973 for the male regular cases (table 10.3) was $190, which was not statistically significant; for the male controverted cases (table 10.4) it was $6,898, which was statistically significant. We estimate actual 1968-73 earnings of the 5,602 workers in our two samples to have been $27.473 million less than they would have been if the workers had not been injured.

For the entire sample of male regular cases, the workers experienced an average 0.5 percent loss of potential earnings because of their injuries (table 10.3, panel E), a loss too small to be considered statistically meaningful. The male controverted sample, on the other hand, experienced on average a 21.1 percent loss of potential earnings during the six-year period (table 10.4, panel E).

A relationship between seriousness of injury and extent of earnings losses for the male controverted sample is shown by the consistent increase in proportional earnings losses as disability ratings increase in

Table 10.4
Florida Controverted Permanent Partial Disability Cases for Men with 1968 Injuries

Classification of workers	Percent rating								Mean ratings	Total
	1–5	6–10	11–15	16–25	26–50	51–70	71–99	100		
Panel A										
	Weighted counts of workers and mean disability ratings									
1. Workers age 20–59	1,308	951	610	492	430	50	31	65	15.29	3,937
2. Workers age 20–29	321	237	124	78	75	5	6	6	12.40	852
3. Workers age 30–39	376	281	164	156	117	16	7	18	15.12	1,135
4. Workers age 40–49	412	242	193	160	148	10	8	24	16.17	1,197
5. Workers age 50–59	199	191	129	98	90	19	10	17	17.44	753
6. Upper extremities	408	194	125	85	52	9	0	5	10.50	878
7. Trunk cases	393	363	287	248	187	27	13	35	17.92	1,553
8. Lower extremities	268	197	104	88	57	8	9	12	14.08	743
9. All other cases	239	197	94	71	134	6	9	13	16.66	763
Panel B										
	Mean potential earnings (1968–73, in dollars)†									
1. Workers age 20–59	31,188	32,782	33,117	34,597	34,829	31,142	31,795	33,325		32,735
2. Workers age 20–29	31,045	34,292	33,761	31,200	33,923	35,362	36,535	29,390		32,664
3. Workers age 30–39	34,153	34,966	36,772	39,881	39,808	34,733	31,598	39,321		36,177
4. Workers age 40–49	30,226	34,102	33,170	34,841	35,212	29,848	33,064	33,079		32,815
5. Workers age 50–59	27,808	26,024	27,555	28,493	28,482	27,688	28,076	28,710		27,503
6. Upper extremities	30,335	31,584	34,213	33,264	32,091	28,962	—	43,798		31,613
7. Trunk cases	31,729	31,506	31,576	34,099	34,807	28,982	35,791	33,866		32,432
8. Lower extremities	32,611	35,002	33,981	36,286	35,770	36,773	30,983	25,923		34,031
9. All other cases	30,161	34,095	35,411	35,843	35,523	36,622	26,836	34,671		33,382

Panel C

Mean earnings losses (1968–73, in dollars)†

1. Workers age 20–59	4,094*	4,614*	7,287*	8,903*	12,607*	18,054*	21,313*	24,687*	6,898*
2. Workers age 20–29	6,296*	6,594*	6,759*	8,400*	9,309*	13,898*	23,922*	22,524*	7,187*
3. Workers age 30–39	2,533	5,317*	8,408*	10,127*	18,065*	18,662*	23,734*	29,388*	7,500*
4. Workers age 40–49	5,517*	2,609	8,255*	6,978*	13,518*	22,178*	25,883*	26,640*	7,254*
5. Workers age 50–59	547	3,661*	4,920*	10,496*	6,761*	16,466*	14,398*	17,715*	5,097*
6. Upper extremities	3,911*	914	3,678	7,464*	5,686*	11,392*	—	17,649*	3,820*
7. Trunk cases	4,013*	3,215	8,662*	10,381*	17,437*	20,462*	23,505*	26,043*	8,265*
8. Lower extremities	3,808	10,203*	7,385*	7,575*	8,040*	17,543*	23,875*	20,895*	7,442*
9. All other cases	4,862*	5,245*	7,778*	7,106*	10,494*	17,895*	15,585*	27,242*	7,129*

Panel D

Standard deviation of mean earnings losses (1968–73, in dollars)†

1. Workers age 20–59	953	1,022	1,137	177	1,129	1,604	2,255	1,458	501
2. Workers age 20–29	2,062	1,912	2,854	2,199	2,648	5,555	3,746	3,487	1,093
3. Workers age 30–39	2,013	2,275	1,932	1,844	3,027	2,977	4,119	2,253	1,068
4. Workers age 40–49	1,599	2,219	2,043	2,657	1,929	3,243	5,246	2,146	975
5. Workers age 50–59	1,877	1,521	1,864	2,158	321	2,370	3,260	3,169	826
6. Upper extremities	1,901	2,575	1,947	2,296	2,460	3,986	—	8,659	1,106
7. Trunk cases	1,811	1,959	1,742	1,766	2,041	1,935	4,037	1,813	854
8. Lower extremities	1,950	1,609	2,170	2,193	2,485	4,668	3,358	3,195	848
9. All other cases	1,886	1,765	2,977	2,593	2,496	3,573	3,149	2,483	1,015

Panel E

Proportional earnings losses

1. Workers age 20–59	.131	.141	.220	.257	.362	.580	.670	.741	.211
2. Workers age 20–29	.203	.192	.200	.269	.274	.393	.655	.766	.220
3. Workers age 30–39	.074	.152	.229	.254	.454	.537	.751	.747	.207
4. Workers age 40–49	.182	.077	.248	.200	.384	.743	.783	.805	.221
5. Workers age 50–59	.020	.141	.179	.368	.237	.595	.513	.617	.185
6. Upper extremities	.129	.029	.107	.224	.177	.393	—	.403	.121
7. Trunk cases	.126	.102	.274	.304	.501	.706	.657	.769	.255
8. Lower extremities	.117	.292	.217	.209	.225	.477	.771	.806	.219
9. All other cases	.161	.154	.220	.198	.295	.489	.581	.786	.214

Table 10.4 (continued)

Classification of workers	1-5	6-10	11-15	16-25	26-50	51-70	71-99	100	Mean ratings	Total
Panel F				Mean benefits net of legal fees (1968–73, in dollars)†						
1. Workers age 20-59	1,106	2,318	3,067	5,340	8,269	11,612	14,331	18,203		3,534
2. Workers age 20-29	1,016	1,963	2,863	4,903	7,778	10,410	17,012	29,643		2,869
3. Workers age 30-39	1,077	2,229	2,894	5,167	8,438	12,274	12,854	19,454		3,468
4. Workers age 40-49	1,156	2,887	3,266	5,523	8,608	12,841	15,299	17,946		3,880
5. Workers age 50-59	1,203	2,169	3,187	5,667	7,903	10,725	12,982	13,202		3,837
6. Upper extremities	906	1,931	2,811	4,724	6,563	9,142	—	16,144		2,280
7. Trunk cases	1,221	2,306	3,015	5,300	8,558	12,569	14,502	16,842		4,001
8. Lower extremities	1,073	2,984	3,428	5,347	8,132	11,520	12,199	20,597		3,520
9. All other cases	1,295	2,055	3,171	6,212	8,588	11,135	16,216	20,448		4,040
Panel G				Replacement rates; benefits as proportion of earnings losses						
1. Workers age 20-59	.27	.50	.42	.60	.66	.64	.67	.74		.51
2. Workers age 20-29	.16	.30	.42	.58	.84	.75	.71	1.32		.40
3. Workers age 30-39	.43	.42	.34	.51	.47	.66	.54	.66		.46
4. Workers age 40-49	.21	1.11	.40	.79	.64	.58	.59	.67		.53
5. Workers age 50-59	2.20	.59	.65	.54	1.17	.65	.90	.75		.75
6. Upper extremities	.23	2.11	.76	.63	1.15	.80	—	.91		.60
7. Trunk cases	.30	.72	.35	.51	.49	.61	.62	.65		.48
8. Lower extremities	.28	.29	.46	.71	1.01	.66	.51	.99		.47
9. All other cases	.27	.39	.41	.87	.82	.62	1.04	.75		.57

*Mean earnings losses differ significantly from zero at the .05 level.

†1968 present value dollars discounted at 6 percent.

table 10.4, panel E, line 1. Also, for the male regular cases, the only proportional earnings loss associated with a statistically significant mean earnings loss is for the most serious disability rating category: workers with 26-50 percent disability ratings experienced a 10.8 percent loss of potential earnings during 1968-73 (table 10.3, panel E, line 1).

Panel F presents the mean benefits net of legal fees for the Florida workers. Attorneys' fees represented about 13 percent of gross benefits for workers in our sample. For the entire sample of regular cases, the average worker received $1,372 in benefits between 1968 and 1973 (panel F of table 10.3); total net benefits received by the sample were $2.284 million. The mean benefits for the controverted cases were $3,534 (table 10.4, panel F), and total benefits for the sample were $13.913 million. The grand total for both samples of Florida male workers was $16.197 million in benefits.

Panel G contains the replacement rates. For all the workers in the male regular sample, the replacement rate is 7.24 ($1,372 ÷ $190). That is, we estimate benefits were 724 percent of earnings losses for the workers in the male regular sample. For all the workers in the controverted sample, benefits are estimated to have replaced 51 percent of the earnings losses (table 10.4).

The Wage-Loss Study of California

The California Workers' Compensation Program[10]

In 1968, the temporary total disability benefits were 65 percent of the worker's average weekly earnings (which were defined as 95 percent of actual earnings), subject to a maximum weekly benefit of $70.00 and a minimum weekly benefit of $25.00. Permanent partial disability benefits were paid for up to 400 weeks depending on the severity of the injury at a rate of four weeks for each percent of permanent disability, and the weekly benefit was 65 percent of the worker's average weekly earnings, subject to a maximum weekly benefit of $52.50 and a minimum weekly benefit of $20.00. Workers with permanent disability ratings of 70 percent or above also received life pension benefits, which began when their permanent partial disability benefits terminated. The weekly pension amount was 1.5 percent of average weekly earnings for each percent of disability rating above 60 percent. In 1968, the maximum average weekly earnings considered in calculating the life pension were $80.77.

The permanent disability ratings in California are determined by a unique approach that is described in chapter 7. One distinctive feature of the California statute is that rather than containing a schedule of certain injuries with a corresponding list of durations, it authorizes the administrative director of the Division of Industrial Accidents to issue a comprehensive schedule to be used to rate all permanent disabilities, and the schedule is to take account of the nature of the injury, the worker's occupation and age, and his diminished ability to compete in an open labor market. The schedule that has been issued pursuant to this statutory provision provides guidance for rating most injuries and diseases on the basis of the resulting impairment or functional limitations or work disability (loss of wage-earning capacity) or a combination of these consequences.

The method of determining the permanent disability ratings in California is also unique. Within the state workers' compensation agency is the Disability Evaluation Bureau (formerly the Permanent Disability Rating Bureau), which applies the rating schedule in many of the cases involving permanent disability benefits. There are five main types of rating procedures used by the Bureau, of which two are of particular relevance here because they help define our samples of California workers. *Informal ratings* (formerly designated advisory ratings) are made in voluntary cases, that is, cases in which no application for adjudication has been filed with the workers' compensation agency. The Bureau prepares the informal rating at the request of the employee and employer (or carrier), normally on the basis of medical reports submitted with the rating request. If the rating is acceptable to both parties, compensation is paid to the employee without further notification to the agency. The parties are not required to obtain informal ratings, are not bound by the ratings, and typically either do not bother to use the procedure or do not accept the ratings they obtain. *Formal ratings* are prepared by the Bureau at the request of a workers' compensation judge during the course of a litigated case. The rating is based on a description of the disability prepared by the judge, and the Bureau does not have access to the medical reports or other information in the case file as a basis for the rating. The judge will consider objections to the rating from the parties and the rating may be modified during the litigation process, but normally the rating serves as a basis for the decision (known as a findings and award).

Most California permanent disability cases pay benefits without informal or formal ratings being prepared by the Disability Evaluation

Bureau. We term these cases "Other WCAB" cases because a Workers' Compensation Appeals Board judge is involved. The judge may issue a findings and award without using the Bureau (a relatively unusual procedure) or, quite commonly, approve a compromise and release agreement or a stipulated findings and award (in these procedures, the judge can approve an agreement reached by the parties without conducting a regular hearing). Some of the Other WCAB cases in our sample contain ratings made by the Bureau other than informal or formal ratings, but the typical Other WCAB case involves a compromise and release or stipulated findings and award that the workers' compensation judge has approved without considering a rating from the Disability Evaluation Bureau.

Empirical Results for California

The methodology used for California was similar to that described for Wisconsin, consisting of drawing a sample of 1968 injuries, collecting data on the sampled cases by examining case folders, and then having the Social Security Administration process the data and prepare tabulations, which include the information in tables 10.5-10.7.[11] The main difference in the California methodology is that tape records of 1968 injuries were available only for those workers with informal ratings or formal ratings, and approximately 40,000 case folders were physically inspected in order to draw the Other WCAB sample.

Male informal cases—those in which an informal rating was received from the Disability Evaluation Bureau and benefits were paid on the basis of the informal rating—are included in table 10.5, and constitute about 10 percent of the male cases in our sample.[12] Male formal cases—those in which formal ratings were received from the Bureau—are included in table 10.6 and constitute about 20 percent of our male cases.[13] The Other WCAB cases, in which permanent disability benefits were received but neither informal nor formal ratings played a part, are included in table 10.7 and constitute about 70 percent of our male cases.

The format of tables 10.5-10.7 is similar to that of tables 10.1-10.4, except that the percent rating intervals that define the columns differ among the states. (For example, California has an 11-25 percent disability rating interval, whereas Florida has both an 11-15 percent interval and a 16-25 percent interval.) The percent disability rating used to classify each California case was constructed by using the dollar amount of the permanent disability award as a proxy for the disability rating. The award was divided by four times the weekly rate for permanent

Table 10.5
California Informal Permanent Partial Disability Cases for Men with 1968 Injuries

Classification of workers	Percent rating						Mean ratings	Total
	1–5	6–10	11–25	26–50	51–69	70+		
Panel A								
Weighted counts of workers and mean disability ratings								
1. Workers age 20–59	885	392	248	59			7.21	1,584
2. Workers age 20–29	223	86	32	0			4.78	341
3. Workers age 30–39	252	68	57	9			6.41	386
4. Workers age 40–49	244	120	75	24			7.82	463
5. Workers age 50–59	166	118	84	26			9.39	394
6. Upper extremities	772	270	139	20			5.87	1,201
7. Back	0	17	47	28			20.43	92
8. Lower extremities	97	93	47	5			7.90	242
9. All other cases	16	12	15	6			11.92	49
Panel B								
Mean potential earnings (1968–73, in dollars)†								
1. Workers age 20–59	45,221	46,375	44,025	48,354				45,436
2. Workers age 20–29	36,680	36,291	(40,590)	—				36,949
3. Workers age 30–39	50,850	51,673	48,549	48,583				50,602
4. Workers age 40–49	49,613	54,176	47,195	51,409				50,497
5. Workers age 50–59	41,695	42,736	39,435	45,454				41,773
6. Upper extremities	45,441	44,331	42,314	45,886				44,837
7. Back	—	51,777	46,569	48,136				48,008
8. Lower extremities	43,947	51,637	44,349	54,640				47,201
9. All other cases	42,321	43,912	50,898	52,356				46,565

Panel C			Mean earnings losses (1968–73, in dollars)†		
1. Workers age 20–59	-2,272	-1,287	-93	2,762	-1,500
2. Workers age 20–29	2,193	-1,941	24	—	943
3. Workers age 30–39	-2,065	1,106	2,898	12,066*	-444
4. Workers age 40–49	-2,613	-3,741	-2,866	2,808	-2,665
5. Workers age 50–59	-8,085*	309	308	-502	-3,281
6. Upper extremities	-2,496	-961	-1,871	5,199	-1,950
7. Back	—	-1,497	3,344	3,213	2,409
8. Lower extremities	-846	-2,367	3,278	-755	-631
9. All other cases	-114	83	-4,954	-4,539	-2,089

Panel D			Standard deviation of mean earnings losses (1968–73, in dollars)†		
1. Workers age 20–59	2,194	1,871	1,273	2,024	1,293
2. Workers age 20–29	5,339	1,797	3,225	—	3,364
3. Workers age 30–39	4,771	4,333	2,249	5,321	3,204
4. Workers age 40–49	2,961	3,767	1,916	2,822	2,074
5. Workers age 50–59	2,327	3,793	2,169	3,059	1,856
6. Upper extremities	2,487	3,300	1,726	3,398	1,698
7. Back	—	2,508	2,411	2,998	1,613
8. Lower extremities	2,164	2,630	2,176	5,495	1,424
9. All other cases	3,222	1,521	3,212	6,093	2,062

Panel E			Proportional earnings losses		
1. Workers age 20–59	-.050	-.028	-.002	.057	-.033
2. Workers age 20–29	.060	-.054	.001	—	.026
3. Workers age 30–39	-.041	.021	.060	.248	-.009
4. Workers age 40–49	-.053	-.069	-.061	.055	-.053
5. Workers age 50–59	-.194	.007	.008	-.011	-.079
6. Upper extremities	-.055	-.022	-.044	.113	-.044
7. Back	—	-.029	.072	.067	.050
8. Lower extremities	-.019	-.046	.074	-.014	-.013
9. All other cases	-.027	.002	-.097	-.087	-.045

Table 10.5 (continued)

Classification of workers	Percent rating						Mean ratings	Total
	1–5	6–10	11–25	26–50	51–69	70+		
Panel F								
Mean benefits net of legal fees (1968–73, in dollars)†								
1. Workers age 20–59	856	2,312	4,358	8,016				2,032
2. Workers age 20–29	659	2,326	4,690	—				1,459
3. Workers age 30–39	865	2,297	4,327	8,104				1,797
4. Workers age 40–49	757	2,326	4,222	8,431				2,123
5. Workers age 50–59	1,253	2,297	4,374	7,603				2,650
6. Upper extremities	805	2,118	4,093	8,020				1,601
7. Back	—	2,633	4,928	8,050				5,454
8. Lower extremities	1,280	2,825	4,593	8,586				2,669
9. All other cases	756	2,233	4,294	7,573				3,011
Panel G								
Replacement rates: benefits as proportion of earnings losses								
1. Workers age 20–59	a	a	a	2.9				a
2. Workers age 20–29	.30	a	191.66	.00				1.55
3. Workers age 30–39	a	2.08	1.49	.67				a
4. Workers age 40–49	a	a	a	3.00				a
5. Workers age 50–59	a	7.42	14.22	a				a
6. Upper extremities	a	a	a	1.54				a
7. Back	—	a	1.47	2.51				2.26
8. Lower extremities	a	a	1.40	a				a
9. All other cases	a	26.99	a	a				a

*Mean earnings losses differ significantly from zero at the .05 level.

†1968 present value dollars discounted at 6 percent.

a. The replacement rate is not shown because the mean earnings loss estimate is negative.

disability benefits to determine a disability rating. This procedure was necessary because for half of the Other WCAB sample, no disability rating of any kind was available in the case folder. This estimating procedure produces ratings identical to the informal ratings and formal ratings when the ratings were used to determine the amount of permanent disability benefits. For other cases, such as compromise and release cases, the procedure produces an approximation of the implicit disability rating that allows comparisons to be made among all types of California cases. [14]

Panel A presents the weighted counts for the workers in each sample. Table 10.5 indicates that the total sample of male informal cases was 1,584 workers, who had an average disability rating of 7.21 percent. Table 10.6 shows that the 3,213 male cases with formal ratings had average disability ratings of 22.08 percent, and table 10.7 reveals that the average disability rating was 12.51 percent for the 11,182 cases in the sample of Other WCAB cases.

In all three samples, the size of the disability ratings is associated with age and injury location. With only one minor exception, mean disability ratings increase with age. Among the four injury locations, upper extremity injuries have the lowest average rating and back injuries the highest average rating in each sample. Comparison of the A panels of tables 10.5-10.7 reveals an association between the size of the rating and the method of resolving the case. Most cases in all ratings categories were resolved without the use of formal or informal ratings and thus fall in the Other WCAB sample. Informal ratings account for 14 percent of the cases with ratings of 5 percent or less, and decline in importance for more serious cases. In contrast, formal ratings account for less than one in ten of the cases with ratings of 5 percent or less, but increase in importance for more serious cases and represent more than four out of ten of the cases with ratings of 51 percent or more. Also, controlling for severity, there is an association between injury location and the method of resolving the case. For example, among cases with 6-10 percent disability ratings, about 15 percent of the upper extremity cases were in the informal sample (270 of 1,641), but only about 2 percent of the back cases were in the informal sample (17 of 985).

As shown in table 10.5, panel B, the mean potential earnings for all of the workers in the male informal sample were $45,436 (measured in 1968 present value dollars discounted at 6 percent, as are all dollar

Table 10.6
California Formal Permanent Partial Disability Cases for Men with 1968 Injuries

Classification of workers	Percent rating						Mean ratings	Total
	1–5	6–10	11–25	26–50	51–69	70+		
Panel A								
	Weighted counts of workers and mean disability ratings							
1. Workers age 20–59	574	660	994	736	129	119	22.08	3,213
2. Workers age 20–29	196	201	238	138	8	8	15.89	789
3. Workers age 30–39	218	186	340	218	36	18	19.86	1,016
4. Workers age 40–49	102	110	250	234	47	49	26.94	842
5. Workers age 50–59	58	113	166	146	38	44	27.43	566
6. Upper extremities	212	185	178	72	5	10	13.30	663
7. Back	124	282	518	530	82	73	27.25	1,609
8. Lower extremities	129	144	226	84	30	19	18.83	632
9. All other cases	109	49	72	50	12	17	20.59	309
Panel B								
	Mean potential earnings (1968–73, in dollars)†							
1. Workers age 20–59	39,478	37,711	39,402	43,337	39,877	43,767		40,144
2. Workers age 20–29	34,205	32,596	39,020	37,447	30,905	46,226		35,903
3. Workers age 30–39	42,724	45,270	42,215	50,672	48,332	58,893		45,210
4. Workers age 40–49	44,055	39,880	39,060	43,236	38,769	45,288		41,251
5. Workers age 50–59	37,805	31,300	34,702	38,111	35,190	35,439		35,280
6. Upper extremities	40,706	38,060	40,686	37,937	24,725	45,937		39,559
7. Back	33,979	36,927	38,476	45,548	39,590	45,017		40,201
8. Lower extremities	42,004	39,207	39,410	44,388	42,064	37,997		40,671
9. All other cases	40,357	36,517	42,868	36,833	42,598	43,573		40,026

Panel C

	Mean earnings losses (1968–73, in dollars)†						
1. Workers age 20–59	3,341*	6,156*	8,717*	17,520*	20,791*	32,958*	10,633*
2. Workers age 20–29	3,149	3,370	12,667*	6,933*	19,451*	35,927*	7,232*
3. Workers age 30–39	2,259	11,621*	10,218*	26,322*	32,972*	41,353*	13,580*
4. Workers age 40–49	6,568	5,464	5,153*	19,373*	10,526*	34,423*	11,343*
5. Workers age 50–59	2,417	3,086	5,367*	11,424*	22,210*	27,352*	9,024*
6. Upper extremities	47	7,791*	6,428*	9,808*	2,577	26,490*	5,411*
7. Back	3,005	6,690*	11,277*	19,584*	19,879*	35,841*	14,125*
8. Lower extremities	4,064	3,327	4,737*	12,657*	22,612*	26,594*	6,851*
9. All other cases	9,274*	5,224	8,431*	14,997*	29,980*	31,497*	11,388*

Panel D

	Standard deviation of mean earnings losses (1968–73, in dollars)†						
1. Workers age 20–59	1,700	1,403	1,260	2,235	2,292	1,612	825
2. Workers age 20–29	2,576	2,235	2,276	2,654	6,414	5,234	1,293
3. Workers age 30–39	3,044	2,967	2,550	5,967	2,916	4,260	1,893
4. Workers age 40–49	4,270	3,076	2,516	3,293	4,207	2,275	1,618
5. Workers age 50–59	3,406	2,070	1,941	3,363	3,695	2,472	1,324
6. Upper extremities	3,345	2,531	2,139	2,474	4,753	5,678	1,488
7. Back	3,216	1,796	1,838	3,095	3,344	2,108	1,375
8. Lower extremities	3,365	3,368	1,946	2,475	3,277	2,535	1,378
9. All other cases	2,539	2,854	2,870	2,558	4,227	4,284	1,479

Panel E

	Proportional earnings losses						
1. Workers age 20–59	.085	.163	.221	.405	.521	.753	.265
2. Workers age 20–29	.092	.103	.324	.186	.629	.777	.201
3. Workers age 30–39	.053	.257	.242	.519	.682	.702	.300
4. Workers age 40–49	.150	.137	.132	.449	.272	.760	.275
5. Workers age 50–59	.065	.098	.155	.299	.631	.772	.256
6. Upper extremities	.001	.205	.158	.260	.104	.577	.137
7. Back	.088	.181	.293	.440	.502	.796	.351
8. Lower extremities	.097	.085	.120	.285	.538	.700	.168
9. All other cases	.230	.143	.197	.407	.704	.723	.285

Table 10.6 (continued)

Classification of workers	Percent rating						Mean ratings	Total
	1–5	6–10	11–25	26–50	51–69	70+		
Panel F								
	Mean benefits net of legal fees (1968–73, in dollars)†							
1. Workers age 20–59	1,155	2,194	4,311	8,148	11,553	16,482		4,934
2. Workers age 20–29	1,245	1,940	4,568	7,266	11,206	21,943		3,790
3. Workers age 30–39	1,085	2,772	4,247	8,304	10,925	16,373		4,621
4. Workers age 40–49	1,111	2,137	4,261	8,857	11,000	16,409		5,839
5. Workers age 50–59	1,189	1,771	4,148	7,610	12,888	15,614		5,747
6. Upper extremities	967	2,106	3,890	8,184	9,684	15,692		3,149
7. Back	1,464	2,027	4,438	8,023	11,497	16,418		5,871
8. Lower extremities	1,334	2,689	4,481	8,810	11,844	16,682		4,728
9. All other cases	958	2,029	3,903	8,299	11,975	16,996		4,312
Panel G								
	Replacement rates: benefits as proportion of earnings losses							
1. Workers age 20–59	.35	.36	.49	.47	.56	.50		.46
2. Workers age 20–29	.40	.58	.36	1.05	.58	.61		.52
3. Workers age 30–39	.48	.24	.42	.32	.33	.40		.34
4. Workers age 40–49	.17	.39	.83	.46	1.05	.48		.51
5. Workers age 50–59	.49	.57	.77	.67	.58	.57		.64
6. Upper extremities	20.47	.27	.61	.83	3.76	.59		.58
7. Back	.49	.30	.39	.41	.58	.46		.42
8. Lower extremities	.33	.81	.95	.70	.52	.63		.69
9. All other cases	.10	.39	.46	.55	.40	.54		.38

*Mean earnings losses differ significantly from zero at the .05 level.

†1968 present value dollars discounted at 6 percent.

figures in tables 10.5-10.7). This amount times the sample size (1,584) yields potential earnings of $71.971 million for the entire male informal sample. For the male formal sample (table 10.6), the mean potential earnings were $40,144 and the aggregate potential earnings were $128.983 million. For the Other WCAB sample (table 10.7), the mean potential earnings were $38,683 and the aggregate potential earnings $432.551 million. The total expected or potential earnings for all three samples were thus $633.505 million.

The meaning of the -$1,500 earnings loss figure for the male informal cases (table 10.5) is that actual earnings exceeded our estimate of potential earnings by $1,500 per worker, a result that was not statistically significant (table 10.5, panels C and D). For the male informal sample of 1,584 workers, actual earnings exceeded our estimates of potential earnings by $2.376 million. For the male formal cases (table 10.6), the mean loss was $10,633 and statistically significant, and the aggregate earnings loss $34.163 million. For the Other WCAB cases (table 10.7), the mean loss was $7,166 and statistically significant, and the aggregate earnings loss was $80.138 million. We estimate that actual earnings of the 15,979 California workers in our three male samples between 1968 and 1973 were $111.925 million less than they would have been if the workers had not been injured.

Panel E provides estimates of proportional earnings losses, which are the mean earnings losses from panel C divided by the mean potential earnings from panel B. For the entire sample of male informal cases, the workers experienced an average 3.3 percent negative earnings loss, which was not statistically significant. Essentially, we found that workers in our sample of male informal cases experienced no earnings losses because of their injuries. Workers in the male formal cases (table 10.6, panel G), however, experienced on average a 26.5 percent loss of potential earnings during 1968-73 because of their injuries, and the male Other WCAB cases had an average loss of 18.5 percent (table 10.7, panel G). A relationship between seriousness of injury and extent of earnings losses for all three samples is shown by the consistent increases in proportional earnings losses as disability increases in panel E, line 1 of tables 10.5-10.7. Of the three samples, it is evident that earnings losses are lowest in the informal sample. When severity of injury is controlled for, neither of the other two samples consistently shows greater earnings losses than the other.

Table 10.7
California "Other WCAB" Permanent Partial Disability Cases for Men with 1968 Injuries

Classification of workers	Percent rating					Mean ratings	Total
	1-5	6-10	11-25	26-50	51+		
Panel A							
	Weighted counts of workers and mean disability ratings						
1. Workers age 20-59	4,681	2,620	2,282	1,280	320	12.51	11,182
2. Workers age 20-29	1,634	914	469	329	61	10.09	3,407
3. Workers age 30-39	1,577	650	693	310	90	12.25	3,330
4. Workers age 40-49	735	751	500	395	115	15.41	2,496
5. Workers age 50-59	735	305	620	236	54	13.47	1,949
6. Upper extremities	2,316	1,186	594	236	42	8.29	4,374
7. Back	730	686	986	707	155	18.20	3,264
8. Lower extremities	671	428	484	178	52	12.74	1,813
9. All other cases	964	320	217	159	71	12.52	1,731
Panel B							
	Mean potential earnings (1968-73, in dollars)†						
1. Workers age 20-59	39,302	38,958	37,838	36,933	40,395		38,683
2. Workers age 20-29	34,919	34,944	35,451	34,275	44,102		35,070
3. Workers age 30-39	45,152	39,801	43,685	44,744	41,088		43,653
4. Workers age 40-49	41,029	42,402	38,209	36,839	41,337		40,163
5. Workers age 50-59	34,716	40,706	32,809	30,270	33,048		34,472
6. Upper extremities	40,151	38,748	35,980	32,959	46,401		38,911
7. Back	41,356	34,762	37,314	37,402	40,176		37,883
8. Lower extremities	41,459	45,629	38,796	39,884	31,560		41,294
9. All other cases	34,166	39,821	43,339	37,440	43,792		37,057

Panel C

Mean earnings losses (1968–73, in dollars)†

1. Workers age 20–59	4,373*	5,358*	9,719*	12,024*	25,214*	7,166*
2. Workers age 20–29	4,386*	4,766	7,276*	7,221*	24,934*	5,527*
3. Workers age 30–39	5,564*	8,311*	12,098*	16,134*	33,342*	9,227*
4. Workers age 40–49	1,551	2,030	7,236*	11,254*	28,416*	5,607*
5. Workers age 50–59	4,610*	9,031*	10,911*	14,438*	5,163	8,508*
6. Upper extremities	3,437*	4,300*	6,146*	7,755*	12,966	4,363*
7. Back	11,321*	9,950*	12,358*	14,229*	31,094*	12,872*
8. Lower extremities	2,451	2,542	6,956*	12,269*	18,185*	5,090*
9. All other cases	2,698	3,208	13,674*	8,266	26,733*	5,666*

Panel D

Standard deviation of mean earnings losses (1968–73, in dollars)†

1. Workers age 20–59	1,049	1,391	1,102	1,425	3,827	650
2. Workers age 20–29	1,683	2,444	2,382	3,147	7,896	1,173
3. Workers age 30–39	2,066	2,532	1,984	2,594	6,688	1,255
4. Workers age 40–49	2,404	2,517	2,310	2,411	3,829	1,308
5. Workers age 50–59	2,197	4,240	2,196	3,123	11,818	1,441
6. Upper extremities	1,340	1,917	2,110	2,616	21,171	979
7. Back	2,882	2,900	1,605	1,939	3,662	1,123
8. Lower extremities	2,698	3,532	2,278	3,718	4,531	1,521
9. All other cases	2,553	3,602	4,310	4,547	6,543	1,853

Panel E

Proportional earnings losses

1. Workers age 20–59	.111	.138	.257	.325	.624	.185
2. Workers age 20–29	.126	.136	.205	.211	.565	.157
3. Workers age 30–39	.123	.209	.277	.361	.811	.211
4. Workers age 40–49	.038	.048	.189	.306	.687	.139
5. Workers age 50–59	.133	.222	.332	.477	.156	.247
6. Upper extremities	.086	.111	.171	.235	.279	.112
7. Back	.274	.286	.331	.380	.752	.340
8. Lower extremities	.059	.056	.179	.308	.576	.123
9. All other cases	.079	.081	.316	.221	.610	.153

Table 10.7 (continued)

Classification of workers	Percent rating					Mean ratings	Total
	1-5	6-10	11-25	26-50	51+		
Panel F							
	Mean benefits net of legal fees (1968–73, in dollars)†						
1. Workers age 20–59	802	1,951	3,886	7,864	14,664		2,905
2. Workers age 20–29	733	1,990	3,863	7,318	13,780		2,370
3. Workers age 30–39	773	2,054	4,120	7,637	14,112		2,739
4. Workers age 40–49	804	1,770	3,979	8,406	15,428		3,607
5. Workers age 50–59	1,019	2,065	3,565	8,030	14,957		3,225
6. Upper extremities	831	1,976	3,964	6,966	12,988		2,014
7. Back	892	1,944	3,871	8,208	15,695		4,301
8. Lower extremities	896	2,057	3,748	8,065	13,661		3,001
9. All other cases	599	1,734	4,043	7,442	14,140		2,425
Panel G							
	Replacement rates: benefits as proportion of earnings losses						
1. Workers age 20–59	.18	.36	.40	.65	.58		.41
2. Workers age 20–29	.17	.42	.53	1.01	.55		.43
3. Workers age 30–39	.14	.25	.34	.47	.42		.30
4. Workers age 40–49	.52	.87	.55	.75	.54		.64
5. Workers age 50–59	.22	.23	.33	.56	2.90		.38
6. Upper extremities	.24	.46	.64	.90	1.00		.46
7. Back	.08	.20	.31	.58	.52		.33
8. Lower extremities	.37	.81	.54	.66	.75		.59
9. All other cases	.22	.54	.30	.90	.53		.43

*Mean earnings losses differ significantly from zero at the .05 level.

†1968 present value dollars discounted at 6 percent.

Panel F presents the mean benefits net of legal fees for the California workers.[15] Attorneys' fees represented about 6 percent of gross benefits for workers in our sample. For the sample of male informal cases, the average worker received $2,032 in benefits between 1968 and 1973 (panel F of table 10.5) and the total net benefits received by the sample were $3.219 million. The mean benefits for the male formal cases were $4,934 (table 10.6, panel F), and aggregate benefits for the sample were $15.853 million. For the Other WCAB cases, the mean benefits were $2,905 (table 10.7, panel F) and aggregate benefits $32.484 million. The grand total for all three samples of California male workers was $51.556 million.

Panel G contains the replacement rates. The replacement rate could not be calculated for workers in the male informal sample, since we estimate a negative earnings loss for that sample. Overall, we estimate that benefits replaced 46 percent of earnings losses for workers in the male formal sample and 41 percent of the earnings losses for workers in the male Other WCAB sample.

Comparisons of the Three States[16]

The panel A data show several similar patterns across the three states. The mean disability rating for the contested case sample is higher than the mean rating for the uncontested sample in each state. (Among the contested samples we include the Florida controverted cases and the California formal and Other WCAB cases; among the uncontested cases we include the Florida regular cases and the California informal cases.) A related finding is that the proportion of cases contested increases with increases in the disability ratings, a phenomenon demonstrated by comparing the number of cases in line 1 for the uncontested and contested cases in each state. Another common pattern is that disability ratings tend to increase with age; this relationship is particularly evident in Florida and California. The data by part of body injured (lines 5-9) also show some consistency across states. Trunk cases (including for this discussion the California back cases) and all other cases are the types most likely to be litigated, and upper extremity cases the least likely. Among contested cases, trunk injuries always have the highest mean rating, and among uncontested cases, upper extremity injuries always have the lowest mean rating.

The panel A data also show some important differences among the states. The total male samples are 15,979 in California, 5,602 in Florida, and 1,970 in Wisconsin, reflecting in part the variations among the states' labor force sizes. Of more significance is the variation in the proportion of cases that are contested in each state. In Wisconsin, 14 percent of the cases were contested (285 of 1,970 cases), compared to 70 percent of the Florida cases (3,937 of 5,602 cases) and 90 percent of the California cases (14,395 of 15,979 cases).[17] Another significant difference involves the mean disability ratings. Among uncontested cases, for example, Wisconsin workers had disability ratings averaging 3.70 percent, whereas Florida workers averaged 5.57 percent and California workers 7.21 percent. For all of the Wisconsin workers—involving both contested and uncontested cases—the average disability rating was 4.63 percent; the corresponding figure for all Florida workers was 12.40 percent and for all California workers 13.91 percent. (Those overall disability ratings for each state were constructed by using the sample sizes for the uncontested and contested cases as weights.) Thus, Wisconsin stands out among the three states for having the fewest contested cases and the lowest disability ratings.

The panel B data show the potential or expected earnings for the workers in the samples. In all three states, workers aged 30-49 had higher expected earnings than younger and older workers, reflecting the normal relationship between age and earnings. As anticipated, in light of previous studies of interstate differences in earnings, California workers in our sample had the highest expected earnings, followed by Wisconsin and then Florida workers. In both California and Florida, potential earnings are markedly higher for workers in the uncontested cases samples than for workers in the contested cases samples, largely because workers in the uncontested samples were relatively high-wage workers before their injuries. In Wisconsin, this differential is less pronounced.[18]

Examination of the data in panels C and D, which show the mean earnings losses and the standard deviations of those losses, reveals further notable similarities and differences among the states. In all three states, the contested cases sample has statistically significant earnings losses for the entire sample and for the workers in each of the disability rating categories in line 1 of panel C (the one exception is for Wisconsin contested cases with 1-2 percent ratings, in which the earnings losses are insignificant). The states differ in the results for uncontested cases, however. In Wisconsin, the entire uncontested sample and all rating categories except 1-2 percent show statistically significant losses. In Florida, except for the 26-50 percent rating category, the earnings losses are not statistically significant, and in California none of the disability rating categories shows earnings losses. In all three states, earnings losses are greater for contested cases than for uncontested cases for workers with the same disability ratings. Also, among contested cases, back cases consistently show the largest earnings losses and upper extremity cases the smallest losses. There is no stable relationship between age and size of earnings losses.

The average earnings loss for all Wisconsin workers was $3,430 (a figure calculated by taking the weighted average of the $2,519 loss for uncontested cases and the $5,128 loss for contested cases); the loss figures for all Florida workers and all California workers are $4,904 and $7,004, respectively. Since, as previously described, the average disability ratings in the three states were 4.63, 12.40, and 13.91 percent, the results indicate that each 1 percent of disability rating is associated with $741 of earnings losses in Wisconsin, $396 in Florida, and $504 in California. Thus Wisconsin disability ratings appear to be rather stringent in terms of the amount of lost earnings associated with a particular rating compared to the ratings in the other states.

The panel E data on proportional earnings losses also show significant patterns and variations across the three states. The proportional earnings losses increase with higher disability ratings in each of the seven samples, as can be seen by moving to the right in line 1 of panel E of tables 10.1-10.7 (only the Florida uncontested cases show some irregularity in this respect). Another consistent pattern is that contested cases have higher proportional earnings losses than uncontested cases, even when disability ratings are held constant. There are 18 instances in which the panel E, line 1 entry for a state's contested cases can be compared to an entry with the same disability ratings for the state's uncontested cases, and in all 18 instances the contested cases show greater proportional earnings losses. Among the contested cases, trunk cases consistently show the greatest proportional earnings losses and upper extremity cases the least. No such stable relationship exists for differences among workers classified by age.

Wisconsin uncontested cases have higher proportional earnings losses than the uncontested cases in Florida and California. All three states have proportional earnings losses of about 20 percent for their contested cases.[19] When the uncontested and contested cases in each state are combined by using sample sizes as weights, the average proportional earnings loss for all Wisconsin workers works out to .082; for all Florida workers, to .150; and for all California workers, to .179. That is, the male Wisconsin workers in our uncontested and contested cases samples combined had earnings losses in 1968-73 that averaged 8.2 percent of their potential earnings during the six-year period, and Florida and California workers experienced 15.0 and 17.9 percent losses, respectively. Carrying the comparisons one step further, recall that the panel A discussion indicated that the average disability rating for all Wisconsin workers (including uncontested and contested cases) was 4.63 percent, for Florida workers 12.40 percent, and for California workers 13.91 percent. Thus the ratio of 1968-73 proportional earnings losses to disability ratings was 1.77 in Wisconsin (8.2 percent earnings losses divided by 4.63 percent disability ratings), and the ratios in Florida and California were 1.21 and 1.29, respectively. This is additional evidence that the Wisconsin ratings are stringent in terms of the extent of earnings losses associated with a particular rating compared to the ratings in Florida and California.

The panel F data on net benefits show some similarities among the states, although the differences are more pronounced. All states pay higher benefits on average to workers with higher disability ratings (as shown by moving to the right on line 1 of panel E), and all states show higher average benefits for contested cases than for uncontested cases, largely reflecting the more serious injuries experienced by typical workers in contested cases. For uncontested cases, the Wisconsin sample had average benefits of $2,150, more than the Florida average of $1,372 and the California average of $2,032. For contested cases, the Wisconsin sample had average benefits of $5,128, more than the Florida average of $3,534 and the California averages for two contested cases samples of $4,934 and $2,905. Because a relatively high proportion of Wisconsin cases is uncontested, however, the average benefit for all Wisconsin workers was $2,580, less than the Florida average of $2,891 and the California average of $3,226. (These averages were constructed by using the sample sizes in each state as weights.) Again extending the comparison, it is interesting that the benefits associated with each 1 percent of disability rating were $557 in Wisconsin ($2,580 average benefits divided by the average disability rating of 4.63 percent), more than twice the benefits per 1 percent of rating of $233 in Florida and $232 in California. The difference between Wisconsin and the other states reflects in part the differences in benefit formulas discussed earlier in this section and the smaller percentage of gross benefits in Wisconsin used to pay attorneys' fees.

The final comparisons among the three states are based on the panel G data, which are the replacement rates (benefits divided by earnings losses). In each state, the replacement rate for the uncontested cases was higher than for the contested cases. The replacement rate is in the range of .4 to .6 for all the samples of contested cases, meaning that benefits replaced between 40 and 60 percent of earnings losses for these workers. The replacement rate is much more variable for uncontested cases: benefits replaced 85 percent of earnings losses for Wisconsin workers and 724 percent of earnings losses for Florida workers; California workers in the uncontested cases sample on average had no earnings losses to replace, and so the replacement rate can be considered infinite.

For contested cases in all three states, the replacement rates tend to increase for workers with higher disability ratings (as shown by moving to the right in line 1 of panel E), although a drop in the replacement rate for the most serious category of injuries occurs for the Wisconsin sample and the two contested cases samples in California. The apparent general tendency for replacement rates to increase with disability severity must be viewed with caution, since for the most serious cases, significant earnings losses probably continue after the 1968-73 period, whereas most workers' compensation benefits were exhausted during that period; if replacement rates were calculated for a period extending beyond 1973, the replacement rates would probably drop more rapidly for serious injury cases than for minor injury cases. There are no obvious and pronounced relationships between replacement rates and age or part of body injured. In both Florida and California, trunk cases have the lowest replacement rates in the controverted cases samples, but this relationship is not found in Wisconsin.

The overall replacement rate for all Wisconsin workers was .75, indicating that benefits replaced 75 percent of lost earnings for the workers. In Florida, benefits replaced 59 percent of lost earnings, while in California the benefits replaced 46 percent of earnings losses. (These averages were constructed by using sample sizes as weights.) Underlying these differences in overall replacement rates is an interesting set of relationships. For a given disability rating, say 10 percent, Wisconsin workers on average experience somewhat greater earnings losses than do workers in Florida or in California ($7,410 in Wisconsin, $3,960 in Florida, and $5,040 in California) but the Wisconsin workers on average received considerably more benefits for the same rating ($5,570 in Wisconsin versus $2,330 in Florida and $2,320 in California), and so the ratio of benefits to earnings losses—the replacement rate—was higher in Wisconsin (.75) than in Florida (.59) or California (.46).

The preceding comparisons have been based on the entire sample line (line 1) or the Total column, but the panel G replacement rates in the cells defined by lines 2-9 and the several rating columns also deserve attention. The dominant characteristic of these rates in all the tables is the considerable variability as comparisons are made by moving down a column or across a row. For example, for the Wisconsin male un-contested cases, the average replacement rate for all workers with 3-5 percent ratings is .90 (table 10.1, panel G, line 1), but when these cases are disaggregated by age (lines 2-5) the replacement rates vary from .33 to 9.91, and when they are disaggregated by part of body injured (lines 6-9) the replacement rates vary from .58 to 1.22. The significance of this characteristic variability is considered in chapter 11.

NOTES

1 More details on the Wisconsin workers' compensation program are included in Berkowitz, Burton, and Vroman (1979), chapter 13, section A, and in chapter 7 of the present study.

2. The idea that a particular consequence of an injury may be the operational basis for compensation because it serves as a convenient proxy for other consequences of the injury is discussed in chapter 2.

3. The methodology for the NSF research and the Wisconsin results are discussed in detail in chapters 10 and 13 of Berkowitz, Burton, and Vroman (1979).

4. A sample of Wisconsin females is discussed in Berkowitz, Burton, and Vroman (1979), chapter 13. The results are less reliable due to the smaller sample size and problems with control methodology.

5. As explained in chapter 10 of the *NSF Report* (Berkowitz, Burton, and Vroman, 1979), data on education, assets, marital status, and work experience (which human capital studies suggest would be useful predictors of EGR behavior) were unavailable for the workers in our sample.

The *NSF Report* also presents results (in appendices to chapters 11-13) of an alternative method of calculating potential earnings that relies on the actual earnings experience of California workers in the Continuous Work History Sample (CWHS) maintained by the Social Security Administration. The results using the CWHS control group methodology are generally consistent with those shown in tables 10.1-10.7 of this report.

6. More details on the Florida workers' compensation program are included in Berkowitz, Burton, and Vroman (1979), chapter 12, section A, and in chapter 9 of the present study.

7. The lack of information in the folders for washout cases about the basis for the settlement causes problems because typically the settlement amount includes an unspecified payment to defray future medical expenses. We adopted the procedure used by the Florida Bureau of Workers' Compensation to allocate the settlement amounts in compromise and release agreements between cash

benefits and medical benefits. For settlements up to $10,000, 70 percent was allocated to cash benefits; for settlements between $10,000 and $15,000, 60 percent was allocated to cash benefits; and for settlements over $15,000, 50 percent was allocated to cash benefits. The estimates of cash benefits were then divided by the weekly benefit rate to produce an implied number of weeks, which then served as the basis for the Florida estimates of the extent of disability. Compared to the procedure used to rate California compromise and release cases, the Florida procedure tends to lower the disability rating and the amount of cash benefits.

8. The Florida cases are discussed in detail in chapter 12 of Berkowitz, Burton, and Vroman (1979), which also includes information on a sample of female controverted cases.

9. For many Florida workers, the Z:16 time charge is derived from the disability rating that is used to determine the duration of permanent disability benefits. This derivation of Z:16 charges from the disability ratings occurs in nonscheduled cases and in cases resolved by compromise and release agreements.

10. More details on the California workers' compensation program are included in Berkowitz, Burton, and Vroman (1979), chapter 11, section A, and in the first section of chapter 7 of the present study.

11. The California cases are discussed in detail in chapter 11 of Berkowitz, Burton, and Vroman (1979), which also includes information on a sample of females with formal ratings.

12. A case that had an informal rating that did not serve as the basis for benefits (because, e.g., the case was subsequently resolved by an award by a workers' compensation judge) was dropped from the male informal sample.

13. Some cases with formal ratings from the Disability Evaluation Bureau were resolved by compromise and release agreements or findings and awards where the amount of permanent disability benefits did not correspond to the disability ratings in the formal ratings. The percent rating for these cases is based on the general procedure discussed *infra* in the text that derives the disability rating from the amount of the permanent disability award.

14. The problems of constructing disability ratings and the implications for comparisons of workers within and among states are discussed in Berkowitz, Burton, and Vroman (1979), chapters 10 and 14.

One problem is that compromise and release agreements often include an unspecified sum to cover future medical expenses. In California, the first state in which we collected data for the NSF study, we were unable to determine from case folders for compromise and release cases how to separate the amounts for future medical expenses from the amounts for cash benefits for permanent disability, and we treated the entire amount of the settlement as cash benefits. This procedure raised the disability rating in any case where part of the settlement was for future medical, since—as explained in the text—the disability rating was calculated by dividing the permanent disability award by four times the weekly rate for permanent disability benefits. In some instances— most notably serious back injuries—our procedure produced implicit disability ratings that exceeded 100 percent. While the estimating procedure for disability ratings thus tended to exaggerate the ratings for those cases in which the compromise and release settlement contained an amount for future medical, the procedure also tended to exaggerate the amount of cash benefits and understate the amount of medical benefits received in these cases. Since the test for adequacy of benefits discussed in section G compares cash benefits to earnings losses, our procedure tends to overstate the adequacy of the California workers' compensation benefits.

Compromise and release cases were handled differently in Florida. There the Bureau of Workers' Compensation had devised a procedure to allocate compromise and release settlement amounts between cash benefits and medical benefits, and we adopted the Bureau's procedure, as discussed in footnote 7.

Compromise and release cases were handled still differently in Wisconsin, where they are unusual. Case folders were examined and settlement amounts were allocated between cash benefits and medical care on a case-by-case basis. The estimates of the permanent disability cash benefits were divided by the weekly permanent disability benefit rate to produce an implied number of weeks, which when divided by 10 produced the permanent disability rating for the case. Because compromise and release cases are unusual in Wisconsin and because the files normally contained sufficient information to permit allocations between cash benefits and medical care, the accuracy of the disability ratings for Wisconsin workers is less of a concern than the accuracy of the disability ratings for California and Florida workers.

15. A worker's disability rating and his permanent disability benefits are essentially simultaneously determined. For workers with identical ratings (informal or formal), total benefits differ only to the extent the workers received different amounts of temporary disability benefits or had different weekly rates for permanent benefits (an uncommon occurrence for the California workers injured in 1968, since most received the $52.50 per week maximum benefit). For workers without disability ratings from the rating bureau or who received an award or settlement subsequent to receiving a rating from the rating bureau, a disability rating was simulated using the procedure described in footnote 14. The inherently close relationship between disability ratings and amounts of benefits means that no particular significance should be attached to the relatively close relationship between benefit amounts and disability ratings shown in panel F of tables 10.5-10.7. What is not inherently close is the relationship between loss of earnings on the one hand and the disability rating or amount of benefits on the other. As panels C, F, and G of tables 10.5-10.7 show, these relationships are not particularly close.

The inherent relationship between disability ratings and benefit amounts and the lack of particular significance for the relationship is also true for the Wisconsin and Florida results shown in tables 10.1-10.4.

16. A more extensive comparison of the empirical results involving California, Florida, and Wisconsin is included in Berkowitz, Burton, and Vroman (1979), chapter 14. The three states are evaluated in terms of adequacy, equity, and efficiency in chapter 11, *infra*.

17. The term "contested cases" is used in this comparison to include all cases in which the parties have indicated to the state agency that they disagree over some aspect of the case that they would like the agency to resolve or in which the parties resolved a disagreement by negotiations and approval of the negotiated settlement by the state agency is required. Thus the term "contested case" includes *inter alia* cases resolved by an agency decision after a formal hearing and compromise and release agreements, which require agency approval in Florida, Wisconsin, and California.

18. California workers in the male informal sample had 1966-67 earnings that on average were $2,633 higher than the 1966-67 earnings of workers in the male formal sample and $3,288 higher than the 1966-67 earnings of workers in the Other WCAB sample (Berkowitz, Burton, and Vroman [1979], chapter 11). Florida workers in the male regular sample had 1966-67 earnings that on average were $2,105 higher than the 1966-67 earnings of workers in the male controverted sample (Berkowitz, Burton, and Vroman [1979], chapter 12). Wisconsin workers in the male uncontested sample had 1966-67 earnings that on average were only $781 higher than the 1966-67

earnings of workers in the male contested sample (Berkowitz, Burton, and Vroman [1979], chapter 13). All of the intrastate differences in sample means were statistically significant.

19. The California male formal cases have proportional earnings losses of .265 and the California Other WCAB cases have losses of .185 (tables 10.6-10.7, panel E). A weighted average of the proportional earnings losses for these two samples of contested cases is .203.

Part IV
Evaluation
and
Possible Reforms

Chapter 11
Evaluation of Permanent
Disability Benefits

This chapter evaluates the performance of the workers' compensation program in providing permanent partial disability benefits. Chapter 12 discusses some of the policy alternatives that could be used to improve the performance.

The criteria we use to evaluate permanent disability benefits are those articulated in chapter 2: permanent partial benefits should be adequate, equitable, and efficiently provided.[1]

Replacement Rates as Tests of Adequacy and Equity

The evaluation of the adequacy and equity of permanent partial disability benefits will largely rely on the replacement rates shown in tables 10.1-10.7 for the workers' compensation programs in California, Florida, and Wisconsin. The adequacy and equity tests will be applied following a review of some conceptual issues and limitations of our data.

(1) *Which consequences should be compensable?* As discussed in chapter 2, there are two possible purposes for permanent disability benefits: to compensate workers for work disability (loss of actual earnings or loss of earning capacity), and to compensate workers for permanent impairments or the other consequences of their injuries or diseases. Our assessment of the adequacy of permanent disability benefits assumes their only purpose is to compensate for work disability. This assumption, which seems warranted since most workers' compensation programs purport to pay benefits only for work disability, tends to improve the Wisconsin, Florida, and California records. If a portion of the benefits were considered payments for impairment, the balance of the benefits (which would be considered payments for work disability) would be less adequate in comparison to the loss of earnings.

(2) *Which is the relevant aspect of work disability?* We assume that actual loss of earnings, as opposed to loss of earning capacity (see chart 1.2), is the proper measure of work disability. Although state programs

are more likely to operationally base the permanent disability benefits on loss of earning capacity, they presumably do so because they expect that loss of capacity will manifest itself in some subsequent actual loss of earnings.

(3) *How should earnings losses be measured?* A fundamental issue in measuring the extent of earnings losses is deciding the reference wage against which the disabled worker's actual earnings will be compared in order to determine the extent of earnings losses. Operationally in workers' compensation, the reference wage almost invariably is the worker's own wage before the occurrence of the work-related disability. A conceptually superior reference wage is the earnings the worker would have earned if he had not experienced the work-related injury or disease. Calculation of this reference wage requires a projection of the worker's predisability wage into the future, ideally on the basis of factors such as the worker's age, sex, education, work experience, and other characteristics that affect age-earnings profiles. In our study, data on many of these factors are unavailable and postinjury potential earnings were estimated on the basis of each worker's preinjury earnings, age, and sex.

Earnings losses should be measured as the difference between the projected earnings and the worker's actual earnings in the postinjury period, where the actual earnings are adjusted to reflect any other factor than the work injury that affects the earnings. If, for example, two years after the work injury the worker is involved in a nonwork accident that affects his earnings, the actual earnings figure should be adjusted. Our data do not permit adjustments on a case-by-case basis for these other influences on postinjury earnings, since our only sources of information are the workers' compensation agency files and the Social Security summary earnings records. Our methodology, however, accounts for these other influences when the results for groups of workers are considered. The workers in our control group are also subject to these postinjury influences on actual earnings, and thus the earnings growth ratios (EGRs) described in chapter 10 that were derived from the actual earnings in 1968-73 of the control group workers have built into them the influence of the factors other than work injuries that affect actual earnings.[2] In short, the earnings losses we show are associated with the 1968 injuries to the workers in our samples and are in excess of earnings losses caused by other adverse events that influenced these workers from 1968 to 1973.[3]

The accuracy of the estimates of earnings losses for individuals is also limited because of the data source we used for earnings. Social Security earnings records do not include information on all types of earnings (for example, some state and local government employees are not covered by the Social Security system). Also, the records only include reports of actual earnings up to the taxable maximum; estimates of total annual earnings were made for workers who reached the taxable maximum.

The limitations of our data mean that our results must be used with some caution. Estimates of potential earnings, actual earnings, and earnings losses for individual workers are particularly vulnerable to error. Results for groups of workers, however, are more reliable, as evidenced by the statistical significance of the earnings losses for many of the groups of workers shown in the C panels of tables 10.1-10.7.

For some cells in the C panels, our estimates of mean earnings losses are negative (the replacement rates in corresponding cells in the G panels are missing). This occurrence is pronounced for the cases with 1-5 percent ratings for the California male informal cases (table 10.5) and the Florida male regular cases (table 10.3). In only one instance, however, are the negative earnings losses statistically significant (table 10.5). In other words, our estimates of actual earnings for some workers in 1968-73 exceed, in all but one case by a statistically insignificant amount, our estimates of potential earnings for these workers. We interpret these negative entries to mean that average earnings losses were essentially zero and that very high average replacement rates (in excess of 100 percent) should be inferred for the workers in these cells.

(4) *What is the proper measure of earnings?* According to the National Commission, the "basic measure of the worker's economic loss is the lifetime diminution in remuneration attributable to the work-related injury or disease. This can roughly be described as wage loss, although remuneration is composed of earnings plus supplements" (National Commission *Report* 1972, p. 36). Supplements include fringe benefits, such as health insurance, and legally mandated employer expenditures. The Commission concluded that the appropriate measure of lost remuneration is not the difference between total remuneration before and after the disability, but the difference in net remuneration. This comparison reflects factors that are affected by disability such as taxes, work-related expenses, some fringe benefits that lapse, and the worker's uncompensated expenses resulting from the work-related impairment.

It is exceedingly difficult to use the National Commission's measure of the worker's economic loss. Data on fringe benefits, taxes, and other factors are not routinely collected by workers' compensation agencies, and are difficult to obtain without extensive contacts with workers and their employers. Also, the Social Security records of earnings have no data on supplements or income taxes.

These difficulties of data collection mean that most researchers do not use the net remuneration concept described by the National Commission, but instead use data that are conceptually less appropriate but operationally much more accessible. Such data are used in part III, because the realistic alternatives are no data at all or better data for a much smaller sample. We believe the data, despite their deficiencies, are reasonably appropriate for evaluation purposes. Nonetheless, we acknowledge that the assessment of the adequacy and equity of the workers' compensation benefits must be made without any direct information for items such as taxes and fringes. The direction of any bias in the assessment because of these omissions is unclear. The absence of information on fringe benefits means the measure of earnings understates the total amount of lost remuneration. On the other hand, since workers' compensation benefits are tax free while the income lost because of the injury would have been taxed if received, the earnings-losses replacement rates may understate the effective proportion of net remuneration replaced by workers' compensation benefits.

(5) *How should attorneys' fees be treated?* Another issue is whether the gross benefits paid by the employer or the benefits net of attorneys' fees received by the worker should be counted. We believe the appropriate measure of benefits for the adequacy test is benefits net of attorneys' fees. For a worker, although the payment of an attorney's fee may be a good investment, only the amount of the award that remains is available to replace lost earnings.

(6) *Should benefits from other programs be considered?* Workers' compensation benefits are not the only source of disability benefits received by workers. Many workers with serious injuries, for instance, may be receiving Social Security Disability Insurance benefits or other forms of government or private assistance. In principle, these benefits should be included when considering the adequacy and equity of benefits. In practice, information on the supplementation of workers' compensation benefits by private or public sources is fragmentary.[4] Our data are for that reason confined to workers' compensation benefits. In general,

supplementation of workers' compensation benefits probably is not significant for most workers with nonserious injuries but is likely to be relatively important for older workers and for workers with serious injuries.

(7) *Over what period should earnings losses and benefits be calculated?* The period over which earnings losses and benefits are calculated will affect the assessment of adequacy. In principle, the data should pertain to the worker's entire life, since losses and benefits may persist over long periods. The data in tables 10.1 to 10.7, however, pertain only to 1968-73 (for reasons explained in chapter 10). Among younger workers and workers with high disability ratings, post-1973 earnings losses are probably much larger than post-1973 benefits. Thus the replacement rates are biased upward for the serious injury cases and for the injuries involving younger workers compared to the replacement rates that would be found if lifetime benefits and lifetime earnings losses were compared. Overall, the limitation of our data to 1968-73 means that our replacement rates overstate the adequacy of the benefits in Wisconsin, Florida, and California.

(8) *Should the individual or the family be analyzed?* Much of the recent literature on labor supply has used the family as the unit of analysis, and this approach has been useful in analyzing topics such as retirement decisions and labor force participation for women. Because of the limitations of our data, our estimates of earnings losses pertain only to the injured workers, and because the disability of the workers may cause other family members to increase their participation in the labor market, our estimates exaggerate the total loss of family income caused by the work-related injuries. Also, other family members may qualify for benefits from a social insurance program because of the worker's injury. If these additional transfer payments and earnings were considered and the family were used as the unit of analysis, the replacement rates probably would increase.

A Recapitulation of the Eight Factors. We recognize there are several limitations to the replacement rates used in this study.[5] (1) If workers' compensation benefits are meant in part to provide compensation for consequences other than work disability, then our replacement rates are too high. (2) We assume that actual loss of earnings—not loss of earnings capacity—is the proper measure of work disability. It is not clear which measure of work disability would be larger, so there is no clear implication for the size of our replacement rates. (3) The accuracy of the replacement rates depends on the accuracy of our estimates of the workers' potential earnings, of their actual earnings, and of the benefits received by workers after their injuries. Particularly for the first of these estimates, we recognize that our data have some limitations. However, there is no reason to believe our estimates of the total earnings losses in each state are too high or too low, and thus no reason to think the estimating problem biases our replacement rates either way. (4) Our estimates of earnings losses probably exaggerate the workers' losses of spendable earnings because of the effect of payroll and income taxes, but understate the loss of total remuneration since fringe benefits that lapse because of the work-related injury are not considered. These factors have contrary implications for the size of our replacement rates and it is not evident which dominates. (5) We assume that attorneys' fees should be deducted before benefits are compared to earnings losses, a decision that tends to reduce our replacement rates, especially for serious injury cases that are more likely to involve litigation. (6) Other transfer payments besides workers' compensation benefits are not considered. In the case of Social Security Disability Insurance benefits, we know that older workers and workers with higher disability ratings are more likely to receive these benefits. (See Vroman 1977.) If all transfer payments were considered, the replacement rates would be higher in general, and probably would increase most substantially for older workers and workers with serious injuries. (7) The replacement rates cover benefits and earnings losses for 1968-73, and not post-1973 developments. Among younger workers and workers with high disabiilty ratings, post-1973 earnings losses are probably much larger than post-1973 benefits. Thus the replacement rates in tables 10.1 to 10.7 are biased upward for the serious injury cases and for the injuries involving younger workers compared to the replacement rates that would be found if lifetime benefits and lifetime earnings losses were compared. (8) Our estimates of earnings losses pertain only to the injured workers, and because the disability of the workers may cause other family members to increase their participation in the labor market, our estimates exaggerate the total loss of family income caused by the work-related injuries.

Implications of the Eight Factors for the Adequacy Test. The adequacy test is primarily concerned with the average replacement rate for all workers in a state included in the restricted universe from which our sample was drawn. Two of the factors just discussed (numbers 2 and 3) have no obvious implications for the size of our replacement rates. Three of the factors (numbers 5, 6, and 8) tend to make our replacement rates too low, while two factors (numbers 1 and 7) tend to make our replacement rates too high. The fourth factor has conflicting components and the net influence of the factor on the size of our replacement rates is unclear. The overall impact of the eight factors on the value of the average replacement rate in each state is also unclear. The only solution that seems feasible is to use the state-wide replacement rates without any adjustments, recognizing that the values may be too high, too low, or just right.

Implications of the Eight Factors for the Equity Test. The equity test is primarily concerned with comparisons among the replacement rates for the different cells of the samples within each state, where the cells are defined by age, sex, nature and severity of injury, and type of administrative procedure used to provide the benefits.

The effect of five factors (numbers 1-4 and 8) should be reasonably uniform across the individual cells in tables 10.1-10.7, and should not seriously affect our equity evaluation. If our exclusion of attorneys' fees is improper (number 5), our replacement rates for serious injuries are too low compared to those for minor injuries.

The implication of the seventh factor is that our replacement rates are too high for cases involving serious injuries and younger workers (since we ignore post-1973 developments), while the sixth factor means that the replacement rates are too low for cases involving serious injuries in older workers (since transfer payments other than workers' compensation are more likely for serious injuries in older workers). The sixth and seventh factors appear to offset each other insofar as they give rise to biases in our replacement rates involving serious versus nonserious injuries, but the two factors both suggest that our replacement rates tend to understate the adverse consequences for younger workers relative to the adverse consequences for older workers.

Although these eight factors complicate the evaluation of the replacement rates on the basis of equity, we believe that the problems are not so serious that evaluation is untenable.

Adequate Permanent Disability Benefits

Before we apply the adequacy test, an additional question must be answered: what proportion of earnings losses should be replaced by workers' compensation benefits? As discussed in chapter 2, the National Commission on State Workmen's Compensation Laws indicated that benefits should "provide substantial protection against interruption of income." But the National Commission did not make specific recommendations for permanent partial disability benefits that would permit a translation of providing "substantial protection against interruption of income" into a numerical or quantitative standard. For temporary total and permanent total disability, the National Commission recommended that, subject to the state's maximum weekly benefits, the total disability benefits be at least 66 2/3 percent of the difference between the worker's earnings before and after the injury or disease.

The National Commission provided a higher standard for the adequacy of disability benefits when it recommended that permanent total benefits be increased through time in the same proportion as increases in the state's average weekly wage. Similar protection for permanent partial disability would require the benefits to be escalated through time. This scheme would roughly approximate the conceptually superior approach previously discussed of basing benefits on the difference between the wages a worker would have earned if he had not been injured and the wages actually earned after the injury.

We consider the replacement of 66 2/3 percent of earnings losses calculated on the basis of the postinjury potential earnings to be the proper test, but we also recognize this is a stringent test in terms of the traditional approach in workers' compensation, which is to relate benefits to preinjury earnings. A more lenient test for adequacy, which may be particularly appropriate for 1968-73, a period when wages probably grew more rapidly than was expected as of 1968, is that at least 50 percent of earnings losses calculated on the basis of postinjury potential earnings should be replaced by benefits.[6] As indicated in chapter 10, the Wisconsin workers in our sample had 75 percent of their lost earnings replaced by benefits, the Florida workers 59 percent, and the California workers 46 percent, which means that these states as of 1968 had benefits that ranged from adequate by the stringent test (Wisconsin) to adequate by the lenient test (Florida) to somewhat inadequate (California). For these three states as of 1968, we conclude that benefits were generally adequate.

Our findings for California workers injured in 1968 can be compared to the results from *Economic Consequences of Job Injury* (1984), a study conducted by the California Workers' Compensation Institute, hereafter CWCI *Economic Consequences*. The sample included 8,364 cases of serious claims incurred under workers' compensation insurance policies issued in 1975-76. Earnings records for each worker were obtained from the State Employment Development Department and 1,076 of the workers were also interviewed. Earnings losses for each worker were determined for the four years after the injury. The procedure to estimate the losses was similar to that described in chapter 10 for our wage-loss study, although the CWCI did not escalate preinjury wages over the four years to determine postinjury potential earnings. The interviews allowed the CWCI to eliminate some of the gross earnings losses due to factors other than the work-injury, such as earnings declines due to voluntary retirements. After adjustment to earnings losses for reasons unrelated to the work injuries, the net earnings losses in the four years after the injury averaged $8,080 per worker. The projected net earnings losses over the working lives of the employees averaged $17,700. The study found that on average, workers' compensation income benefits (for both temporary and permanent disability) replaced only 49 percent of the net earnings lost by permanently disabled workers over their working lives, a replacement rate that the CWCI termed inadequate. The CWCI study also extrapolated its results through 1984, considering the general increase in wages after the injury dates for the workers in its sample and the infusion of nearly $1 billion in additional benefits into the California program as a result of 1983-84 benefit changes (described in chapter 7). The net result of the offsetting factors was that the proportion of earnings losses replaced by benefits dropped to 47 percent in 1984 from the previous 49 percent. These results, although based on a methodology somewhat different from ours, are consistent with the replacement rate of 46 percent we found for California workers injured in 1968 and reinforce the conclusion that the state's benefits for permanently disabled workers are inadequate.

Equitable Permanent Disability Benefits

The most straightforward test of equity for disability benefits has two dimensions: *horizontal equity* requires that workers with equal losses of earnings (or losses of earning capacity) should receive equal benefits; a narrow test of *vertical equity* requires that workers with different losses should receive benefits proportional to their losses. A more general test for vertical equity only requires that there be a consistent relationship between losses and benefits. Society may decide, for example, that the proportion of benefits to losses should increase (or decrease) as losses increase. Although the general formulation of vertical equity is more difficult to translate into empirical tests than the narrow test, reasonable requirements appear to be (1) that the ratio of benefits to earnings losses consistently increase (or decrease) as earnings losses increase, and not fluctuate (that is, that the relationship between the replacement rates and earnings losses be monotonic[7]) and (2) that there should be no abrupt changes in the ratio of benefits to earnings losses as earnings losses increase.

It is possible to have benefits that are inadequate yet equitable. For example, as we use those terms, benefits that replace 10 percent of lost wages for all workers, no matter their ages or types of injury, would be inadequate yet equitable. It is also possible to have benefits that are adequate yet inequitable. For example, on the average for all workers in a state, benefits may replace 70 percent of lost wages, and we would consider such an overall figure to be adequate. If some workers received 100 percent of their lost wages replaced by benefits and others only 40 percent, however, the benefits would be inequitable.

Applying the equity criterion properly requires some sensitivity to the conceptual issues and data limitations discussed above. Of particular relevance are the facts that (1) the replacement rates cover benefits and earnings losses for 1968-73, and not post-1973 developments, and (2) transfer payments other than workers' compensation benefits are not considered. The first factor means our replacement rates are too high for cases involving serious injuries and younger workers, while the second factor means that the replacement rates are too low for cases involving serious injuries and older workers. The two factors appear to offset each other insofar as they introduce biases into our replacement rates involving serious versus nonserious injuries, but they both suggest that our replacement rates tend to understate the adverse consequences for younger workers relative to the adverse consequences for older workers.

Application of the Equity Test. An obvious way to begin applying the equity test is to compare the replacement rates for the entire male samples in the three states. The differences in the replacement rates— .75 for Wisconsin, .59 for Florida, .46 for California—suggest that workers injured in different states in 1968 fared quite differently. There is, in short, interstate inequity.

The Wisconsin results provide a model of how the equity test can be applied within a state.[8] The relationship between replacement rates and severity of disability can be determined by moving across the rows in panel G of tables 10.1 and 10.2. Examination of each male sample in total (panel G, line 1) reveals a tendency for replacement rates to increase with the size of the disability rating. Although the relation is not strictly monotonic, the results can be considered consistent with the general test of vertical equity.[9] The regularity of the relationship between size of the disability rating and the replacement rates dissolves, however, when the male samples are disaggregated by age or part of body. In other words, moving across the replacement rate values in rows 2 to 9 in panel G of tables 10.1 and 10.2 reveals fluctuations that are inconsistent with any acceptable version of a vertical equity test.

A horizontal equity test is provided by moving down the columns in panel G. The results indicate that workers with similar disability ratings, but with different ages or parts of body injured, experience widely varying rates in terms of the proportion of their earnings losses replaced by workers' compensation benefits: horizontal equity is lacking.

Comparisons of replacement rates by type of administrative procedure are also possible for the two male samples. Not only is the replacement rate higher overall for the uncontested sample than the contested sample (85 percent versus 58 percent), the replacement rate is consistently higher for the uncontested sample for each of the entries in line 1 of panel G of tables 10.1 and 10.2. Contested cases do not fare as well as uncontested cases in Wisconsin in terms of replacement rates.

Overall conclusions about the equity of Wisconsin workers' compensation benefits must be made with some caution, both because of the previously remarked problems in calculating the replacement rates and because of the choices for equity standards, particularly in determining the appropriate tests for vertical equity. Subject to these cautions, several conclusions can be drawn from the Wisconsin data. First, there is some evidence from Wisconsin consistent with the equity test. For example, the Total column of the male contested cases (table 10.2, panel G) indicates a reasonable consistency in replacement rates across workers classified by age and by injured part of body. Also, there is an overall relationship between replacement rates and severity of disability that is reasonably consistent with a vertical equity test for both the male uncontested and male contested cases (tables 10.1 and 10.2, panel G, line 1). Second, there is some evidence of systematic differences in replacement rates among workers that violate the equity test in Wisconsin. For example, the replacement rates for males in the uncontested sample consistently exceed those for males in the contested sample, even when severity of disability is held constant, and this appears inconsistent with the horizontal equity test. Third, the Wisconsin results provide numerous examples of unsystematic differences in replacement rates among groups of workers that violate horizontal and vertical equity. Both tables demonstrate erratic movement in replacement rates as one moves down the columns in panel G, which violates the test for horizontal equity, for example. Fourth, the comparisons made so far pertain to differences among the mean replacement rates for groups of workers. Given the problems of estimating earnings losses for individual workers, we feel more comfortable about equity tests involving groups of workers. If, however, variations in replacement rates were examined at the individual worker level, the large dispersion within cells would suggest extreme problems of achieving equity on an individual basis. (See Berkowitz, Burton, and Vroman 1979, chapter 15, appendix B.)

Similar conclusions about horizontal and vertical equity are appropriate for the Florida male samples shown in tables 10.3 and 10.4. First, the Total column of the male regular cases (table 10.3, panel G) indicates a reasonable consistency in replacement rates across workers classified by age and part of body injured. Also, there is an overall relationship between replacement rates and severity of disability that is reasonably consistent with a vertical equity test for the male controverted cases (table 10.4, panel G, line 1). Second, there is some evidence from Florida of systematic differences in replacement rates among workers that violate the equity test. For example, the replacement rates were consistently low for workers with injuries to the trunk and consistently high for workers with injuries to the upper extremities, after adjusting for age and severity of injury. Also, the replacement rates for males in the regular sample consistently exceed those for males in the controverted sample, even when severity of disability is held constant, and this also violates horizontal equity. Third, there are numerous violations of horizontal and vertical equity shown by the unsystematic fluctuations in replacement rates as one moves down the columns or across the rows in tables 10.3 and 10.4. Finally, even worse equity problems are evident from the variations in replacement rates among the individuals in the cells of the two tables.

The California data in tables 10.5-10.7 also indicate a mixed record of compliance with the horizontal and vertical equity tests, although more effort is needed to find evidence of compliance with the criterion than in the other states. First, there is an overall relationship between replacement rates and severity of disability that is reasonably consistent with a vertical equity test for the male formal cases and male Other WCAB cases (line 1, panel G, of tables 10.6 and 10.7). The replacement rates tend to increase with severity, meeting the general test of vertical equity, although the increase in the replacement rate from .18 to .58 as one moves across table 10.7, panel G, line 1 seems to represent a pronounced inclination to favor serious injuries. In Wisconsin and Florida there was a reasonable consistency in replacement rates across workers classified by age and injured part of body for the Total column of the contested cases, but the two contested case samples in California show much less consistency. To illustrate, the overall replacement rate for the Wisconsin contested cases was .58, and the variation among the eight components of the sample was from .52 to .82 (table 10.2, panel G, Total column); for Florida workers in the controverted case sample, the overall replacement rate was .51 and the variation among the eight components was from .40 to .75 (table 10.4, panel G, Total column); whereas for California workers in the male formal cases sample, the overall replacement rate of .46 when disaggregated into the eight components showed a greater than two-to-one variation (.34 to .69), and the California Other WCAB sample, with an overall replacement rate of .41, reflected a similar variation (.30 to .64) in the disaggregated sample (Total columns of panel G, tables 10.6 and 10.7).

There are some patterns of systematic differences in replacement rates among groups of California workers that violate the equity test. Thus, in the male formal cases and the Other WCAB cases (tables 10.6 and 10.7), workers with back injuries consistently have lower replacement rates than workers in the samples with other types of injuries, but equivalent disability ratings. More compelling than the pattern of inequity are the apparently unsystematic variations in replacement rates among groups of California workers that violate tests of horizontal and vertical equity. These inequities can be found by moving across the rows or down the columns of panel G in tables 10.5-10.7. Finally, if intracell variations in replacement rates were examined, further evidence of inequity would be found.

We conclude that the equity criterion was seriously violated for the benefits provided to the workers injured in 1968 who were in our samples. Although Wisconsin appears to have done somewhat better than Florida, which in turn did somewhat better than California, none of the states appears to have done a satisfactory job of meeting the tests of horizontal and vertical equity. One interesting finding that is consistent with the alternative test of vertical equity is that in all three states, replacement rates rather consistently increase with the severity of injuries in the contested case samples. This finding casts some doubt on one of the most widely dispensed shibboleths of the workers' compensation field, namely, that permanent partial disability benefits tend to overcompensate minor injuries relative to major injuries. As previously noted, however, the results do not reflect any developments after 1973, when wage losses for serious injuries were likely to continue and benefits were largely ended, which means the earnings-losses replacement rates are likely to decline over time for serious injuries. Even if a modicum of vertical equity is provided by the relationship between severity and replacement rates, our overall assessment of the permanent partial disability benefits on the equity criterion is that there are relatively serious shortcomings. We do not suggest that the benefits will not provide even a rough sort of justice. We do believe, however, that the deficiencies on the equity criterion are much more serious than the deficiencies on the adequacy criterion.

Our findings of inequitable benefits for California workers were supported by the evidence in the recent study by the California Workers' Compensation Institute, CWCI *Economic Consequences*. As described in the adequacy section, the CWCI methodology was somewhat different from the methods used in our wage-loss study (chapter 10). The CWCI, for example, projected earnings losses over the working lives of the employees, whereas we confined our estimates to the six-year period after date of injury. This probably explains why we found that replacement rates increased with severity, while the CWCI found that the replacement rates for permanently and partially disabled workers declined with the severity of the injury: from 88 percent for workers with permanent disability ratings of 1-9 percent to a replacement rate of 32 percent for workers with 70-99 percent ratings. The replacement rate for permanent total disability cases was 64 percent, reflecting the higher maximum weekly benefit for total disability than for partial disability. The CWCI (*Economic Consequences*) found that "replacement rates vary widely according to injury severity and the age of the worker" (p. 7), which led the Institute to criticize the California benefits as inequitable because "replacement of earnings loss due to the injury is not accomplished in any rational matter" (p. 8). Although the particulars of our results and those in the CWCI *Economic Consequences* differ, the central message does not: there are serious inequities in the permanent disability benefits for injured workers.

Efficient Permanent Disability Benefits

The question of efficiency concerns the administrative costs of providing benefits incurred by the participants in the workers' compensation delivery system, including employers, insurance carriers, workers, attorneys, and governmental agencies. The term *efficiency* is used to describe two concepts, as explained in chapter 2. One meaning of efficiency, termed *myopic efficiency,* is that administrative costs are at the lowest possible level without regard to the quality of benefits provided. Although this disregard for quality is usually not made explicit, it appears that what some people mean by maximum efficiency is the cheapest delivery system. The other meaning of efficiency, termed *panoramic efficiency,* is that a particular quality of benefits is provided at the least possible administrative costs. Thus, if two delivery systems provide benefits of equal adequacy and equity, the delivery system that does so with lower administrative costs has greater panoramic efficiency.

We do not believe it is meaningful to say that one delivery system has lower administrative costs than another delivery system unless the differences in the quality of the benefits are specified. Only with the latter information can judgments be made about the relevant concept, namely the panoramic efficiency of the delivery systems.

There are other criteria for judging a delivery system that can be considered part of a broadly defined efficiency test. First, the delivery system should not aggravate the problem the benefits are meant to remedy. Thus, if a particular delivery system induces workers to prolong unnecessarily their periods of work disability or to exacerbate their functional limitations, that system *ceteris paribus* is less efficient than a delivery system without these inducements. Second, the delivery system should facilitate (or at least not impede) the achievement of the objectives of workers' compensation other than providing adequate and equitable cash benefits. Thus, a particular delivery system that helps achieve the safety objective is preferable to a system that does not, *ceteris paribus*.

Evaluation using the efficiency criterion is especially difficult. For one thing, data on the expenses of administering the program that are borne by employers and others in the private sector, the amount of attorneys' fees, and the lags in payments of permanent disability benefits after a workers' condition is permanent and stationary, as well as a variety of other types of data relevant to the assessment of the efficiency of the delivery system, are scarce. Another reason the efficiency criterion is hard to apply is that the quality of benefits and the administrative costs must be simultaneously considered in order to evaluate the panoramic efficiency of a state's workers' compensation program. It would be foolish, for example, to prefer one jurisdiction merely because its administrative costs are lower than the costs in a second jurisdiction. The first jurisdiction's administrative costs may result from lower-quality benefits, and thus represent no greater panoramic efficiency. (In terms of graph 2.2, the two jurisdictions could simply be at different points on the Quality/Costs Constraint line.)

Application of the Efficiency Test. An important aspect of the efficiency test concerns the types of delivery system used to provide workers' compensation benefits. One model (typified by Wisconsin) relies on an active state agency that makes many decisions itself, closely supervises the operation of employers and private carriers, and limits the role for attorneys. A considerably different mode (typified by the federally operated Longshore and Harbor Workers' Compensation Act) relies on the private parties, particularly attorneys, to make most of the decisions about benefit payments. The agency is essentially passive, although it will resolve disputes brought to it by the private parties. An intermediate model (typified by Florida prior to the 1979 reforms and by California) involves a state agency that conducts a minimal review of the decisions made by the private parties and that resolves disputes in a relatively high proportion of the cases, but that nonetheless relies on extensive attorney involvement to make the delivery system operate.

How attorneys are used is an important feature differentiating these three delivery system models. As recounted by many commentators on the history of workers' compensation, the original notion was that the elimination of the fault concept and the prescription of benefits by statute would enable employees to protect their interest without external assistance. From that standpoint, the substantial reliance on lawyers in California and Florida before 1979 suggests at the minimum a lack of myopic efficiency. And yet the involvement of attorneys can also be viewed as a *prima facie* indictment of the idea that workers' compensation laws can be self-administering; attorneys may be in the system because they help achieve the criteria of adequate and equitable benefits. In other words, their involvement may represent a lack of myopic efficiency but not a lack of panoramic efficiency. Whether, in fact, attorneys help achieve the equity and adequacy of benefits is not clear *a priori.* On one hand, they receive fees that generally are subtracted from the workers' awards, which, in a nominal sense, reduces the adequacy of the benefits. On the other hand, attorneys increase the awards in some cases in which they are involved and probably have an indirect impact on the amount of benefits in other cases in which they are not involved (similar to the "threat" effect that unions have on wages in nonunionized firms). Thus on *a priori* grounds, the impact of attorneys on the adequacy of benefits is unclear. Likewise, the impact of attorneys on the equity of benefits is unclear. They may take cases in which benefits would otherwise be inappropriately low, or alternatively their involvement may be on a basis unrelated to the relative undercompensation of the case, such as the worker's membership in a union.

The data from Wisconsin, Florida, and California shed some light on the question of whether the use of attorneys improves panoramic efficiency. In terms of the ability to deliver benefits without litigation, Wisconsin clearly surpassed California and Florida before 1979. As shown by the distribution of cases between tables 10.1 and 10.2, more than 5 out of 6 permanent partial disability cases in Wisconsin were resolved without a contest (including use of compromise and release agreements). By contrast, more than 2 out of 3 Florida permanent disability cases were controverted, and only 1 in 10 California permanent disability cases was resolved by use of informal ratings rather than reliance on a more litigious approach, such as use of a compromise and release agreement or a formal hearing before an Administrative Law Judge. A related finding is that legal fees amounted to only about 3 percent of benefits for the workers in our Wisconsin sample, compared to about 12 percent in Florida and about 6 percent in California.

Wisconsin thus appeared to be superior to California and Florida in the handling of permanent partial disability benefits without excessive litigation, thus providing some evidence that it had greater myopic efficiency. Moreover, the Wisconsin benefits for the workers in our samples were more adequate and more equitable than the Florida and California benefits, suggesting that the Wisconsin delivery system also provided greater panoramic efficiency than the delivery systems in the other two states. We believe this conclusion is valid even when consideration is taken of the administrative expenditures in both the public and private sectors, including the expenses of operating the state workers' compensation agencies and state courts as well as the cost of attorneys' fees for claimants, employers, and carriers. The Wisconsin agency has a particularly impressive record in terms of budget and staff compared to the other jurisdictions in our study (table 4.1).

The Florida and California delivery systems are representative of the systems in most of the jurisdictions in our ten-state study. There appears to be a general concern for myopic efficiency in workers' compensation, which manifests itself in inadequate resources for state agencies and undue reliance on litigation. The consequence of this narrow concern appears to be a loss of panoramic efficiency.

Conclusions

Our overall evaluation of permanent partial disability benefits in the workers' compensation jurisdictions included in our wage-loss study and in our 10-state study is based on the criteria of adequacy, equity, and efficiency. *Adequacy* was not a major problem as of 1968, the date when the workers in the three states in our wage-loss study were injured. The major failing we have documented is the lack of *equity* of the permanent partial disability benefits. The three states we examined most intensively—California, Florida, and Wisconsin—provide considerable evidence that the benefits were not closely matched to the workers with earnings losses. This judgment is based to a large extent on our sample of workers injured in 1968, but there is little reason to believe that workers injured more recently would have done any better on the equity criterion. Only in Florida have the criteria used to determine the amount of permanent partial disability benefits and the procedures used to provide these benefits changed significantly since 1968, and—as stressed in chapter 9—there are no data indicating the impact of these changes on equity. *Efficiency* was also a significant problem in most jurisdictions, although Wisconsin did reasonably well on this criterion.

The balance of the section attempts to identify the causes of the deficiencies of adequacy, equity, and efficiency.

Lack of Adequacy was not a major problem in the three states in the wage-loss study. Underlying this conclusion are some interesting findings. One is that the adequacy of permanent partial disability benefits is almost impossible to evaluate simply by looking at the statutory provisions of a workers' compensation program. For example, the Wisconsin statute as of 1968 had a maximum weekly benefit for permanent partial disability benefits of $47.50, and the benefits were paid for a maximum duration of a thousand weeks. This was in contrast to Florida, where the weekly maximum for permanent partial disability benefits was $49.00 and the maximum number of weeks was 350. The statutory provisions suggest that Wisconsin permanent partial disability benefits would be much more adequate than those in Florida. Our evidence suggests, however, that the permanent partial disability rating standards are much more stringent in Wisconsin than in Florida,[10] and so for a given injury the apparently greater benefits provided by the Wisconsin statute were partially offset by a lower disability rating. The end result was that the adequacy of the Florida and Wisconsin benefits in practice appears to be much more similar than the statutes would suggest.

We draw two implications from this comparison of Wisconsin and Florida. An obvious one is that any attempt to assess the differences among states in the adequacy of permanent partial disability benefits must go beyond comparisons of statutory matters such as weekly benefits and maximum durations and must also consider the standards used to rate disabilities. A less obvious implication, and one that the data only suggest and do not prove, is that, given the extent of discretion inherent in most rating systems for permanent partial disabilities, workers' compensation programs have some ability to be self-correcting on the adequacy criterion. If adequacy of permanent partial disability benefits is widely considered a problem in the state because of low weekly maximums and limited durations, the participants in the delivery system have some opportunities to increase the size of the disability ratings in order to compensate for the low statutory provisions and thus provide a rough sort of justice. This phenomenon is hard to document; there are limits to the parties' ability to carry out such a self-correcting practice; and such a strategy is surely not the ideal way to deal with an adequacy problem (especially since the self-correction mechanism probably aggravates any problems of equity); but we sense that this sort of countervailing activity is taking place in some jurisdictions.

Lack of Equity is a major problem, and the causes appear to be a mixture of the procedures used by the state and the criteria for permanent partial disability benefits. Chapter 4 discusses four aspects of the procedures used by state workmen's compensation agencies, namely record-keeping, monitoring, evaluation, and adjudication. A major source of the lack of equity appears to be inattention by state agencies to the monitoring and evaluation aspects of procedure, and too much emphasis on adjudication. The result is inconsistent treatment of similar injuries because the amount of benefits a worker receives is affected by the policies of his employers or the insurance carrier and by whether the employee hires a lawyer. As we indicated earlier, Wisconsin appears to do better on the equity criterion than California and Florida, and one reason is that the Wisconsin workers' compensation agency's greater attention to monitoring reduces the importance of employers, carriers, and attorneys in determining the outcome of cases.

Probably even more important than procedural deficiencies as a cause of inequity are the characteristics of the criteria used to evaluate the extent of permanent partial disability (see Burton 1983, pp. 24-28). In general, states use criteria that permit and even require a considerable exercise of discretion, and the almost inevitable result is that similar injuries receive dissimilar ratings. Here again Wisconsin shines in comparison to most states because of its emphasis on objective factors in rating and its use of comprehensive guidelines to evaluate a wide range of impairments and functional limitations. In most states, there is more opportunity for subjective factors (such as pain and lack of endurance) to be considered in evaluating the seriousness of the impairments and functional limitation, and these subjective factors allow the evaluator more room to exercise discretion, which in turn results in inconsistent treatment. Probably the worst of all possible criteria in terms of ensuring consistent treatment is the approach used in most jurisdictions for nonscheduled injuries. This approach allows the loss of wage-earning capacity to be assessed on the basis of facts relevant for the particular case: almost invariably reasonable people can and do differ about the extent of disability for a given worker. Thus the rating criteria now used in most states contain a number of subjective elements or require the assessment of imponderables such as loss of wage-earning capacity, and the considerable exercise of discretion required to apply the criteria results in inconsistent ratings of similar injuries.[11]

Another apparently important source of inequity is the timing of application of the criteria used to evaluate permanent partial disabilities. Ordinarily, a worker's permanent partial disability is rated as soon as his permanent injury is considered stable. This approach requires an *ex ante* assessment of the consequences of a particular injury on a worker's earnings. After reviewing the results in California, Florida, and Wisconsin of these *ex ante* evaluations, we conclude that in a high proportion of cases the states are not able to predict with any reasonable degree of accuracy what the consequences of work-related injuries will be for the workers' labor market experience.

Panoramic *efficiency* is achieved to the extent that benefits of a specified level of adequacy and equity are provided with the least administrative cost.[12] As evidenced by the extent of litigation in most jurisdictions compared to Wisconsin, inefficiency seems to be a serious problem, since there is no apparent gain in adequacy or equity in these other states compared to Wisconsin. The inefficiency also appears to be caused by a mixture of the procedures and the criteria used to provide permanent partial disability benefits.

The emphasis in most state workers' compensation agencies is on adjudication, not on the other administrative functions such as monitoring and evaluation. Many state agencies fell into this role of being primarily an adjudicatory body by accident. When workers' compensation was established, the view was widely held that the program would be largely self-administrating since benefits amounts and durations were specified in the statute. Unfortunately, in practice the workers' compensation program was complex and required numerous controversial decisions, especially in the area of permanent partial disability benefits. A substantial delivery system was needed to make these decisions, and essentially states had to choose between two types of delivery systems. One allowed the private parties to work out their own arrangements for the administration of the act with state agencies acting as quasi-courts to adjudicate those disputes the parties could not resolve by negotiations. This approach was taken in most states. The alternative type of delivery system turned to the state workers' compensation agency to fill the emerging need for administration; the state agency pursued the record-keeping, monitoring, and evaluation roles. This approach was chosen in only a few states, of which Wisconsin is probably the best example.

The delivery system that makes the workers' compensation agency primarily a quasi-court was chosen in most states for a mixture of reasons. It reflects in part the interest of attorneys and others who benefit from a delivery system that operates largely on the basis of private negotiations and litigation. Another reason is that in most jurisdictions, state administrators have not pursued the model of an active state workers' compensation agency, often because these administrators were drawn from the ranks of practitioners who had never seen the active-agency model in operation. And certainly another important reason is that efficiency is often equated with a small budget—that is, the goal is myopic efficiency, not panoramic efficiency. State legislators often see the cost of running a state agency as the only relevant cost of the delivery system, and by holding down agency costs they provide a strong incentive for the litigation-based approach to a delivery system. What is often not appreciated is that a low-cost agency is not cheap when the total resource costs of the delivery system are considered.

Another possible reason for the use of a litigious delivery system is that workers may assume they are unlikely to be injured on the job. As a result, they may be unwilling to support an active agency, which requires both time to be established successfully and resources on a continuing basis. When, however, workers are injured on the job (to their surprise), they can obtain crucial assistance from lawyers on short notice. Thus, unwillingness to think about the unpleasant topic of work-related injuries fosters litigation, since legal services can be purchased after the injury occurs, but good administration cannot.

The criteria used to provide permanent partial disability benefits also encourage litigation, which in many jurisdictions appears excessive. Lawyers can make a big difference in the outcome of a case when the criteria are loose, and naturally lawyers are attracted to the program under these circumstances. Again, part of the success of Wisconsin in reducing the incentive to litigation is that comprehensive rating guidelines reduce the chance for disagreement and thus limit the usefulness of lawyers.

We have concluded that the state workers' compensation programs have deficiencies in their permanent partial disability benefits in terms of adequacy, equity, and efficiency, and we have attempted to delineate some of the causes of these deficiencies. The final chapter will examine some policy issues that states can consider in attempting to improve their permanent partial disability programs.

NOTES

1. One qualification of the evaluation in chapter 11 is that the emphasis is on cash benefits, and little attention is given to other objectives of workers' compensation, such as the provision of adequate medical care and the encouragement of safety.

2. We are not able to adjust our estimates of earnings losses to reflect the reduction in labor supply that may be caused by the receipt of workers' compensation benefits. If such a reduction in labor supply occurs, actual earnings after the injury will be reduced and our estimates of the earnings losses caused by the work-related injuries could be exaggerated. We have partially controlled for this benefits-induced reduction in labor supply because the earnings growth ratios (EGRs) for our control group reflect any such reductions for workers with minor permanent partial disability ratings. To the extent that the higher benefits for more serious injuries induce even greater reductions in labor supply, we exaggerated the wage losses caused solely by these injuries.

3. Technically, our control methodology did not follow the procedure described in the text that calculated earnings losses as the difference between potential earnings and actual earnings adjusted to show the adverse impact of factors such as nonwork injuries. We calculated the earnings losses by subtracting unadjusted actual earnings from potential earnings that were adjusted to reflect the impact of the adverse factors. For individual cases the procedure may yield different estimates of earnings losses, but on average the amount of earnings losses in the two procedures is the same.

4. One study of workers who receive multiple benefits is Johnson, Cullinan, and Currington (1979).

5. The eight factors discussed in the text are not the only possible limitations to our replacement rates. Another potential problem is the limitation of our data to those workers injured in 1968 who received permanent disability awards. Some workers may have been injured that year at work and sustained permanent disabilities that were never compensated because, e.g., they worked for uncovered employers or they never filed claims. These workers, in effect, had replacement rates that were zero. If there were such workers, our replacement rates are higher to an unknown degree than the replacement rates for all workers who sustained permanent disabilities because of 1968 work injuries.

6. The data in tables 10.1-10.7 are six-year aggregates and thus are not appropriate for an adequacy test that compares a worker's actual earnings prior to the work-related injury with the worker's actual earnings subsequent to the injury. Many workers with minor permanent injuries experience most or all of their wage losses the first year or two after the injury and then their earnings resume their normal growth pattern. For example, suppose a worker earns $1000 in 1967 (the year before injury) and that his earnings would have increased $100 a year thereafter if he had not been injured. Assume that the worker has no earnings in 1968 and earns only $200 in 1969 as a result of the injury, but then his earnings rebound to $1300, $1400, $1500, and $1600 for 1970-73. This worker would show $1800 of earnings loss if his preinjury wages are compared with his postinjury actual earnings over a two-year period (1968-69) but no earnings losses if his preinjury wages are compared with his postinjury actual earnings over a six-year period (1968-73). Suppose the worker received $1200 of workers' compensation benefits (all paid in 1968 and 1969). This would produce a replacement rate of .67 if earnings losses and benefits are compared over a two-year period but an infinitely large replacement rate if earnings losses and benefits are compared over a six-year period.

The procedure we use to measure earnings losses and replacement rates is not as sensitive to the length of the period during which the adequacy and equity assessments are made. Using the example in the previous paragraph, we would show $1100 of earnings losses in 1968 and $1000 of earnings losses in 1969, and no earnings losses in subsequent years. Thus the dollar amount of earnings losses ($2100) and the replacement rate of .48 ($1000 of benefits divided by $2100 of earnings losses) would be the same whether calculations were done over 1968-69 or over 1968-73. (Proportional earnings losses would vary depending on whether a two- or six-year period were used, but this variable is not used in the adequacy and equity assessments.) Our estimates of replacement rates shown in tables 10.1-10.7 are deficient to the extent that benefit payments and earnings losses extend beyond the period for which we have data (1968-73); this point is discussed in this chapter.

7. As discussed in the text, the definition of vertical equity that requires a strict proportionality of benefits to losses is a special case. More generally, vertical equity only requires that there be a consistent relationship between losses and benefits. Ultimately, policy makers must decide what is a consistent relationship between losses and benefits. In general, little guidance has been provided by policy makers about their intentions for vertical equity. The use of minimum and maximum weekly benefits implies, however, that the desired policy is to replace a higher propor-

tion of lost earnings for low-wage workers than for high-wage workers. Also, the use in most states of maximum durations for benefits for serious permanent partial disabilities implies that the desired policy is to replace a higher proportion of lost earnings for workers with minor injuries than for workers with serious injuries. In California, however, workers with permanent disabilities rated at 70 percent or more of total disability are eligible for life pensions, which suggests that the intent is to replace a higher proportion of lost earnings for more serious injuries.

These examples suggest that it is difficult if not impossible to infer the definition of vertical equity that policy makers explicitly or implicitly intended when they established the various state workers' compensation programs. Absent the guidance about what policy makers intended, we will use two alternative definitions of vertical equity: first, the narrow test of vertical equity implied by the National Commission's definition of equitable, namely the requirement of a strict proportionality of benefits to losses; and second, when appropriate, a more general formulation of vertical equity, which assumes that, among workers who differ in terms of the severity of their work disabilities, the desired relationship between earnings losses and benefits is monotonic. That is, if workers with moderate work disabilities have a higher proportion of their lost earnings replaced by benefits than do workers with minor work disabilities, then workers with severe work disabilities should have at least as high a proportion of their lost earnings replaced by benefits as workers with moderate work disabilities. Thus, a state that replaced 20 percent of lost earnings for workers with minor work disabilities, 60 percent for workers with moderate work disabilities, and 40 percent for workers with severe work disabilities would violate the more general test of vertical equity.

8. Application of the equity test within a state largely involves an analysis of the cell-to-cell variations in the mean replacement rates in the various rows and columns of panel G in tables 10.1-10.7. When the source of this variability is related to the data in panels C and F of the tables, it is evident that the benefits in panel F show a much more regular pattern down columns and across rows than do the earnings losses in panel C, and that the irregularities in earnings losses are primarily responsible for the lack of regularity in the panel G values.

The conclusion that the source of variability in replacement rates is the erratic pattern of earnings losses must be used with some caution, however, since the result is in one sense a statistical artifact caused by the format of our tables. There are three variables reflected in tables 10.1 to 10.7: (1) the permanent disability rating explicitly or implicitly assigned by the workers' compensation program to each worker in our sample, (2) the total amount of workers' compensation benefits received by each worker, including temporary and permanent disability benefits, and (3) the earnings losses between 1968 and 1973 for each worker. In practice, the first two of these variables are highly correlated with each other across workers, while neither is highly correlated with the extent of earnings losses. Our tables use (1) disability ratings to establish the column intervals, and, not surprisingly, show that mean benefits (2) can be "predicted" reasonably well but that (3) mean earnings losses cannot. It would have been possible to construct tables that defined column intervals by the amount of earnings losses in each case; if panels C, F, and G of tables 10.1 to 10.7 had then been constructed using the same data, panel F (showing mean benefits) would have appeared erratic, panel C (showing mean earnings losses) would have shown a regular relationship across rows and down columns, and panel G (showing replacement rates) would have had the same values in the Total column as panel G in the present version of tables 10.1 to 10.7 and would have had values in other columns that demonstrated no pattern of regularity. This approach to a formatting of the tables might be considered evidence that the irregularity of the replacement rates can be traced back to erratic variations in benefits, rather than erratic variations in earnings losses.

We believe our approach to tabulation (using the size of the disability ratings to set the column intervals) is more appropriate than the alternative approach (using the extent of earnings losses to set column intervals) for at least two reasons. First, the research design virtually dictated this approach, since we wanted a sample of permanent disability cases in each state, not the universe of cases, and at the time the sample was drawn, we had information on the disability ratings but not the earnings losses. In other words, the only way to reduce our overall sample size by applying sampling fractions to certain cells was to rely upon information available from the agency tape records, which included no information on earnings losses. Second, the use of disability ratings as column headings implicitly reflects a model in which disability ratings are used to predict earnings losses, and that operationally is the way workers' compensation programs are designed. In other words, the disability ratings are assigned on a prospective basis before the actual loss of earnings occurs, and the ratings are *ex ante* predictions of lost earnings.

Although we believe our approach to tabulation is appropriate, we do not believe the crucial elements of our findings depend on it. Among workers who receive workers' compensation benefits, there are three variables with large standard deviations relative to their means: (1) disability ratings, (2) workers' compensation benefits, and (3) earnings losses. The values of the first two variables are closely correlated, and neither of them is closely correlated with the extent of wage loss. One way to demonstrate the lack of correspondence between benefits and earnings is reflected in our tables, to which the analysis in the text of the chapter now turns.

9. If the replacement rates were calculated for lifetime earnings losses and lifetime benefits, the replacement rates would probably be more similar across the disability rating categories. This result would be more consistent with the narrow test for vertical equity.

10. As discussed in chapter 10, each 1 percent of disability rating is associated with $741 of earnings losses in Wisconsin and $396 in Florida.

11. The recent conversion of Wisconsin from ratings for nonscheduled permanent partial disabilities based on extent of impairment to ratings based on loss of earning capacity (discussed in chapter 7) is not a propitious development in our view.

12. As discussed above, a broadly defined test of efficiency requires that the delivery system should provide adequate and efficient cash benefits without impeding other objectives of workers' compensation. By such a test, in addition to the high costs of litigation, another deficiency of the delivery system approach described in the text that relies on extensive litigation is the interference with the rehabilitation process that is caused by a litigious environment.

Chapter 12
Possible Reforms of Permanent
Partial Disability Benefits

The preceding chapter characterized permanent partial disability benefits in the jurisdictions we examined as generally adequate, seriously inequitable, and apparently provided with great variations in efficiency among the jurisdictions. The judgments of adequacy, equity, and, to a lesser extent, efficiency are based on the data from our wage-loss study of California, Florida, and Wisconsin. The judgments of efficiency and, to a lesser extent, equity are based on the evidence from the 10-state study.

The question to be considered in this chapter is, given the deficiencies in the current handling of permanent partial disability benefits, what are the policy alternatives that should be considered in the quest for benefits that are adequate, equitable, and efficiently provided?

Issues in Designing a Program

Each jurisdiction must resolve a number of issues when a program for permanent partial disability benefits is designed or revised. Resolution of these issues is difficult because the criteria of adequacy, equity, and efficiency on which the decisions must rest often come into conflict.

Complicating the decisionmaking process is that efficiency has two meanings: myopic efficiency—in which the only concern is the reduction of administrative cost without regard to the quality of the program, and panoramic efficiency—in which the goal is the lowering of administrative cost without reducing the program's quality. (Chapter 2 provides an extended discussion of these concepts.)

Given the inadequate level of workers' compensation benefits in many jurisdictions and the extensive reliance on litigation, policy makers sometimes face policy options in which a change in administrative procedures will reduce the program's administrative cost without undermining adequacy or equity—thus achieving both myopic and panoramic efficiency.

Policy makers nonetheless will often face choices in which the only way to cut administrative cost is to reduce the quality of benefits. Such a choice has lower administrative costs and thus higher myopic efficiency, but the lower quality of benefits may reduce panoramic efficiency.

Equity is the aspect of the quality of benefits that seems most likely to deteriorate as myopic efficiency is increased (by reducing administrative costs). Several examples of the myopic efficiency-equity trade-off will be offered in this section.

One useful way to array policy makers' alternatives is to pose a series of questions that must be resolved in designing a program providing permanent partial disability benefits.

1. Which Consequence (or Consequences) of Injuries and Diseases Should Be Compensated? As catalogued in chart 1.2 and discussed in chapter 1, there are several consequences of injuries and diseases, including impairment, functional limitations, work disability, and nonwork disability. Some of these consequences can be further divided; work disability, for example, can be subdivided into loss of earning capacity and loss of actual earnings. Policy makers must decide which of these consequences warrant compensation.

Chapter 2 examined some opinions on this question. Larson argues that the sole basis for workers' compensation benefits should be work disability. In contrast, the National Commission concluded that, although work disability should be the primary basis for benefits, there is a secondary role for impairment. (As explained in chapter 2, *impairment* as used by the National Commission is broad enough to include *functional limitations* and *nonwork disability* as those terms are used in this report.)

Most state workers' compensation programs have never explicitly decided which consequences should be compensable, and the implicit decisions reflected in their statutes, regulations, and practices are often ambiguous or conflicting. Obviously, workers' compensation programs can survive without directly answering the question about the purpose of the benefits, but the failure to do so is one source of problems. Moreover, explicitly deciding the purpose of the benefits will make it easier to answer the balance of the questions that must be resolved in designing policy.

2. Which Consequence (or Consequences) of Injuries and Diseases Should Operationally Be Made the Basis for Benefits? Question 1 was concerned with the underlying purpose for benefits: that is, which consequences warrant compensation. Once that question has been answered, it must be decided whether the consequences that warrant compensation should be compensated directly or indirectly. To compensate indirectly means to make one consequence the operational basis for benefits because it serves as a convenient proxy for another consequence.

Assume, for example, that the first question is resolved with a decision to compensate work disability. The second question requires deciding whether work disability should be compensated directly or indirectly (by, for instance, relating benefits to the extent of impairment). The answer to this question is important, because the incentives built into the program depend upon what is operationally the basis for benefits. If benefits are linked to the extent of impairment, then workers have an incentive to exaggerate the extent of their impairments, and employers and carriers have an incentive to reduce those impairments. On the other hand, linking benefits to the extent of work disability encourages employees to exaggerate the extent of disability and employers and carriers to reduce the residual work disability experienced by workers. This incentive may encourage employers to provide vocational rehabilitation services and reemploy the workers, since these actions should reduce the extent of disability.

The decision about what operationally is made the basis for benefits starkly poses the trade-off between equity and low administrative costs (myopic efficiency). Suppose the answer to the first question is that the underlying purpose of benefits is to compensate workers for their actual loss of earnings. Operationally, this could either be done directly, by compensating the actual loss of earnings, or indirectly, using one of three other measures as a proxy for or approximate estimate of the actual loss of earnings: loss of wage-earning capacity, functional limitations, or impairment. Probably the least expensive strategy is to base benefits on impairment. (The use in workers' compensation programs of schedules that purport to pay benefits because of work disability can be understood as an attempt to obtain efficiency.) But benefits determined in this way are likely to be inequitable.

Probably the most equitable operational basis for benefits, assuming the purpose of the benefits is to compensate for actual loss of earnings, is actual earnings losses. But a wage-loss system that pays benefits for an extended period of time as actual wage losses develop requires considerable resources. Case files must be maintained for long periods, an estimate must be made of the worker's potential earnings (what he would have earned had he not been injured), and the source of the worker's earnings losses must be determined when actual earnings are less than the estimated potential earnings. If the estimate of a worker's potential earnings is to be realistic, the estimating procedure must recognize the complex relationship between earnings and factors such as the worker's age, education, and labor market experience. Also, as suggested in chapter 1, the causes of wage loss are complex and numerous. No one seriously proposes that every worker whose postinjury earnings fall below his estimated potential earnings (or even below his preinjury earnings) should receive benefits. The immense problems of administering the pure wage-loss system have not, to our knowledge, been successfully solved in any jurisdiction. In Michigan, cited with favor by the National Commission, the wage-loss system appears to work only because many workers sign redemption agreements that end their eligibility for subsequent wage-loss benefits. The same problem of premature termination of eligibility for wage-loss benefits is emerging in Florida under the guise of washouts, as discussed in chapter 9.

The premature closing of potential wage-loss claims may not be an inevitable consequence of a wage-loss system,[1] but the evidence from our 10-state study indicates that workers, employers, and carriers are strongly averse to the long-term risks inherent in a pure wage-loss system.[2] If these risks are accepted and eligibility for wage-loss benefits is provided for an extended duration after the injury occurs, the administrative costs will be high—which will discourage states solely concerned with myopic efficiency. Even so, because the potential gains in equity appear to be substantial, the administrative costs may be justifiable in terms of panoramic efficiency.[3]

3. If More Than One Consequence of Injuries and Diseases is Compensable, Should There Be Multiple Benefits? If more than one of the consequences of work-related injuries and diseases warrant compensation, then policy makers must decide if there should be one type of benefit that attempts to compensate two or more consequences, or whether there should be multiple benefits.

Suppose that both impairment and work disability are judged to warrant compensation. One operational approach would base benefits solely on impairment; this means that the benefits would be designed to compensate impairment directly and to compensate impairment as a proxy for work disability. This approach would be a relatively inexpensive way to provide benefits for both impairment and work disability, but appears to be unlikely to meet the equity criteria insofar as compensating work disability is concerned. The problems inherent in the use of one benefit to compensate two consequences, and the virtues of a dual benefit system, were discussed by the National Commission.

We believe that the primary basis for workmen's compensation benefits should be the worker's loss of wages. We also believe that limited payments for permanent impairments are appropriate. A major difficulty with present permanent partial benefit provisions is that most seem to use one formula which bases benefits on both the impairment and disability bases. Combining both bases into one formula appears unworkable.

Consideration should be given to the use of two types of benefits:

permanent partial impairment benefits, paid to a worker solely because of a work-related impairment

permanent partial disability benefits, paid to a worker because he has both a work-related impairment and a resultant disability.

A worker might be eligible for both types of benefits. The impairment benefits would be based on the worker's impairment relative to the whole man. If, for example, the whole man was defined as 400 weeks, and . . . a worker was 50 percent impaired, then he would be eligible for 200 weeks of benefits.

Impairment benefits are justified because of losses an impaired worker experiences that are unrelated to lost remuneration. . . . Since impairment benefits have no relationship to wage loss, there would be no necessity to link the value of the weekly benefits to the worker's own weekly wage; the weekly benefit could be the same amount for all workers in the State.

In contrast, the disability benefits could be based on actual wage loss or loss in wage-earning capacity. (National Commission 1972, pp. 68-69)

More than two consequences of injuries and diseases may be considered worthy of compensation, and a benefit scheme could be designed accordingly. For example, a "modest proposal" for reform might include three types of benefits: (1) Type A benefits, based on the extent of the worker's impairment; (2) Type B benefits, based on the loss of wage-earning capacity (Type B benefits could be calculated by using the impairment ratings from the Type A benefits and modifying the ratings by factors such as age and education); and (3) Type C benefits, paid in the event of continuing wage loss after the Type B benefits expire. A worker might be eligible for all three types of benefits. The rationale for the threefold approach to benefits is that the Type A and Type B benefits compensate workers for impairment and work disability with relatively low administrative expenses, while the Type C benefits provide a safety valve when the Type B benefits result in highly inequitable benefits for a worker whose actual wage loss far exceeds the amount expected on the basis of injury, age, and education.

4. What Standard Should Be Used to Evaluate Cases? Answers to questions 2 and 3 determine which consequences will be operationally important for determining permanent partial benefits. The next question concerns the standards to be used in evaluating these consequences.

Impairments are likely to be an operationally important basis for benefits in a workers' compensation program, whether or not they are serving as a proxy for something else. One device used in almost every jurisdiction to rate some impairments is the schedule. The inclusion of scheduled injuries in a statute presumably reflects a desire for myopic efficiency.[4] But schedules have been subject to criticism in recent years. The National Commission argued that although schedules may cut corners, those currently (in 1972) in use included only a fraction of "medically identifiable permanent impairments" and typically had gone unrevised for years despite major medical advances (National Commission 1972, p. 69). To these drawbacks of schedules, we would add that their application in various states shows great inconsistency (see chapter 5).

If schedules were expunged from workers' compensation statutes, what would be used in their place? One alternative would be to allow the jurisdiction's workers' compensation agency to adopt a comprehensive set of guidelines that could be used to evaluate a large variety of impairments, not just the limited number appearing in the typical schedule. One possible set of guidelines is the AMA *Guides to the*

Evaluation of Permanent Impairment. California is an example of a state that has not included a list of scheduled injuries in its statute, but rather has relied on a comprehensive set of guidelines for evaluating the consequences of injuries or disease.

Both the California approach and the AMA *Guides* go beyond the rating of impairments and also provide standards for rating functional limitations, as those terms are defined in chapter 1. Assuming that states that decide to use impairments as an operational basis for benefits also intend to use functional limitations for the same purpose, it should be noted that the AMA *Guides* approach and the California approach to rating differ significantly. The AMA *Guides* confine the ratings almost exclusively to impairments and objective manifestations of functional limitations. California's guidelines allow, in addition, consideration of subjective manifestations of functional limitations, such as pain and lack of endurance. For the policy maker, the difference between the AMA approach and the California approach can be posed as a choice between myopic efficiency and equity. Abandonment of the current California schedule in favor of the AMA approach could be viewed as a sacrifice of equity (since the argument is made that the subjective manifestations can provide useful guidance concerning the seriousness of the consequences of the injury) for lower administrative costs. The policy maker is again faced with alternatives that reflect conflicting values.

The California schedule can illustrate another of the choices that has to be made in deciding what standards should be used to evaluate consequences. The purpose of the California schedule is to provide an estimate of the loss of earning capacity that a worker experiences because of an injury or disease. The rating of the impairment (or functional limitation) is combined with information on the worker's age and occupation to provide an estimate of the loss of earning capacity.[5] This is a relatively inexpensive way to estimate the loss of earning capacity compared to the procedure used in some states to evaluate "unscheduled" permanent partial injuries. As indicated in chapter 7, the factors considered in some states to evaluate unscheduled injuries are quite extensive: the worker's injury, age, occupation, experience, and the state of the labor market, for example. Since these factors are complex and must be applied on a case-by-case basis, considerable discretion arises in the application of these provisions. Exercise of that discretion invites the use of lawyers, referees, and claims managers, among others, which makes the resolution of many unscheduled injury cases an expensive process. The result may be greater equity than that obtained by using the California approach, but also more expense. The myopic efficiency-equity trade-off is again posed.[6]

5. *Who Should Apply the Standards?* After a jurisdiction decides such questions as which consequences shall be compensable and what standards shall be used to evaluate these consequences, a decision must be made about who shall be given the authority to apply the standards in individual cases.

Employers (and carriers) could be given primary responsibility to evaluate their own employees and compensate them on the basis of the seriousness of the consequences of their injuries and diseases. Until about 20 years ago, California had a procedure known as "self-rating" that was used by employers to evaluate some workers, with little review of the determinations by the workers' compensation agency. Although such an approach is probably the least expensive way to apply workers' compensation standards, most jurisdictions have not followed it, probably because of a concern about the equity and adequacy of the benefits that would result.

Another approach would assign primary responsibility for the application of the standards to employers (and carriers) and to plaintiffs' attorneys, with involvement by the state agency only when the private parties cannot reach a settlement of their own. This approach, exemplified by Florida before 1979 and by California today, reduces the need for an active state agency. When the costs of administering the program are defined to include attorneys' fees, however, the approach is not inexpensive. Data on the operation of the programs in Florida and California presented in part III indicate that benefits are relatively adequate but highly inequitable. Thus the approach that relies on the parties negotiating their own settlements appears to lack panoramic efficiency: administrative costs (including attorneys' fees) probably could be lowered without reducing the adequacy and equity of the benefits.

Another approach to the application of standards would assign primary responsibility to the state workers' compensation agency, which would closely monitor the decisions made by the private parties, or even evaluate the extent of disability in each case, subject to a review of the exercise of its discretion by appeals to the court system. This approach is consistent with the National Commission's view that the "key to an effective delivery system is the agency's active pursuit of the administrative obligations" (National Commission 1972, p. 101). The resources devoted to administering the system are probably no greater in this approach than if employers (and carriers) were given primary authority for applying the standards, but the result of active agency participation should be greater equity of benefits. Wisconsin has an active state agency—stressing record keeping, monitoring, and evaluation—and our results suggest the active agency approach provides more panoramic efficiency because the quality of the benefits is superior. (Chapter 4 discusses the various administrative tasks performed by state workers' compensation agencies.)

The three approaches just described—primary reliance on employers (and carriers); primary reliance on negotiations between the private parties; and primary reliance on the state agency—are models that represent the outer limits of what states can do. Most states, in practice, use a mixture of these approaches. California, for example, places primary reliance on the state agency to determine the benefits for one type of permanent partial disability benefits ("voluntary" benefits, based on informal ratings from the Disability Evaluation Bureau), while the private parties largely determine the benefits for another type of permanent partial disability benefits (compromise and release settlements, which are generally accepted by the state agency with minimal supervision).

6. What Meaning Shall Be Given to the Criteria of Adequacy, Equity, and Efficiency, Especially When the Criteria Come into Conflict? In order to answer the previous questions, and to resolve the other issues that arise in designing a program to provide permanent partial disability benefits, policy makers must decide what interpretations should be given to the criteria of adequacy, equity, and efficiency, and how conflicts among these criteria should be resolved. Answers to these questions are, to a large extent, value judgments: there are no "right" answers.

The adequacy criterion requires policy makers to decide which consequences of injuries and diseases should be compensable, and what proportion of the losses should be replaced. The National Commission concluded that a substantial proportion of lost income (work disability) should be replaced by workers' compensation benefits, and that a limited amount of benefits for impairment should also be provided.[7] The National Commission distinguished workers' compensation from other social insurance programs as to the proportion of lost income to be replaced by benefits. The reason for higher benefits in workers' compensation is that "in exchange for the benefits of workmen's compensation, workers renounced their right to seek redress for economic damages and pain and suffering under the common law. In no other social insurance program such as Social Security or unemployment compensation, did workers surrender any right of value in exchange for benefits'' (National Commission 1972, p. 37).

It is clear that the National Commission's reasoning would justify workers' compensation benefits much higher than the benefits in other social insurance programs, which is a result some policy makers may find unacceptable.[8] It is also clear that if workers' compensation were abolished and employees were allowed to sue their employers under current doctrines of liability, the workers' compensation benefits recommended by the National Commission would appear trifling compared to the damages awarded to plaintiffs when the employers were held liable for damages. (Whether, on the average, injured workers would fare better under liability suits as opposed to the workers' compensation benefits recommended by the National Commission is unclear, since many workers eligible for workers' compensation benefits could not prevail in court suits. Even if workers would do better on average by relying on liability suits, thus improving adequacy, the all-or-nothing element of the approach would aggravate the problem of equity.)

As indicated earlier, the trade-off between equity and administrative costs is likely to appear when a decision has been made that the underlying basis for benefits should be work disability, and a choice must be made of an operational basis for the benefits. At one extreme, using impairment as a proxy for work disability is inexpensive but likely to be inequitable. At the other extreme, using actual wage loss as a basis for the work-disability benefits is likely to be more equitable but expensive, thus reducing myopic efficiency.

What is the right mixture of equity and myopic efficiency under these circumstances? Support for an emphasis on equity can be found in the National Commission's discussion of permanent partial benefits. The Michigan approach was described as paying benefits on the basis of actual wage loss as it develops over an extended period, and praised because the method ''has the substantial merit of matching benefits to a worker's actual loss of wages, rather than basing benefits on guesses about future wage loss'' (National Commission 1972, p. 69).

There are arguments to counter the National Commission's devotion to equity, however. For one thing, the Commission's description of the Michigan approach seems rather naive. As discussed in chapter 8, the practice in Michigan deviates substantially from the theory. Another reason for accepting imperfect equity was stated by Berkowitz (1975):[9]

> One goal of workers' compensation . . . is prompt and certain payment of compensation due the worker. Given such a goal, we should expect to sacrifice some equity. As the Bradley Commission Report put it, "Social insurance relies on the 'magic of averages' to arrive at an overall equity in social justice. This means inescapably that one individual may get somewhat more and another somewhat less than precise individual justice would indicate."

This section has posed six questions that must be answered explicitly or implicitly in the design of a program that provides permanent partial disability benefits. Answers to these questions will determine the extent of adequacy, equity, and efficiency of a state's program. In some instances, proper answers will enable a state to improve its program on one of these criteria without reducing its accomplishments on the other criteria. In other instances, a state will have to sacrifice its accomplishments on one criterion in order to improve on another: the decision on the proper trade-off is essentially a value judgment for which there is no right answer. In this section we have tried to avoid imposing our value judgments.

In the next section we will present some policy prescriptions that reflect, among other things, our views on the proper trade-offs among adequacy, equity, and efficiency.

Evaluation of Policy Alternatives

This section provides our answers to the six questions and discusses other matters.

The Compensable Consequences of Injuries and Diseases

We accept the view that work disability should be the primary basis for permanent partial disability benefits, and that there is also a legitimate secondary role for compensation based solely on impairment. Even when there is no possibility that a permanent impairment will result in the loss of wage-earning capacity or actual earnings losses, it should not be ignored in the design of a workers' compensation program. We are not as concerned about whether the benefits are considered a payment for the impairment per se or a payment for the function limitations and non-work disability that are likely to flow from the impairment, because we believe either view of the impairment represents a justifiable basis for benefits.

Like most commentators who argue there is some role for compensation for impairment, we view the role as secondary to compensation for the worker's loss of earning capacity or loss of actual earnings. The argument that workers can receive benefits even when their employers are not at fault justifies some limitations on the amount of compensation for impairments per se, functional limitations, and nonwork disability. Thus, most of the permanent partial disability benefits should be directed to the compensation of work disability.

The Operational Basis for Work Disability Benefits. We will review the advantages and disadvantages of three approaches to operationalizing work disability benefits, and then will offer a hybrid approach that we believe is desirable.

Work disability criterion I (WDI): a comprehensive schedule of impairments and functional limitations. A comprehensive schedule of impairments and functional limitations, such as the American Medical Association's *Guides to the Evaluation of Permanent Impairment,* could be used to rate the permanent consequences of every work-related injury and disease, and the rating could serve as the basis for permanent partial disability benefits designed to compensate for work disability. Obviously, in this approach, impairments and functional limitations are a proxy for work disability. Although rating systems other than the AMA *Guides* can be used, the *Guides* represent probably the epitome of the search for consistency in ratings, since they are comprehensive and place little reliance on subjective factors, such as residual pain, over which raters are more likely to disagree.

The primary advantage of the WDI criterion is that it greatly limits the rater's opportunity to exercise discretion, which means less opportunity for litigation. In our terms, this approach probably would result in the greatest efficiency in the narrow sense of minimizing administrative costs. There are, however, a number of disadvantages to the WDI criterion. If the primary purpose of permanent partial benefits is to compensate for work disability, then this approach has serious problems, because our evidence from the wage-loss study indicates that similar or identical impairments result in quite disparate earnings losses. Furthermore, our field work in the 10-state study leads us to believe that it is unrealistic to expect the participants to look only at "objective" factors (such as amputation or total loss of use of a bodily member) when determining the extent of impairment or functional limitations, and equally unrealistic to think that only impairments and functional limitations will be considered in making ratings, and not matters such as age, occupation, and the likely prospects for reemployment—even when these factors are not included in the state's rating system. As a result, much of the purported gain in efficiency for a "pure" impairment rating system is illusory. Apparently the basic reason is that the parties rebel at the rating that would be produced if the only factors that could be considered were objective evidence of the extent of impairment and functional limitations.

One way to modify the WDI criterion would be to explicitly incorporate certain objective factors, such as the worker's age, education, and amount of work experience, along with the rating of the worker's impairment, into a formula that produces an estimate of the worker's loss of wage-earning capacity. This can be considered a scheduled assessment of the loss of earning capacity. This operational criterion for work disability benefits (labeled the WDIa approach) is similar to the California rating system. As envisaged here, however, the formula would use age, education, and work experience rather than age and occupation as factors to modify the "standard rating" of impairment or functional limitations. We also would have the standard rating based on objective factors associated with the impairment or functional limitation, and not on subjective factors, as in California. WDIa-type benefits are likely to do a better job than WDI-type benefits in predicting the amount of earnings losses that workers will experience, but our California results suggest that the predictions will still be seriously wrong in many cases.

Work disability criterion II (WDII): nonscheduled assessment of loss of earning capacity. A second basic approach to the quest for operational criteria for work disability benefits is to assess the loss of earning capacity on the basis of the facts in each case. This is essentially the approach used now in many states to rate nonscheduled injuries, as described in chapter 7. Statutes provide that for those injuries not included in the schedule, the extent of disability shall be determined on the basis of the worker's loss of earning capacity. The statutes sometimes list factors to be considered, such as the extent of the worker's impairment, his age, his ability to compete in the open labor market, and so on. The main purported advantage of this loss of earning capacity approach is the ability to consider much more information about the worker than can be considered in the WDI or WDIa approaches. But we do not believe that accurate predictions can be made about the extent of earnings losses a worker will experience on the basis of this information when the judgments are made on an *ex ante* basis. The relationships among type and severity of injury, age, sex, education, prior work experience, motivation, and other factors are so complex that meaningful predictions about how particular workers will fare in the labor market are often impossible. As a result, we think that the added information that can be incorporated into the loss of earning capacity approach where each case considers all the relevant facts is not very helpful. The disadvantage of the approach is that disagreements are almost inevitable about the impact of these various factors, and as a result litigation is virtually invited. The end result is an approach that is expensive to administer and produces little equity in the sense of matching wage loss and workers' compensation benefits. We conclude that the approach that assesses the loss of earning capacity on the basis of the facts in the particular case is the worst possible solution to the quest for operational criteria to compensate work disability. We pronounce this harsh judgment cognizant that this is the approach used in most jurisdictions for rating nonscheduled permanent partial disability cases.

Work disability criterion III (WDIII): "pure" wage-loss. A "pure" wage-loss approach is another possible operational criterion for work disability benefits. The essence of this approach is that the worker's actual earnings after his injury are monitored and a proportion of the difference between these actual earnings and an estimate of his potential earnings had he not been injured are paid as workers' compensation benefits. Benefits are paid retroactively as the worker experiences wage loss that can be attributed to the work-related injury or disease. The "pure" wage-loss approach would keep cases open until retirement age. To protect the right to file claims during this extended period, compromise and release agreements would be prohibited.

The greatest potential advantage of the "pure" wage-loss approach is that it improves the chances of matching permanent partial disability benefits with actual wage loss. In our terms, this closer correspondence between benefits and wage loss would represent an improement in the quity of the benefits. It must be stressed, however, that the search for equity in the wage-loss approach must face pitfalls. Although the preceding paragraph provided the essence of the wage-loss approach, the operational version in invariably more complicated. In the normal approach to wage-loss benefits (described in chapter 8), the amount of compensable wage loss is the difference between the postinjury potential earnings the worker would have been able to earn but for the injury and the greater of (1) postinjury actual earnings or (2) postinjury potential earnings in light of the worker's injury. As discussed in chapter 9, Florida does not compare (1) and (2), but nonetheless does not always accept postinjury actual earnings at face value; the wage-loss approach there must somehow sort out the incidents of wage loss due to the work-related injury from those due to other causes.

Determining what a worker would have been able to earn but for a work-related injury is also a difficult task, particularly if the law does not just mechanically equate postinjury potential earnings with preinjury actual earnings. The problem of estimating postinjury potential earnings is especially difficult for workers who are very young or very old or female. Younger workers are more likely to be working less than full time because of their attendance in school, and older workers are likely to retire. Historically, women have been more likely than men to have intermittent spells of withdrawal from the labor force, and although the differences have been narrowing substantially in recent years, nonetheless the stability of employment is still higher for men than for women. For these groups of workers—the young, the old, and women—predictions of postinjury potential earnings are especially challenging. In some instances, extrapolation into the postinjury period on the basis of the worker's earnings before injury will exaggerate the earnings the worker would have earned if he or she had never been injured. For example, a worker who was working full time up to the date of injury may have been on the verge of retiring or returning to school. In other instances, extrapolation on the basis of the preinjury earnings may underpredict the potential earnings that a worker would have earned if he or she had not been injured. This might occur, for example, for a student who had been working part time prior to the injury and was on the verge of entering the labor force on a full-time basis, or for a woman who had temporarily left the labor force to raise children and who experienced a work-related injury just as she was beginning to phase back to a full-time job.

Because of these complications in determining the extent of wage loss associated with a particular work-related injury or disease, the wage-loss approach may fail to match benefits with wage loss, and thus may fail to achieve the goal of equity.[10] The complications also mean the wage-loss approach can be relatively expensive to administer. If, for example, any worker were eligible for benefits who had even a slight deficiency in actual earnings after his injury compared to the estimate of his potential earnings, many cases could qualify for benefits, since even without the impact of injuries there are considerable variations in wages that would trigger the benefit system. Another concern is that the wage-loss system can provide undesirable disincentives to work. The disincentive occurs because the greater the wage loss, the higher the benefits. The rational response of workers to incentives to limit their labor supply and thus increase their benefits is an especially acute problem for workers who are still recovering from their work-related injury and in the process of rehabilitation when they need every incentive to regain their confidence and productive skills.[11]

Another aspect of the wage-loss system that must be considered is the general aversion to the approach shown by workers, employers, and carriers. As discussed in our 10-state study, the experience in states such as Michigan, Ohio, and Florida suggests that the parties are not enamored with a system that prolongs the period during which there is uncertainty about the amount of benefits to be paid. A course commonly followed to avert the uncertainty is to terminate prematurely the potential eligibility for wage-loss benefits through devices such as compromise and release agreements. Thus a wage-loss system, if it is going to provide benefits for the entire duration of the loss of earnings, will require careful monitoring by the state agency to keep the parties from opting out of the system.

It is possible to think of modifications that can blunt some of the criticisms of a pure wage-loss approach. For example, a delay between the date that the worker is considered to have reached maximum medical improvement and the date when the wage-loss benefits begin would allow the rehabilitation process to proceed without the work disincentives operating at the critical stages of rehabilitation. It must be recognized, however, that such a lag would be indefensible if no other benefits were being paid during that period.

Another modification that would improve the efficiency of the wage-loss approach is a requirement that a nontrivial minimum level of earnings losses must be experienced before a worker is eligible for wage-loss benefits. For example, a wage loss of only 10 or 20 percent of the estimated potential earnings might be considered an amount likely to have been caused by factors other than the work-related injury and thus would not establish eligibility for benefits. Such a threshold for eligibility would substantially reduce the number of cases that could receive benefits if a pure wage-loss system were adopted.[12] (A more detailed example of a system with a threshold limit of losses is described below.)

Work Disability Criterion: A Hybrid Approach. We have described three approaches to operational bases for work disability benefits: a comprehensive schedule of impairments (WDI), a nonscheduled assessment of loss of earning capacity (WDII), and a "pure" wage-loss approach (WDIII). Each approach has some merits and disadvantages, although we can see little of merit in the WDII approach despite its general use in most states. We believe the best solution combines elements of the WDI and WDIII approaches. These two approaches can be combined in a number of ways, as the balance of this subsection indicates.

Our hybrid approach begins with a period of *presumed disability benefits* that commence as soon as the worker's permanent condition is rated. The amount and duration of the benefits do not depend on demonstration of actual loss of earnings. The worker is rated on the severity of his impairment and functional limitations based on a comprehensive set of guidelines issued by the state workers' compensation agency. These guidelines should emphasize objective factors for rating (such as loss of motion) and minimize the use of subjective factors (such as loss of endurance). The obvious example of the rating guidelines we have in mind is the American Medical Association's *Guides to the Evaluation of Permanent Impairment.* These guidelines cover all types of injuries and thus eliminate the distinction between scheduled and nonscheduled injuries. We think there is no convincing reason to maintain the conventional distinction between scheduled and nonscheduled injuries. Also, we would not draw a distinction between permanent partial disability and permanent total disability: the same set of guidelines should be used to evaluate all degrees of permanent disability between 1 percent and 100 percent.

The evaluation of the seriousness of the worker's impairment or functional limitations produces a standard rating that varies between 1 percent and 100 percent. (The benefits are intended only for a worker with at least a minimal permanent impairment.) Although the standard rating could be used without modification, an acceptable alternative approach would modify the rating on the basis of objective information such as the worker's age, level of education, and years of work experience. These factors are used to provide an approximation of the influence of personal characteristics on a worker's labor market experience, given the seriousness of the injury. The factors would be incorporated by use of a formula, such as the one used in California, and their influence on the standard rating would not vary from case to case because of an assessment by the administrative law judge about their likely impact for particular workers. The formula incorporating the adjustment factors would be designed so that *on average* the standard ratings would translate into the same level of modified ratings. In short, the modification factors would be as likely to increase as to decrease the standard rating.

Once the modified rating (or standard rating, if the jurisdiction decides not to incorporate other factors into a formula) is determined, the amount and duration of the presumed disability benefits depend on the size of the modified rating (for example, each 1 percent of rating might result in four weeks of benefits). The weekly benefit could be 66 2/3 percent of the worker's preinjury wage, subject to a maximum benefit of 100 percent of the state's average weekly wage. An alternative approach that we prefer pays the initial benefits for a fixed duration for all cases (for example, six months), with the amount of the weekly benefit varying as a function of the size of the modified rating. Thus a 5 percent rating would produce six months of benefits, with the weekly benefit equal to 5 percent of the worker's preinjury wage, subject to a maximum benefit of 100 percent of the state's average weekly wage. It may be that a fixed duration of longer than six months for the presumed wage-loss benefits would be desirable. An important principle is that these presumed disability benefits are paid without requiring the worker to demonstrate any actual loss of earnings, and it is important that the period of presumed disability benefits be long enough for most workers to recover their strength and earning capacity so that they are unlikely to be experiencing actual wage loss by the end of the period.

The weekly benefit amounts just described are meant to illustrate how the approach operates: the appropriate amounts for a particular state are a consequence of several matters, including the generosity of the rating system used to evaluate the impairments and functional limitations. The AMA *Guides* are relatively strict compared to the rating standards used in most states, and if the AMA *Guides* are used, then the weekly benefit amounts for each 1 percent of rating can be relatively large. The proper combinations of weekly benefit amount, duration of benefits, and rating system must be worked out on a state-by-state basis. As a rough guide to the desired combination, we believe that the benefits produced by the presumed disability benefits provisions should be no more than the amounts currently paid in most states under their present permanent partial disability benefit provisions (and perhaps should be even less), because in our scheme these presumed disability benefits can be followed by a second type of benefit for many workers.

In our scheme, the second type of benefits are *modified wage-loss benefits*. Table 12.1 provides information on a number of aspects of a wage-loss program that must be considered by policy makers, and indicates two types of modified wage-loss benefits. The extensive type represents the most developed form of wage-loss benefits that we can envisage a state adopting. Because so little is known about the operation of wage-loss benefits, however, we also indicate how a number of aspects of wage-loss benefits could be handled in a more limited fashion.

The wage-loss benefits described in table 12.1 are designed to complement the presumed disability benefits of the type just described that begin on the date of MMI and continue for six months, with the weekly amount of benefits varying in proportion to the worker's permanent disability rating. Because of the general lack of experience with wage-loss benefits, a state initially may want to restrict the benefits to workers with ratings that are at least moderately serious. Aspect 1 in table 12.1 indicates that a limited type of wage-loss benefit might use an 11 percent permanent disability rating as a minimum level for eligibility for these benefits. (Workers with ratings of 10 percent or less will be receiving presumed disability benefits during the first six months after their injuries are rated.) The extensive type of wage-loss benefits is available to all workers with a permanent disability rating of 1 percent or greater.

The worker is first eligible for the wage-loss benefits at the end of the six months of presumed disability benefits under both our limited and extensive types of wage-loss benefits (aspect 2). Aspects 3-7 pertain to a method of calculating the amount of wage-loss benefits. The earnings shortfall is the difference between potential earnings and actual postinjury earnings (or postinjury earning capacity if that figure is greater than actual earnings). The earnings shortfall must exceed 20 percent of potential earnings before the worker is eligible for wage-loss benefits in the limited type of wage-loss benefits; the excess amount above the 20 percent threshold is defined as compensable wage loss. The wage-loss benefits are calculated as 80 percent of the compensable wage loss. One difference between the limited and extensive types of wage-loss benefits pertains to the threshold, which is only 10 percent of potential earnings in the extensive type. Another crucial difference

Table 12.1
Variations in Wage-Loss Benefits

Aspect of benefits	Type of wage-loss benefits	
	Limited	Extensive
1. Workers potentially eligible for wage-loss benefits	Workers with permanent disability ratings (PDR) over 10%	Workers with permanent disability ratings (PDR) of at least 1%
2. Earliest date of eligibility (EDI)	Six months after date of maximum medical improvement	Same
3. Potential earnings	Worker's preinjury earnings	Worker's preinjury earnings increased through time to reflect changes in wages or prices
4. Earnings shortfall	Potential earnings minus greater of (1) worker's actual earnings after EDI or (2) worker's earning capacity after EDI	Same
5. Threshold	20% of potential earnings	10% of potential earnings
6. Compensable wage loss	Earnings shortfall minus threshold	Same
7. Amount of wage-loss benefits	80% of compensable wage loss	Same
8. How soon after EDI must earnings shortfall commence or elibibility ends	PDR 11–25% one year PDR 26–50% two years PDR 51–100% three years	PDR 1–10% one year PDR 11–25% two years PDR 26–50% three years PDR 51–100% five years
9. Duration of break in shortfall that will cause eligibility to lapse	PDR 11–25% one year PDR 26–50% two years PDR 51–100% three years	PDR 1–10% one year PDR 11–25% two years PDR 26–50% three years PDR 51–100% five years

10.	Maximum duration for benefits	350 weeks after EDI or until worker reaches normal retirement age, whichever is sooner	Until worker reaches normal retirement age
11.	Burden of proof on whether earnings shortfall is work-related	PDR 11–50%, employee must show shortfall is work-related PDR 51–100%, employer must show shortfall is not work-related	PDR 1–40%, employee must show shortfall is work-related PDR 41–100%, employer must show shortfall is not work-related
12.	Burden of proof on whether worker's earning capacity after EDI is greater than actual earnings	PDR 11–50%, employee must show actual earnings equal earning capacity PDR 51–100%, employer must show earning capacity is greater than actual earnings	PDR 1–40%, employee must show actual earnings equal earning capacity PDR 41–100%, employer must show earning capacity is greater than actual earnings
13.	Compromise and release	Yes, if approved by appeals board as in best interests of worker	PDR 1–25%, yes if approved by appeals board as in best interests of worker PDR 26–100%, no
14.	Rehabilitation requirements	Worker must accept rehabilitation approved by state agency or not eligible for benefits	Same
15.	Financing of wage-loss benefits	Employer responsible for all benefits	Employer responsible for first 350 weeks of benefits; special fund responsible thereafter

involves the calculation of potential earnings. In the limited type, the potential earnings are equal to the worker's preinjury earnings, whereas in the extensive type the potential earnings are the worker's preinjury earnings adjusted through time to reflect changes in the state's wages or prices. The most obvious adjustment method is to increase the worker's preinjury wages by the same percentage that the state's average weekly wage has increased between the year when the worker was injured and the year when the potential earnings are calculated.

To illustrate how the limited wage-loss benefits would be calculated, assume a worker is injured in 1987 when his preinjury earnings are $400 a week. In 1990 his actual earnings are $200 a week and he is eligible for wage-loss benefits. Then the worker's earnings shortfall is $400–$200 = $200; the compensable wage loss is $200–(20 percent x $400) = $120; and the wage-loss benefit is 80 percent x $120 = $96.

To illustrate the extensive wage-loss benefit, assume that the state's average wages increase 25 percent between 1987 and 1990. Then potential earnings for the worker are equal to 125 percent x $400 = $500; the earnings shortfall is $500–$200 = $300; the compensable wage loss is $300–(10 percent x $500) = $250; and the wage-loss benefit is 80 percent x $250 = $200.

The purposes of the 20/80 formula in the limited wage-loss approach are several. A 20 percent earnings loss is a minimum requirement to warrant any benefits because we do not want the benefit payments to be triggered by the minor fluctuations of earnings that many workers experience for reasons having nothing to do with work-related injuries or diseases. But once the worker does have a substantial earnings loss, then a relatively high proportion (80 percent) of the loss should be replaced. For those jurisdictions that conclude the 20/80 formula is too parsimonious, the extensive type of wage-loss benefit provides an alternative formula, namely a 10 percent threshold of earnings loss and an 80 percent replacement rate above this figure. Burton (1983, pp. 41-46) argues that increasing the replacement rate above 80 percent is not an appropriate method to improve the generosity of the benefits because of the disincentives to return to work caused by an excessive replacement rate.

Several decisions must be made concerning the time limits within which workers much establish their eligibility for wage-loss benefits and the potential duration for the benefits. As a practical matter, the wage-loss system cannot be expected to provide compensation to a worker whose initial earnings losses occur 25 or even 10 years after his work-related injury.[13] Aspect 8 suggests some time limits. For example, the limited type of wage-loss benefits could require a worker with a 51 to 100 percent permanent disability rating to experience earnings shortfall within three years after his earliest date of eligibility for wage-loss benefits or he cannot thereafter claim the benefits. The time by which initial eligibility must be established is extended for the more extensive type of wage-loss benefits. It will be necessary to include a provision in the state laws to protect employees against their employers maintaining them on the payroll until the eligibility period is over and then discharging or demoting them in an obvious ploy to avoid payment of wage-loss benefits.

Aspect 9 concerns the duration of employment at wages high enough to cause no earnings shortfall that will extinguish the continuing eligibility for the benefits for a worker who has qualified for the benefits. In the case of the limited type of wage-loss benefits, for example, a worker with a permanent disability rating of 11 to 25 percent who experiences a one-year period of employment at wages that produce no earnings shortfall will lose eligibility for additional benefits.

Another important aspect of wage-loss benefits is the maximum duration for the benefits. A limited type of wage-loss benefit could use a maximum of 350 weeks. Although this means that some workers will have their wage-loss benefits terminated after approximately seven years, which could cause severe hardship, nonetheless the hardship is probably much more severe under most current workers' compensation programs. Further, after some experience with a maximum duration of 350 weeks, a state would have enough information to decide whether to move to the unlimited duration that is a component of the extensive wage-loss benefits. For either the limited or extensive wage-loss benefits, however, eligibility for benefits would terminate at the worker's normal retirement age. That age would presumably be 65 for most workers (the age when they would be eligible for full Social Security benefits), but the age might be earlier or later if the worker or employer can demonstrate that the standard age for retirement in a particular industry or occupation is not 65. The provision concerning the maximum age for eligibility would have to be drawn carefully so that workers would not receive wage-loss benefits during their normal retirement years.[14]

Another aspect of wage-loss benefits concerns who has the burden of proof to establish whether an earnings shortfall is caused by the work-related injury or disease, or by other (noncompensable) reasons, such as unemployment due to adverse economic conditions associated with a business cycle. For the limited type of wage-loss benefit, the employee must demonstrate that the shortfall is work-related if his permanent disability rating is from 11 to 50 percent, but the employer must show that the shortfall was *not* work-related if the permanent disability rating is greater than 50 percent (see aspect 11). For the extensive type of wage-loss benefits, the level of rating at which the burden of proof shifts from the employee to establish his eligibility to the employer to establish the lack of eligibility is lowered. Aspect 12 deals with the associated legal issue of the relationship between actual earnings in the postinjury period and postinjury earning capacity. For the limited type of wage-loss benefit, a worker with a permanent disability rating from 11 to 50 percent has the burden to show that actual earnings are equal to earning capacity (if actual earnings are found to be less than earning capacity, then the earnings shortfall is calculated as the difference between potential earnings and postinjury earning capacity); and the employer has the burden of proof to establish that earning capacity is greater than actual earnings if the employee has a permanent disability rating greater than 50 percent. The burden of proof shifts to the employer at a lower permanent disability rating in the case of the extensive type of benefits. In a case in which the employer has this burden and fails to establish that postinjury earning capacity exceeds postinjury actual earnings, the earnings shortfall is calculated as the difference between potential earnings and actual earnings. Aspects 11 and 12 will have to be carefully translated into legislation in light of the state's legal philosophy and the stringency of the permanent disability rating standards used in the workers' compensation program. The purpose is to allow employers to defend themselves against claims for wage-loss benefits based merely on the circumstance that the workers' actual earnings in the postinjury period are less than the workers' potential earnings. The difficult task, however, is to find statutory language that provides employers this protection without placing undue requirements on workers to demonstrate that their earnings losses are work-related. The Florida experience examined in chapter 9 indicates that this balancing of employer and employee interests is one of the most difficult tasks in a wage-loss system. Aspects 11 and 12 in table 12.1 may provide solutions that are too simplistic, but at least they make explicit certain critical legal issues that are implicit in any wage-loss approach but that are often given inadequate attention in drafting statutory language.

An essential part of the wage-loss approach is that earnings losses are assessed after they occur, and then benefits are paid on a retrospective basis. This approach obviously will not work if before the earnings losses occur the employee signs a compromise and release agreement waiving his right to any such benefits. At a minimum (aspect 13, table 12.1), a compromise and release agreement should be approved only if the appellate level of the state workers' compensation agency judges that it is in the best interest of the worker. An extensive type of wage-loss benefit could require such approval for workers with permanent disability ratings of 1 to 25 percent, and absolutely prohibit compromise and release agreements for more serious injuries.

One of the main advantages of the wage-loss approach is that employers have a strong incentive to reemploy and rehabilitate workers in order to reduce their potential liability for benefits. In order to complement this incentive for employers, the wage-loss benefit program should provide strong encouragement to workers to undergo rehabilitation. Our recommendation is that workers lose their eligibility for wage-loss benefits unless they accept rehabilitation services approved by the state workers' compensation agency (aspect 14, table 12.1). These services would be paid for by the employer, carrier, or state.

Finally, decisions must be made about the financing of wage-loss benefits. One reason for the strong pressure for compromise and release agreements and premature termination of eligibility for long-term benefits is employers' and carriers' concern about the uncertainty associated with long-term cases. We suggest that for a limited type of wage-loss benefits, in which the maximum duration is 350 weeks, the employer (or its carrier) can assume all of the financial liability for its own workers (aspect 15). On the other hand, for the extensive type of wage-loss benefits, in which payments can continue for decades, the employer (or its carrier) can be responsible for the initial phase of the benefits (for example, 350 weeks) and then liability for the continuation of the benefits is assigned to a special fund financed by assessments on carriers and employers.

It should be evident that the recommendations summarized in table 12.1 are not meant to be unalterable solutions. Each state must design its own wage-loss benefits in light of the economic and legal conditions in the state. Some of the elements from the Limited Benefits column in table 12.1 can be combined with some of the elements from the Extensive Benefits column in order to meet a state's particular needs.

It also should be stressed that a state that does not want to move immediately to permanent partial disability benefits reform as substantial as that represented in the Limited Benefits column of table 12.1 can nonetheless begin to move toward a wage-loss approach. That is, smaller increments toward the wage-loss approach are feasible than even the limited wage-loss benefits envisaged in table 12.1. A state with a typical program for permanent partial disability benefits that incorporates scheduled and nonscheduled benefits can graft some elements of the wage-loss program onto its current system. For example, the state may change its law so that workers who receive a relatively high disability rating under their current state law (e.g., equivalent to 40 percent or more of total disability) could be eligible for wage-loss benefits after their benefits under the current state law expire. A high cutoff point in terms of the disability ratings would limit the potential claimants to a small number, so that the plan would not be very expensive or disruptive to the current state program. Thus, a worker who now receives permanent partial disability benefits for 150 weeks would become eligible for wage-loss benefits if he has continuing actual wage loss after the 150 weeks. The wage loss could be determined on the basis of the 20/80 formula summarized in table 12.1, and some of the other matters, such as burden of proof and the duration of wage-loss benefits, also could be resolved by using table 12.1 as a guide. This incremental approach to a wage-loss system would allow the state to monitor its own experience and determine how many workers have substantial continuing wage loss for long periods of time, and as evidence accumulates the state may decide to move further in the direction of the limited or extensive wage-loss benefits spelled out in table 12.1.

The Operational Basis for Impairment Benefits. The preceding discussion is concerned with several alternative operational bases for work disability benefits. If a state decides to compensate explicitly for impairment, an operational basis for this type of benefits must also be determined. We think the choice is clear: namely, the extent of impairment or functional limitation should be determined by use of comprehensive guidelines, such as the AMA *Guides.* Even if the purpose of the impairment benefits is to compensate for the subsequent consequence, nonwork disability, it is difficult to imagine an operational way to measure nonwork disability directly other than by an expensive and almost invariably arbitrary case-by-case analysis of each worker's life style and how it was affected by his work-related injury or disease. As a practical matter, the only feasible approach is to measure the impairment and functional limitations and use the rating as a proxy for nonwork disability.

Each worker with a permanent disability rating of 1 percent or more could receive impairment benefits. Since these benefits are not designed to compensate for work disability, there is no reason to relate the amount of the benefits to the level of preinjury earnings. Rather we would use the same amount of benefits per percent of disability for all workers. A simple formula would give each worker $200 for each 1 percent of his standard rating; thus a 15 percent rating would result in $3000 of impairment benefits. A more complex formula would provide proportionally greater benefits for more serious impairments. For example, a 1 to 10 percent standard rating could receive $100 per percent; an 11 to 25 percent rating could receive $200 for each percent in this interval; a 26 to 50 percent rating could receive $400 per percentage point in this interval; and ratings over 51 percent could receive $500 per percent in excess of 50 percent. Thus a 30 percent rating would result in $5,500 of impairment benefits. The impairment benefits could be paid in a lump sum at the time of the rating.

The Use of Multiple Benefits

We have stated our belief that permanent partial benefits are warranted both because the worker experiences a work disability and because of the impairment per se. How should this dual purpose be translated into an operational basis for benefits?

One possibility would be to have a three-tiered benefits system, paying (1) impairment benefits that are operationally based on the standard rating of the worker's impairment and functional limitations; (2) presumed work-disability benefits that are paid for six months with the amount of the weekly benefit determined by the size of the modified impairment rating; and (3) wage-loss benefits that are paid after the six months for those workers who qualify on the basis of the criteria in table 12.1. Thus every worker with a permanent disability rating of at least 1 percent would receive two types of benefits (impairment and presumed disability), and some would also receive a third type (wage-loss).

A simpler dual-benefit system would collapse the impairment benefits and presumed disability benefits into IPD benefits (impairment/presumed disability benefits). All workers with a permanent disability rating of at least 1 percent would receive IPD benefits, and some workers would also qualify for wage-loss benefits. Since the primary purpose of permanent partial disability benefits is to compensate for work disability, the IPD benefits would be wage-related. If there were a dual-benefit system, the amount of the IPD benefits would be somewhat larger than the amount of the presumed disability benefits under a three-tiered system in order to incorporate both purposes—compensating work disability and compensating impairment—into the IPD benefits.

An advantage of the three-tiered benefits approach is that the judgments of adequacy and equity would be simplified. The total amount of the presumed disability benefits and wage-loss benefits can be compared to the worker's actual loss of earnings, since the sole purpose of these two types of benefits is to compensate for work disability. Awarding the initial six months of permanent disability benefits with the purpose of compensating for impairment and work disability (the IPD benefits) complicates judgments, since some proportion of the benefits are payment not for work disability, but for the other consequences of the work-related injury or disease.

If a dual-benefit approach is selected, the preferred method collapses the impairment and presumed work-disability benefits into IPD benefits and then allows wage-loss benefits to start after six months. An alternative dual-benefit approach uses impairment benefits and wage-loss benefits, with the latter commencing immediately after the worker reaches MMI. This approach is not desirable, however, because, as indicated earlier, we believe that granting eligibility for wage-loss benefits immediately after MMI can represent a disincentive to rehabilitation.

Standards to Be Used in Evaluating Impairments and Functional Limitations

The previous discussion made clear our preference for evaluating impairments and functional limitations by using comprehensive guidelines, such as the AMA *Guides,* that primarily rely on objective factors, rather than subjective factors such as pain and lack of endurance. A major reason for use of these guidelines is that they minimize the amount of discretion available to the personnel rating injured workers. In most workers' compensation programs today, reducing the existing discretionary scope could often work to an employee's disadvantage. In our approach, however, the lack of flexibility at the rating stage is not critical, because the actual wage-loss benefits serve as a safety valve. That is, if the initial prediction of presumed work disability is unduly low, the wage-loss benefits can help offset the error.

Application of the Rating Standards

Most of our recommendations discussed so far in this section have concerned the appropriate standards for rating impairments and work disability and the types of benefits that should be paid to workers with permanent partial disabilities. Administrative arrangements and procedures are also an important component of our recommendations. One particularly important matter concerns who should make the decision on a case-by-case basis about the appropriate rating. The typical pattern in most jurisdictions is for the employee and employer (or the lawyers or carriers representing these parties) to negotiate an agreement about the extent of permanent disability. When an agreement cannot be reached, the issue is resolved by an administrative law judge in the workers' compensation agency.[15] In view of the expense of litigation and the inconsistencies among ratings that occur, depending on such vagaries as whether the worker is represented by a lawyer and who his employer is, we do not think this approach is appropriate. In order to reduce litigation and inconsistencies, we would assign primary responsibility for assigning ratings to an impairment rating division (IRD) that is a component of the workers' compensation agency.

The IRD would be required to rate the extent of the worker's permanent disability (or the extent of the worker's impairment and functional limitations, if that is the basis of the rating) before permanent partial disability benefits are paid or before the case can be taken to a hearing before the administrative law judge when the amount of permanent partial disability benefits is an issue. The IRD would make a rating based on medical evidence from the treating physician, from an examining doctor selected by the worker, or from a doctor chosen by the employer. When there is a conflict in medical evidence, the IRD must resolve it, either by using a doctor who is a staff member of the workers' compensation agency or by obtaining evidence from an impartial doctor the IRD selects.

The rating assigned by the impairment rating division must be used by the parties and the workers' compensation agency (including administrative law judges) unless the worker or the employer can demonstrate by a preponderance of evidence that the rating is capricious, arbitrary, or grossly inappropriate. If the parties can convince the administrative law judge that the rating is defective, then the case must be returned to the IRD for further consideration. The parties and the administrative law judge may submit additional information for consideration by the IRD, but the IRD also must have the right to obtain additional medical information if the case is referred back to it, and the IRD is ultimately responsible for deciding the appropriate rating. This scheme provides the impairment rating division with an amount of authority that is found in none of the workers' compensation programs we examined. We are convinced that such centralization of rating authority and protection of the IRD's rating are necessary if consistency among awards is to be assured and the incentive for litigation is to be reduced. The ultimate justification for this degree of centralization of authority over the ratings in our scheme is that if the IRD seriously underestimates the adverse economic consequences of a work-related injury or disease, the wage-loss benefits are available to the worker after six months, a safeguard that is missing now in almost every state workers' compensation program. In short, we place considerable emphasis on efficiency of the rating process and consistency among the ratings (even though they may be inaccurate predictors of the extent of work disability) because the wage-loss benefits can deal with the equity problems caused by seriously deficient predictions of earnings losses.

There are several complementary policies that will facilitate the role we have specified for the impairment rating division. One is that the IRD would train physicians in the state to apply the rating standards being used, which should help reduce the potential for disagreement between the parties concerning the appropriate ratings. Also, inappropriate litigation can be discouraged by limiting attorneys' fees in cases involving disputes over the extent of the permanent disability ratings to an amount that is proportional to the increase in the disability rating between the IRD's initial rating in the case and the rating ultimately assigned by the IRD. If the initial rating is not changed as a result of the hearing, the attorney is not entitled to any fee for the part of the case concerned with the extent of the disability rating. (In most permanent partial disability cases that is the sole issue.) If this stringent requirement for attorneys' fees were used by a state, the fees could appropriately be added to the worker's award rather than subtracted, as is the practice in most workers' compensation programs now.

We recognize that some states will be reluctant to move to an impairment rating bureau of the sort we prescribe, at least initially. A transition stage could involve the use of neutral doctors approved by the state workers' compensation agency to make ratings based upon a comprehensive set of guidelines issued by the state. These physicians could be in private practice and would be certified because of their neutrality between the parties. They could be approved by a selection committee that includes representatives of workers and employers. We do not believe that the use of such doctors is ideal, especially if a state uses a rating formula that incorporates factors other than the extent of impairment and functional limitations, such as age and education. Also, even if standards are widely promulgated, their application may be inconsistent among doctors. The use of an impairment rating division is likely to reduce such inconsistencies.

Other Prerequisites for a Wage-Loss System

A state that adopts the benefit proposals we have suggested must be willing to expend administrative resources for their implementation. The benefit proposals are new and relatively complex, and there is considerable potential for litigation and thus for the system to be undermined. The key to the successful operation of the program is an active state workers' compensation agency. The components of such an agency have been described in some detail in chapter 4, and only a few points will be reemphasized here. One is that an active state agency requires adequate resources and manpower. As we have stressed in part IV of this report, the practice in many states of equating efficiency with low budgets for workers' compensation agencies is a clear instance of false economy; the almost inevitable consequence of an underfunded agency is the encouragement of litigation, which in turn requires the utilization of considerable resources in the private sector to administer the program.

Another point is that it is important to separate the adjudication function in the agency from the administrative function. In some states, administration takes second place to adjudication partially because the chief administrator is also a member of the appeals board. Although such an arrangement does not always undermine administration, we believe that such matters as record keeping, monitoring, and evaluation usually receive due attention only when there is an administrator who understands these are his responsibilities and that one measure of his success is the extent to which he can reduce adjudication.

Another important aspect of a workers' compensation program that incorporates wage-loss benefits is the encouragement of rehabilitation. One of the most desirable consequences of a program that potentially involves wage-loss benefits of substantial amounts paid over long durations is that there is a strong incentive for employers to avoid unnecessary payment of benefits by providing rehabilitation at an early stage of the case.

A final prerequisite for a wage-loss system worth stressing is that the wholesale reliance on compromise and release agreements to resolve disagreements about the extent of disability and to prematurely end potential claims should by all means be avoided, because of the threat to equity it represents. An essential attribute of the wage-loss approach is that some protection is provided for workers with unanticipated wage loss that occurs long after the permanent disability ratings are made. The best way to overcome the poor record of *ex ante* predictions about the extent of wage loss is to begin to supplement the initial benefits with *ex post* benefits for workers who have unusually large earnings losses. This requires that cases be open longer, which means that employers and carriers have greater potential long-term liability and thus higher risks. Devices other than compromise and release agreements must be sought to enable the parties to live with risk, such as separate funds for cases with extended durations of wage-loss benefits.

Some Tests for the Operational Versions of Our Proposals

The proposals we have made concerning the types of permanent partial disability benefits that are appropriate and the procedures that should be used to provide these benefits would involve significant modifications of the permanent partial disability benefit programs in most states. There are several ongoing tests that could be used to monitor the performance of our proposals and decide whether they have achieved their goals. If these tests are not being met, the evidence will help the participants in the system redesign the program. We recognize that our proposals will initially need to be adapted to each state and will require continuing monitoring and modification.

The criterion of efficiency is reflected in two tests. One concerns the extent of litigation in permanent partial disability cases over the extent of disability. If, at the stage of the case where the permanent ratings are being determined, litigation occurs in more than 15 or 20 percent of the cases, the system is not serving the purpose of reducing litigation. The program would then have to be modified either by making the standards more comprehensive or objective or by increasing the protection afforded to the ratings made by the impairment rating division.

Another test of efficiency concerns the proportion of cases that qualify for wage-loss benefits after the initial six months of presumed disability benefits expire. If more than 20 or 25 percent of the cases that qualify for presumed disability benefits also qualify for wage-loss benefits, adjustments are probably needed. One possible adjustment is to extend the duration of the presumed disability benefits from six months to a longer period, such as a year. Some workers experiencing actual wage loss after six months would have recovered their earning capacity by the end of the year and thus would not qualify for wage-loss benefits. Extending the duration of the presumed disability benefit would probably require a reduction in the amount of the weekly benefit in order to avoid substantially increasing the cost of the system.

The equity criterion that requires benefits to be matched to wage loss can best be evaluated by monitoring the earnings losses of workers. This might require an examination similar to the procedure used in this research project, in which earnings reported to the Social Security system are evaluated periodically to see if earnings losses are matched by permanent disability benefits. That form of monitoring requires considerable effort, however, and there are other simpler tests that will provide at least some evidence about whether the equity goal is being achieved. For example, the proportion of cases that are terminated by compromise and release agreements is an indicator of potential lack of equity, since those cases in which unanticipated wage loss occurs after the compromise and release agreement is signed are bound to involve equity problems. A system in which more than 5 or 10 percent of the permanent partial disability cases are terminated by compromise and release agreements is not likely to provide sufficient equity.

Finally, assessment of adequacy (which concerns the proportion of lost earnings replaced by benefits) probably requires monitoring of actual wage loss and comparison between the losses and the benefits. Our study has convinced us that examination of statutory benefit amounts and durations provides little guidance to adequacy because of the critical importance of the rating system in determining the amount of benefits a particular injury will receive.

The Wage-Loss Concept in Florida

The Florida legislation of 1979 is the most widely discussed innovation in providing permanent partial disability benefits in the last decade, and so warrants special attention. The legislation provides impairment benefits that are paid to workers with certain types of permanent impairments (amputations, loss of 80 percent or more of vision, or serious head or facial disfigurements) but are not paid to workers with other types of permanent impairments (such as total or partial loss of use of a body member). The impairment benefits as of 1986 were $250 for each percent of permanent impairment for 1 to 10 percent ratings, and $500 for each percent over 10 percent. Thus a worker with a 60 percent impairment rating receives $27,500. These impairment benefits can be paid in a lump sum as of the date of maximum medical improvement.

Workers with permanent impairments are also eligible for wage-loss benefits as of the date of MMI if sufficient wage loss occurs. Wage-loss benefits are paid to workers with at least a 15 percent loss of earnings. Benefits are 95 percent of the earnings losses in excess of the 15 percent threshold. The maximum wage-loss benefit is the lesser of 66.66 percent of the worker's preinjury wage or 100 percent of the state's average weekly wage. There is, in effect, a 5 percent per year escalation in potential earnings used to calculate wage loss (this figure was 3 percent a year for injuries that occurred before July 1, 1980).

The maximum duration for the wage-loss benefits is 525 weeks (an increase from 350 weeks for injuries that occurred before July 1, 1980). When the worker becomes eligible for Old Age benefits from Social Security (normally at age 62), the wage-loss benefits are reduced by the amount of the Old Age benefits. Workers lose their eligibility for additional wage-loss benefits if they do not experience at least three consecutive months of compensable wage loss in each two-year period.

The 1979 Florida legislation thus establishes two types of benefits for workers with permanent consequences of their work-related injuries or diseases. Impairment benefits are paid to workers with the specified types of permanent impairments. Wage-loss benefits are paid to workers with wage losses that meet the statutory prerequisites. An individual worker may be eligible for impairment benefits, or wage-loss benefits, or both types of benefits, or neither type of benefit, depending upon the exact nature of the permanent impairment and the timing and amount of the earnings losses.

Evaluation of Florida Wage-Loss Benefits

The Florida wage-loss benefits will be evaluated here on the basis of some of the aspects for such benefits included in table 12.1.[16] The record is mixed. Florida's system conforms with the first aspect of the extensive type of wage-loss benefits because the law makes all workers with permanent disability ratings of at least 1 percent potentially eligible for wage-loss benefits. The Florida legislation also conforms with the fifth aspect, which requires that wage-loss benefits be paid only to workers with at least moderate lost earnings (the requisite in Florida that there be at least a 15 percent loss before any wage-loss benefits are paid is midway between the thresholds for the limited and extensive types of wage-loss benefits). The Florida law also largely complies with aspect eight, which prescribes a reasonable deadline after the date of MMI by which wage loss must be established in order for a worker to be eligible for wage-loss benefits. Similarly, there is substantial compliance with the ninth aspect, which specifies the duration of the break in earnings losses that will cause the worker's eligibility for wage-loss benefits to lapse.

The Florida law partially complies with the third aspect, which requires the potential earnings of workers to be adjusted through time to reflect changes in wages or prices. There is also compliance with the tenth aspect of the limited type of wage-loss benefits, which requires that benefits be paid for 350 weeks or until the worker reaches the normal retirement age, whichever is sooner. The maximum duration of 525 weeks does not yet bring Florida into compliance with the tenth aspect for the extensive type of wage-loss benefits, however, which requires wage-loss benefits until the worker reaches normal retirement age even if the worker is injured ten or more years before that date.

The Florida legislation fails to meet several of the desirable aspects for wage-loss benefits included in table 12.1. The second aspect, requiring a lag between the date of MMI and the initial date of eligibility for wage-loss benefits, is clearly violated since workers are immediately eligible for benefits. Many workers will begin to receive benefits in the rehabilitation phase of their postinjury recovery period and are likely to face serious disincentives to undergo rehabilitation and to return to work. The disincentive problem is aggravated because 95 percent of earnings losses above the threshold are replaced, a clear violation of the seventh aspect. This is especially troublesome since the benefits in Florida are tax-free. With a 95 percent replacement rate, some workers will actually be worse off financially by increasing the amount of time they work. (See Burton 1983, pp. 41-46.)

It is particularly difficult to evaluate the Florida legislation in terms of aspects 4, 11, and 12. These aspects pertain to the definition of earnings shortfall and the assignment of burdens of proof to establish the cause and magnitude of postinjury earnings losses. The statutory provisions and the court decisions in Florida were examined in chapter 9, and the best brief characterization is that Florida has not yet successfully resolved the problems of distinguishing compensable from non-compensable earnings losses. Unfortunately, the 1983 amendments appear to have raised serious obstacles to workers in establishing their eligibility, and we concluded these amendments were inappropriate. Whether the Florida courts will apply the 1983 amendments in the spirit in which they were apparently intended remains to be seen. Taken at face value, the recent changes stand as a serious challenge to a primary purpose of the wage-loss approach: to compensate workers who experience losses of earnings that would not have occurred but for their work-related injuries or diseases.

An overall evaluation of the 1979 Florida legislation dealing with permanent disabilities is obviously difficult and dependent on subjective values. We have identified some attributes of the law that agree with our recommendations and some that do not, but the day when the actual performance of the law can be evaluated in terms of adequacy, equity, and efficiency may be long in coming, since (as remarked in chapter 9) no data on the operation of the Florida law are being collected that will permit such an evaluation.

Conclusions

Several of our conclusions deserve to be briefly restated. One set of conclusions addresses the criteria that are currently used in most jurisdictions to provide permanent partial disability benefits. Our 10-state study has made clear that the dominant approach to compensating permanent partial disabilities relies on proxies for wage loss that are evaluated before the period when the actual wage loss occurs. The data from our wage-loss study of California, Florida, and Wisconsin suggest that the prospective (or *ex ante*), proxy approach does a poor job of matching benefits to actual wage loss and thus results in serious inequity. The results also suggest that the *ex ante* approach can provide benefits that on average are adequate, inadequate, or excessively generous. In short, nothing inherent in the *ex ante*, proxy approach precludes success on the adequacy criterion, but the prospects of achieving equity appear virtually nonexistent.

Another set of conclusions concerns the procedures that are currently used in most jurisdictions to provide permanent partial disability benefits. In terms of the administrative functions identified in chapter 4, most jurisdictions place primary emphasis on adjudication rather than record keeping, monitoring, and evaluation. The emphasis on adjudication is seen to result in high delivery system costs, once expenditures in the private sector, most notably attorneys' fees, are figured in. Our data from part III indicate that California and Florida, which were much more litigious than Wisconsin at the time of our wage-loss study, do not achieve greater adequacy or equity as a result of the devotion of substantial resources to litigation. In short, those delivery systems, which are typical of most states' procedures for permanent partial disability benefits, suffered from substantial inefficiency. Inefficiency is not inherent in the provision of such benefits, as the example of Wisconsin proves. With much less litigation than Florida and California, Wisconsin provided benefits that were more adequate and equitable than those in the other jurisdictions.

The previous paragraphs provide a serious indictment of the criteria and procedures used to provide permanent partial disability benefits in most jurisdictions at the present time. The procedures and criteria produce benefits that sometimes are inadequate, often are provided inefficiently, and invariably are inequitable. We would like to end this study by providing an easy solution, or an obvious solution, or at least a solution that we are convinced will work, even if complicated and obscure. Alas, we cannot even provide that degree of certitude. What we can provide are some general guidelines that we believe represent the best possible hope for reform of permanent partial disability benefits.

One set of guidelines concerns the procedures that hold the best promise for adequate, equitable, and efficient benefits. Most states need to significantly redirect the efforts of their workers' compensation agencies away from adjudication in favor of record keeping, monitoring, and evaluation. Let justice be served by avoiding adjudication! And coupled with this redirection of effort must be a recognition that tight budgets for a workers' compensation agency often are a sign of myopia, not fiscal prudence. We surely do not endorse every possible item in a workers' compensation agency's budget, but we are convinced that excessive stringency will curtail the ability of the agency to perform the necessary record keeping, monitoring, and evaluation functions and drive the delivery system toward excessive litigation. To be sure, the cost of an agency subject to a tight budget may be less, but only at the price of undue resources devoted to litigation. Needless to say, any workers' compensation system will involve some litigation, but the use of adjudication to process permanent partial disability claims should be the exception rather than the rule.

Another set of guidelines concerns the criteria that show the greatest promise of promoting adequacy, equity, and efficiency. We have roundly rejected the dominant approach currently used, namely the *ex ante* approach. Although we do not believe this approach holds much promise for reform, we have offered suggestions for an improved *ex ante* approach in this chapter. Much more noteworthy is the wage-loss (or *ex post*) approach, which provides benefits to workers after they have demonstrated actual wage loss. This approach holds promise for greater equity. Because of its adoption in Florida in 1979, the wage-loss approach has generated considerable enthusiasm. The wage-loss approach is not inherently adequate, and thus is not necessarily superior to the *ex ante* approach on this ground. Nor is the wage-loss approach inherently less expensive than the *ex ante* approach. Burton (1983) has demonstrated that the nonscheduled permanent partial benefits in New York are now accounting for more than half of all the dollars spent on cash benefits in the state, and that these costs have increased rapidly in the 1970s in response to deteriorating labor market conditions. These nonscheduled permanent partial disability benefits in New York are a variant on the wage-loss approach, and are obviously providing a lesson different from that provided by the cost-reducing experience that Florida has had with its version of wage-loss benefits.

In addition to these reservations concerning the adequacy and expense of wage-loss benefits, a lesson from Florida concerning the difficulties of administration bears repeating: the application of the wage-loss concept is not as easy as might appear at first glance. The problems Florida has had in sorting out compensable from noncompensable wage loss are not going to be easily solved elsewhere.

There are additional drawbacks to the pure wage-loss approach that would begin permanent partial disability benefits on this basis as of the date of maximum medical recovery. We have indicated our concern over the disincentive to engage in rehabilitation or to return to work that is aggravated if the wage-loss approach begins too soon. Our preferred solution is a hybrid approach, which would provide benefits without regard to actual wage loss for a limited duration (perhaps six months) after the date of MMI and then give way to benefits based on actual wage loss. Like the *ex ante* and wage-loss approaches, there can be considerable variations in design and administration of the hybrid approach. The hybrid approach has a limited counterpart in New York (See Burton 1983) and an intellectual history that predates our research.[17] We believe there is sufficient evidence to justify states in abandoning the traditional criteria and procedures for providing permanent partial disability benefits, with their deficiencies in adequacy, equity, and efficiency, and sufficient understanding of the wage-loss and hybrid approaches to warrant the adoption of those approaches in more jurisdictions. With sufficient experimentation and with appropriate monitoring of the experiments, there is hope that the proper criteria and procedures for permanent partial disability benefits can be identified with more certainty in the next decade.

NOTES

1. Pennsylvania uses a limited wage-loss approach and yet does not permit compromise and release agreements. As discussed in chapter 8, however, the Pennsylvania wage-loss benefits are limited in duration and amount.

2. See the discussions of Michigan and Florida. Also see the evidence from Ohio discussed in chapter 8.

3. Even those gains in equity may be illusory, however. Given the substantial problems in deciding, even on a retrospective basis, what was the contribution of a work-related injury or disease to a particular loss of earnings, it may be that weighing all the evidence pertaining to that issue on a case-by-case basis may not do much to improve the record of matching workers' compensation benefits to the wage losses caused by work-related injuries and disease. The recent court decisions in Florida discussed in chapter 9 illustrate the problems of identifying earnings losses due to work-related causes.

4. The apparent purpose of the schedules is to use a relatively inexpensive procedure that provides a rough estimate of earnings loss associated with certain injuries. In terms of graph 2.2, the use of schedules can be considered a decision to choose a point in the lower portion of the Quality/Cost Constraint Line because of a desire to minimize administrative costs. A policy that pursues low administrative costs without regard for the consequences of the quality of benefits represents myopic efficiency.

5. The specific factors used in California (age and occupation) may not be the best available predictions of the differences in earnings losses that will occur for workers with similar impairment ratings. Other relatively "objective" factors that could be used include sex, educational level, and extent of prior work experience. The essence of the California approach is not the specific factors used, but the reliance on a formula approach to estimate the extent of work disability for all types of injuries and diseases. In other states, nonscheduled injuries are often rated on the basis of a relatively time-consuming investigation of the facts of each case.

6. There may be, however, no improvement in equity from evaluating the loss of earning capacity by considering on a case-by-case basis all the factors that affect earning capacity, rather than using a California-type schedule to estimate loss of earning capacity. Given our limited understanding about the relationships between earnings and a worker's age, occupation, experience, etc., it is not clear that consideration of all of these factors improves the accuracy of predictions about earnings losses compared to predictions based on formulas that consider only a few factors. The data from chapter 10 indicate that California (which estimated loss of earning capacity by use of a

schedule) and Florida (which estimated loss of earning capacity by using all of the relevant facts in a case) both had serious equity problems with the statutes in effect in 1968.

7. The National Commission argued that when workers gave up their common law remedies, they received the right to receive workers' compensation benefits without regard to the employer's fault. As a result, the employer's liability for the consequences other than work disability should be limited. (National Commission 1972, p. 38.)

8. Historically, the benefit levels in workers' compensation were inadequate (National Commission 1972, pp. 60-62) and generally no higher than the benefits in other social insurance programs. But the recent increases in workers' compensation benefits have made them generally higher than benefits in other programs, according to Berkowitz (1977).

9. The contrast between the National Commission's view and Berkowitz's view on equity versus efficiency is in effect a debate about whether policy option 2 or policy option 4 in graph 2.2 is preferable. Policy option 4 involves greater equity and higher administrative costs, while policy option 2 involves less equity and lower administrative costs. Since both options are on the quality/costs constraint line, they represent equal panoramic efficiency.

10. The adequacy goal is also not achieved if there is a general tendency for a workers' compensation program to fail to distinguish between wage losses due to work-related injuries or diseases and wage losses due to other causes. For example, the average replacement rate in a state could be too high if the program provides benefits to many cases in which "wage losses" are due to factors such as retirement at the normal retirement age.

11. For an extended discussion of the incentives to employees and employers in a wage-loss approach, see Burton (1983), pp. 34-35.

12. A potential problem of an eligibility threshold is that the behavior of workers can be significantly affected if, e.g., a small additional amount of earnings losses establishes the worker's eligibility for a sizeable amount of benefits. This "notch" effect can be minimized if the workers who barely qualify for some benefits only receive a nominal amount, as in the plan for wage-loss benefits encompassed in table 12.1.

13. Work-related diseases pose a more serious problem for designing appropriate time limits for eligibility for wage-loss benefits than do work-related injuries. In principle, the eligibility date for a work-related disease should be based on the date when a worker is first disabled, rather than on the date of exposure to the substance that produced the disease. In practice, given the long latency period for some diseases and the multiple causes of many diseases, a well-designed wage-loss system will have to consider such issues as the use of presumptions that help decide whether the wage loss is due to a work-related disease or not. Thus a worker exposed to a particular toxic substance at work who is subsequently disabled from a disease that might have been caused by the toxic substance could use a presumption that the disease is work-related if the period between exposure and disability is 10 years or less, but would have to overcome a presumption that the disease is not work-related if the period is over 10 years.

14. A minimum duration of wage-loss benefits may be appropriate for workers injured near or after their normal retirement ages. For example, a worker injured at age 68 in an industry in which the normal retirement age is 65 could be eligible for a minimum of one year's wage-loss benefits (assuming he met the other prerequisites for such benefits, such as demonstration of an earnings shortfall). The minimum duration provision would have to be drawn carefully in order to prevent wage-loss benefits from becoming a general retirement bonus.

15. Wisconsin is an obvious exception to the typical pattern described in the text, and much of the discussion concerning desirable changes in agency structure and procedure is inapplicable to Wisconsin.

16. For an evaluation of the impairment benefits plus additional evaluations of the wage-loss benefits, see Burton 1983, pp. 41-49.

17. Although the hybrid system has only limited counterparts in actual practice, it does have an intellectual history that provides some reassurance for those concerned about sharp breaks in tradition. Perhaps the most compelling precedent is the Report of the Permanent Partial Disabilities Committee of the IAIABC (Reid 1966). Although the particulars of the Reid committee report differ from the hybrid proposal in this chapter, its purposes and approaches are similar.

Bibliography

Alpert, Jonathan L., and Murphy, Patrick J. 1978 with 1984 Supp. *Florida Workmen's Compensation Law.* 3rd ed. Norcross, Calif.: Harrison.

American Medical Association. 1971. *Guides to the Evaluation of Permanent Impairment.* Chicago: AMA.

American Medical Association. 1984. *Guides to the Evaluation of Permanent Impairment.* 2nd ed. Chicago: AMA.

Barbieri, Alexander. 1975. *Pennsylvania Workmen's Compensation.* Philadelphia: G. T. Bisel.

Berkowitz, Monroe. 1960. *Workmen's Compensation: The New Jersey Experience.* New Brunswick: Rutgers University Press.

Berkowitz, Monroe. 1975. "Requiem for the Schedule." *1975 Convention Proceedings of IAIABC,* pp. 136-44. International Association of Industrial Accident Boards and Commissions.

Berkowitz, Monroe. 1977. "Workers' Compensation in a General Disability System." *Proceedings of the Twenty-Ninth Annual Winter Meeting of the Industrial Relations Research Association,* pp. 212-18. Madison, Wis.: Industrial Relations Research Association.

Berkowitz, Monroe, Burton, John F., Jr., and Vroman, Wayne. 1979. *Permanent Disability Benefits in the Workers' Compensation Program.* Final report for a project supported by the National Science Foundation.

Blackman, Philip, trans. 1983. *Mishnayoth.* 3rd ed. New York: Judaica Press.

Burton, John F., Jr. 1966. *Interstate Variations in Employers' Costs of Workmen's Compensation.* Kalamazoo, Mich.: W. E. Upjohn Institute.

Burton, John F., Jr. 1983. "Compensation for Permanent Partial Disabilities." In Worrall, John D., ed., *Safety and the Work Force,* pp. 18-60. Ithaca, N.Y.: ILR Press.

Burton, John F., Jr., Hunt, H. Allan, and Krueger, Alan B. 1985. *Interstate Variations in the Employers' Costs of Workers' Compensation, with Particular Reference to Michigan and the Other Great Lakes States.* Ithaca, N.Y.: Workers' Disability Income Systems, Inc.

Burton, John F., Jr., and Krueger, Alan B. 1986. "Interstate Variations in the Employers' Costs of Workers' Compensation, with Particular Reference to Connecticut, New Jersey, and New York.'' In Chelius, James, ed., *Current Issues in Workers' Compensation,* pp. 111-208. Kalamazoo, Mich.: W. E. Upjohn Institute.

Burton, John F., Jr., Larson, Lloyd W., and Moran, Janet P. 1980. *Final Report on a Research Project on Permanent Partial Disability Benefits.* (mimeo.) Ithaca, N.Y.: New York State School of Industrial and Labor Relations, Cornell University.

Burton, John F., Jr., and Partridge, Dane M. 1985. *Workers' Compensation Benefits in Michigan and the Other Great Lakes States.* Ithaca, N.Y.: Workers' Disability Income Systems, Inc.

Burton, John F., Jr., Partridge, Dane M., and Thomason, Terry. 1986. *Final Report of a Research Project on Nonscheduled Permanent Partial Disability Benefits Provided by the New York State Workers' Compensation Program.* (mimeo.) Ithaca, N.Y.: New York State School of Industrial and Labor Relations, Cornell University.

Burton, John F., Jr., and Thomason, Terry. 1986. *Cash Benefits in the New York State Workers' Compensation Program: Estimates of the Costs of Possible Changes.* (mimeo.) Ithaca, N.Y.: New York State School of Industrial and Labor Relations, Cornell University.

Burton, John F., Jr., and Vroman, Wayne. 1979. ''A Report on Permanent Partial Disabilities Under Workers' Compensation.'' In *Research Report of the Interdepartmental Workers' Compensation Task Force,* Vol. 6, pp. 11-77. U.S. Department of Labor, Employment Standards Administration.

California Joint Study Committee on Workers' Compensation. 1986. *Workers' Compensation: A Staff Report.*

California Senate Interim Committee. 1953. *Report to the Senate on Workmen's Compensation Benefits.*

California Workers' Compensation Institute. 1984. *Economic Consequences of Job Injury.* San Francisco: California Workers' Compensation Institute.

California Workers' Compensation Institute. 1985-86. *Bulletin.* San Francisco: California Workers' Compensation Institute.

California Workers' Compensation Reporter. 1985-86. Berkeley, Calif.: Melvin S. Witt.

Council of State Governments. 1963 and 1965. *Workmen's Compensation and Rehabilitation Law.* Chicago: Council of State Governments.

Dodd, Walter F. 1936. *Administration of Workmen's Compensation*. New York: Commonwealth Fund.

Driver, G. R., and Miles, John C. 1960. *The Babylonian Laws*. Oxford: Clarendon Press.

Falk, Zeen W. 1964. *Hebrew Law in Biblical Times*. Jerusalem: Wahrman Books.

Florida. Department of Labor and Employment Security, Division of Workers' Compensation. 1979. *Analysis of Work Injuries Covered by Workers' Compensation, 1977-1978* [also titled *1977-1978 Cases Causes Costs*].

Florida. Department of Labor and Employment Security, Division of Workers' Compensation. 1985. *1984 Workers' Compensation Injuries: A Statistical Report*.

Florida. The Workers' Compensation Experience Review Committee. 1984. *Report of the Workers' Compensation Experience Review Committee*.

Fratello, Barney. 1955. "The 'Workmen's Compensation Injury Table' and 'Standard Wage Distribution'—Their Development and Use in Workmen's Compensation Insurance Rate-Making." In *Proceedings of the Casualty Actuarial Society* XLII.

Geerts, Achilles, Kornblich, Borris A., and Urmson, W. John. 1977 *Compensation for Bodily Harm: A Comparative Study*. Brussels: Fernand Nathan.

Gifford, Courtney D., ed. 1982. *Directory of U.S. Labor Organizations, 1982-83 Edition*. Washington: Bureau of National Affairs, Inc.

Ginnold, Richard. 1979. "A Follow-up Study of Permanent Disability Cases Under Wisconsin Workers' Compensation." In *Research Report of the Interdepartmental Workers' Compensation Task Force*, Vol. 6, pp. 79-93. U.S. Department of Labor, Employment Standards Administration.

Gmeinder, Henry J. 1983. *100th Anniversary of the Department of Industry, Labor and Human Relations*. Madison, Wis.: State of Wisconsin, Workers' Compensation Division.

Gmeinder, Henry J., and Tatarsky, Stephen. 1986. *Five Pillars to 75 Years of Worker's Compensation*. Madison, Wis.: State of Wisconsin, Worker's Compensation Division.

Hertz, J. H., ed. 1975. *Pentateuch and Haftorahs*. 2nd ed. London: Soncino Press.

Hunt, H. Allan. 1982. *Workers' Compensation System in Michigan.* Kalamazoo, Mich.: W. E. Upjohn Institute.

Hunt, H. Allan, Krueger, Alan B., and Burton, John F., Jr. 1985. "The Impact of Open Competition in Michigan on the Employers' Costs of Workers' Compensation." Presented at 1985 seminar sponsored by National Council on Compensation Insurance.

Jaffy, Stewart R., and Smith, Warren J. 1981. *Workers' Compensation Manual.* 11th ed. Columbus, Ohio: Ohio State AFL-CIO.

Johnson, William G., Cullinan, Paul R., and Currington, William P. 1979. "The Adequacy of Workers' Compensation Benefits." In *Research Report of the Interdepartmental Workers' Compensation Task Force,* Vol. 6, pp. 95-121. U.S. Department of Labor, Employment Standards Administration.

Journal of American Insurance. Summer 1982. "Florida's Bold Experiment in Cutting Worker [sic] Compensation Costs."

Kessler, Henry H. 1970. *Disability Determination and Evaluation.* Philadelphia: Lea and Febriger.

Krueger, Alan B., and Burton, John F., Jr. 1984. "Interstate Differences in the Employers' Costs of Workers' Compensation: Magnitudes, Causes, and Cures." Presented at 1983 seminar sponsored by National Council on Compensation Insurance.

Larson, Arthur. 1973. "Basic Concepts and Objectives of Workmen's Compensation." In *Supplemental Studies for the National Commission on State Workmen's Compensation Laws,* Vol. I, pp. 31-39. Washington: Government Printing Office.

Larson, Arthur. 1986 revision. *Workmen's Compensation (Desk Ed.).* New York, N.Y.: Matthew Bender.

Larson, Lloyd W., and Burton, John F., Jr. 1985. "Special Funds in Workers' Compensation." In Worrall, John D., and Appel, David, eds., *Workers' Compensation Benefits: Adequacy, Equity, and Efficiency,* pp. 117-57. Ithaca, N.Y.: ILR Press.

Lefelt, Steven. 1975. "Toward a New Method of Awarding Compensation Benefits." *Rutgers Law Review* 28: 587-615.

Lewis, John H. 1973. "A Workmen's Restoration System." In *Supplemental Studies for the National Commission on State Workmen's Compensation Laws,* Vol. III, pp. 499-516. Washington: Government Printing Office.

Lieb, Saul B. 1975. "Medical Aspects of New Jersey's Workers' Compensation." In Valore, Carl, ed., *Aspects of Representing the Petitioner in Workers' Compensation*. New Brunswick: Institute for Continuing Legal Education, Rutgers University.

Malone, Wex S. 1970. "Ruminations on the Role of Fault in the History of Torts." In *The Origin and Development of the Negligent Action*. U.S. Department of Transportation Automobile Insurance and Compensation Study. Washington: Government Printing Office.

McBride, Earl D. 1942. *Disability Evaluation*. Philadelphia: J. B. Lippincott.

Mintner, Jim. 1982. *The Circle Solution*. Tallahassee: Florida Association of Insurance Agents.

Nackley, Jeffrey V. 1985. *Ohio Workers' Compensation Claims*. Rochester, N.Y.: Lawyers Co-operative.

Nagi, Saad Z. 1975. *An Epidemiology of Adulthood Disability in the United States*. Mershon Center Information Publications. Columbus: Mershon Center, Ohio State University.

Napier, Alfred J. 1981. "The Impact of the Reform Act of 1980." Unpublished manuscript.

National Commission on State Workmen's Compensation Laws. 1972. *The Report of the National Commission on State Workmen's Compensation Laws*. Washington: Government Printing Office.

National Commission on State Workmen's Compensation Laws. 1973. *Compendium on Workmen's Compensation*. Washington: Government Printing Office.

National Council on Compensation Insurance. 1984. *Workers' Compensation Claim Characteristics*. New York: National Council on Compensation Insurance.

Neal, John D. 1983 with 1985 Supp. *Worker's Compensation Handbook*. Madison, Wis.: State Bar of Wisconsin.

Neufeld, E. 1951. *The Hittite Laws*. London: Luzac.

New Jersey Workmen's Compensation Study Commission. 1973. *Report of the New Jersey Workmen's Compensation Study Commission*. Newark.

New York. Temporary State Commission on Workers' Compensation and Disability Benefits. 1986. *Final Report of the Temporary State Commission on Workers' Compensation and Disability Benefits*. Albany.

New York. Workers' Compensation Board. 1984. *Compensated Cases Closed, 1982.* New York City.

Ohio. Industrial Commission of Ohio. 1981. *Medical Examination Manual.* (mimeo.)

Pollock, Frederick, and Maitland, Frederic W. 1895. *The History of English Law.* Cambridge: Cambridge University Press.

Popkin, William. 1975. "Counsel and the Welfare State: A Statistical and Legal Analysis of the Role of Representatives in Administrative Decision-Making Based on a Study of Five Disability Programs." Preliminary draft. Washington: Administrative Conference of the United States.

Pound, Roscoe. 1914. "The End of Law as Developed in the Legal Rules and Doctrines." *Harvard Law Review* 27: 605-28.

Price, Daniel N. 1980. "Workers' Compensation: 1978 Program Update." *Social Security Bulletin* 43 (October 1980): 3-10.

Price, Daniel N. 1984. "Workers' Compensation: 1978-80 Benchmark Revisions." *Social Security Bulletin* 47 (July 1984): 3-23.

Price, Daniel N. 1987. "Workers' Compensation: Benefits and Coverage, 1984." *Social Security Bulletin* (forthcoming).

Reede, Arthur H. 1947. *Adequacy of Workmen's Compensation.* Cambridge, Mass.: Harvard University Press.

Reid, James J. 1966. "Report of the Permanent Partial Disabilities Committee." *1966 Convention Proceedings of IAIABC,* pp. 27-71. International Association of Industrial Accident Boards and Commissions.

Rubinow, I. M. 1916. *Social Insurance.* New York: Henry Holt.

St. Antoine, Theodore J. 1984. *Workers' Compensation in Michigan: Costs, Benefits, and Fairness.* Ann Arbor, Mich.: University of Michigan Law School.

Somers, Herman M., and Somers, Anne R. 1954. *Workmen's Compensation.* New York: John Wiley and Sons.

Stander, Erwin. 1976. "The 'No Compromise' Mess in Pennsylvania Workmen's Compensation." *The Legal Intelligencer,* Sept. 9, 1976.

Stiles, Mary Ann. 1982. *Employers' Handbook on the Florida Workers' Compensation Law, 1982-1983 Edition.* Tallahassee: Associated Industries of Florida Service Corporation.

Stiles, Mary Ann. 1983. *Workers' Compensation Report.* Three-page unpublished manuscript.

Swezey, Charles L. 1985 with 1986 Supp. *California Workers' Compensation Practice.* Berkeley, Calif.: California Continuing Education of the Bar.

Tebb, Alan. 1986. "The 1982 Changes in California." In Chelius, James R., ed., *Current Issues in Workers' Compensation,* pp. 45-54. Kalamazoo, Mich.: W. E. Upjohn Institute.

U.S. Chamber of Commerce. 1986. *Analysis of Workers' Compensation Laws.* Washington: U.S. Chamber of Commerce.

U.S. Department of Labor, Bureau of Labor Statistics. 1914. *Workmen's Compensation Laws in the United States and Foreign Countries.* Bull. 126.

U.S. Department of Labor, Employment Standards Administration, Division of State Workers' Compensation Programs. 1985. *State Workers' Compensation: Administration Profiles.*

U.S. Department of Labor, Employment Standards Administration, Division of State Workers' Compensation Programs. January 1986. *State Workers' Compensation Laws.*

U.S. Department of Labor, Employment Standards Administration, Division of State Workers' Compensation Programs. January 1986. *State Workers' Compensation Laws in Effect on January 1, 1986 Compared with the 19 Essential Recommendations of the National Commission on State Workmen's Compensation Laws.*

U.S. Department of Labor, Employment Standards Administration, Division of State Workers' Compensation Programs. Forthcoming 1987. *State Compliance with the 19 Essential Recommendations of the National Commission on State Workmen's Compensation Laws, 1972-1984.*

Vroman, Wayne. 1977. "Work Injuries and Wage Losses for Partially Disabled California Workers." *Proceedings of the Twenty-Ninth Annual Winter Meeting of the Industrial Relations Research Association,* pp. 228-35. Madison, Wis.: Industrial Relations Research Association.

Welch, Eli P. 1964. "Presentation on Permanent Disability Ratings." Presented to the California Workmen's Compensation Study Commission.

Welch, Eli P. 1973. "Permanent Disability Evaluation." In Witt, Melvin S., ed., *California Workmen's Compensation Practice,* pp. 531-71. Berkeley, Calif.: California Continuing Education of the Bar.

440

World Health Organization. 1980. *International Classification of Impairments, Disabilities, and Handicaps.* Geneva: World Health Organization.

Young, James L. 1971 with 1984 Supp. *Workmen's Compensation Law of Ohio.* 2nd ed. Cincinnati: W. H. Anderson.

INDEX

Abdomen, 178
Ability
    to pay, 105
    to work, 217
Absence from work, 112
Accident policies, 106
Acosta v. Kraco, Inc., 287
Adequacy, 22-24, 26-27, 81, 83, 89, 138, 204-207, 365, 368, 370-373, 379, 381-386, 391, 398-401, 418, 423, 426-429
Adjudication, 83-84, 93-94, 97-98, 165-166, 385, 421, 427
Adjusted manual rates, 69
Administration, 77, 95, 421
    private, 75
Administrative
    costs, 26-28, 398, 400, 402, SEE ALSO Costs
    function, 83, 96-97
    law judge, SEE Judge, administrative law
    organizations, 162, 280
    procedures, 138
Admissibility, 80
Advance payment, 307-308
AFL-CIO, 138, 276-277
Age, 9-10, 26, 81, 107-108, 117, 124-125, 127, 131, 135, 137, 140, 146, 160, 172-174, 180, 183, 196, 198, 267, 330, 340, 345, 366, 371, 376, 394, 397, 403-404, 407, 421
Aging process, 129, 230
Agreement system, 133
Alaska, 188
ALJ Qualification Advisory Committee, 223
AMA Guides, SEE American Medical Association
American Academy of Orthopedic Surgery, *Manual,* 284-286
American Medical Association, *Guides to the Evaluation of Permanent Impairment,* 3, 8, 45, 101, 112, 116, 118, 120, 123, 126, 130, 141, 147-148, 155, 174-175, 177, 182, 203, 258, 283-285, 396-397, 402, 407-408, 416, 418
Amputation, 6, 79, 100, 118, 140, 155, 181, 203, 275, 278, 282, 319, 330, 403, 423
Anatomical loss, 79
Anderson v. S & S Diversified, Inc., 289
Anglo-Saxon, 104
Ankylosis, 6-7
Appeal, 82, 94, 98
Appeals officer, 139, 144
Appellate
    body, 82, 98
    court, 167
Apportionment, 181
    statute, 129
Arizona, 41, 107, 233
Arkansas, 107
Arm, 99, 108-109-113, 116-119, 140, 153, 203, 214, 224, 242, 251-252, 266, 284
Assistance sources, 9-10
Associated Industries of Florida, 274-275, 293
Assumption of risk, 17
Attorney, 75, 135, 137, 144, 147, 153, 170, 181, 183, 185, 196, 199, 218, 228, 268-269, 271, 274-276, 281, 311, 320, 330, 353, 356, 380-381, 385-386, 397-398, 419-420

458

Vocational
    expert, 76, 80-81, 199
    rehabilitation , 15, 112, 185, 393
Voluntary limitation of income, 288-290
Vroman, Wayne, 44, 273

Wage
    preinjury, 108
    rates, 131
    reference, 366
Wage-earning capacity, SEE Earning capacity
Wage loss, 81, 88, 126, 184, 191-192, 212-213, 229, 235, 245, 255, 300, 317-361,
    367, 395, 404, 424
    actual, 101, 106, 123-124, 131,186, 190, 206, 220, 226, 234, 254, 258, 259, 261,
    267,279, 287, 295, 311, 400, 404, 426, 428
    approach, 100, 211-213, 257, 260, 265-267, 271-277, 295, 309, 311-312, 405, 407,
    414-415, 426, 428-429
    benefits, 101-102, 131, 152, 221, 226, 234, 257, 259, 262, 273, 276, 278-279, 282-
    283, 285-287, 289-290, 293-294, 299, 308, 311-312, 409, 412-416, 418, 420-425,
    428. SEE ALSO Benefits
    legislation, 277
    method, 118
    permanent, 102
    provision, 106
    states, 45, 89, 92, 124, 211-263
    study, 317-361
    SEE ALSO Earnings loss
Wage-replacement approach, 185
Waiting period, 159
Walker v. Electronic Products & Engineering Co., 267
Walking, 7, 179
Walsh v. New York Telephone, 248
War wounds, 106
Washington, 107-108
Washout, SEE Compromise and release agreement
Weakness, 6, 8
Welfare, 9-10
West Virginia, 107
Whole man, 45, 100, 141
Wisconsin, 44-46, 49, 52, 54, 57, 60, 63, 66, 84, 86-87, 90-91, 94-95, 105-107, 109,
    113, 116, 119, 124-125, 193, 210, 317-330, 353-361, 365, 369, 372, 374-375, 380-
    386, 399, 426-427
Wisconsin Department of Industry, Labor and Human Relations, 199
Wisconsin Industrial Commission, 197
Wisconsin Labor and Industry Review Commission, 197
Wisconsin Medical Society, 201
Wisconsin Study Commission, 207
Wisconsin Supreme Court, 195, 197, 206
Wisconsin Workers' Compensation Act, 193, 203
Wisconsin Workers' Compensation Division, 195, 200
Woodward v. Dade County Board of Public Instruction, 267-268
Work, 178-179, 182
    ability, 138
    experience, 9-10, 100, 124, 131, 198, 366, 397, 403-404, 407